# Cybercrime and Criminological Theory

## Fundamental Readings on Hacking, Piracy, Theft, and Harrassment

Edited by Thomas J. Holt

cognella

San Diego, CA

Bassim Hamadeh, CEO and Publisher
Christopher Foster, General Vice President
Michael Simpson, Vice President of Acquisitions
Jessica Knott, Managing Editor
Kevin Fahey, Cognella Marketing Manager
Jess Busch, Senior Graphic Designer
Jamie Giganti, Project Editor
Brian Fahey, Licensing Associate
Kate McKellar, Interior Designer

First published in the United States of America in 2013 by Cognella, Inc.

Printed in the United States of America

ISBN: 978-1-60927-496-2

www.cognella.com  800.200.3908

# contents

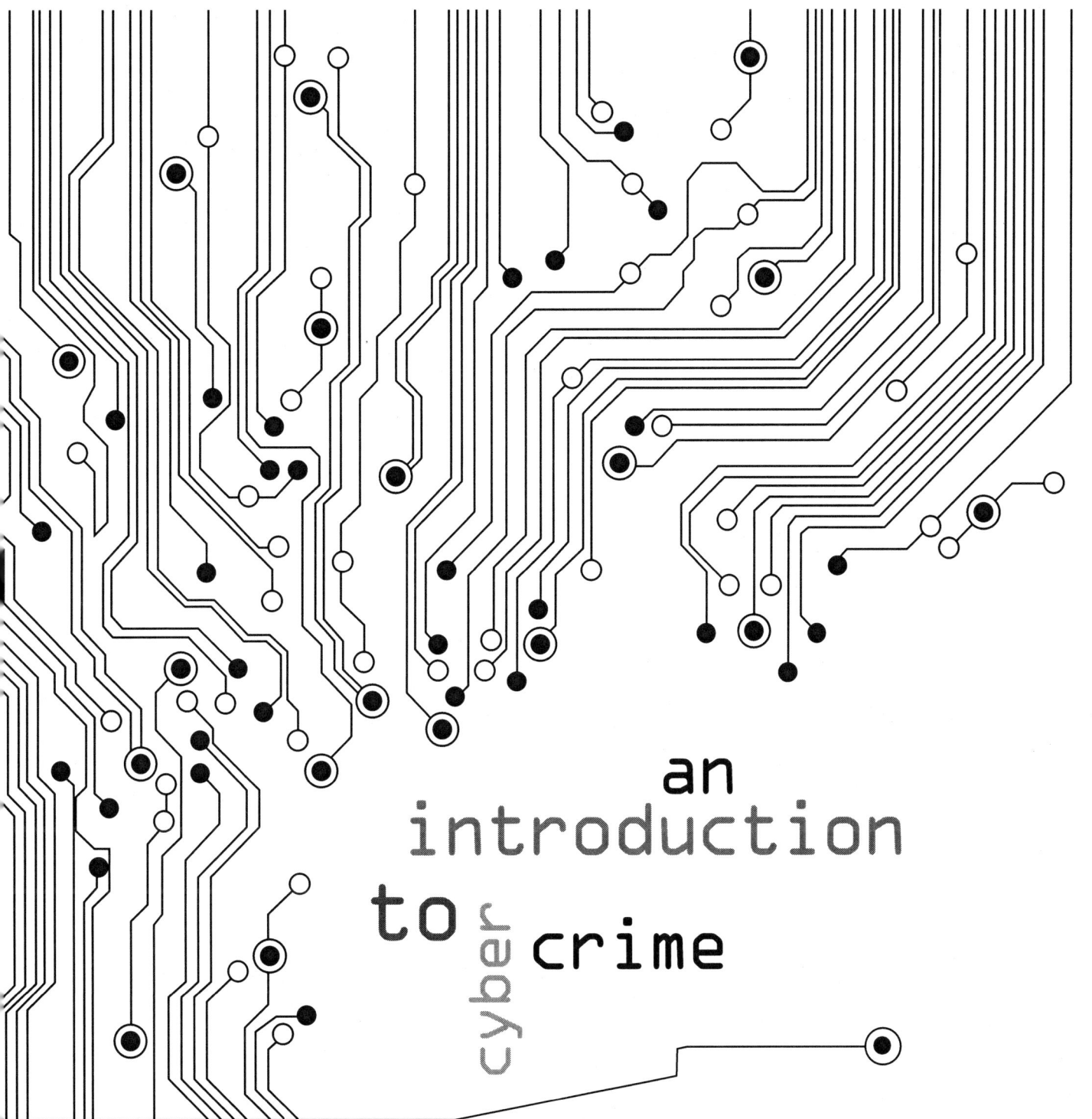

# an
# introduction
# to cyber crime

thomas j. holt

# general

# cyber crime

Over the last three decades, computer technology has become an entirely ubiquitous component of modern life. Individuals regularly utilize laptops, desktops, tablet computers, and smartphones to engage in all facets of life, from communications to finance (Moore, 2011; Smith, 2011). Social networking sites like Facebook allow us to stay in touch with friends and family around the world, while streaming media services keep individuals entertained 24 hours a day on demand. On-line retail generates billions of dollars in income every year, and most consumers now utilize electronic banking services to manage their accounts and pay bills (Anderson, 2010). In fact, government and industry now depend on the Internet and computers to maintain sensitive records and provide real-time information to consumers and citizens about any issue that may be of interest.

The increasing dependence on technology to support and manage our lives has created unparalleled opportunities for crime and misuse. In fact, most any form of crime now involves technology in some way, whether through the use of cell phones and text messages or more novel applications of technology to commit crimes that are not otherwise possible outside of digital devices (Taylor, Fritsch, Liederbach, & Holt, 2010; Wall, 2007). The World Wide Web and the Internet also provide a venue for individuals who engage in crime and deviance to communicate and share information; this would not otherwise be possible in the real world (Quinn & Forsyth, 2005). As a result, it is vital that we begin to understand how these changes are occurring, and what this means for offending in the 21st century.

To that end, it is necessary to define and classify the crimes that involve computers in some fashion. The terms "cybercrime" and "computer crime" are most frequently used to identify these offenses and have become nearly synonymous, although they technically refer to different behaviors. Cybercrime refers to crimes "in which the perpetrator uses special knowledge of cyberspace," whereas computer crimes are offenses where "the perpetrator uses special knowledge about computer technology" (Furnell, 2002: 21; Wall, 2001). Many in the popular media treat these terms interchangeably (Furnell, 2002). However, this text will use the term "cybercrime" because of the large number of offenses that can occur in on-line environments and the overwhelming number of computers that are connected to the Internet.

Understanding what acts constitute cybercrime has led to a great body of research on the various offenses that fall under this term. One of the most well-referenced and -constructed frameworks to understand cybercrimes is Wall's (2001) four-category typology to identify the wide range of behaviors involving technology and the Internet in some fashion. The first category is cyber-trespass, encompassing the crossing of invisible, yet salient, boundaries of ownership on-line (Wall, 2001). Computer hackers are most likely to engage in acts of cyber-trespass due to their desire to penetrate computer systems. Defined broadly, hackers are individuals with a profound interest in computers and technology who have used their knowledge to access computer systems for malicious or ethical purposes (Holt, 2007; Jordan & Taylor, 1998). Though hackers engage in and develop security tools, many in the general public only view hacking in its malicious context because of the economic and personal harm they may cause (Furnell, 2002). In fact, malicious hacking is often tied to the creation and distribution of malicious software, or malware, that can automate attacks against computer systems (Bossler & Holt, 2010; Chu, Holt, & Ahn, 2010). These programs can disrupt e-mail and network operations, access private files, delete or corrupt files, and generally damage computer software and hardware (Computer Security Institute, 2012). Thus, acts of cyber-trespass are a significant concern for home users, businesses, and governments alike.

The second and related category is cyber-deception and -theft. This form of computer crime includes all the various criminal acquisitions that may occur on-line, particularly for thefts due to trespass. For example, businesses lost over $5 million to theft of proprietary or confidential information in 2007 (Computer Security Institute, 2008). Similarly, there are several different types of fraud that are perpetrated on-line, including electronic auction or retail-based fraud schemes, stock scams, and the sale of counterfeit goods (Newman & Clarke, 2003; Wall, 2004). Another high-profile form of cyber-theft is digital piracy, or the illegal copying of digital media such as computer software, digital sound recordings, and digital video recordings without the explicit permission of the copyright holder (Higgins, 2005; Hinduja, 2003). Pirated materials can be downloaded easily in a variety of outlets via the Web, and are thought to cause billions of dollars in losses through lost revenue and jobs (Higgins, 2005).

The third category within Wall's (2001) typology includes cyber-porn and obscenity. Sexually explicit images and video are immediately accessible on-line and constitute a multibillion dollar industry (Edelman, 2009; Lane, 2000). Though these materials may not be illegal, the Internet has also fostered the growth of a wide range of communities supportive of deviant sexual behaviors (DiMarco, 2003). On-line spaces enable individuals to find others who share their interests, creating supportive communities where individuals can be part of a group that validates their practices (Rosenmann & Safir, 2006). For instance, the customers of prostitutes regularly use technology to communicate with others who share their interests and solicit illicit sexual services in the real world (Holt & Blevins, 2007). The Internet has also become a popular venue for pedophiles and sexual predators to gain access to potential child victims or child pornography (Durkin, 1997; Quayle & Taylor, 2002).

The final form of crime within Wall's (2001) typology is cyber-violence, representing the distribution of a variety of injurious, hurtful, or dangerous materials on-line. For example, individuals can now use the Internet as a means to threaten, bully, or harass others (Bocij, 2004; Finn, 2004). Harassment can take a variety of forms, such as threatening or sexual messages delivered via e-mail, instant messaging services, or posts in chatrooms. In addition, social networking sites engender individuals to post hurtful or mean comments for everyone to see without any direct contact with the intended target (Hinduja & Patchin, 2009). Victims of stalking and harassment may feel physical or emotional stress as a consequence, while others may report being able to ignore such comments entirely (Finn, 2004; Hinduja & Patchin, 2009). Estimates of on-line harassment and stalking appear to be on the rise, particularly among young people and college students, due in part to frequent Internet use among this population (Bocij, 2004; Finn, 2004; Wolak, Mitchell, & Finkelhor, 2006).

This text provides an exploration of activities from each of these four forms, with particular emphasis on participation in and victimization by hacking, fraud, theft, piracy, bullying, and stalking. These works provide an overview of the correlates and predictors of cybercrime victimization and offending, as well as the utility of traditional theories of crime for these emerging activities. But first, it is necessary to give adequate context to the evolution of research perspectives on cybercrime. Thus, selections from two seminal works are provided to frame the challenges that cybercrime poses to our concepts of law, policing, and criminality as a whole. The first article, by Grabosky (2001), provides one of the first discussions of cybercrimes during the earliest periods of investigation in this field. In this work, he argues that crime in cyberspace is "old wine in new bottles," in that traditional forms of offending are enabled through new tools. Computer technology simply provides another medium by which such information can be obtained from potential victims (Grabosky, 2001). In turn, this creates substantive challenges for police and private industry to investigate these offenses. In the second piece, Brenner (2007) provides a more recent discussion on the issue of cybercrime and its relationship to cyberterrorism, whereby extremist groups can engage in cyber-attacks to affect government and civilian targets. The inherent challenges these offenses pose to law enforcement require a reconceptualization of how cyberspace can be policed, and the role of civilians in order maintenance on-line. Thus, Brenner (2007) discusses these issues in detail and provides a model for the future of policing on- and off-line.

The fundamental insights provided by these pieces demonstrate the myriad threads in cyberspace and the difficulties that traditional criminal justice models face in combating cybercrimes. In order to improve the justice system's response to the constant shifts in offender behavior on-line, it is critical that researchers identify the causes and nature of participation in cybercrimes generally. Insights into the root causes of offending can be used to develop targeted enforcement strategies that may more effectively detect active criminals and deter prospective offenders. As a result, criminologists have created a number of theories to account for a range of deviant and criminal behaviors in the real world. There is, however, a lack of clarity as to the value of this body of knowledge to account for offenses in virtual environments. Thus, the remainder of this text presents seminal and cutting edge tests of traditional theories of both crime victimization and offending to consider their applicability to cybercrimes. In turn, this should enlighten our knowledge of cybercrime and criminological theories and identify key questions within each theoretical perspective that can advance the field as a whole.

## discussion questions

1. What are some of the factors that immediately differentiate cybercrimes from more traditional real-world offenses? For instance, does the anonymity afforded by the Internet make it more difficult to identify an individual responsible for an act of cybercrime?

2. What potential forms of cybercrime victimization do you think you may be exposed to on a daily basis? For instance, how frequently do you receive questionable e-mail messages with links to websites you have never seen before?

3. Why are cybercrimes such a challenge for traditional models of policing and criminal justice processing? Do you agree with Brenner's (2007) argument that citizens be greater incorporated into the regulation of on-line spaces?

## references

Anderson, J. (2010). *Understanding the Changing Needs of the U.S.Online Consumer, 2010. An Empowered Report: How Online and Mobile Behaviors Are Changing.* Forrester Research. [Online] Available at: http://www.forrester.com/rb/Research/understanding_changing_needs_of_us_online_consumer%2C/q/id/57861/t/2

Bocij, P. (2004). *Cyberstalking: Harassment in the Internet Age and How to Protect Your Family.* Westport, CT: Praeger.

Bossler, A. M., & Holt, T. J. (2009). On-line activities, guardianship, and malware infection: An examination of routine activities theory. *International Journal of Cyber Criminology, 3*, 400–420.

Brenner, S. W. (2007). At Light Speed: Attribution and Response to Cybercrime/Terrorism/Warfare. *Journal of Criminal Law and Criminology, 97*, 379–475.

Chu, B., Holt, T. J., & Ahn, G. J. (2010). *Examining the Creation, Distribution, and Function of Malware On-Line.*Washington, DC: National Institute of Justice. [Online] Available online at: www.ncjrs.gov./pdffiles1/nij/grants/230112.pdf

Computer Security Institute (2008). *Computer Crime and Security Survey.* [Online] Available at: http://www.cybercrime.gov/FBI2008.pdf

Computer Security Institute (2012). *Computer Crime and Security Survey.* [Online] Available at: http://www.cybercrime.gov/FBI2012.pdf

DiMarco, H. (2003). The electronic cloak: Secret sexual deviance in cybersociety. In Y. Jewkes (ed.), *Dot.cons: Crime, Deviance, and Identity on the Internet* (pp. 53–67). Portland, OR: Willan Publishing.

Durkin, K. F., & Bryant, C. D. (1999). Propagandizing pederasty. A thematic analysis of the on-line exculpatory accounts of unrepentant pedophiles. *Deviant Behavior, 20*, 103–127.

Edelman, B. (2009). Red Light States: Who Buys Online Adult Entertainment? *Journal of Economic Perspectives, 23*, 209–220.

Finn, J. (2004). A Survey of Online Harassment at a University Campus. *Journal of Interpersonal Violence, 19*, 468–483.

Furnell, S. (2002). *Cybercrime: Vandalizing the Information Society.*London: Addison-Wesley.

Grabosky, P. N. (2001). Virtual criminality: Old wine in new bottles? *Social and Legal Studies, 10*, 243–249.

Higgins, G. E. (2005). Can low self-control help with the understanding of the software piracy problem? *Deviant Behavior, 26*, 1–24.

Hinduja, S. (2003). Trends and Patterns among Software Pirates. *Ethics and Information Technology, 5*, 49–61.

Hinduja, S., & Patchin, J. W. (2009). *Bullying Beyond the Schoolyard: Preventing and Responding to Cyberbullying.* New York: Corwin Press.

Holt, T.J. (2007). Subcultural evolution? Examining the influence of on- and off-line experiences on deviant subcultures. *Deviant Behavior, 28*, 171–198.

Holt, T. J., & Blevins, K. R. (2007). Examining sex work from the client's perspective: Assessing johns using online data. *Deviant Behavior, 28*, 333–354.

Jordan, T., & Taylor, P. (1998). A sociology of hackers. *Sociological Review, 46*, 757–780.

Lane, F. S. (2000). *Obscene Profits: The Entrepreneurs of Pornography in the Cyber Age.* New York: Routledge.

Newman, G., & Clarke, R. (2003). *Superhighway Robbery: Preventing E-Commerce Crime.* Cullompton, UK: Willan Press.

Quayle, E., & Taylor, M. (2002). Child pornography and the Internet: Perpetuating a cycle of abuse. *Deviant Behavior, 23*, 331–361.

Quinn, J. F., & Forsyth, C. J. (2005). Describing sexual behavior in the era of the internet: A typology for empirical research. *Deviant Behavior, 26*, 191–207.

Rosenmann, A., & Safir, M. P. (2006). Forced Online: Pushed Factors of Internet Sexuality: A Preliminary Study of Paraphilic Empowerment. *Journal of Homosexuality, 51*, 71–92.

Taylor, R. W., Fritsch, E. J., Liederbach, J., & Holt, T. J. (2010). *Digital Crime and Digital Terrorism, 2nded.* Upper Saddle River, NJ: Pearson Prentice Hall.

Wall, D. S. (2001). Cybercrimes and the Internet. In D. S. Wall (ed.), *Crime and the Internet* (pp. 1–17). New York: Routledge.

Wall, D. S. (2004). Digital realism and the governance of spam as cybercrime. *European Journal on Criminal Policy and Research, 10*, 309–335.

Wall, D. S. (2007). *Cybercrime: The Transformation of Crime in the Information Age.* Cambridge: Polity Press.

Wolak, J., Mitchell, K., & Finkelhor, D. (2006). *Online Victimization of Youth: Five Years Later.* Washington, DC: National Center for Missing & Exploited Children.

peter n. grabosky

# virtual criminality: old wine in new bottles?

## interpersonal relations in cyberspace

Digital technology has, to some extent, impacted on interpersonal relations. The illusion of anonymity seems to have elicited more candour over the internet than one would expect in face-to-face communications. But whether the role play that occurs in some chatrooms constitutes something completely different from good theatre, in which the actors are immersed in their roles, is open to question. To be sure, some of this role play is extremely aggressive, or otherwise antisocial. But any more so than a performance of Hamlet?

The internet has indeed brought about significant changes in human interaction. Ordinary investors are now able to buy and sell shares online without dealing through intermediaries such as underwriters, brokers and investment advisers. While this may enhance the efficiency of securities markets, it also provides opportunities for criminal exploitation. But the fundamental criminality is still reducible to the basics: misrepresenting the underlying value of a security at the time of the initial public offering, or market manipulation during secondary trading of a security, through the dissemination of false information, or engineering a deceptive pattern of transactions to attract the attention of the unwitting investor. One hears anecdotes about children who have been lured from the safety of their homes by paedophiles after an initial encounter in an internet chatroom, or women who, after an electronically arranged assignation, meet with foul play at the hands of a predator. But is this really new? Cyberspace serves the same function as the busstop, the schoolyard or the disco.

There is another sense in which digital criminality may be similar to conventional criminality. At the risk of oversimplification, one may divide conventional criminals into two classes: the competent and the incompetent. Sooner or later, most of the latter wind up in prison. The competent ones avoid detection, or at the very least, prosecution and conviction. So it is with cybercriminals. The most adept are never noticed, much less identified. By contrast the inept cybercriminal leaves his footprints all over cyberspace.

## new challenges for the state

The digital age has begun to pose new challenges for the state. Blasphemous, seditious, salacious, and otherwise offensive communications have long been the focus of governmental preoccupation. In an era where many governments seek to shed functions and devolve powers, the urge to control digital technology remains strong. And yet the ability of governments and legal systems to adapt to new media for the transmission of offensive content is somewhat limited. Of course, one could always 'pull the plug', and severely restrict citizens' access to cyberspace. But those governments which seek to maximize the economic well-being of their citizenry realize that it is futile to try to hold back the tide of globalization, and that failure to get in on the ground floor of electronic commerce may retard economic development.

The challenges faced by governments are by no means limited to the regulation of online content. In English-speaking societies at the very least, the capacity of public police is now acknowledged to be limited. Most victims of residential burglary are aware that they stand little chance of recovering their lost possessions; they harbour few illusions that 'their' offender will eventually be brought to justice. The role of the police is often limited to that of legitimizing insurance claims and providing a few kind words (and perhaps some crime prevention advice) to the victim. Individuals are, to an extent that few wish to acknowledge openly, largely on their own as far as crime prevention is concerned. And so those who can afford it acquire sophisticated alarm systems and live in 'gated' communities. The necessity of self-reliance in crime control is no less in cyberspace than in one's physical neighbourhood.

## paradoxes of the digital age

In addition to the tension between the shrinking state, and the imperative to direct traffic on the information superhighway, the digital age has given rise to other paradoxes. Technologies of anonymity and pseudonymity such as remailers and cryptography can provide a modicum of cover for someone wishing to mask his or her identity and the content of his or her communication.

But not everyone avails themselves of such technologies, and capacities of surveillance exceed all but the most determined users.

Cryptography, regarded by law enforcement as a threat, is one of the fundamental pillars of electronic commerce. Without this secure technology, electronic payments, much less the transmittal of one's credit card details, would be that much riskier. Cryptography may be a boon to criminals, but it is arguably an even greater boon to legitimate business.

Arguably, the internet constitutes a greater threat to privacy than was ever thought possible. The possibility of remaining anonymous in cyberspace, far from being endless, appears significantly constrained. Moreover, the threat to privacy may come from private as well as governmental sources. Much is made of so-called 'hacker sites' and chatrooms devoted to 'teensex', many of which are essentially accessible to the public. The fact remains that these can be wonderful sources of intelligence for law enforcement agencies or information security specialists. The annals of law enforcement are expanding with examples of police officers posing as 13-year-old girls who arrange online assignations with those who were once described as 'dirty old men'.

## the private threat to privacy

Of perhaps even greater significance is the exploitation of personal information by private commercial interests. The amount of personal information available about individuals' spending patterns and consumer preferences is surprising to many. In the past, information privacy was protected by data dispersion (Clarke, 1988). A great deal of personal information may have been stored here and there in various locations (whether public or private), but aside from major investigations, the cumbersome logistics of sorting through rooms full of forms in one place and another precluded collation on any significant scale. Technologies of data manipulation that permit merging of databases and matching of individual identities now facilitate the aggregation of data from disparate sources (Clarke, 1988). The term 'data mining' is commonly used to refer to such practices. The linkage of disparate data is facilitated by the existence of identification numbers that are common in most industrial societies. The nine-digit Social Security Number in the United States is a classic example. Through the collation of disparate personal details, the whole becomes greater than the sum of its parts.

One suspects that most individuals are not resorting increasingly to anonymity, and that their personal details are accessible in abundance. Moreover, these details are traded freely by marketing firms.

Many people who use electronic mail do so with unusual candour. In the words of Bennahum (1999, 102) 'Email is a truth serum'. But unlike a face-to-face conversation, electronic communications are not evanescent. Records persist, and may return to haunt one or more participants in the communication. Even when a message is erased, it may have been retained by another party to the communication, or it may have been 'backed up' on one or more system files. Moreover, many communications are accessible merely by using readily available search technology. One estranged husband searched the internet for his ex-wife's account name and collected 30 pages of messages that she had posted in chatrooms, not all of which reflected well on her as a parent. Seeking greater visiting rights with his children, he presented them unsuccessfully to the mediator in his custody hearing (Glod, 1999).

## the transnational dimension

One of the greatest challenges posed by the advent of digital criminality is the enormously enhanced potential for transnational offending. Many, if not most, cybercrimes can now be committed from the other side of the world as easily as from the building next door. Not only will this tend to make identification of the perpetrator somewhat more difficult, it will greatly impede prosecution of the offender.

Despite the hackneyed contention that the world is shrinking, laws differ. Some jurisdictions prohibit unauthorized access to a computer system, while others do not. Some make it a crime to alter or erase data, while others do not. Nations such as Germany make it a crime to disseminate neo-Nazi propaganda. As distasteful as such material may be, the right to do so is protected by the Constitution of the United States of America. Some nations criminalize online gambling, while others see it as a wonderful source of export income.

A degree of common legal ground is required in order to mobilize the law of a foreign state on one's behalf. Without 'dual criminality', assistance of the jurisdiction in which the offender is situated is most unlikely to be forthcoming. But even if there is a degree of consistency, enforcement by officials in the host nation may by no means follow automatically. All law enforcement agencies have their priorities. If I, comfortably situated in Australia, were foolish enough to fall victim to an online investment fraud originating in Albania, the Australian authorities and/or their Albanian counterparts may have more pressing demands. 'My' case may never receive serious investigative consideration by authorities in either jurisdiction.

## references

Bennahum, D. (1999) 'Daemon Seed: Old Email Never Dies', *Wired* 7.05 (May) 100–11.

Clarke, R. (1988) Information Technology and Dataveillance. Commun. ACM 31,5 (May 1988) 498–512 http://www.anu.edu.au/people/Roger.Clarke/DV/CACM88.html (visited 30 December 1999)

Glod, M. (1999) 'Spouses may delete their marriage, but e-mail lives on as evidence', *Seattle Times* 28/4/99. http: //archives.seattletimes.com/cgi-bin/texis.mummy/ web/vortex/display? StoryID = 3733259942 &query = internet + and + privacy (visited 13 June 1999)

Grabosky, P., R. G. Smith and G. Dempsey (2001) *Electronic Theft: Unlawful Acquisition in Cyberspace*. Cambridge: Cambridge University Press.

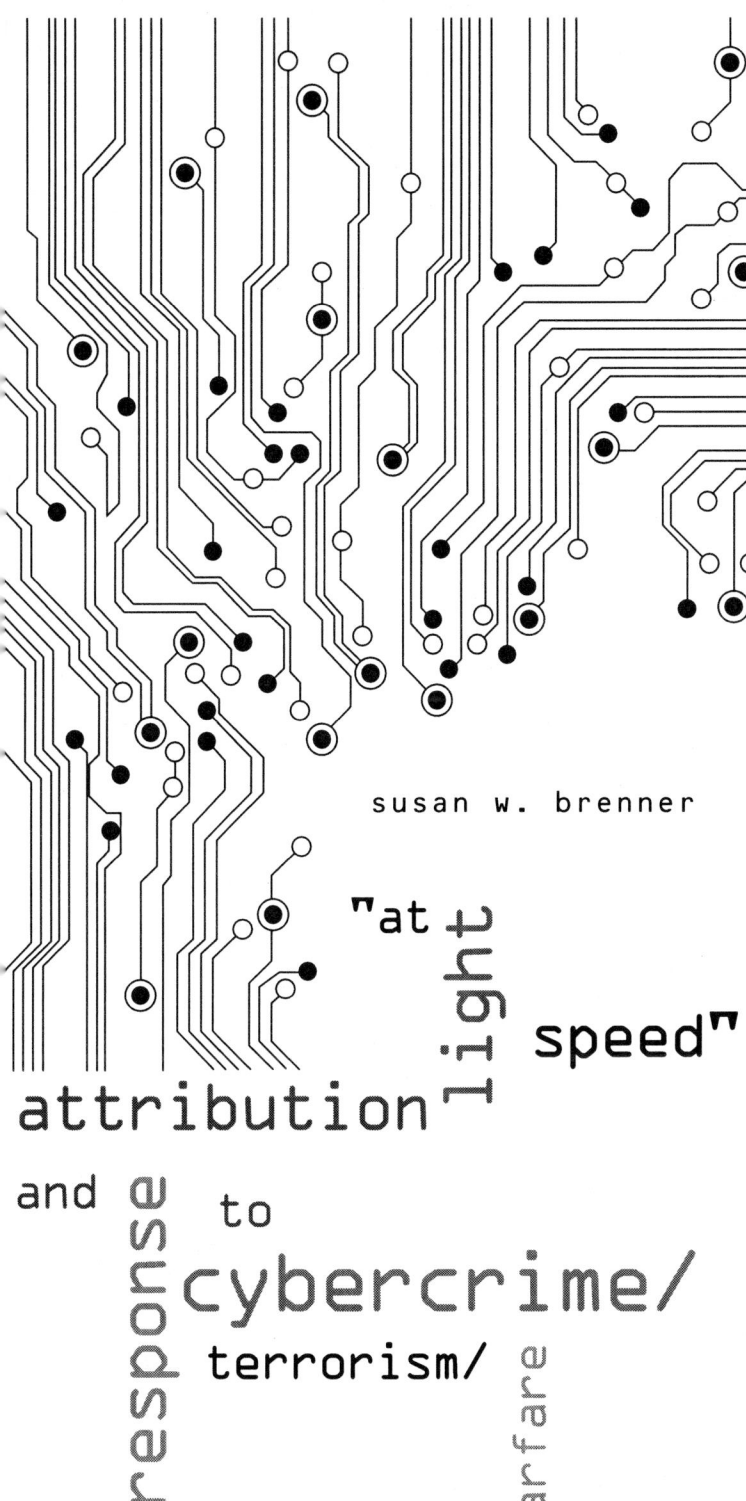

susan w. brenner

"at light speed"

attribution

and response to cybercrime/terrorism/warfare

Societies have historically used a two-pronged strategy to maintain the order they need to survive and prosper. Societies maintain internal order by articulating and enforcing a set of proscriptive rules (criminal law enforcement) that discourage the members of a society from preying upon each other in ways that undermine order, such as by killing, robbing, or committing arson.[1] Societies maintain external order by relying on military force (war) and, to an increasing extent, international agreements.[2] I call this the internal–external threat dichotomy, and the choice between law enforcement and military the attack-response dynamic.

As we will see, computer technology erodes the empirical realities that generated and sustain this dichotomous approach to maintaining order. This approach is based on the assumption that each

---

1   See Brenner, *Toward a Criminal Law for Cyberspace*, *supra* note 5 at 6–49.
2   See id.

Susan W. Brenner, "At Light Speed: Attribution and Response to Cybercrime/Terrorism/Warfare," *Journal of Criminal Law & Criminology*, vol. 97, no. 2, pp. 382-400, 405-424, 427-430, 441-468, 472-474. Copyright © 2007 by ProQuest. Reprinted with permission.

society occupies a territorially-defined physical locus—that, in other words, sovereignty and "country" are indistinguishable.[3] One consequence of the presumptive isomorphism between sovereignty and territory is that threats to social order are easily identifiable as being *either* internal (crime/terrorism) or external (war). Computer-mediated communication erodes the validity of this binary decision tree by making territory increasingly irrelevant; as a study of cybercrime laws noted, "In the networked world, no island is an island."[4] In the twenty-first century, those bent on undermining a society's ability to maintain order can launch virtual attacks from almost anywhere in the world. As a result, these attacks may not fit neatly into the internal–external threat dichotomy and the attribution hierarchy (crime/terrorism, war) derived from that dichotomy.

Section II outlines a taxonomy of the three categories of cyberthreats: cybercrime, cyberterrorism, and cyberwarfare. Section III explains how these online variations of real-world threat categories challenge the processes we currently use for threat attribution.

## cybercrime

An online dictionary defines "cybercrime" as "a crime committed on a computer network."[5] The basic problem with this definition is that American lawyers need to be able to fit the concept of "cybercrime" into the specific legal framework used in the United States and into the more general legal framework that ties together legal systems around the world in their battle against cybercrime.[6] That leads me to ask several questions: Is cybercrime different from regular crime? If so, how? If not, if cybercrime is merely a boutique version of crime, why do we need a new term for it?

The first step in answering these questions is parsing out what cybercrime is and what it is not. When we do this, we see that the definition quoted above needs to be modified for two reasons.

The first reason is that this definition assumes every cybercrime constitutes nothing more than the commission of a traditional crime by non-traditional means (using a computer network instead of, say, a gun). As I have argued elsewhere,[7] that is true for much of the cybercrime we have seen so far. For example, online fraud such as the 419 scam[8] is nothing new as far as the law is concerned; it is simply "old wine in new bottles."[9] Until the twentieth century, people had only two ways of defrauding others: they could do it face to face by offering to sell someone the Brooklyn Bridge for a *very* good price; or they could do the same thing by using snail mail.[10] The proliferation of telephones in the twentieth

---

3 *See* Restatement (Third) of Foreign Relations Law § 201 (1987); *see, e.g.,* Black's Law Dictionary 377 (8th ed. 2004) (defining "country" as "a nation or political state"); *see also* Country—Wikipedia, http://en.wikipedia.org/wiki/Country (last visited Apr. 21,2007).

4 McConnell Int'l, Cyber Crime … and Punishment? Archaic Laws Threaten Global Information 8 (2000), *available at* http://www.witsa.org/papers/McConnell-cybercrime.pdf.

5 Cybercrime—definitions from Dictionary.com, http://dictionary.reference.com/browse/cybercrime (last visited Apr. 21, 2007).

6 It might be more accurate to cite the *evolving* framework that is intended to unite legal systems in the battle against cybercrime. *See* Convention on Cybercrime, Council of Europe, Nov. 23, 2001, C.E.T.S. No. 185, *available at* http://conventions.coe.int/Treaty/en/Treaties/Html/185.htm [hereinafter Convention on Cybercrime Treaty]; Convention on Cybercrime, Council of Europe, Signatures and Ratifications, Nov. 23, 2001, C.E.T.S. No. 185, *available at* http://conventions.coe.int/Treaty/Commun/ChercheSig.asp?NT = 185&CM = 8&DF = 12/11/2006&CL-ENG.

7 *See* Susan W. Brenner, *Is There Such a Thing as Virtual Crime?*, 4 Cal. Crim. L. Rev. 1 pp. 120–29 (2001), http://www.boalt.org/CCLR/v4/v4brenner.htm [hereinafter Brenner, *Virtual Crime*].

8 *See* Advance fee fraud—Wikipedia, http://en.wikipedia.org/wiki/Advance_fee_fraud (last visited Apr. 21, 2007); Nigeria—The 419 Coalition Website, http://home.rica.net/alphae/419coal/ (last visited Apr. 21, 2007).

9 *See* Advance fee fraud—Wikipedia, *supra* note 18.

10 *See, e.g.,* David W. Maurer, The Big Con 31–102 (1999).

century made it possible for scam artists to use the telephone to sell the bridge, again at a *very* good price.[11] And we now see twenty-first century versions of the same scams migrating online.

The same is happening with other traditional crimes, such as theft, extortion, harassment, and trespassing.[12] Indeed, it seems reasonable to believe that many, if not most, of the crimes with which we have traditionally dealt will migrate online in some fashion. Admittedly, a few traditional crimes—such as rape and bigamy—probably will not migrate online because the commission of these particular crimes requires physical activity that cannot occur online (unless, of course, we revise our definition of bigamy to encompass virtual bigamy).[13]

The same cannot be said of homicide: while we have no documented cases in which computer technology was used to take human life, this scenario is certainly conceivable and will no doubt occur.[14] Those who speculate on such things have postulated instances in which someone would hack into the database of a hospital and kill people by altering the dosage of their medication.[15] The killer would no doubt find this a particularly clever way to commit murder because the crime might never be discovered. The deaths might well be put down to negligence on the part of hospital staff;[16] and even if they were identified as homicide, it might be very difficult to determine which of the victims were the intended targets of the unknown killer and thereby begin the investigative process.

My point is that while most of the cybercrime we have seen to date is simply the commission of traditional crimes by new means, this will not be true of *all* cybercrime. We already have at least one completely new cybercrime: a distributed denial of service (DDoS) attack. A DDoS attack overloads computer servers and "make[s] a computer resource [such as a website] unavailable to its intended users."[17] In February 2000, a Canadian known as "Mafiaboy" launched attacks that effectively shut down websites operated by CNN, Yahoo!, Amazon.com, and eBay, among others.[18]

DDoS attacks are increasingly used for extortion.[19] Someone launches an attack on a website, then stops the attack and explains to the website owner that the attack will continue unless and until the owner pays a sum for "protection" against such attacks.[20] This is the commission of an old crime

---

11  *See, e.g.,* Fed. Trade Comm'n, Putting Telephone Scams ... On Hold (2004), *available at* http://www.ftc.gov/bcp/conline/pubs/tmarkg/target.htm.

12  *See* Brenner, *Virtual Crime, supra* note 17, ¶¶ 39–50, 61–68.

13  *Id.* ¶¶ 104–26.

14  There are reports of attempts to use computer technology to cause injury or death: "[H]ackers have infiltrated hospital computers and altered prescriptions. ... [A] hacker prescribed potentially lethal drugs to a nine-year-old boy who was suffering from meningitis. The boy was saved only because a nurse caught the deviation prior to the drug being administered." Howard L. Steele, Jr., *The Prevention of Non-Consensual Access to "Confidential" Health-Care Information in Cyberspace,* 1 Comp. L. Rev. & Tech. J. 101, 102 (1997), *available at* http://www.smu.edu/csr/Steele.pdf. This same interloper had also prescribed unnecessary antibiotics to a seventy-year-old woman. *Id.*

15  *Stealing the Network: How to Own A Continent* outlines a creative cyber-homicide scenario: *Uber-hacker* Bob Knuth tricks Saul, a student, into hacking into a hospital's wireless network. FX et al., STEALING THE NETWORK: HOW TO OWN A CONTINENT 39–75 (2004).

16  *See id.*

17  Denial of service attack—Wikipedia, http://en.wikipedia.org/wiki/Denial-of-service_attack (last visited Apr. 21, 2007).

18  *See, e.g.,* Pierre Thomas & D. Ian Hopper, *Canadian Juvenile Charged in Connection with February "Denial of Service" Attacks,* CNN.com, Apr. 18, 2000, http://archives.cnn.com/2000/TECH/computing/04/18/hacker.arrest.01/.

19  *See, e.g.,* McAfee NA Virtual Criminology Report 6–19 (2005), *available at* http://www.softaart.eom/mcafee/docs/Mort.pdf; Paul McNamara, *Addressing "DDoS Extortion,"* Network World, May 23, 2005, *available at* http://www.networkworld.com/columnists/2005/052305buzz.html; Jose Nazario, *Cyber Extortion, A Very Real Threat*, IT-Observer, June 7, 2006, http://www.it-observer.com/articles/1153/cyber_extortion_very_real_threat/.

20  *See, e.g.,* Erik Larkin, *Web of Crime: Enter the Professionals,* PC WORLD, Aug. 22, 2005, *available at* http://pcworld.about.com/news/Aug222005idl22240.htm.

(extortion) by a new means, little different from tactics the Mafia used over half a century ago, though they relied on arson instead.[21]

But a "pure" DDoS attack, such as the 2000 attacks on Amazon.com and eBay, is not a traditional crime. It is not theft, fraud, extortion, vandalism, burglary, or any crime that was within a pre–twentieth century prosecutor's repertoire.[22] It is an example of a new type of crime: a "pure" cybercrime.[23] As such, it requires that we create new law that would make it a crime to launch such an attack.[24]

To summarize, one reason why the definition quoted above is unsatisfactory is that it does not encompass the proposition that cybercrime can consist of committing "new" crimes—crimes we have not seen before and therefore have not outlawed—as well as "old" crimes. The other reason I take issue with this definition is that it links the commission of cybercrime with the use of a computer network.[25]

Certainly, use of computer networks is usually true for cybercrime. In fact, it is probably the default model of cybercrime. But it is also possible that computer technology, not network technology, can be used for illegal purposes. A non-networked computer can, for example, be used to counterfeit currency or to forge documents.[26] In either instance, a computer—but not a computer network—is being used to commit a crime. Here, the computer is being used to commit an "old" crime, but it is at least conceptually possible that a non-networked computer could be used to commit a "new" crime of some type.

Thus, a better definition of cybercrime is the use of computer technology to commit crime; to engage in activity that threatens a society's ability to maintain internal order. This definition encompasses both traditional and emerging cybercrimes. It also encompasses *any* use of computer technology, not merely the use of networked computer technology.

This generic definition does not, of course, provide the legal predicate needed to respond to cybercrime, as it is a conceptual definition of a category of crime rather than the definition of a particular offense or particular offenses. To ensure they can respond to new types of cybercrime, societies must monitor online activity in an effort to identify emerging activities that constitute a threat to their ability to maintain internal order. Once identified, these activities should be criminalized, just as the United Kingdom recently criminalized DDoS attacks.[27]

## cyberterrorism

[G]et ready ... terrorists are preparing ... cyberspace based attacks. ...[28]

Generically, cyberterrorism consists of using computer technology to engage in terrorist activity.[29] This definition mirrors the generic definition of cybercrime articulated in the previous section, which is

21   *See, e.g.,* President's Comm'n on Law Enforcement and Admin, of Justice, Crime in a Free Society: Excerpts from the President's Commission on Law Enforcement and Administration of Justice 192–209 (1968).
22   *See* Brenner, *Virtual Crime, supra* note 17, ¶¶ 73–76.
23   *See id.*
24   Otherwise, there is no crime. In fact, until recently this was the case in the United Kingdom: the U.K.'s 1990 Computer Misuse Act outlawed hacking and other online variants of traditional crime, but it did not address DDoS attacks. Tom Espiner, *U.K. Outlaws Denial-of-Service Attacks,* CNET News.com, Nov. 10, 2006, http://news.com/2100-7348_3-6134472.html.
25   *See* Cybercrime—definitions, *supra* note 15.
26   *See, e.g.,* Convention on Cybercrime Treaty, *supra* note 16; United States Secret Service: Know Your Money—Counterfeit Awareness, http://www.secretservice.gov/money_technologies.shtml (last visited Apr. 21, 2007).
27   *See, e.g.,* Espiner, *supra* note 34.
28   John Arquilla, *Waging War Through the Internet,* S.F. Chron, Jan. 15, 2006, at E1, *available at* http://ww.sfgate.com/cgi-bin/article.cgi7f-/c/a/2006/01/15/ING2AGLP 021.DTL [hereinafter Arquilla, *Waging War Through the Internet*].
29   *See, e.g.,* Clay Wilson, Cong. Research Serv., Computer Attack and Cyberterrorism: Vulnerabilities and Policy Issues for Congress (2005).

appropriate given that societies treat terrorism as a type of crime. However, societies conflate crime and terrorism because both threaten their ability to maintain internal order. The assumption, which derives from the dichotomy noted earlier, is that all threats to internal order should be dealt with in the same way.[30]

Although societies conflate crime and terrorism, we need to distinguish them because they differ in ways that are relevant to how societies need to respond to them. Basically, crime is personal while terrorism is political.[31] Crimes are committed for individual and personal reasons, the most important of which are personal gain and the desire or need to harm others psychologically and/or physically.[32]

Terrorism often results in the infliction of harms indistinguishable from those caused by certain types of crime (such as death, personal injury, or property destruction), but the harms are inflicted for very different reasons.[33] A federal statute, for example, defines "terrorism" as committing acts constituting crimes under the law of any country to intimidate or coerce a civilian population; to influence government policy by intimidation or coercion; or to affect the conduct of government by mass destruction, assassination, or kidnapping.[34] We will return to the issue of terrorism-as-crime in a moment, but first we need to focus on what precisely is involved in the commission of terrorist acts.

As the above definition suggests, terrorism is usually intended to directly or indirectly demoralize a civilian population;[35] this distinguishes terrorism from warfare, which is not supposed to target

---

30  For the proposition that crime and terrorism both threaten internal order, see *supra* Section I.
The move to criminalize terrorism began in the 1930s as a reaction to the assassination of King Alexander I of Yugoslavia. *See* Ben Saul, *The Legal Response of the League of Nations to Terrorism,* 4 J. Int'l Crim. Just. 78, 79 (2006). It resulted in the adoption of the 1937 League of Nations' Convention for the Prevention and Punishment of Terrorism, which required parties to adopt legislation criminalizing terrorism. *See* Reuven Young, *Defining Terrorism: The Evolution of Terrorism as a Legal Concept in International Law and Its Influence on Definitions in Domestic Legislation,* 29 B.C. Int'l & Comp. L. Rev. 23, 35–36 (2006). One proponent of the 1937 Convention, Czechoslovakia, said that "criminalization was necessary to protect 'security of life and limb, health, liberty and public property intended for the common use.'" Saul, *supra,* at 81 (quoting J. Starke, *The Convention for the Prevention and Punishment of Terrorism,* 19 British Year Book Int'l. L. 60 (1938)). As one author noted, "Ordinary criminal offences aim to achieve the same object." Saul, *supra,* at 82.
The 1937 Convention never went into effect, but its approach proved influential; its successor, the United Nations, has consistently defined terrorism as criminal activity. *See* Young, *supra,* at 36–40; see, *e.g.,* G.A. Res. 49/60, U.N. Doc. A/RES/49/60 (Feb. 17, 1995), *available at* http://www.un.org/documents/ga/res/49/a49r060.htm.

31  *See, e.g.,* Paul R. Pillar, Terrorism and U.S. Foreign Policy 13–14 (2001).

32  Id.

33  *See, e.g.,* Pippa Norris, Montague Kern & Marion Just, *Introduction: Framing Terrorism, in* Framing Terrorism: The News Media, the Government, and the Public 3, 8 (Pippa Norris, Montague Kern & Marion Just eds., 2003) [hereinafter Framing Terrorism] (distinguishing terrorism from "crimes motivated purely by private gain, such as blackmail, murder, or physical assault directed against individuals, groups, or companies, without any political objectives").

34  18 U.S.C. § 2331 (2000). For more definitions, see, *e.g.,* Mohammad Iqbal, *Defining Cyberterrorism,* 22 J. Marshall J. Computer & Info. L. 397 (2004).

35  We are familiar with terrorist acts that are intended directly to demoralize a civilian population, such as the 9/11 attacks in the United States and the 3/11 Madrid bombings. In both instances, violence was used for symbolic purposes, and the goal was to shock and demoralize the populace of societies with which Al-Qaeda deems itself to be at war—an ideological war aimed at allowing the restoration of the "ancient Islamic caliphate." *See* Lawrence Wright, The Looming Tower: Al-Qaeda and the Road to 9/11 175, 234–35 (2006); *see also* Norris, Kern & Just, *supra* note 43, at 7–8.
The goal in these and similar attacks is to demoralize civilians by directly demonstrating their vulnerability through the inability of their government to protect them from seemingly random violence. One source explains how this demoralization ties into the terrorists' goals:

> Terrorists may create … fear … to influence their negotiations with … governments, but fear has secondary consequences that further undermine government authority. … [F]ear fragments and isolates society into anxious groups of individuals concerned only with their personal survival. … "Terrorism destroys the solidarity, cooperation, and interdependence on which social functioning is based, and substitutes insecurity and distrust." The breakdown of social trust and cooperation could have serious effects on how society functions.

Leonie Huddy et al., *Fear and Terrorism, in* Framing Terrorism, *supra* note 43, at 255, 255 (quoting Martha C. Hutchinson, *The Concept of Revolutionary Terrorism,* 6 J. Conflict Resol. 288 (1973)); *see also* Information Operations: Warfare and

civilians.[36] In the real-world, terrorism usually achieves its primary goal[37] of demoralizing civilians by destroying property and injuring or killing civilians[38] The 9/11 attacks on the World Trade Center are a perfect example of real-world terrorism; they were intended to destroy a premier symbol of capitalism and in so doing undermine the morale of U.S. citizens and the stability of the U.S. society.[39]

To date, there have been no known instances of cyberterrorism.[40] There have been cases which media has incorrectly described as cyberterrorism: in 2000, an Australian man hacked into a municipal waste-management system and dumped "millions of litres of raw sewage" into parks, rivers, and businesses.[41] Elsewhere, in 1997 a Massachusetts hacker shut down all communications to a Federal Aviation Administration (FAA) control tower at an airport for six hours.[42] These and similar cases, however, involved *cybercrime*, not cyberterrorism. In each instance, the perpetrator acted out of individual motivations—a desire for revenge or power—instead of out of a desire to advance a particular ideology by demoralizing segments of a civilian population.[43]

---

the Hard Reality of Soft Power 92 (Leigh Armistead ed. 2004) [hereinafter Information Operations] ("[Terrorism is an attack on the legitimacy of the established order."). For more on this, see *infra* Sections II.B.2–3.

36   *See* U.N. Office of the High Comm'r for Human Rights, *Geneva Convention Relative to the Protection of Civilian Persons in Time of War*, Aug. 12, 1949, *available at* http://www.unhchr.ch/html/menu3/b/92.htm; *see also* Terrorism—Wikipedia, http://en.wikipedia.org/wiki/Definition_of_terrorism (last visited Apr. 21, 2007).

37   It is important to realize—especially when analyzing cyberterrorism—that terrorists also have secondary goals. Their secondary goals involve the successful conducting of activities that sustain and promote their ability to work toward achieving their primary goal. These goals include disseminating propaganda; recruiting news members of a terrorist group and retaining existing members; fundraising to support terrorist activities and the terrorists themselves; training terrorists in attack strategies; coordinating attacks; and researching attack targets. *See, e.g.,* Eben Kaplan, Council on Foreign Rel., Terrorists and the Internet (2006), *available at* http://www.cfr.org/publication/10005/; *see also* U.S. Dep't of State, Country Reports on Terrorism 2005 17 (2006), *available at* http://www.state.gov/documents/organization/65462.pdf [hereinafter Country Reports on Terrorism 2005] ("Terrorists exploit electronic infrastructure ... for recruitment, training, planning, resource transfer, and intelligence collection between and among ... terrorist groups. ... Harnessing the Internet's potential for speed, security, and global linkage gives terrorists the ability to conduct many of the activities that once required physical haven, yet without the associated security risks. With the ability to communicate, recruit, train, and prepare for attacks, any computer may function essentially as a 'virtual' safe haven.").

This Article focuses exclusively on terrorists' use of computer technology to further their primary goal of demoralizing civilians for two reasons: 1) brevity; and 2) using computer technology to further primary goals is the essence of cyberterrorism.

38   "[A]cts done to advance an ideological ... cause and to induce terror in any population ... are terrorism if they cause one of the following outcomes: death or serious injury; serious risk to public health or safety; destruction or serious damage to property." Young, *supra* note 40, at 86 (summarizing Terrorism Suppression Act, 2002, § 5 (N.Z.)).

39   *See, e.g.,* Wright, *supra* note 45, at 308.

40   But see Arquilla, Waging War Through the Internet, supra note 38, at E1.

41   Tony Smith, *Hacker Jailed for Revenge Sewage Attacks*, Register, Oct. 31, 2001, http://www.theregister.co.uk/2001/10/31/hackerJailed_for_revenge_sewage/.

42   Bill Wallace, *Next Major Attack Could Be Over Net*, S.F. Chron., Nov. 12, 2001, at A1, *available at* http://www.sfgate.com/cgi-bin/article.cgi?file=/chronicle/archive/ 2001/11/12/MN29929.DTL.

43   Probably the closest thing we have to a reported cyberterrorist attack came in 1998 when:

> Tamil guerrillas swamped Sri Lankan embassies with 800 e-mails a day over a two-week period. The messages read, "We are the Internet Black Tigers and we're doing this to disrupt your communications." Intelligence authorities characterized it as the first known ... attack by terrorists against a country's computer systems.

Rohas Nagpal, *Cyber Terrorism in the Context of Globalization*, 2 World Congress on Informatics & L. 22 (2002), *available at* http://www.ied.org/congreso/ponencias/Nagpal,%20Rohas.pdf. The Tamil Tigers have certainly proven to be terrorists, and their email bombing was undertaken to promote an ideological agenda. See Council on Foreign Rel., Liberation Tigers of Tamil Eelam (2006), *available at* http://www.cfr.org/publication/9242/. Some might argue that this attack did not constitute cyberterrorism because it targeted computer systems at embassies located in countries other than Sri Lanka and therefore did not impact Sri Lanka's civilian populace. But the attack did shut down the embassy computers and "had the desired effect of generating fear in the embassies." Dorothy E. Denning, *Activism, Hacktivism, and Cyberterrorism: The Internet as a Tool for Influencing Foreign Policy, in* Networks and Netwars: The Future of Terror, Crime, and Militancy 236, 239 (John Arquilla & David F. Ronfeldt eds., 2001), *available at* http://www.nautilus.org/archives/info-policy/workshop/papers/denning.html.

To understand what cyberterrorism can and will be, we must parse out how terrorists can use computer technology to demoralize a civilian population and thereby undermine a society's ability to sustain internal order.[44] Conceptually, computer technology's use for this purpose falls into three categories: (1) weapon of mass destruction; (2) weapon of mass distraction; and (3) weapon of mass disruption.[45] I now examine each, in order.

## weapon of mass destruction

This is a conceptual option, but not a real possibility. The notion that computer technology can be a weapon of mass destruction is based on a flawed premise: the concept that computers, alone, can be used to inflict the kind of demoralizing carnage the world saw in New York and Washington, D.C., on 9/11 or in Madrid on 3/11.[46] Computers, as such, cannot inflict physical damage on persons or property; that is the province of real-world implements of death and destruction.[47]

However, computers *can* be used to set in motion forces that produce physical damage. Instead of hacking into a municipal waste-management system for revenge, cyberterrorists could disable the systems that control a nuclear power plant and cause an explosion like the one at Chernobyl in 1986.[48] By claiming responsibility for the catastrophe, the cyberterrorists could exploit the resulting illness, death, and radioactive contamination to undermine citizens' faith in their government's ability to protect them and maintain order.

This is a viable terrorism scenario, but it is not a *cyber*terrorism scenario. While computer technology would be used to trigger the explosion, the victims would recall it as a *nuclear* catastrophe, not as a *computer* catastrophe. Here, as in other computer as weapon of mass destruction scenarios, computer technology plays an incidental role in the commission of a terrorist act, serving merely as a detonator. To describe this scenario as cyberterrorism is as inappropriate as describing the 1998 U.S. embassy

---

44   While some dismiss the possibility of cyberterrorism, others correctly understand that it is not merely a possibility, but an inevitability. *See, e.g.,* Arquilla, *Waging War Through the Internet, supra* note 38, at E1.

> Despite ... al Qaeda's long-standing interest in cyber terror, we have been ... dismissive of this burgeoning threat. In part, that's because we doubt terrorists will focus on using computers to attack computer systems, believing instead that "real terrorists" want to kill people and blow things up. ...
>
> From a purely psychological point of view, this idea makes sense, as traditional terrorists have been leg-breakers. ... But over the past four years, we have made it very hard for al Qaeda to mount new attacks within the United States.
>
> So, if Osama bin Laden wants to pursue his goal of attacking our economy, disruptive cyber-terror strikes via the Internet are likely to be an increasingly important element in his offensive.

*Id.* Arquilla also attributes our tendency to dismiss cyberterrorism to our misplaced confidence "in our defensive capabilities." *Id.*

45   The discussion that follows focuses on terrorists' use of computer technology to further their *primary* goal of advancing an ideological agenda. It does not address the use of computer technology to further the secondary goals noted earlier.

46   2004 Madrid train bombings—Wikipedia, http://en.wikipedia.org/wiki/11_March_2004_Madrid_train_bombings (last visited Apr. 21, 2007).

47   The erroneous assumption that computer technology is merely another mode of mass destruction accounts for the skepticism many express about the prospects of a "digital Pearl Harbor" or a "digital 9/11." *See, e.g.,* Drew Clark, *Computer Security Officials Discount Chances of "Digital Pearl Harbor,"* GovExec.com, June 3, 2003, http://www.govexec.com/dailyfed/0603/060303td2.htm.

48   *See, e.g.,* Chernobyl disaster—Wikipedia, http://en.wikipedia.org/wiki/Chernobyl_accident (last visited Apr. 21, 2007); *see also* Barton Gellman, *Cyber-Attacks by Al-Qaeda Feared,* Wash. Post, June 27, 2002, at A1, *available at* http://www.washingtonpost.com/ac2/wp-dyn/A50765-2002Jun26?start=24&per=24 (reporting that in 1998 a twelve-year-old hacker "broke into the computer system that runs Arizona's Roosevelt Dam" and could have released 489 trilliion gallons of water, which would have flooded the cities of Mesa and Tempe).

bombings carried out by Al-Qaeda as automotive-terrorism because vehicles were used to deliver the bombs to the target sites.[49]

## weapon of mass distraction

This is both a conceptual and a realistic possibility. Here, computer technology plays a pivotal role in the commission of a terrorist act, an act that differs in essential ways from the real-world terrorism to which we are accustomed. Computer technology is used to manipulate a civilian population psychologically. This manipulation saps civilian morale by undermining citizens' faith in the efficacy of their government.[50] Depending on the type of manipulation involved, it can also result in the infliction of personal injury, death, and property destruction.

To understand how computer technology could be used purely for psychological manipulation, consider this scenario: on September 11, 2001, as planes crashed into the World Trade Center and the Pentagon, millions of Americans watched the events unfold on television; many also used the Internet to try to find out more about what was happening.[51] The CNN site experienced particularly heavy traffic that day.[52] What if, instead of finding CNN-generated content, these visitors had encountered a Web page that announced, in appropriately terrifying graphics, "World War—Nuclear Holocaust in Europe and Australia, Japan Devastated by Chemical Attack"?[53]

As this was 2001, an over-the-top Orson Welles "War of the Worlds" reaction would have been unlikely,[54] since for the last decade, people typically have been obtaining their news from several types of media and from various sources within each type. But the posting of such a falsified page could have acted as a terror multiplier, enhancing the unnerving effects of the day's real-world terrorist events.[55] It could also have left lingering doubts in the public's mind as to whether "the government" had actually "covered up" the extraterritorial disasters once reported on CNN. These doubts could have provided the predicate for a long-term campaign of eroding public confidence in public officials and news outlets.

Now consider a scenario coupling psychological manipulation with injury, even death. At 1:00 p.m. on a Wednesday in San Francisco, the local Office of Emergency Services and Homeland Security receives messages via a secure government computer system informing them that a "suitcase nuclear device" is on the Bay Area Rapid Transit (BART) system, the public transportation system that serves San Francisco and surrounding cities.[56] The officials are told the device is in the hands of terrorists who will detonate it in two hours, at 3:00 p.m. If such a device were detonated, the death and destruction would be unimaginable—far greater than that inflicted on 9/11. The officials issue an immediate evacuation order for the San Francisco area. This produces chaos as panicked citizens desperately try to flee an impending nuclear disaster: cars clog the streets and accidents ensue, while those without cars clamor for other means of public transportation, leading to stampedes. Death, injury and property damage result—except that there is no impending disaster, no suitcase nuke. Terrorists hacked the government

---

49   *See, e.g.,* Wright, *supra* note 45, at 270–72.

50   Susan W. Brenner & Marc D. Goodman, In Defense of Cyberterrorism: An Argument for Anticipating Cyber-Attacks, 2002 U. ILL. J.L. Tech. & Pol'y 1, 31–40.

51   *See, e.g.,* September 11, 2001 timeline for the day of the attacks—Wikipedia, http://en.wikipedia.org/wiki/September_11,_2001_timeline_for_the_day_of_the_attacks (last visited Apr. 21, 2007) ("8:49:34 a.m.—CNN and MSNBC's websites receive such heavy traffic that many servers collapse.").

52   See id.

53   For analogous, but much less dramatic attacks, see Brenner & Goodman, *supra* note 60, at 32–34.

54   The War of the Worlds (radio)—Wikipedia, http://en.wikipedia.org/wiki/The_War_of_the_Worlds_(radio) (last visited Apr. 21, 2007).

55   *See* Brenner & Goodman, *supra* note 60, at 26.

56   Bay Area Rapid Transit—Wikipedia, http://en.wikipedia.org/wiki/Bay_Area_Rapid_Transit (last visited Apr. 21, 2007).

computer system and sent credible, fake messages, which the local officials reasonably believed. The net result is that the terrorists could achieve injury, death, and destruction as well as a dramatic erosion in the public's confidence in the government's ability to ensure their security without having to deploy an actual weapon.[57]

In these and other computer as weapon of mass distraction scenarios, computer technology is used primarily for psychological manipulation. The first scenario is a "true" computer as weapon of mass distraction scenario; the second scenario tends to blend weapon of mass distraction with hypothesized weapon of mass disruption effects. The point, though, is that neither scenario involves the actual use of real-world weapons; the computer is the only implement the terrorists employ.

## weapon of mass disruption

When terrorists use computer technology as a weapon of mass disruption, their goal is to undermine a civilian populace's faith in the stability and reliability of essential infrastructure components such as mass transit, power supplies, communications, financial institutions, and health care services.[58] Although the weapon of mass disruption and weapon of mass distraction alternatives both target civilians' faith in essential aspects of their society, they differ in how computer technology is used to corrode civilian confidence in societal infrastructure and services.

As we saw in the previous section, terrorists launch a psychological attack when they use computer technology as a weapon of mass distraction; the goal is to undermine civilians' confidence in one or more of the systems they rely on for essential goods or services. The cyberterrorists accomplish this by making citizens *believe* a system has been compromised and is no longer functioning effectively. The terrorists do not actually impair the functioning of the system. Their goal is to inflict psychological, not systemic, damage.

However, when computer technology is used as a weapon of mass disruption, terrorists' goal *is* the infliction of systemic damage on one or more target systems. This version of cyberterrorism is closer to the scenarios that sometimes appear in the popular media in which cyberterrorists shut down an electrical grid or the systems supplying natural gas or petroleum to a particular populace.[59]

Like the weapon of mass distraction alternative, this scenario is a conceptual yet realistic possibility. Here, terrorists utilize computer technology in a fashion that is analogous to, but less devastating than, their utilization of real-world weapons of mass destruction. Their goal is not to inflict the catastrophic carnage and destruction we saw on 9/11.[60] Rather, it is more insidious: to demoralize a civilian populace by making civilians question the government's ability to keep things working. In other words, terrorists seek to undermine citizens' faith in their government's ability to maintain the essential fabric of their lives by ensuring that the systems on which they rely function as they are intended to.

As many have noted, our increasingly urbanized, increasingly technologized lifestyle makes us more vulnerable to this type of terrorism than traditional, rural societies:

> The key to unlocking the disruptive potential of cities ... is to attack key points ... within target
> infrastructure ... to force a change in the city's dynamic. Infrastructure attacks, particularly on

---

57  For a similar, equally-Active account of how false information can be used to create confusion and a resulting risk of injury, see Chris Suellentrop, *Sim City: Terr or town,* Wired, Oct. 2006, at 103, 103–04, *available at* http://www.wired.com/wired/archive/14.10/posts.html?pg = 2.

58  *See* Brenner & Goodman, *supra* note 60, at 26.

59  *See, e.g.,* Dan Verton, Black Ice: The Invisible Threat of Cyber-Terrorism 1–16 (2003); *see also* Jeremy Kirk, *Russian Expert: Terrorists May Try Cyberattacks,* InfoWorld.com, Dec. 13, 2006, http://www.infoworld.com/article/06/12/13/HNcyberterroralert_l.html?sour.

60  See supra note 57.

power/fuel/water, negate the ability of the government to deliver political goods. ... This halts economic activity and ... damages the ability of the government to deliver political goods, which are the key to legitimacy.[61]

In this excerpt, the author is assuming attacks of a more drastic character, such as those inflicted in war.[62] He cites contemporary Baghdad as an example of how cities can

be engineered to radiate instability. ... This is accomplished through acts that leverage three attributes of modern cities. These include:

- Extreme mobility and interconnectedness (for example, high rates of automobile and cell phone ownership).
- Complete reliance on high volume infrastructure networks.
- Complex and heterogeneous social networks that are held together under pressure.[63]

The same effect can be achieved, less dramatically, with cyberterrorist attacks that disrupt the functioning of infrastructure components. A recent exercise conducted by the U.S. Secret Service and Department of Homeland Security demonstrates this. In February 2006, more than three hundred participants from the American public and private sectors and from four other countries conducted a simulated cyberterrorism assault, called Cyber Storm, on U.S. government agencies and businesses.[64] The attacks were meant to disrupt "critical infrastructure, ... leading to cascading effects" within the participating countries' "economic, societal, and governmental structures."[65] The exercise revealed problems in coordination between the public and private sectors and between different agencies in the public sectors. It also showed that talented, determined attackers can inflict serious damage on components of the United States' infrastructure.[66]

---

61   John Robb, *The Role of Cities*, Global Guerrillas, Oct. 21, 2006, http://globalguerrillas.typepad.com/globalguerrillas/2006/10/the_role_of_cit.html.

62   See id.

63   *Id.*.

64   U.S. Dep't of Homeland Security, National Cyber Exercise: Cyber Storm 1 (2006), *available at* www.automationalley.com/MiRSA/Studies/prep_cyberstormreport_sep06.pdf [hereinafter Cyber Storm Report] :

Cyber Storm was a coordinated effort between international, Federal and State governments, and private sector organizations to exercise their response, coordination, and recovery mechanisms in reaction to ... cyber events. ...

Over 100 public and private agencies, associations, and corporations participated in the exercise from over 60 locations and 5 countries. ...

The ... scenario simulated a large-scale cyber campaign affecting or disrupting ... critical infrastructure elements primarily within the Energy, Information Technology (IT), Telecommunications and Transportation sectors. The exercise was conducted primarily on a separate exercise network without impacting real world information systems.

65   *Id.* at 1.

The exercise simulated a sophisticated cyber attack campaign through ... scenarios directed against critical infrastructures. The intent ... was to highlight the interconnectedness of cyber systems with the physical infrastructure and to exercise coordination ... between the public and private sectors. Each of the scenarios ... was executed in a closed and secure environment.

*Id.* at 11.

66   See *id.* at 6–9.

The Cyber Storm attacks were launched by a loosely knit coalition of domestic terrorists and opportunistic attackers, including a "cyber saboteur," a disgruntled airport employee, and German hackers.[67] Among other things, the disparate attackers crashed the FAA computer control system, caused electrical power and Internet outages, shut off the heat in government buildings, compromised medical data, posted a false Amber alert, altered one "No Fly" list and posted another one online, shut down commuter trains, and altered account balances in financial institutions.[68]

Cyber Storm was intended to test how collaborating government agencies and private sector representatives would respond to cyberattacks.[69] The exercise demonstrated that these cyberattacks can be launched with a fair degree of efficacy.[70] The Cyber Storm report noted that while the "good guy" players were "generally effective in addressing single threats/attacks, ... [p]layers were challenged when attempting to develop an integrated situational awareness picture and cohesive impact assessment across sectors and attack vectors."[71] It also noted that improved "processes, tools and technology" would "enhance the quality, speed and coordination of response," particularly for "cascading attacks or consequences."[72] The Cyber Storm report at least implicitly indicates that improvements are needed in interagency (and inter-sector) coordination, contingency planning, risk assessment, and definition of "roles and responsibilities across the entire cyber incident response community."[73]

The effects of the Cyber Storm attacks were localized and somewhat limited because the goal of the exercise was to test responses, not to explore how cyberattacks can demoralize civilians.[74] Still, shutting down FAA systems, commuter trains, electrical power, Internet access, and heat would unnerve the victim populace. Arguably, one of the most effective ways to mount a weapon of mass disruption attack would be to structure outages or other interferences of essential services in a way that dramatically demonstrates that these systems are now under the control of some anonymous, hostile agency.

One way to do this would be to launch sequenced, synchronized attacks shutting down ATMs and other financial systems in carefully selected U.S. cities.[75] They should be minor cities, perhaps Des Moines, Ithaca, Tulsa, Lexington, Eugene, and Fresno. The reason for this is that we are more likely to expect terrorist attacks on major cities. The bombing of the Oklahoma City federal building was especially horrific because until then, we had not expected catastrophes in the Heartland. Many still do not.

---

67   *Id.* at 14 ("The simulated adversaries did not represent a specific ... terrorist group. ... The[y] ... were a loose coalition of well financed 'hacktivists.'").
The Cyber Storm attackers are consistent with emerging threats that have been identified elsewhere. A recent State Department report notes that "technologically empowered ... 'micro actors'" who are "extremely difficult to detect or counter" are an emerging trend in terrorism. See Country Reports on Terrorism 2005, *supra* note 47, at 11.
68   See U.S. Dep't of Homeland Sec., Presentation, National Cyber Exercise: Cyber Storm, New York City Metro ISSA Meeting 11 (June 21, 2006), available at http://www.cryptome.org/cyberstorm.ppt [hereinafter Cyber Storm powerpoint].
69   See Cyber Storm Report, *supra* note 74, at 1.
70   We are left to wonder how effectively these entities would have responded had they not been anticipating such attacks and/or had the attacks targeted more than three infrastructure sectors. *See supra* note 74.
71   Cyber Storm Report, *supra* note 74, at 2.
72   *Id.* at 10 (italics omitted).
73   *See id.* at 1–2. Interestingly, the Cyber Storm report also concluded that "[p]ublic messaging must be an integral part of ... incident response to ... empower the public to take appropriate individual protective or response actions consistent with the situation." *Id.* at 2.
74   See generally id. at 1.
75   *See* Brenner & Goodman, *supra* note 60, at 39–40. In 2003, the Slammer worm "disrupted more than 13,000 Bank of America" ATMs, apparently as an unintended consequence of its propagation. Clay Wilson, Cong. Research Serv., Computer Attack and Cyber Terrorism: Vulnerabilities and Policy Issues for Congress 34 n.90 (2003), *available at* http://www.fas.org/irp/crs/RL32114.pdf ("[T]he effects would likely have been more severe had Slammer carried a malicious payload."). In August 2003, the Nachi worm compromised ATMs at financial institutions "in the first confirmed case of malicious code penetrating cash machines." Kevin Poulsen, *Nachi Worm Infected Diebold ATMs,* Register, Nov. 25, 2003, http://www.theregister.co.Uk/2003/11/25/nachi_worm_ infected_diebold_atms/.

As the financial system attacks progressed from city to city, it would become increasingly apparent they were neither random, nor the product of software bugs, nor otherwise explainable, but were instead the product of terrorist activity. While attacks such as these would not inflict the sheer horror of the 9/11 attacks, they could further terrorist goals by creating a climate of insecurity and anger at the government, something analogous to what we saw with the Hurricane Katrina fiasco. The negative effects could be magnified if the attacks were sporadically repeated in other cities or if they were coupled with similar attacks on other non-financial systems, such as electrical power, telephone communication, or air traffic control.[76]

Another kind of attack might target health care systems. We have already seen an inadvertent example of this. In 2005, a botnet, a network of compromised computers,[77] controlled by Christopher Maxwell attacked a Seattle hospital.[78] The botnet shut down computers in the Intensive Care Unit and caused operating room doors and doctors' pagers not to function.[79] Maxwell did not intend for his botnet to attack Seattle's Northwest Hospital or any other hospital; rather, he was using it to earn commissions for surreptitiously installing adware on users' computers.[80] The attack, if such it was, occurred because the botnet was searching for computers to add to its system; in so doing, it overloaded the hospital's computer systems and shut down various functions.[81] Because the attack was inadvertent, its effects were not as serious as they would have been had there been a sustained attack. Hospital staff was therefore able to improvise solutions that prevented patients from being harmed and ensured uninterrupted quality patient care.[82]

As the Seattle episode illustrates, weapon of mass disruption attacks can cause personal injury or even death (along with property damage).[83] They can also be, but are not necessarily, blended attacks, which combine the infliction of real harms with psychological manipulation.[84]

## cyberterrorism as crime

Having analyzed how terrorists can use computer technology to advance their primary goals of demoralizing civilians and destabilizing governments, by logical extension, it is fair to define terrorism as a crime rather than as war. Terrorism is defined and prosecuted as a crime in the U.S. and elsewhere.[85] A federal statute makes terrorism a federal crime in the United States.[86] Other countries criminalize

---

76   See Brenner & Goodman, *supra* note 60, at 39–42.

77   "Botnet" refers "to a collection of compromised machines running programs ..., under a common command and control infrastructure. A botnet's originator ... can control the group remotely, usually through a means such as IRC, and usually for nefarious purposes." Botnet—Wikipedia, http://en.wikipedia.org/wiki/Botnet (last visited Apr. 21, 2007).

78   Press Release, U.S. Attorney, W. Dist. of Wash., California Man Pleads Guilty in "Botnet" Attack that Impacted Seattle Hospital and Defense Department (May 4, 2006), *available at* http://seattle.fbi.gov/dojpressrel/2006/botneck050406.htm.

79   Id.

80   Id.

81   Id.

82   See Maureen O'Hagan, Three Accused of Inducing Ill Effects on Computers at Local Hospital, Seattle Times, Feb. 11, 2006, at A1, available at http://seattletimes.nwsource.com/html/localnews/2002798414_botnetllm.html; see also Michael S. Mimoso & Marcia Savage, Today's Attackers Can Find the Needle, Info. Sec., June 2006, at 24, available at http://informationsecurity.techtarget.com/magPrintFriendly/0,293813,sid42_gci1191313,00.html.

83   The prosecutor handling the case noted afterward that while no patients were harmed, "this kind of attack could easily endanger lives." O'Hagan, *supra* note 92.

84   See Brenner & Goodman, *supra* note 60, at 39–42.

85   See, e.g., Note, Responding to Terrorism: Crime, Punishment, and War, 115 Harv. L. Rev. 1217, 1224 (2002).

86   18 U.S.C. § 2332b (2000). Section 1030(a)(5) of title 18 can also be used to prosecute cyberterrorism. *See* 18 U.S.C.S. § 1030(a)(5) (LexisNexis 2006). The USA PATRIOT Act made modifications to § 1030 that were intended to enhance its applicability to cyberterrorism. *See* Uniting and Strengthening America by Providing Appropriate Tools Required to

terrorism, and both the United Nations and the European Union have defined terrorism in a criminal context.[87]

The practice of treating terrorism as crime no doubt evolved for two reasons. First, terrorists historically tended to be home-grown; they might, like the first-century Zealots or eleventh-century Hashhashin, target foreigners in their own country, but they were still a local, domestic threat.[88] Second, their efforts generally target a society's ability to maintain order in the face of internal threats, and the activities in which they engage are functionally indistinguishable from many crimes.[89] Real-world terrorists kill, injure, and kidnap people and destroy property. The activity is the same as that conducted by criminals—only the motivation differs.

It seems reasonable to continue this approach of treating cyberterrorists as criminals, even though cyberterrorism, unlike most traditional, real-world terrorism, can be committed remotely.[90] For example, in the Cyber Storm exercise, three hackers operating from Germany contributed to the disruption of services in the United States.[91] One might argue that this remote commission capacity warrants treating cyberterrorism differently—approaching it as an external, rather than an internal, threat to social order. To do that, we would have to define "remote" cyberterrorism as something other than crime.[92] Alternatively, we could expand our definition of crime to encompass at least one type of external threat.[93]

As I noted earlier, cybercrime can also be committed remotely. This has certain consequences for how we approach the investigation and apprehension of those who commit cybercrime,[94] but for "mere" cybercrime, the capacity to act remotely is clearly irrelevant to the inherent nature of the phenomenon itself. Theft is theft, fraud is fraud, and extortion is extortion, regardless of whether they are committed

---

Intercept and Obstruct Terrorism Act of 2001 (USA PATRIOT Act), Pub. L. No. 107–56, Title V, § 506(a), Title VIII, § 814, 115 Stat. 366, 382 (codified as amended at 18 U.S.C.S. § 1030(a)(5)).

87   See *supra* note 40; *see also* Terrorism—Wikipedia, *supra* note 46.

88   *See, e.g.,* Sharon Harzenski, *Terrorism, A History: Stage One,* 12 J. Transnat'l L. & Pol'y 137, 140 n.17 (2003); History of Terrorism—Wikipedia, http://en.wikipedia.org/wiki/History_of_terrorism (last visited Apr. 21, 2007); Terrorism—Wikipedia, http://en.wikipedia.org/wiki/Terrorism (last visited Apr. 21, 2007).

89   *See, e.g.,* United States v. Sarkissian, 841 F.2d 959, 965 (9th Cir. 1988) ("[Terrorism,] by definition, requires the investigation of activities that constitute crimes.").

90   Note that real-world terrorism *can* be committed remotely, as Ramzi Yousef proved in 1994, when he left a triggered time-bomb on a Philippines Airlines plane bound from Manila to Tokyo. *See, e.g.,* Dennis Piskiewicz, Terrorism's War with America: A History 91 (2003). The bomb went off two hours after Yousef had disembarked from the airliner; it killed the man who had taken his seat, seriously injured other passengers, and nearly disabled the airplane (which had been Yousef's goal). *See id.* Fortunately, the pilot was able to safely land the plane, saving the lives of all those who survived the explosion. *See id.*
Yousef also triggered the bomb he used in the first World Trade Center attack remotely by lighting a twelve-minute fuse. *See id.* at 87. But while these and similar instances involve the remote commission of terrorist acts in the literal sense, they still require that the terrorist be, or have recently been, in physical proximity to the attack target. Real-world terrorist attacks simply cannot be committed by terrorists who are spatially remote from the attack site. (By "spatially remote," I mean that they are in another country or in another part of the country from where the attack is carried out.) These real-world remote terrorist attacks are therefore functionally more analogous to crime than they are to cyberterrorism. Here, as with real-world crime, the terrorist-perpetrators' physical proximity to the attack site increases the risk that they will be identified and apprehended; it also makes the task of carrying out the attack more difficult, as they have to deal with constraints imposed by acting in the real, physical world. *See* Brenner, *Toward a Criminal Law for Cyberspace, supra* note 5, at 65–76.

91   *See* Cyber Storm powerpoint, *supra* note 78, at 10.

92   This, in turn, might result in our employing a dichotomous approach to cyberterrorism in which non-remote cyberterrorism was defined as crime, while remote cyberterrorism was defined as something other than crime.

93   If we were to do this, we would also have to decide how we should respond to this new, not-crime phenomenon. We would presumably not prosecute apprehended not-criminal cyberterrorists in our domestic courts because these courts are reserved for criminals. We might set up specialized tribunals—perhaps analogous to war crimes tribunals—to prosecute them. We will return to this issue later, when we analyze the process of responding to cybercrime/cyberterrorism/cyberwarfare. *See infra* Section IV.

94   See Brenner, Toward a Criminal Law for Cyberspace, supra note 5, at 65–76.

by the victim's next-door neighbor or by someone halfway around the world. The same is true for the other categories of harm-infliction we define as crime. As long as the remote (or local) perpetrator acts out of personal motives, the dynamic is that of crime—the victimization of one individual by another.[95] Therefore, instead of focusing on means (how harm is inflicted), we focus on the harm itself, because it is the infliction of these types of harm (criminal harms) that threatens internal order.[96]

The same should be true for terrorism. Insofar as terrorist acts are designed to undermine a society's ability to maintain internal order, they are indistinguishable from, and should be treated as, crime regardless of whether they are perpetrated locally or remotely.

\* \* \*

## attacker-attribution

The task of identifying those who are responsible for an attack has been, and will remain, a constant. As we will see, identification of the attacker can play an integral role in ascertaining the nature of an attack; and ascertaining the nature of an attack is usually the first step in formulating a response to an attack, of whatever type.

\* \* \*

We will divide our consideration of attacker-attribution into two stages. First, we review how attacker-attribution is currently approached for real-world attacks. Second, we will consider how attacker-attribution becomes problematic as attacks migrate online, in whole or in part.

### real-world attribution

Attacker-attribution has historically been less problematic for war than for crime or terrorism.[97] The laws of war require states launching an attack on another state to identify themselves, though this convention is apparently honored more in the breach than in its realization.[98] Even if that is true, it is

---

95   *See id.* at 40–65. When I say "individual," I mean to denote, at least as far as the victim is concerned, both real and fictive persons. So far anyway, the victimizers are necessarily human, but the victims could be human, corporate, or another artificial entity.

96   *See also id.* If citizens do not believe their society can protect them from crime "harms," they are likely to resort to self-help measures, which can lead to chaos. *See, e.g.,* Andrew Ashworth, *Responsibilities, Rights and Restorative Justice,* 42 Brit. J. Criminology 578, 585 (2002) (stating that societies undertake "the duty of administering justice and protecting citizens in return for citizens giving up their right to self-help").

97   Here, as earlier, we are using "war" to denote an armed conflict between two or more nation-states. *See* Nabulsi, *supra* note 117, at 9–21.

98   *See* Hague Convention No. III Relative to the Opening of Hostilities art. I, Oct. 18, 1907, 36 Stat. 2259, 2271, T.S. 598, *available at* http://www.yale.edu/lawweb/avalon/lawofwar/hague03.htm; Yoram Dinstein, *Comments on War,* 27 Harv. J.L. & Pub. Pol'y 877, 885–86 (2004); *also* Dinstein, *supra* note 111, at 29–32 (declaration of war is not essential to establish state of war; armed attack suffices). A declaration of war "served the legal function of triggering international law governing neutral and belligerent states ..." William C. Peters, *On Law, Wars and Mercenaries: The Case for Courts-Martial Jurisdiction over Civilian Contractor Misconduct in Iraq,* 2006 BYU L. Rev. 367, 404 (quoting Curtis A. Bradley & Jack L. Goldsmith, Foreign Relations Law 177,178 (2003)). The United Nations Charter "abolished" war "as a category of international law," so declarations of war no longer serve any legal purpose. *See* Paul W. Kahn, *War Powers and the Millennium,* 34 Loy. L.A. L. Rev. 11,17 (2000).

generally not difficult to identify the state responsible for an act of war in the real-world. The initial attack may be a surprise, as with Pearl Harbor, but attributing the attack to a specific state tends to be a relatively simple process. Military attackers wear distinctive, uniform clothing and use equipment with insignias or characteristics indicating their national affiliation. The language the attackers use will be another indicator of their country of origin, as well as circumstances of the attack itself.[99] The location from which an attack is launched can be another clue: if Nation-State A is under attack by missiles being launched from Nation-State B, Nation-State A's decision-makers can reliably infer that either Nation-State B, or another nation with which Nation-State B is affiliated (Nation-State C, say) is responsible for the attack.[100]

Identifying those responsible for a crime is usually much more difficult. Criminals have a strong incentive to avoid identification because it is generally the first step to being apprehended, tried, convicted, and sanctioned for their misdeeds.[101] With rare exceptions,[102] criminals do not intentionally identify themselves as the architects of their crimes (though they may do so indirectly by using a *nom de crime*, such as "the Zodiac Killer").[103] Since crime control is essential for the maintenance of internal order, nation-states have developed a standardized, generally effective approach for identifying those who commit crimes in their territory.[104]

This criminal investigation approach assumes activity in the real-world because, until recently, physical reality was the only arena of crime commission.[105] The approach therefore focuses on finding attribution evidence at a physical crime scene by locating witnesses who saw the perpetrator and can describe and hopefully identify him, and physical evidence (such as DNA or fibers) that can be traced to a particular individual who was suspiciously at the crime scene. Since it is predicated on conduct in the real-world, this approach assumes that the perpetrator of an attack—a crime—was, and still is, physically in the local geographical area.[106] The latter assumption gives rise to the "dragnet" tactic, in which officers comb the area for sightings of the perpetrator and for people who know him.[107] If attacker-attribution fails for a crime, officers will assume the attacker remains in the local area and will consequently be alert for the possibility that he will re-offend and then be identified.[108]

With regard to attacker-attribution, terrorism occupies a middle ground between war and crime. While those who carry out a terrorist attack may not identify themselves personally,[109] they often iden-

---

99   These attribution factors apply whenever a classic state of war exists, and can also apply when nations are embroiled in "incidents short of war." Dinstein, *supra* note 111, at 3–13.

100   *See, e.g.,* Gulf War—Wikipedia, http://en.wikipedia.org/wiki/Desert_Storm (last visited Apr. 21, 2007) (illustrates real-life example where U.S.-led coalition forces, representing "Nation-State A," launched initial air sorties against Iraq, "Nation-State B," from Saudi Arabia, "Nation-State C").

101   *See* Brenner, Toward a Criminal Law for Cyberspace, *supra* note 5, at 49–59.

102   *See, e.g.,* Bonnie and Clyde—Wikipedia, http://en.wikipedia.org/wiki/ Bonnie_and_Clyde (last visited Apr. 21, 2007) (Bonnie Parker wrote poems about the pair's exploits and sent them to newspapers, which published them).

103   *See, e.g.,* Zodiac Killer—Wikipedia, http://en.wikipedia.org/wiki/Zodiac_killer (last visited Apr. 21, 2007). The *nom de crime* tactic is not, of course, intended to reveal the perpetrator's true identity. Instead, it is a compromise—a way of letting the perpetrator "take credit" for the crimes she commits while still retaining the anonymity that increases her chances of avoiding capture.

104   *See* Brenner, *Toward a Criminal Law for Cyberspace, supra* note 5, at 55–65; *see also* Denning, *supra* note 132, at 5–6 (discussing the Uniform Crime Reporting program for real-world crimes). We will review the basic tactics used in this approach in the next section.

105   *See* Brenner, Toward a Criminal Law for Cyberspace, supra note 5, at 65–76.

106   *See id.*

107   *See id.*

108   *See id.* Officers can also rely on identifiable geographical and offense patterns in local crimes to assist in identifying perpetrators. *See id.*

109   Terrorists are more likely to identify themselves if they do not anticipate escaping to commit further attacks. Terrorists whose goal is to commit further attacks eschew self-identification for the same reason crime-perpetrators try to avoid

tify themselves as acting on behalf of a terrorist group so the group can take credit for the attack.[110] Increasingly, terrorism-perpetrators identify themselves as representatives of a particular terrorism group in "martyrdom messages" recorded prior to an attack, especially a suicide attack.[111] It is also increasingly common for the group sponsoring a terrorist attack to claim credit for it in a message posted online or on a videotape delivered to media outlets.[112] And if the sponsoring group does not claim credit for an attack, the structure and style of the attack may inferentially identify the organization responsible for it.[113] In terrorism, as in war, it is usually possible to identify the entity responsible for an attack; but, as with crime, it can be difficult to identify the individuals who actually carried out an attack. Since the current strategy treats terrorism as a type of crime, the criminal investigation approach outlined above is often used to identify and apprehend individual terrorists.[114]

## online attribution

The BIS episode[115] illustrates how online attacks complicate attacker-attribution across all three dimensions of crime, terrorism, and war. Attacker-attribution becomes problematic at each level because the approaches we use to identify attackers implicitly assume territorially-based activity in the physical world. Since cyberattacks do not take place in physical reality, the attack signatures[116] of cybercrime, cyberterrorism, and cyberwarfare generally display few of the empirical characteristics common to their real-world counterparts.

To understand why that is true, we need to parse the BIS attacks. As we saw in the previous section, the real-world crime-terrorism and war attacker-attribution calculi rely on the "place" where an attack

---

identifying themselves. Identification facilitates apprehension, which, for terrorists, negates their ability to commit further acts of terrorism. *See, e.g.,* Carlos the Jackal—Wikipedia, http://en.wikipedia.org/wiki/Ilich_Ram%C3%ADrez_S%C3%A1nchez (last visited Apr. 21, 2007).

110  Terrorist groups differ in terms of their attitude toward publicly taking credit for attacks. *See, e.g.,* Kim Cragin & Sara A. Daly, The Dynamic Terrorist Threat 37–38 (2004) (explaining that RIRA, the "Real Irish Republican Army," and Hamas take credit for the attacks they sponsor, while FARC, the Revolutionary Armed Forces of Colombia, and al-Qaeda generally do not).

111  *See id.* at 38; *see also Video Shows Laughing 9/11 Hijackers in Afghan Hideout,* CNN.com (Oct. 1, 2006), http://edition. cnn.com/2006/WORLD/meast/10/01/hijackers.video/index.html; Martyrdom Video—Wikipedia, http://en.wikipedia.org/ wiki/Martyrdom_video (last visited Apr. 21, 2007).

112  *See, e.g.,* 7 July 2005 London bombings—Wikipedia, http://en.wikipedia.org/wiki/7_July_2005_London_ bombings#Claims_of_responsibility (last visited Apr. 21, 2007) (explaining that multiple groups claimed responsibility for the London subway bombing attacks via statements posted online and that two of the bombers left videotaped messages). The increasing tendency of groups to claim responsibility can produce conflicting claims of responsibility for an attack. *See, e.g.,* Hugh Miles, *"We Heard a God Almighty Bang. Then Another, and Then Another,"* Telegraph (London), July 23, 2005, *available at* http://www.telegraph.co.uk/news/main.jhtml?xml=/news/2005/07/24/wegyptl24.xml; John Ward Anderson, *Suicide Blast Kills Four in Tel Aviv,* Wash. Post, Feb. 26, 2005, at A01, *available at* http://www.washingtonpost. com/wp-dyn/articles/A55514-2005Feb26.html.

113  *See, e.g.,* Scott MacLeod, *Is Al-Qaeda in Sinai?,* Time, Oct. 12, 2004, at 17, 17, *available at* http://www.time.com/ time/magazine/article/0,9171,1101041018-713210,00.html (reporting that "synchronized attacks are a common al-Qaeda tactic"); *World Nations Beef Up Security after London Bombings,* Al Jazeera (Qatar), July 8, 2005, http://www.aljazeera. com/me.asp?service_ID=8870 (quoting a security expert who explains that synchronized attacks are "pretty classic for al Qaeda"). It is also possible to infer responsibility for an attack from the likely motive for the attack.

114  *See, e.g.,* Dennis Piszkiewicz, Terrorism's War with America: A History 85–96 (2003) (describing the investigation and apprehension of 1993 World Trade Center bomber Ramzi Yousef, which mirrors the steps involved in the criminal investigation approach).

115  *See supra* Section I.

116  Essentially, an attack signature encompasses the essential elements of an attack. *See, e.g.,* Bryan Sartin, *Tracking the Cybercrime Trail,* Sec. Mgmt., Sept. 2004, at 95, 95–96 ("FBI agents ... looked at ... audit logs to find the hacker's ... attack signature—that is, how the hacker broke in and what the hacker did once he ... had access.").

occurred or originated from in determining attacker identity. With virtual attacks, a "place" tends to be at once more ambiguous and less conclusive than in real-world analyses.

### attack origin

With cybercrimes, a "place" is ambiguous because while attacks may be routed through Internet servers located in China, this does not necessarily mean that they originated in China. It is common for online attackers to use "stepping stones"—computers the attacker controls but that are owned by innocent parties—in their assaults.[117] These "stepping stone" computers can be located anywhere in the physical world because real-space is irrelevant to activity in cyberspace. So, while use of the Chinese servers might mean the attacks came from China, it also might mean they did *not* come from China. Rather, the attacker might be in Russia, Brazil, or Peoria. Indeed, an attacker located somewhere other than in China and who knew of U.S. concern about China's efforts to develop cyberwarfare capabilities might use Chinese servers deliberately to mask the true source of the attack and mislead the investigators trying to identify him.[118] Unless and until investigators reliably establish that the attacks originated in Chinese real-space, we cannot predicate attacker-attribution on inferences drawn from the place of attack origin.[119]

What if BIS-style attacks were repeated over a period of time, with each attack coming from Chinese servers and each targeting computers used by U.S. government agencies? Can we now predicate attacker-attribution on inferences drawn from the repetitive use of what seems to be the same point of origin? It would be risky to rely on mere repetition; aside from anything else, a virtual Machiavelli might be "framing" China by routing structurally similar attacks through its real-space.[120]

Repetition coupled with other circumstances might support using point of attack origin inferences to establish attacker-attribution. Assume that BIS-style attacks are launched against another U.S. government agency's computers. Investigators trace these attacks to servers in Guangdong, China. Over the last, say, six years, sporadic attacks targeting U.S. government and civilian computers have been traced to Guangdong; some say the attacks were conducted by Chinese military hackers, others say Guangdong University students were responsible for them.[121] Can we predicate attacker-attribution inferences on the discontinuous repetition of similar target attacks coming from the same real-world locus in China? Does the (reasonably reliable) identification of a single point of origin support the inference that the recent BIS-style attacks came from Guangdong?[122]

---

117   *See, e.g.,* Denning, *supra* note 132, at 7.

118   *See, e.g.,* Nathan Thornburgh, *The Invasion of the Chinese Cyber spies,* Time, Sept. 5, 2005, at 34, 34, *available at* http://www.time.com/time/magazine/article/0,9171,1098961-1,00.html ("China ... is known for having poorly defended servers that outsiders from around the world commandeer as their unwitting launchpads.").

119   News reports of the attacks indicate that investigators were able to determine that they came "through Chinese servers" but not necessarily from China. *See, e.g.,* Gregg Keizer, *Chinese Hackers Hit Commerce Department,* Tech Web, Oct. 6, 2006, http://www.techweb.com/showArticle.jhtml;jsessionid=OM4E5LCHY4WOWQSNDLRCKHSCJU NN2JVN?articleID=193105174.

120   *See, e.g.,* Jeremiah Grossman—The devil made me do it, http://jeremiahgrossman.blogspot.com/2006/07/devil-made-me-do-it.html (July 18, 2006) (describing how XSS exploitation could be used to frame someone for launching attacks on government or other websites).

121   *See, e.g.,* Robert Vamosi, *Is China's Guangdong Province Ground Zero for Hackers?,* ZD Net, Aug. 30, 2001, http://techupdate.zdnet.com/techupdate/stories/main/0,14179,2808609,00.html; *Hacker Attacks in U.S. Linked to Chinese Military,* Breitbart.com, Dec. 12, 2005, http://www.breitbart.com/news/2005/12/12/051212224756.jwmkvntb.html.

122   One can argue that basing attacker-attribution on the above facts produces errors analogous to those known as the "prosecutor's fallacy." *See* Michael N. Schmitt & Laura H.Crocker, *DNA Typing: Novel Scientific Evidence in the Military Courts,* 32 A.F.L. Rev. 227, 301 (1990) ("The prosecutor's fallacy is essentially overstating the statistical case ... [A]ssume a blood match results in a ninety percent probability of the accused being the source of the sample found at the crime scene.

Of course, one can still argue that Guangdong's status as the point of origin of the attacks has not been conclusively established. But while certainty is reassuring, it is a luxury decision-makers often cannot afford. In the cyber-world (and the real-world), it can be difficult to conclusively establish the circumstances of an event; here, as is often true for real-world events, decision-makers will sometimes have to rely on inference. For the purposes of analysis, therefore, we will assume the facts in the previous paragraph support the inference that the hypothesized BIS-style attacks were launched by "someone" in Guangdong. That brings us to the next question: how, if at all, does the inference that the attacks came from Guangdong advance the process of identifying the "someone" who is responsible for the attacks?

\* \* \*

### crime-terrorism

This leaves the role that point of attack origin plays in the crime-terrorism calculus. While crime and terrorism are conceptually distinct phenomena, we will consider them jointly in this analysis because both represent threats to internal order (and, as discussed earlier, law treats terrorism as crime). Unlike war, which threatens a society's ability to maintain external order, crime and terrorism are the product of individual rather than state action.[123]

Point of attack origin has historically played a much more limited role in crime and terrorism attacker-attribution than in war attribution. While point of attack origin can inferentially indicate who may have been responsible for a crime or an act of terrorism, the link between origin and attribution is much more attenuated than in war analysis.

The primary reason for this is that in the real-world, point of attack origin and point of attack occurrence are often so closely related as to be indistinguishable for crime, and even for terrorism.[124] A crack dealer buys and sells crack in his neighborhood;[125] the points of origin and occurrence of his drug crimes are functionally identical. In 1982, the Irish National Liberation Army (INLA), a terrorist group, bombed a disco frequented by British soldiers in Ballykelly, Northern Ireland, killing eleven soldiers and six civilians; the INLA agents who carried out the bombing operated out of nearby Deny.[126] Since the points of attack origin and occurrence for this act of terrorism were separated by only a short distance, one can argue that they are functionally identical here as well.

If there is little or no differentiation between the point of attack origin and the point of attack occurrence, identifying the point of origin is unlikely to markedly advance the process of identifying the attacker. Assume a woman is raped as she leaves Ladies Night at a neighborhood bar. She left at

---

The prosecutor's fallacy is citing this figure without taking into account exculpatory evidence."); *see also* State v. Bloom, 516 N.W.2d 159, 162–63 (Minn. 1994).

123   This proposition becomes problematic for state-sponsored crime and state-sponsored terrorism, which we will consider briefly in Section III.A.2.a.iii, *infra*, and in more detail in Section III.B.2, *infra*.

124   As I have explained elsewhere, spatial proximity between attacker and victim has historically been an inevitable element of real-world crime and, to a somewhat lesser extent, of real-world terrorism. *See* Brenner, *Toward a Criminal Law for Cyberspace, supra* note 5, at 65–76. Proximity has been unavoidable because both have required direct physical action by the attacker against the victim. *See id.; see also* History of Terrorism—Wikipedia, *supra* note 98. The development of timing devices created a limited potential for the remote commission of crime and terrorism, but physical proximity remains the norm for real-world activity. *See, e.g.,* discussion *supra* note 100.

125   *See, e.g.,* George F. Rengert, The Geography of Illegal Drugs 67–90 (1996).

126   *See* Dominic McGlinchey—Wikipedia, http://en.wikipedia.org/wiki/Dominic_McGlinchey (last visited Apr. 21, 2007); Irish National Liberation Army—Wikipedia, http://en.wikipedia.org/wiki/INLA (last visited Apr. 21, 2007).

closing time and was attacked in the nearby parking lot where she left her car.[127] Police are likely to infer that the attacker is an opportunistic local who is familiar with the bar's closing time, with its Ladies Nights, and with the fact that patrons use the rather isolated parking lot.[128] This inference establishes that, insofar as an attack such as this has a distinct point of origin, it is in the local area. This inference would also play a role in the police's attempt to identify the rapist by focusing their efforts on the area the bar serves. Police would interview people who might have seen someone in the area that night or might have heard someone talking about the rape. They would also check the location and alibis of locals with sex crime convictions and pursue other, similar leads.

As this hypothetical illustrates, point of attack origin tends to be merely one factor in the inferential and evidence-gathering processes law enforcement officers use to identify those responsible for real-world crime and terrorism. It has played a lesser, implicit role in crime and terrorism attacker-attribution because these threats to internal order have, at least until recently, come primarily, if not exclusively, from domestic actors.[129] Domestic actors are presumptively in the nation-state where the attack occurred, and investigators tend to assume that the domestic actors responsible for an attack remain in the locality where it occurred. Even when there is significant spatial differentiation between point of origin and point of occurrence, identifying the former serves at most as a clue—an inferential datum that can contribute to the identification of the attackers and, if terrorism, of the sponsoring terrorist organization.[130]

As crime and terrorism migrate online, point of attack origin can assume more importance in attacker-attribution. As we saw in our discussion of war attribution, cyberspace eliminates the need for physical proximity between attacker and victim and thereby creates the potential for increased differentiation between point of attack origin and point of occurrence.

In 1994, workers at the Rome Air Development Center (Rome Labs) in upstate New York discovered that the lab's computer systems had been hacked by unknown persons.[131] The hackers had, among other things, copied data from computers containing sensitive Air Force research and development data.[132] Since hacking (unauthorized access) is a federal crime, Air Force, Secret Service, and Federal Bureau of Investigation agents immediately began investigating the incidents, hoping to identify the perpetrators.[133] They found a complex attack signature: the attackers had routed their attacks through multiple computers in various countries.[134] Through a process too intricate to describe here, the U.S. investigators eventually traced the attacks to the United Kingdom where, with Scotland Yard's assistance, they identified two adolescents as the Rome Labs attackers.[135] Both were prosecuted, though with mixed results.[136]

---

127   We will assume that the victim cannot identify her attacker and that he left no DNA for searching within police databases.

128   It is possible he is an out-of-towner who simply happened to be driving by when the victim was walking to her car. While this inference is logically permissible, experience tells us that it is less likely to be correct than the inference given above. The police will, therefore, base their investigation on the higher probability inference.

129   *See* Brenner, *Toward a Criminal Law for Cyberspace, supra* note 5, at 65–76; Larry Copeland, *Domestic Terrorism: New Trouble at Home*, USA Today, Nov. 15, 2004, at 1A, *available at* http://www.usatoday.com/news/nation/2004-11-14-domestic-terrorism_x.htm.

130   *See generally Search Continues for Witness in Clinic Bombing*, CNN.com, Jan. 31, 1998, http://www.cnn.com/US/9801/31/clinic.bombing/?related; World Trade Center bombing—Wikipedia, http://en.wikipedia.org/wiki/World_Trade_Center_bombing (last visited Apr. 21, 2007) (in these bombings, identification of the point of origin was merely a clue in the process of identifying the attacker).

131   *See, e.g.,* Richard Power, Tangled Web: Tales of Digital Crime From the Shadows of Cyberspace 66–75 (2000).

132   *See id.*

133   *See id.*

134   *See id.*

135   *See id.* For more on the investigation, see *infra* notes 231–239 and accompanying text.

136   *See* Power, *supra* note 170, at 70–75 (one pled guilty, charges were dropped against the other).

The Rome Labs case illustrates how and why the use of cyberspace can make attacker-attribution more difficult. Cyberspace erodes law enforcement's ability to assume that an attacker is parochial. The viability of that default assumption still holds for real-world crime, and *can* also hold for real-world terrorism, but its applicability to online crime and terrorism is increasingly problematic.

When it comes to cybercrime and even some types of cyberterrorism, the parochial-attacker assumption is most likely to hold for "personal" attacks: crimes and acts of terrorism in which the perpetrator's motives are idiosyncratically emotional.[137] In these cases—where John uses cyberspace to stalk his former girlfriend or Jane uses it to attack her employer—the perpetrator and victim are in the same area, but instead of using physical activity in that real-space to conduct the attack, the perpetrator vectors it through cyberspace.[138]

This creates an epistemological issue: When attacker and attacked are in the same real-space area throughout an attack conducted online, did the attack originate in the real-space occupied by attacker and victim, online, or in both? For the purposes of attacker-attribution, the answer should be both.

In "personal" attack cases, the connections between attacker and victim mean that the parochial-attacker assumption is likely to be very useful in identifying the attacker. Thus far, cyber-vendettas seem primarily to originate in real-world contacts between attacker and victim.[139] This assessment means that investigators can profitably rely on the approach used for real-world crime and terrorism, focusing on inferences derived from a real-world context. Therefore, for the purposes of this approach, the attack should be construed as originating in the real-space occupied by attacker and victim.[140]

But the origin of the attack should not be the only focus of their investigation. When a "personal" attacker uses cyberspace, it, too, becomes a "place" of origin of the attack. Its role in the investigation of "personal" attacks is analogous to the role that a physical point of attack origin plays in the traditional investigative process. Cyberspace, like a real-world point of attack origin, becomes a source of inferential data that can be used to identify the attacker.[141] If, for instance, a stalker consistently uses a specific website in tormenting his victim, that website becomes "a" point of origin of the attack and should be

---

137    These cybercrimes include revenge attacks by former spouses/lovers and current or former employees, as well as more generalized cyberstalking and harassment. *See* Susan W. Brenner, *Should Criminal Liability Be Used to Control Online Speech?*, 76 Miss. L.J. (forthcoming 2007); Drew Cullen, *UBS Logic Bomber Jailed for Eight Years*, Register (London), Dec. 13, 2006, http://www.theregister.co.Uk/2006/12/13/ubs_logic_bomber_sentenced/; Devin Smith & Marsha Kranes, *Match.creep: Cop Hounded Ex on Dating Site*, N.Y. Post, Apr. 4, 2006, at 19, *available at* 2006 WLNR 6494179.
Terrorist attacks of this type can include the efforts of groups such as the Red Hackers Association, a "revolutionary" organization that seems primarily to target Turkish government and political websites. *See, e.g.,* Press Release, Red Hackers Ass'n (Dec. 24, 2006) (on file with author); Press Release, Red Hackers Ass'n (Dec. 18, 2006), *available at* http://istanbul. indymedia.org/news/2006/12/161565.php. In December 2006, for example, the Red Hackers Association posted messages on target sites condemning the 2000 "massacre" of revolutionaries being held in Turkish prisons. *See* Justus Leicht, *Turkish State Suppresses Prison Revolts*, World Socialist Web Site, Dec. 22, 2000, *available at* http://www.wsws.org/articles/2000/ dec2000/turk-d22.shtml; Press Release, Red Hackers Ass'n (Dec. 24, 2006), *supra*. Since their efforts are intended to promote an ideological agenda, the Red Hackers might be characterized as domestic terrorists, given their focus on localized issues. Their latest efforts would fall within the category noted above because they have a specific emotional component, that is, the efforts are reactions to the 2000 prison "massacre."
138    *See* Paul Shukovsky, *Cyberstalker Just out of Reach of Law, But Finally, He Stops*, Seattle Post-Intelligencer, Feb. 11, 2004, *available at* http://seattlepi.nwsource.com/local/16020l_cyberstalking11.html; Press Release, Office of the U.S. Attorney, S. Dist. of Cal. (Aug. 28, 2006), *available at* http://www.usdoj.gov/usao/cas/press/cas60828-l.pdf.
139    *See also* Leroy McFarlane & Paul Bocij, *An Exploration of Predatory Behaviour in Cyberspace: Towards a Typology of Cyber stalkers*, First Monday, Sept. 2003, *available at* http://www.firstmonday.org/issues/issue8_9/mcfarlane/index.html (writing that investigators are in fact likely to assume a real-space point of origin for a "personal" attack case and proceed accordingly).
140    *See, e.g.,* People v. Vijay, No. H024123, 2003 WL 23030492 (Cal. Ct. App. Dec. 19, 2003); State v. Hoying, No. 2004-CA-71, 2005 WL 678989 (Ohio Ct. App. Mar. 25, 2005); State v. Cline, No. 2002-CA-05, 2003 WL 22064118 (Ohio Ct. App. Sept. 5, 2003), *rev'd*, 816 N.E.2d 1069 (Ohio 2004); State v. Askham, 86 P.3d 1224 (Wash. 2004).
141    It can also, as noted earlier, become a source of physical evidence. *See supra* note 169.

treated as such.[142] Even if the attacker has not revealed his identity to the site operator, his use of that particular website may provide inferential data as to his identity.[143]

What about attacks in which the attacker is *not*, by any definition, in the same real-space as the victim? In the BIS attacks, the target was in Washington, D.C., while the attackers were (presumably) in China; in the Rome Labs attacks, the target was in upstate New York, while the attackers were in Cardiff, Wales, and London.[144] An identified point of attack origin serves a very different function in cases like these, for several reasons.

First, identifying the point of attack origin in attacks such as these serves an initial, essentially negative function in attacker-attribution. It tells the investigators that the parochial-attacker assumption and derivative investigative approach that they use for real-world crime and terrorism will probably be of little use in identifying the attackers. When an attack presents functionally coterminous points of attack origin and occurrence, we have a localized crime scene that becomes the focal point of the investigation. Evidence, inferences, observations of witnesses, and connections between victim and attacker all radiate from and revolve around this unitary crime scene. It creates a comprehensible focus for the investigation and, in so doing, makes the investigation a manageable task. In complex serial-killer cases, we have seen how expanding a single crime scene into a variegated network of geographically-dispersed, victim-idiosyncratic, real-space crime scenes can test the limits of the traditional investigative approach.[145]

But even ambitious serial killers operate on a limited geographical scale: in the U.S., they have tended to confine their activities to a smaller area within a state, sometimes to the state itself, and in unusual instances, to surrounding states.[146] The physical constraints of the real-world limit the frequency and geographical dispersion of the attacks real-world serial killers can successfully carry out.[147] However, this limitation is not true for other offenses once cyberspace becomes a component of criminal and/or terrorist activity. Instead, one can strike anonymously from any point connected to the Internet and iterate the attacks with a frequency impossible in the real-world.[148]

Cyberspace fractures the crime-scene into shards, the number of which depends on the particular circumstances of an attack. One constant shard is the alpha point of attack origin—the place where the attacker is physically located and from which she launches the attack. Other, variable crime scene shards (beta, gamma) are the intermediary points of transmission used in the attack; each represents the occurrence of a constituent, spatially diverse event that contributed to the success of the ultimate

---

142  *See, e.g.,* Smith & Kranes, *supra* note 176.

143  *See id.*

144  *See, e.g., Targeting the Pentagon,* Sunday Times (London), Mar. 30, 1998, *available at* http://marc.theaimsgroup.com/?l = isn&m = 100434567710396&w = 2-.

145  *See, e.g.,* Ann Rule, Green River, Running Red: The Real Story of the Green River Killer—America's Deadliest Serial Killer (2004); *see also* Andrei Chikatilo—Wikipedia, http://en.wikipedia.org/wiki/Andrei_Chikatilo (last visited Apr. 21, 2007). Serial killers are a useful analog here because while their attacks take place in real-space, they are not "personal" in the sense used earlier:

> Murder is usually either a crime of personal relationships ... or an unintended consequence of other crimes. Because of this, most murders are ... simple to solve; in most familial deaths, the murderer makes little ... effort to conceal the crime ...; in other cases, the murderer is usually a local. ... These assumptions, with which any law enforcement officer naturally approaches a single murder, are barriers to catching a serial killer.

> Another barrier to serial killers' early capture is their ... choices of victim. ... They almost never have any links to their victims—they pick by whim or impulse, seeking types or opportunity rather than any easily detectable link.

Serial killer—Wikipedia, http://en.wikipedia.org/wiki/Serial_killer (last visited Apr. 21, 2007).

146  *See, e.g.,* Ted Bundy—Wikipedia, http://en.wikipedia.org/wiki/Ted_Bundy (last visited Apr. 21, 2007) (Bundy is an example of a serial killer who murdered in several states).

147  See Brenner, Toward a Criminal Law for Cyberspace, supra note 5, at 65–76.

148  See id.

attack.[149] The other constant shard, the omega shard, is the place of attack occurrence, which we will examine in the next section.

Fracturing the crime scene into shards makes identifying the point of attack origin and linking it to the attacker much more difficult. Aside from anything else, a fractured crime scene can result in false positives—in investigators assuming that an intermediary point of transmission of an attack is the originating point for the attack.

This situation could have happened in the Rome Labs case. Here, the investigators initially traced the two intruders back to an ISP, "mindvox.phantom.com, in New York City."[150] The provider allegedly had ties to the Legion of Doom, a hacker group several members of which had been convicted of unlawful intrusion crimes a few years earlier.[151] The investigators could logically have assumed that this ISP was the originating point for the attack on the Rome Labs computers, given its immediate connection to the attack and its apparent ties to hackers.[152] This assumption would have been consistent with the real-world approach to investigating crime because it tends to incorporate the notion that point of attack origin is a binary concept. Real-world "places" tend to be mutually exclusive: a real-world "place" is either the point of attack origin or it is not; if it is the point of attack origin, other "places" cannot be. Since it was clear that the immediately-proximate source of the attack was the New York ISP, it could, logically, have been deemed to be "the" point of attack origin for the Rome Labs attack.

Identifying the New York ISP as the point of origin would have been a false positive, one that most certainly would have derailed the investigation. Fortunately, the investigators continued to investigate and eventually identified a trail of attack increments that utilized many computers in various countries.[153] However, they were not able to track the increments back to their true points of origin. Ironically, the Rome Labs investigators ultimately identified the perpetrators—"Datastream Cowboy" and "Kuji"—the old-fashioned way: by using informants.[154] They knew that the attackers used these *noms de hack*, so the investigators sent people to chat rooms to see if either was taking credit for the attacks.[155] Datastream Cowboy not only took credit, he also revealed that he was from the United Kingdom and gave an informant his home telephone number.[156] It became a simple matter to identify and apprehend him, though doing the same for Kuji took a while longer.[157] This episode illustrates the way that cyberspace can fracture the crime scene into shards, which makes it more difficult to determine the point of origin of an attack.[158] Making this determination proved impossible for the Rome Labs investigators because of the intricate paths the attackers used.[159]

---

149  *See supra* note 124 and accompanying text; *see also* Jeanne Sahadi, *Credit Card Breach: Tracing Who Dunnit*, CNN/ Money.com, June 29, 2005, http://money.cnn.com/2005/06/28/pf/security_hackers/.

150  Power, *supra* note 170, at 68. Investigators also traced part of the attack to a Seattle ISP. *Id.* This discussion focuses only on the New York ISP because it provides a better illustration.

151  See id. at 68.

152  Indeed, it could also have seemed a logical choice for the point of attack origin because it was in the same state where the attack occurred.

153  *See* Power, *supra* note 170, at 68–69.

154  *See id.* at 70.

155  *See id.* at 71–75.

156  *See id.*

157  *See id.*

158  *See, e.g.,* Daniel A. Morris, U.S. Dep't. of Justice, Tracking a Computer Hacker (2001), http://www.cybercrime.gov/ usamay2001_2.htm.

159  Difficulty unraveling the point of origin in an attack is not unique to the Rome Labs case. *See, e.g.,* Tom Young, *IT Industry Core to Global E-Crime Battle,* IT Week, Nov. 9, 2006, http://www.itweek.co.Uk/computing/analysis/2168266/ industry-core-global-crime (quoting an FBI Special Agent who "estimates that fewer than five per cent of international e-criminals are caught." The agent also notes that "evidence is in many different areas—personal PCs, corporate databases, all over the world—which makes it particularly difficult.").

Another issue that can complicate the process of backtracking through a series of incremental attack stages is the legal process involved.[160] Incremental attack stages will almost certainly involve the use of computers in different countries.[161] To gain access to the necessary information to trace an attack back through those computers, law enforcement will have to obtain assistance from government and civilian entities in the countries in which the computers were used.[162] This process can be difficult and time-consuming. The formal methods used to obtain assistance can take months or even years when digital evidence is fragile and can disappear by the time the investigators obtain the assistance they need.[163] Furthermore, not all countries have criminalized hacking or other computer malfeasance, sometimes making it impossible to obtain assistance from the authorities.[164]

Even if the investigators obtain the assistance they need and are confident they have traced an attack back to its true point of origin, this may not markedly advance their effort to identify the attacker. The BIS attacks are instructive in this regard. Investigators in that case accurately ascertained that the attacks came from servers in China. However, this information could neither directly nor inferentially establish who was responsible for the attacks or, indeed, what *kind* of attacks they were.

In some instances, identifying the ultimate extraterritorial point of attack origin can serve the same function an identified point of origin serves in investigating real-world crime—it can become an inferential datum that contributes to identifying the attacker.[165] Assume the FBI has information independently derived from informants or from other online investigations that a Romanian gang is engaged in phishing.[166] If the FBI then traces a phishing attack to Romania, it would be reasonable to infer that it came from the gang already under suspicion.[167] The inference would be strengthened if, say, the attack were traced to the city out of which the gang is known to operate or if the attack signature displayed elements peculiar to this gang's operations.

In sum, while point of attack origin can play a role in identifying the attackers in a cybercrime or cyberterrorism event, its function tends to be limited, and will probably become more so as cyberattackers become more sophisticated about hiding their tracks.[168]

### state-sponsored crime/terrorism

In the previous sections, we considered attacker-attribution and other issues presented by crime and terrorism, cyber and otherwise. We have assumed for the purpose of analysis that there is a distinct conceptual divide between war, which is conducted by nation-states, and crime and terrorism, which

---

160   See, e.g., Morris, supra note 197.

161   *See, e.g.,* Young, *supra* note 198 (reporting that the FBI Special Agent said international cybercriminals "are specialists in … covering their tracks").

162   See, e.g., Susan W. Brenner & Joseph J. Schwerha IV, Transnational Evidence-Gathering and Local Prosecution of International Cybercrime, 20 J. Marshall J. Computer & Info. L. 347, 354–88 (2002).

163   See id.; see also Young, *supra* note 198.

164   *See* Brenner & Schwerha IV, *supra* note 201.

165   *See supra* note 169 and accompanying text.

166   *See, e.g.,* Rene Millman, *Half of all phishes from Romanian cyber gang,* PC Pro, Dec. 18, 2006, http://www.pcpro.co.uk/news/100351/half-of-all-phishes-from-romanian-cyber-gang.html. Phishing is, essentially, using online techniques to trick people into giving online criminals useful information, such as their credit card numbers, Social Security number, passwords, and usernames. *See, e.g.,* Phishing—Wikipedia, http://en.wikipedia.org/wiki/Phishing (last visited Apr. 21, 2007).

167   This example suggests a longitudinal way in which point of attack origin can contribute to the identification of an attacker or attackers. If investigators can establish point of attack origin with a high level of confidence for successive attacks, then they should be able to use the repeated occurrence of attacks emanating from this same point of origin to infer some consistency in the identity of the person or persons responsible for those attacks. *But see supra* Section III.A.2.a.

168   *See generally* Brian Krebs, *Cyber Crime Hits the Big Time in 2006*, Wash. Post, Dec. 28, 2006, *available at* http://www.washingtonpost.com/wp-dyn/content/article/2006/12/22/AR2006122200367_pf.html (reporting that 2006 saw an "unprecedented spike" in "sophisticated online attacks").

are carried out by individuals. While this distinction is still useful for analyzing attacker-attribution in real-world and online attacks, it is not as stable as it once was.

Over the last several decades, the hybrid phenomena of state-sponsored terrorism and state-sponsored crime have emerged as increasingly serious threats.[169] Both present distinct legal issues, most notably with regard to the efficacy of attempting to use criminal sanctions to deter an activity sponsored by a nation-state.[170] Aside from anything else, a sponsoring state may not cooperate in the investigation, apprehension, and extradition of those who acted on its behalf in committing criminal or terrorist acts.[171]

Notwithstanding the complexities associated with the mechanics of bringing these offenders to justice,[172] analysis of attacker-attribution for individually-perpetrated attacks and for acts of war can be useful in a state-sponsored cybercrime and cyberterrorism context. Yet, the ultimate determination of responsibility for attacks falling into these categories will require ascertaining the nature of the attacks—an issue we take up below.

To understand why this is true, reconsider the BIS attacks. We are assuming they were launched from Guangdong, China. We know they targeted computer systems used by a sensitive U.S. government agency in Washington, D.C. We analyzed how the attacker-attribution calculus should proceed if the attacks were cyberwarfare or "personal" cybercrime/cyberterrorism. Inherent in this analysis was the need to differentiate the two categories of attacks. The act of distinguishing involves both identifying an attacker and identifying the nature of an attack, because for cyberwarfare, the same factor establishes both. If the attacker-attribution calculus indicated that an attack "came from" a nation-state (command and control), we concluded it was war; otherwise, it fell into the residual category of cybercrime or cyberterrorism.

One problem with this analysis is that determining whether a cyberattack "comes from" a specific nation-state can be difficult because territorial point of attack origin can be ambiguous in this context. An attack from Guangdong might "come from" China itself or it might "come from" sport hackers[173] who are adventitiously in Guangdong. Essentially, point of attack origin's utility in attacker-attribution has, to this point, been limited to negating the proposition that an attack is an instance of cyberwarfare. If we conclude with some confidence that an attack did not "come from" a nation-state actor, we inferentially assign it to the cybercrime/cyberterrorism category and embark upon the tasks of determining precisely what it is and who is responsible for it.

The other problem with our earlier analysis is that nation-state "involvement" in an attack is no longer synonymous with warfare.[174] In the real-world, we now have intermediate categories of nation-state involvement that, among other things, have given us state-sponsored crime and state-sponsored

---

169    *See, e.g.,* Christopher C. Joyner & Wayne P. Rothbaum, *Libya and the Aerial Incident at Lockerbie: What Lessons for International Extradition Law?,* 14 Mich. J. Int'l L. 222, 229 (1993) ("State-sponsored terrorism has emerged since the 1970s as a dangerous strain of international violence."). *But see* Susan W. Brenner & Anthony C. Crescenzi, *State-Sponsored Crime: The Futility of the Economic Espionage Act,* 28 Hous. J. Int'l L. 389 (2006) (economic espionage as state-sponsored crime); Douglas R. Burgess, Jr., *Hostis Humani Generi: Piracy, Terrorism and a New International Law,* 13 U. Miami Int'l & Comp. L. Rev. 293, 302–03 (2006) (writing that sixteenth-century British government regarded piracy "in much the same way as state-sponsored terrorism is viewed today"). In the discussion above "state-sponsored crime" denotes state involvement in the commission of conventional crimes, such as the theft of intellectual property. *See* Brenner & Crescenzi, *supra.* This Article is not concerned with the distinct phenomenon of state-sponsored war crimes or crimes against humanity. For more on that topic, see, e.g., Jean-Marie Simon, *The Alien Tort Claims Act: Justice or Show Trials?,* 11 B.U. Int'l L.J. 1, 50 (1993).
170    *See* Brenner & Crescenzi, *supra* note 208. *But see* Country Reports on Terrorism 2005, *supra* note 47 (describing the use of economic and other sanctions against state supporters of real-world terrorism).
171    *See* Brenner & Crescenzi, *supra* note 208.
172    For an examination of this issue, see *infra* Section IV.
173    *See Secure Your Wi-Fi Network,* Accent, Aug. 2005, http://www.emphasisonsuccess.com/htmlArchive/aug2005/aug2005page3.html.
174    *See supra* note 208 and accompanying text.

terrorism.[175] State-sponsored crime has already migrated online, and state-sponsored terrorism will certainly follow.[176] The problem, for the moment, is parsing out whether an attack is "mere" cybercrime or state-sponsored cybercrime, "mere" cyberterrorism or state-sponsored cyberterrorism.

State sponsorship necessarily involves a level of state participation in a cyberattack, but identifying a nation-state's involvement in a less-than-cyberwarfare attack will surely be difficult. Point of attack origin is unlikely to be helpful in this effort, for at least two reasons. First, the fact that an attack originates in the territory of a nation-state, even one known to be inclined to sponsor terrorist activity, is inconclusive. Attack origination on its territory *might* mean the state is involved in the attack, but it might not;[177] territorial origination is inferentially even less significant here than it is for cyberwarfare. Second, the fact an attack originates *outside* the territory of a particular nation-state does not necessarily mean the nation-state is not sponsoring the attack. As we have seen in the real-world, state sponsorship can take many forms, such as providing terrorists with "funding, weapons, training and sanctuary."[178]

A Machiavellian nation could fund and otherwise support terrorists (or criminals) who launch cyberattacks from outside its territory on a nation-state it wants to see "harmed"—economically undermined, harassed, rendered vulnerable to overtures, or intimidated in the real-world.[179] The point of attack origin might be traced and used to identify the individual attackers, but it would reveal nothing about the sponsoring nation-state's complicity in the attack; indeed, since the attacks originated outside the physical "presence" of this rogue nation-state, this nation-state would plausibly be able to deny any association with them.[180]

If the attacks were launched from within its territory, our hypothetical state sponsor of cybercrime and cyberterrorism could still credibly deny involvement with them. Physical attacks involve detectable staging efforts that can be difficult to conceal, which can make it challenging for a nation-state to disavow knowledge of (and at least tacit complicity in) activity within its borders.[181] State-sponsored cyberattacks, like their civilian counterparts, are presumably clandestine in staging and in execution, and, unlike physical attacks, involve computer activities which are harder to detect and easier to conceal. The sovereign-sponsor of such domestically-launched attacks could therefore plausibly deny knowledge of and involvement with them in the same way and for the same reasons nation-states concede their inability to identify cybercriminals ex ante (or even ex post).[182] A devious nation-state might even be able to conceal its involvement in self-interested cyberattacks by encouraging "civilian" cybercriminals and cyberterrorists to conduct their operations from within its borders since the fog of "civilian" cyberattacks would obscure the purpose and origins of the state-sponsored attacks.

As these examples illustrate, point of attack origin will not be particularly helpful in attributing state responsibility for sponsored cyberattacks because we are dealing with tiered responsibility: primary responsibility for an attack rests with the individuals who carry it out, while secondary responsibility

---

175    *See supra id.;* see also *supra* note 111.

176    See, e.g., Rollins & Wilson, *supra* note 8.

177    *See* Country Reports on Terrorism 2005, *supra* note 47, at 16 ("The presence of terrorist safe havens in a nation ... is not necessarily related to state sponsorship of terrorism.").

178    State Sponsors: Iran—Council on Foreign Relations, http://www.cfr.org/publication/9362/ (last visited Apr. 21, 2007).

179    *See* Brenner & Crescenzi, *supra* note 208; *see, e.g.,* Office of the Nat'l Counterintelligence Executive, Annual Report to Congress on Foreign Economic Collection and Industrial Espionage—2005 10 (2006), *available at* http://www.ncix.gov/publications/reports_speeches/reports/fecie_all/Index_fecie.html.

180    This becomes easier as the state's level of sponsorship diminishes. *See, e.g.,* Pillar, *supra* note 41, at 157–96 (distinguishing state-sponsors of terrorism, state-enablers of terrorism, and state-cooperators in terrorism).

181    *See, e.g.,* Michael Elliott, *They Had a Plan,* Time, Aug. 2, 2002, *available at* http://www.time.com/time/covers/1101020812/story.html (discussing al-Qaeda in Afghanistan prior to 9/11); Bay of Pigs Invasion—Wikipedia, http://en.wikipedia.org/wiki/Bay_of_Pigs_Invasion (last visited Apr. 21, 2007).

182    See Brenner, Toward a Criminal Law for Cyberspace, supra note 5, at 65–76.

rests with the nation-state that sponsored their efforts.[183] As discussed earlier, an identified point of attack origin can play a role in primary attacker-attribution for cybercrime and cyberterrorism; however, that role diminishes for secondary attacker-attribution because of the sponsor's indirect participation in the attack.

\* \* \*

### crime-terrorism

Point of attack occurrence is an integral component of attacker-attribution for crimes and acts of terrorism. Real-world investigations concentrate on the scene of the crime or terrorist event, on the place where the attack occurred. This investigative model is based on the assumption that the players in the attack dynamic (criminals/terrorists and victims) occupied shared real-space; this assumption derives from the inescapable fact that physical proximity is an essential prerequisite for the commission of real-world crime or terrorism.

Thus, the point of attack occurrence plays a central role in the investigation of these real-world events. It is the most likely source of physical evidence and eyewitness testimony that can be used to identify an attacker and link him to the crime/act of terrorism. The larger spatial context in which the immediate crime scene resides provides a potential source of further testimony and data that can become the basis of inferential linkages between victim and attacker. And sometimes the place where the attack occurs can itself become a source of inference as to the likely identity of an attacker. If someone is murdered in a home with an armed alarm system, this suggests the attacker knew the victim; but if jewelry disappears from a locked safe in a jewelry store, this suggests the thief was an insider who had access to the safe's combination.[184]

Here, again, the importance of point of attack occurrence diminishes as attacks move online. A real-space attacker's gaining entry to a home that has an armed alarm system suggests the attacker knew the victim, but a cyberspace attacker's gaining entry to a home computer hooked to a cable modem does not. Similarly, a hacker's transferring funds from online bank accounts is likely not an inside job. Although the bank presumably had measures in place that were intended to limit virtual access to the accounts, the compromise of those measures, unlike the compromise of the jewelry store safe, did not necessarily involve privileged physical access either to the accounts or to "inside" information needed to access them. Investigators can infer with a high degree of confidence that the compromise of the jewelry store safe came from an employee or a former employee who was given the combination as a routine part of his employment or from someone with whom that employee shared the information. The physical constraints that govern action in the real-world make it eminently reasonable to draw certain inferences from the place where an attack occurred; the absence of those constraints makes it problematic, if not impossible, to predicate similar inferences on the place where a virtual attack occurred. Cyberspace nullifies the influence of the three spatial dimensions that constrain action in the real-world and, in so doing, erodes the significance of place in attacker-attribution.

The point of attack occurrence still plays a role in attacker-attribution for online crimes and acts of terrorism because it is literally the place where an attack occurred. More precisely, it is the place where the virtual attack was consummated. Real-world attacks are initiated and consummated in a single

---

183   *See* Country Reports on Terrorism 2005, *supra* note 47, at 173, 176–77 (listing Iran and Syria as nation-states with secondary responsibility).
184   See, e.g., Sex, Lies And The Doctor's Wife, CBS News, June 6, 2006, http://www.cbsnews.com/ stories/2005/11/09/48hours/mainl 028132.shtml; Ali Winston, *$13G "Inside Job " Jewelry Theft*, Jersey J. (Jersey City, N.J.), Dec. 8, 2006, *available at* http://www.nj .com/news/jjournal/index.ssf?/base/news-3/116556105967210.xml&coll = 3.

physical place, which then becomes the crime scene. As we saw earlier, the utilization of cyberspace breaks the crime scene into shards. Here, the place where the attack actually occurs—where the harm is inflicted on the victim—is part of a larger crime scene. Like a real-world crime scene, it will contain evidence that can be used in an attempt to track the person(s) responsible for the attack. Unlike a real-world crime scene, however, it is not self-contained; the evidence found at this virtual crime scene is part of a sequence of digital evidence that is strewn around cyberspace and stored on the computers used in the attack. Since the ultimate crime scene accounts for only part of the available evidence, its role in the inferential process of identifying the attacker is accordingly reduced.

And as with cyberwarfare, determining the identity of the attacker responsible for crimes or acts of terrorism will often be bound up with determining the nature of an attack. I return to this issue in Section III.B.

### state-sponsored crime/terrorism

The role of point of attack occurrence in attacker-attribution for state-sponsored cybercrime and cyberterrorism is functionally indistinguishable from the role it plays in assigning individual responsibility for online crime and acts of terrorism. Here, too, it is simply part of the total crime scene—the point at which an attack is consummated. Digital evidence retrieved from the point of attack occurrence can be used in efforts to backtrack the attack to its source and can be the basis for an inference as to primary and secondary responsibility for an attack, once investigators determine that it was state-sponsored. In making this determination, investigators should factor the analog of the Willie Sutton rule into the calculus because, as we saw earlier, point of attack occurrence cannot itself sustain a finding of nation-state responsibility.

\* \* \*

External order was a purely sovereign concern; nation-states challenged each other in the international arena and resolved matters with military combat. Non-state actors were limited to challenging a state's ability to maintain internal order; criminals' pursuit of self-gratification and the more doctrinaire activities of terrorists threatened to erode social order in varying ways and to varying degrees. For at least a century and a half, nation-states have employed a unique strategy—civilian law enforcement—to control internal threats.[185] This two-pronged strategy consists of adopting laws that criminalize crime and terrorism and using a specialized, quasi-military force to identify and apprehend those who violate the laws.[186] Violators are prosecuted, convicted, and sanctioned, which presumptively deters them from re-offending and others from following their example.[187]

The sections below examine attacker-attribution, in the real-world and then in the virtual world of cyberspace. As part of this analysis, the first section incorporates some consideration of the response mechanisms we employ for each category of threats in the real-world; the next section continues that approach by demonstrating how the attribution ambiguity in online attacks impacts response mechanisms.

\* \* \*

---

185  See Brenner, Toward a Criminal Law for Cyberspace, supra note 5, at 49–65.
186  See id.
187  See id.

In the United States response authority is scrupulously bifurcated between military and civilian law enforcement personnel,[188] with military personnel responding to external threats (acts of war) and law enforcement personnel responding to internal threats (crime and terrorism). Further, "pure" civilians have absolutely no role in responding to crime or terrorism, and the only role they play in responding to acts of war is as recruits for a country's military forces.

This seems an eminently logical state of affairs to us because it is all we know. In the United States, the basic components of this model have been in place since the Revolutionary War ended, though they have been refined somewhat over the years. The two sections below briefly review the legal principles that are responsible for this bifurcated response authority; the first examines the military–law enforcement bifurcation, while the second examines the non-role "pure" civilians have in attack response processes.

## military–law enforcement bifurcation

The United States' commitment to bifurcated response authority has its roots in English common law and more immediate origins in the American colonists' experience with the British military.[189] In the Declaration of Independence, colonists complained that the King's actions had "render[ed] the military independent of and superior to the Civil Powers."[190] According to one scholar, the Declaration of Independence's "'repudiation of military intervention in domestic law enforcement,' which the founders viewed as an offense against civil liberties, became 'the bedrock of due process on which the American government was built.'"[191]

The concern with limiting military power carried over to the drafting of the Constitution. The delegates to the Constitutional Convention accepted the need for a standing military force, but only "on the condition that there be safeguards established to keep the military under civilian control."[192] The Constitution consequently "allowed for a standing army and navy, but restricted military appropriations to two years, and ... appointed a civilian commander-in-chief."[193] While the Constitution itself "did not include an explicit provision regarding the domestic use of military forces,"[194] some argue that the Bill of Rights achieves this indirectly: "Hamilton chose the Fifth Amendment's due process clause to satisfy the delegates who demanded a clear separation between civil and military authority. The Amendment's emphasis on the full and unhindered process of the law implies the superiority of the civil sphere over ... military authority."[195]

---

188  The discussion that follows makes explicit what has been implicit in what I have written so far; that is, it explicitly assumes the model of response authority in effect in the United States, both because it is the model with which I am the most familiar and because it seems to be the most extreme instance of the partitioned response authority model. The partition is not as defined, nor as rigid, in some countries. See, e.g., Donald E. Schulz, The United States and Latin America: Shaping an Elusive Future 37 (2000). But see Daniella Ashkenazy, The Military in the Service of Society and Democracy: The Challenge of the Dual-Role Military 5 (1994) ("[T]he military in democratic societies have not been assigned a role as a domestic law enforcement agency, with the exception of extreme circumstances of insurrection or collapse of domestic public order beyond the capabilities of civilian police.").

189  See, e.g., Nathan Canestaro, Homeland Defense: Another Nail in the Coffin for Posse Comitatus, 12 Wash. U. J.L. & Pol'y 99, 101–10 (2003).

190  The Declaration of Independence para. 14 (U.S. 1776); see also id. at para. 13, 16 & 27.

191  Canestaro, supra note 278, at 108 (quoting David E. Engdahl, Foundations for Military Intervention in the United States, 7 U. puget sound L. Rev. 1, 7 (1983)). The dichotomization of the civilian–military spheres of authority and the military's consequent subservience to civilian authority are essential organizing principles in democratic societies. See Ashkenazy, supra note 277, at 4–5.

192  Canestaro, supra note 278, at 109.

193  Id.

194  Id.

195  Id.

Notwithstanding these efforts, in "the first ninety years of the republic, there was no clear … legal barrier to the use of federal troops to enforce the laws."[196] The Militia Act of 1792 authorized federal marshals to use state militias in enforcing civil law on the premise that the militia members were acting "as private citizens, not as soldiers."[197] In the years leading up to the Civil War, federal marshals' use of army troops to enforce federal law "became commonplace," and in 1854, the Attorney General issued an opinion upholding the legality of the practice.[198]

The use of federal military personnel for law enforcement continued until its abuse in the post–Civil War South brought calls for a change.[199] "As a result, in 1878 the post-Reconstruction Congress passed the Posse Comitatus Act … to put an end to the use of military for ordinary law enforcement purposes."[200] The Posse Comitatus Act (PCA) is still in force, and currently provides as follows: "Whoever, except in cases … expressly authorized by the Constitution or Act of Congress, willfully uses any part of the Army or the Air Force … to execute the laws shall be fined … or imprisoned not more than two years, or both."[201] While the PCA only applies to the Army and Air Force, Department of Defense regulations extend its restrictions to the Navy and Marines.[202] It has not been applied to the Coast Guard because the Coast Guard has traditionally functioned more as a law enforcement agency than as a military entity.[203]

As many commentators have noted, the restrictions imposed by the PCA have eroded over the last several decades: "Since the 1970s, the courts have narrowed the scope of the Act's application, and during the 1980s, Congress specifically exempted certain military actions from the PCA, particularly in the context of the war on drugs."[204] In 1981, for example, Congress passed the Military Cooperation with Law Enforcement Officials Act, which let the military

---

196 *Id.* at 109–10 (quoting Edward F. Sherman, Contemporary Challenges to Traditional Limits on the Role of the Military in American Society, in Military Intervention in Democratic Societies 216, 219 (Peter J. Rowe & Christopher J. Whelan eds., 1985)).

197 *Id.* at 110; see Militia Act of 1792, ch. 28, § 2, 1 Stat. 264 (1792). The Act only permitted use of the militia "in limited circumstances where law enforcement officers … could not suppress a violent internal disorder." Sean J. Kealy, *Re-examining the Posse Comitatus Act: Toward a Right to Civil Law Enforcement*, 21 Yale L. & Pol'y Rev. 383, 392 (2003). And it drew a "clear distinction between the citizen soldiers who may be used in emergencies and the standing army, indicating that Congress sought to exclude the regular army from law enforcement matters." *Id.*

198 Canestaro, *supra* note 278, at 110 (citing 6 Op. Att'y Gen. 466, 473 (1854)); *see also* Kealy, *supra* note 286, at 392–93.

199 *See, e.g.*, Comment, *The Posse Comitatus Act Applied to the Prosecution of Civilians*, 53 U. Kan. L. Rev. 767, 771 (2005) [hereinafter *The Posse Comitatus Act*] ("Never before or after, within the continental boundaries of the United States, did [the military] exercise police … functions … on the scale it did in the eleven ex-Confederate states from 1865 to 1877" (quoting Robert W. Coakley, The Role of Federal Military Forces in Domestic Disorders 1789–1878 268 (1988))).

200 *The Posse Comitatus Act, supra* note 288, at 772 (citing Army Appropriations Act, ch. 263, § 15, 20 Stat. 145, 152 (1878)). As one author notes, "the PCA was rarely mentioned for a century after its passage, and the courts so rarely had to interpret the law that one court described the PCA as 'obscure and all-but-forgotten.' The obscurity may have been a result of the Act's effective curtailment of military involvement in law enforcement." Kealy, *supra* note 286, at 398 (quoting Chandler v. United States, 171 F.2d 921, 936 (1st Cir. 1948)).

201 18 U.S.C. § 1835 (2000).

202 *See The Posse Comitatus Act, supra* note 288, at 772–73 (citing U.S. Dep't of Defense, Directive No. 5525.5, DoD Cooperation with Civilian Law Enforcement Officials, encl. 4 at 4.3 (Jan. 15, 1986)). A federal statute requires the Secretary of Defense to establish regulations which ensure that law enforcement activity "does not include or permit direct participation by a member of the Army, Navy, Air Force or Marine Corps." 10 U.S.C. § 375. Prior to the enactment of the Department of Defense regulations, the Fourth Circuit had held that the Act applies all branches of the armed services. *See* United States v. Walden, 490 F.2d 372, 375 (4th Cir. 1974).

203 *See The Posse Comitatus Act, supra* note 288, at 773; *see also* United States v. Chaparro-Almeida, 679 F.2d 423, 425–26 (5th Cir. 1982); Jackson v. State, 572 P.2d 87, 93 (Alaska 1977). At least two circuits have held that the Posse Comitatus Act does not apply to the Navy when it is under the control of or supporting the Coast Guard. *See* United States v. Klimavicius-Viloria, 144 F.3d 1249, 1259 (9th Cir. 1998); United States v. Kahn, 35 F.3d 426, 432 (9th Cir. 1994); United States v. Mendoza-Cecelia, 963 F.2d 1467, 1477–78 (11th Cir. 1992).

204 Kealy, *supra* note 286, at 398; see, e.g., Laird v. Tatum, 408 U.S. 1, 19 (1972).

help enforce drug, immigration, and tariff laws. The Act ... [allowed] the military to cooperate with law enforcement by providing equipment, research facilities, and information; by training and advising police on the use of loaned equipment; and by assisting law enforcement personnel in keeping drugs from entering the country.[205]

After 9/11, there were calls to abandon the PCA to let the military play a "greater role" in homeland defense,[206] but the general sentiment seems to be that it should neither be repealed nor further eroded.[207]

The PCA is the primary legal principle barring the military from participating in civilian law enforcement, but other federal statutes and regulations also contribute to the bifurcation.[208] The correlate aspect of this bifurcation—law enforcement's exclusion from the conduct of military operations—is a fundamental principle of the modern laws of warfare.[209] It is also implicit in the Constitution's authorizing Congress to "raise and support Armies."[210] The military is, as a treatise notes, "separate from civilian society, with a jurisprudence that exists ... apart from the law which governs" the civilian realm.[211] Its unique and exclusive function is, as the Supreme Court said, "to fight or be ready to fight wars."[212]

## civilian exclusion from attack response

The sections below examine civilian exclusion from the law enforcement and military response processes. The first section considers law enforcement; the second analyzes the military.

### law enforcement

Until the nineteenth century, civilians not only participated in law enforcement, they essentially *were* law enforcement.[213] As I have explained in more detail elsewhere, until Sir Robert Peel established the first professional police force in early nineteenth-century London, civilian law enforcement was an ad hoc process that relied heavily on the efforts of citizens.[214] Pre–nineteenth century England and the American colonies had laws that required able-bodied men to participate in apprehending criminals; American civilians, at least, were initially reluctant to surrender this function to armed professionals for fear of government overreaching.[215] Their reluctance waned, and by the twentieth century, policing had become the sole province of law enforcement officers.[216]

---

205 Kealy, *supra* note 286, at 409 (citing Department of Defense Authorization Act of 1982, Pub. L. No. 97–86, § 905, 95 Stat. 1115 (codified as amended at 10 U.S.C. §§ 371–78).

206 *See, e.g., id.* at 424; see also Stewart M. Powell, Bush Considers Changes to Posse Comitatus Act, Hous. Chron., Oct. 2, 2005, available at 2005 WLNR 24636542.

207 *See, e.g.,* Dan Bennett, Comment, *The Domestic Role of the Military in America: Why Modifying or Repealing the Posse Comitatus Act Would Be a Mistake,* 10 Lewis & Clark L. Rev. 935 (2006); *see also* Michael T. Cunningham, *The Military's Involvement in Law Enforcement: The Threat Is Not What You Think,* 26 Seattle U. L. Rev. 699, 717 (2003) (arguing that utilizing the military in domestic law enforcement would threaten the military's ability to "project effective, overwhelming force" in the interests of national defense).

208 *See, e.g.,* Adam Burton, *Fixing FISA for Long War: Regulating Warrantless Surveillance in the Age of Terrorism,* 4 Pierce L. Rev. 381, 389 (2006) (asserting that the Foreign Intelligence Surveillance Act creates "a 'wall' of separation between agencies responsible for law enforcement and those responsible for military and foreign intelligence").

209 *See, e.g.,* Hague Convention No. IV, *supra* note 115.

210 U.S. Const, art. I, § 8, cl. 12.

211 6 C.J.S. Armed Services § 11 (note omitted).

212 Toth v. Quarles, 350 U.S. 11,17 (1955).

213 *See* Brenner, Toward a Criminal Law for Cyberspace, supra note 5, at 65–76.

214 *See id.*

215 *See id.*

216 *See id.*

The process of professionalizing policing has been so successful that civilians no longer need to assume any responsibility for controlling or preventing crime.[217] Those tasks are now monopolized by professional police forces organized in a hierarchical, quasi-military fashion.[218] Civilians' only roles in this model of crime control and prevention are as sources of evidence—witnesses or victims.[219]

Indeed, civilian exclusion from law enforcement is so complete that when citizens *do* participate, their actions have been given a distinct, pejorative descriptor: vigilantism. Vigilantism is essentially a civilian's "taking the law into her own hands": engaging in action that would be lawful if it were carried out by an authorized law enforcement agent.[220] Since the vigilante is not an authorized law enforcement agent, she will be prosecuted for her conduct if it violates an established criminal prohibition and she cannot raise a statutory defense to criminal charges.[221]

"Pure" vigilantism almost always involves "volunteers"—untrained, rogue actors who have taken it upon themselves to "assist" law enforcement by operating on their own.[222] Societies have long deemed "pure" vigilantism intolerable for several reasons, one of which is that the activities of "pure" vigilantes create unacceptable risks of error in offender identification and apprehension.[223] Another argument against tolerating "pure" vigilantism is that it tends to undermine legal guarantees that are designed to safeguard civil liberties. It also undermines respect for lawfully-established authority, such as law enforcement and the judicial system. For these and other compelling reasons, societies have rigorously, and successfully, discouraged "pure" vigilante efforts for the last century or so, in large part as a function of professionalizing law enforcement.

Our suppression of "pure" vigilantism will, however, continue to be successful only so long as law enforcement is perceived as effective in combating crime.[224] This is so far not a problem for real-world crime, at least not in most countries, but it is for cybercrime. As we saw earlier, cybercrime represents a significant challenge for law enforcement because it differs in several critical respects from the real-world crime that shaped the current law enforcement model.[225] Law enforcement is losing its battle with

---

217 *See id.*

218 *See id.*

219 *See id.* The model of "community policing" that emerged at the end of the last century seeks to incorporate a level of civilian participation into the law enforcement process, but here, too, the civilians function almost exclusively as sources of information about actual or potential crimes. *See id.* Even when they take a rather more active role in crime control, civilian participants in community policing do not participate in the processes of investigating crime and apprehending perpetrators. *See id.; see, e.g.,* Community Policing, http://www.hawaiipolice.com/topPages/cpo.html (last visited Apr. 21, 2007).

220 One scholar characterizes vigilantism as "lawless law." Lawrence M. Friedman, Crime and Punishment in American History 172 (1993). He describes it as follows: "'Taking the law into one's own hands' ... expresses two thoughts: first, that the action is *private*, the action of individuals ... who seize ... the state's role as enforcer of law. But equally important is the second idea, that it is *law* that one is taking into one's hands" *Id.*

221 See Kelly D. Hine, Vigilantism Revisited: An Economic Analysis of the Law of Extrajudicial Self-Help or Why Can t Dick Shoot Henry for Stealing Jane s Truck?, 47 Am. U. L. Rev. 1221, 1227-28(1998).

222 *See, e.g.,* Vigilante—Wikipedia, http://en.wikipedia.org/wiki/Vigilante (last visited Apr. 21, 2007).

223 It can also, in extreme circumstances, create the potential for the erroneous application of sanctions to those whom "pure" vigilantes have misidentified as offenders.

224 Although the *perception* that law enforcement is effectively combating crime necessarily encompasses the premise that law enforcement *actually* enjoys a level of success in this regard, it does not mean law enforcement must apprehend the perpetrator of every crime it is unable to prevent. Modern societies rely on a crime-control, not a crime-negation, strategy to maintain the baseline of internal order they require to survive and prosper. *See* Brenner, *Toward a Criminal Law for Cyberspace, supra* note 5, at 65–76. Crime-control strategies maintain that baseline of internal order by persuading citizens that the risks of apprehension are high enough that they dissuade all but a subset of the population from engaging in criminal activity. *See id.* This keeps crime at an acceptable level. *See id.* There can be a disconnect between the actual and perceived risks of perpetrator apprehension, but the disconnect will be irrelevant to the efficacy of the crime-control strategy as long as the perceived risk of apprehension is significant enough to act as a default crime-deterrent.

225 *See id.*

sophisticated, transnational cybercrime, and will continue to do so unless and until we can adapt our current law enforcement model to an increasingly online environment.[226]

While many citizens remain unaware of this reality, others understand that online law enforcement is failing. Some of those in the latter category have consequently become "pure" online vigilantes: rogue actors whose goals are, variously, to frustrate online criminal activity or to initiate the apprehension and prosecution of online perpetrators. And the incidence of "pure" online vigilante activity is almost certain to increase unless we improve the efficacy of online law enforcement; "pure" vigilantism emerges when citizens perceive that there is a law enforcement vacuum, that crime control is ineffective.[227] The already-notable online vacuum encourages "pure" vigilantism, as do several other factors. One is the ease with which online vigilantes can affiliate with like-minded others; websites and e-mail let them share information and join in collaborative vigilante activity directly targeting online offenders. Another factor prompting online vigilantism is that it is a relatively low-risk activity. Since they have no reason to be in physical proximity with those they pursue, online vigilantes run little risk of physical violence from their prey; a vigilante can be in a different city, a different state, or a different country from those he targets. And because online vigilantes can conceal their identities as well as their locations, they are unlikely to be identified and prosecuted as vigilantes.

The eroding efficacy of our current model of law enforcement is therefore compounding the problem of maintaining internal or external order online: the model's increasing inefficacy in controlling crime qua crime is eroding societies' disparate abilities to discourage criminal activity in cyberspace; this not only undermines the perception that social order is being maintained "in" cyberspace, it also erodes the perception that societies are maintaining order in the real-world. Criminal laws are designed to prevent the citizens of a society from preying on each other;[228] the problem we now confront is that while the enforcement of these laws in their real-world societal context continues to be efficacious enough to maintain order within a given society, the inefficacy with which criminal laws are enforced in cyberspace bleeds into the real-world, where it undermines our faith in our government's ability to protect us. That, in turn, encourages "pure" vigilantism, which itself threatens societies' ability to maintain internal order; while vigilantes claim to be acting on behalf of the law, their conduct actually erodes the fabric and integrity of the law.

It would seem, then, that we must continue to exclude civilians from law enforcement because to do otherwise would at least implicitly sanction vigilantism.[229] And that is true as far as it goes: For the reasons noted above, we cannot tolerate "pure" vigilantism in the real-world, in cyberspace, or in the intersection of the two. But "pure" vigilantism—vigilantes substituting for law enforcement officers—is not our only option. Another possibility is to return to the past—to institute a limited revival of the traditional Anglo-American system in which civilians legitimately participated in (rather than replaced) law enforcement.

One of the reasons law enforcement is struggling with cybercrime is a lack of resources and trained personnel. Agencies operating essentially on the same budgets that barely sufficed for real-world crime must now respond to real-world crime *plus* cybercrime. Cybercrime also increases the complexity, as well as the quantity, of the crime with which officers must deal; because cybercriminals exploit computer technology in more or less sophisticated ways, investigators need special training and

---

226  *See id.*

227  *See, e.g.,* Friedman, *supra* note 309, at 158–68.

228  See Brenner, Toward a Criminal Law for Cyberspace, *supra* note 5, at 65–76.

229  As I note in Section IV.B, *infra*, an early twentieth-century experiment with bringing civilians into law enforcement had the apparently unintended effect of sanctioning—and thereby encouraging—the worst kind of "pure" vigilantism.

equipment, both of which must be continually upgraded. The obvious solution would be to increase law enforcement budgets so that they can support the personnel, resources, and training necessary to increase the efficacy with which law enforcement responds to cybercrime. Unfortunately, this appealingly straightforward solution is ultimately impracticable because the cost would be prohibitive, at least in terms of what taxpayers in the United States and elsewhere would be willing to bear.[230]

We could achieve essentially the same end indirectly if we were to utilize the above noted approach, that is, incorporating a level of civilian participation into law enforcement. The Anglo-American practice of incorporating such participation derived from the then-acknowledged need to supplement available law enforcement resources. Of course, at that time officers needed manpower, weapons, and horses, while today's officers need hardware, software, and individuals trained in their use. The principle, though, remains the same: civilian participation can serve as an in-kind supplement to formal law enforcement resources.

We will assume for the purpose of analysis that corporate and individual civilians are able and willing to participate in the law enforcement response to cybercrime. Therefore, the difficulty, if any, of implementing this strategy lies in (1) identifying precisely *how* civilians would participate in that endeavor and (2) resolving any legal obstacles to such participation. We will defer the first issue for now, and return to it later in Section IV.B. Our concern here is with how the law does, and should, approach civilian participation in what has long been a purely sovereign function. It seems that re-establishing the principle of civilian participation in law enforcement would, at a minimum, require resolving two legal issues. One is the vigilantism issue noted earlier: how can we integrate civilian participation into law enforcement without sanctioning vigilantism and its attendant evils? The other issue is perhaps more straightforward: what, if any, statutory or other obstacles currently ban civilian participation in law enforcement?

### vigilantism

The vigilantism issue is concededly problematic, as history demonstrates. I address this issue in more detail in Section IV.B, when I speculate about the mechanics of integrating civilians into the cyberconflict attack processes. For now, I want to note only that the strategy currently under consideration involves utilizing civilians to *supplement*, rather than *replace*, law enforcement efforts. It

---

230   There are several reasons why taxpayers would not—and probably could not—fund the personnel and other resources needed to maintain an effective law enforcement response to cybercrime.

One is the sheer magnitude of the problem: Criminal law enforcement in the United States primarily takes place at the state and local level; there are, consequently, over 17,500 state and local law enforcement agencies in the United States. Bringing these agencies up to speed in the battle against cybercrime would require hiring and training an appropriate number of officers in each agency and equipping each agency with some to-be-identified quantum of specialized computer hardware and software. The initial costs would be staggering because the process would certainly require purchasing new equipment and would almost certainly require hiring new officers; new hires would be necessary both because of the need to maintain current force levels to deal with real-world crime and because traditional officers often have neither the interest nor the aptitudes needed to pursue cybercrime. As to personnel costs, we can only speculate as to how many officers would need to be hired, but if it averaged, say, two officers per agency, 35,000 officers would have to be hired for this purpose. The initial costs of bringing the agencies up to speed would, therefore, encompass salaries, benefits, and initial training for these new hires, as well as the purchase of the hardware and software they would need in their work.

If we were dealing with real-world law enforcement, the initial costs would basically be a one-time expense. While officers do continue to train in the use of weapons and other tactics, their equipment and police vehicles last for years. Cybercrime, on the other hand, is an exponentially evolving arms race: computer hardware and software evolve at an amazing pace, a circumstance cybercriminals exploit. Optimally, cybercrime investigators should be equipped with and trained in the latest technology, and their efficacy as investigators will decline if they do not have access to current technology and training. But providing them with what they need is an expensive proposition; more precisely, it is a recurring expensive proposition since hardware and software quickly become obsolete. It is conceivable, but exceedingly unlikely, that taxpayers could and would bear the expense involved in keeping law enforcement competitive with cybercriminals.

does not legitimize "pure" vigilantism. The critical distinction between "pure" vigilantism and the hypothesized strategy is that the civilians work under the supervision of authorized law enforcement officers.[231] Whatever else they do, civilians do not initiate or control the course of investigations; the adoption and rigorous implementation of this proposition should eliminate the evils associated with "pure" vigilantism. Since the civilians remain subordinate to law enforcement officers, the perception will be that crime control—efficacious crime control—is being implemented by law enforcement.[232]

### existing law

Does existing law create any obstacles to the strategy posited above? There is a federal statute, the Anti-Pinkerton Act, that seems to prohibit such an effort, but probably does not. To understand why, we need to review a bit of history.

When the Civil War began, the federal government had no law enforcement officers of its own. Because it was written before professional policing had been invented, the Constitution requires Congress to create and maintain "Armies" but not law enforcement agencies.[233] As a result, when President Lincoln's life was threatened, federal authorities had to turn to a private agency for help. Allan Pinkerton, founder of what would become Pinkerton's National Detective Agency, was hired to guard the President.[234] Pinkerton then not only guarded Lincoln, he also took over the Secret Service—"the Union army's intelligence operation."[235] As a result, throughout the Civil War, "the United States continuously employed 'Pinkertons' as security officers, intelligence gatherers, and counterintelligence operatives" because there was no other alternative.[236]

After the war, Pinkerton and his agents returned to providing security and guard services for businesses, which led to their involvement in "strikebreaking" for companies opposed to unionization.[237] Pinkerton's anti-labor activities, combined with an infamous riot in which Pinkerton guards and strikers were killed, caused "great public concern over the use of private security forces." [238] This concern and union pressure resulted in Congress' adopting what is known as the Anti-Pinkerton Act.[239] The Act, which has changed very little since it was adopted in 1893, states that "[a]n individual employed by the Pinkerton Detective Agency, or similar organization, may not be employed by the Government of the United States."[240]

While the Act seems to bar the federal government from hiring private individuals to participate in federal law enforcement activities, this may not be true. The only court so far to interpret the

---

231  Federal law, for example, already allows this practice with regard to the execution of search warrants. *See* 18 U.S.C. § 3105 (2000) (private citizen may assist an officer in executing a search warrant); *see, e.g.,* United States v. Schwimmer, 692 F. Supp. 119, 12627 (E.D.N.Y. 1988) (holding that the execution of search warrant by "computer expert" acting under supervision of federal agent was proper).

232  This negates the "perceived law enforcement vacuum" which, as noted earlier, tends to encourage the rise of vigilantism.

233  *See supra* notes 298, 302–307 and accompanying text.

234  *See* David Sklansky, The Private Police, 46 UCLA L. Rev. 1165, 1212 (1999).

235  *See id.*

236  Gregory L. Bowman, Transforming Installation Security: Where Do We Go from Here?, 178 Mil. L. Rev. 50, 55 (2003).

237  *See id.*

238  *See id.*

239  *See id.* It was also "spurred in part by the employment of 25 Pinkerton guards at the 1889 presidential inauguration." Sklansky, *supra* note 323, at 1214 n.297. Hostility toward Pinkerton and its strikebreaking activities was a factor in changing American attitudes toward the professionalization of policing. *See id.* ("Hostility to private policing mounted during the second half of the nineteenth century, fueled by ... stories of malfeasance and by a growing notion that the responsibility for peacekeeping should not be placed in private hands.").

240  5 U.S.C. § 3108 (2000).

Anti-Pinkerton Act held that an organization "is not 'similar' to the ... Pinkerton Detective Agency unless it offers quasi-military armed forces for hire."[241] The then-Fifth Circuit based its holding on the premise that the Act was meant to prevent the federal government from hiring the kind of "armed guards" who precipitated injury and death in the nineteenth century labor riots, not from retaining the services of companies (or individuals) who merely provide investigative services.[242]

The *Weinberger* court's holding is one reason why the Anti-Pinkerton Act is presumably not an impediment to implementing the civilian participation strategy outlined above, at least not at the federal level. Since the strategy contemplates civilian participation in law enforcement investigations, the civilians' efforts should fall within the "safe harbor" this court carved out for investigative services.

The other reason why the Anti-Pinkerton Act does not seem to preclude implementation of a civilian participation strategy derives from the language of the Act itself: as noted above, it bars the federal government from "employing" individuals who work for the Pinkerton Agency or similar organizations. This prohibition does not apply to the strategy outlined above because it does not contemplate "employing" civilians; "employing" individuals denotes paying them for their efforts, and that would be impracticable in this context for the same reasons increasing law enforcement budgets is impracticable.[243] Since the strategy is predicated on volunteer civilian participation, the Anti-Pinkerton Act seems inapposite. It is also inapposite insofar as the strategy does not encompass hiring civilians to act as "quasi-military armed forces."

No statutory obstacles seem to exist at the state level. States do not seem to have adopted analogs of the Anti-Pinkerton Act.[244]

The de facto exclusion of civilians from the law enforcement process is apparently more a product of custom or culture rather than of law—a byproduct of the professionalization of policing that emerged in the nineteenth century and evolved in sophistication in the last century.

### military

Civilian participation in the military attack response process falls into two categories. In one, civilians surrender their civilian status and become members of the armed forces; a civilian who joins the military is not only authorized, but required, to participate in responding to attacks of war.[245] The more problematic category involves participation by civilians who have remained civilians, that is, who have not officially joined the military.

As one author notes, the law of war "attempts to regulate state utilization of civilians in combat operations in the course of international armed conflicts by prohibiting civilians from directly participating in combat."[246] The goal is to protect civilians from retaliatory attacks, but the "effectiveness of this prohibition has been substantially undercut ... by the failure of the law of war to provide a clear

---

241   United States ex rel. Weinberger v. Equifax, Inc., 557 F.2d 456, 463 (5th Cir. 1977).

242   *See id.* at 462–63.

243   *See supra* note 319 and accompanying text. Hiring civilians to supplement law enforcement efforts could be even more expensive than increasing law enforcement budgets, since civilian consultants would probably cost more, per hour, than would law enforcement investigators.

244   In the late nineteenth century, some states adopted laws restricting the use of private, armed guards "brought in from out of state," but these laws seem to have had little effect and have apparently disappeared. *See* Sklansky, *supra* note 323, at 1215 n.296.

245   *See* Jeffrey F. Addicott, *Contractors on the Battlefield*, 28 Hous. J. Int'l L. 323, 340–41 (2006) (writing that the Geneva Conventions require "militaries to distinguish between combatants (armed forces) and noncombatants (civilians)"); *see also* 10 U.S.C. § 802(a); 32 C.F.R. §§ 1624.9 & 1627.1 (2002).

246   J. Ricou Heaton, Civilians at War: Reexamining the Status of Civilians Accompanying the Armed Forces, 57 A.F.L. Rev. 155, 157 (2005). For more on this, see id. at 168–84.

definition of what constitutes direct participation in combat."[247] Until relatively recently, no precise definition was needed because the demarcation between civilians as noncombatants and civilians as combatants was quite apparent in an era of "simple weapons systems operating at short range."[248]

As warfare becomes more sophisticated and remote warfare becomes more common, the distinction between civilian noncombatants and civilian combatants has eroded.[249] In order to "save money and gain access to superior technical expertise," countries are increasingly using civilians "to operate and maintain sophisticated military equipment and to support combat operations."[250] The increasing integration of civilians into military efforts can create uncertainty as to whether a civilian is acting as a "civilian" or as a military actor.[251]

Under the current law of war, a "civilian" is someone who is not a member of a country's armed forces.[252] Ambiguity as to someone's status is resolved by construing him as a civilian.[253] Civilians involved in military efforts fall into two classes: employees and contractors.[254] "Civilian employees are hired and supervised by the armed forces and have an employment relationship with them. Contractors work independently or for a private company and have a contractual relationship with the armed forces."[255] Civilian employees are "subject to supervision, control, and discipline" by military personnel to a far greater degree than are civilian contractors.[256]

In the U.S. military, the role of civilian employees has been limited to providing combat support for real-world military operations; consequently, they work in "areas such as weapons system maintenance, logistics, and intelligence."[257] Civilian contractors, on the other hand, are "involved in almost every aspect of military activity."[258] They "train, feed, equip, and house" soldiers; they also "maintain weapons, gather intelligence, provide security at forward locations, and even fight."[259] Civilian contractors who train military units may accompany the units into combat, and contractor-consultants can be "actively involved" in planning combat operations.[260]

The roles contractors are assuming in real-world military operations can conflict with the law of war; under current law, civilians cannot participate directly in military activities.[261] Civilian employee participation in U.S. military endeavors generally comports with this requirement, but contractor participation may not, depending on how one defines "direct" participation in military activities.[262] The extent to which civilians of either type can participate in cyberwarfare is even more uncertain:

---

247  *Id.*
248  *Id.*
249  *See id.* at 157, 159–63. "Combatants" and "noncombatants" are all members of the armed forces, the distinction being that one engages in combat activities while the other does not. *See id.* at 172–73. Noncombatant members of a military force are barred from engaging in combat by the laws of their own state, not by the laws of war. *See id.*
250  *Id.* at 157; *see also id.* at 191–92.
251  *See id.* at 157, 159–63.
252  *Id.* at 173 (citing 1977 Geneva Protocol I Additional to the Geneva Conventions of Aug. 12, 1949, and Relating to the Protection of Victims of International Armed Conflicts, Dec. 12, 1977 arts. 43 and 51, 1125 U.N.T.S. 3 (entered into force Dec. 7, 1978)).
253  *See id.*
254  *See id.* at 184.
255  *Id.* at 174 (citation omitted).
256  *Id.* at 184.
257  *Id.*
258  *Id.* at 186.
259  *Id.*
260  *Id.* at 184.
261  *Id.* at 192–93.
262  *Id.* at 190–93.

The law of war provides limited guidance to help determine when computer network attack and exploitation [CNAE] actions are considered combat. No treaties specifically regulate CNAE, but it is governed by the law of war. Those aspects of CNAE which cause physical damage can be treated like attacks with more conventional weapons, with the consequence that carrying out such attacks is limited to combatants. Other types of CNAE, particularly those involving attacks on networks to steal, destroy, or alter information within them, do not necessarily constitute direct participation in hostilities and are arguably open to lawful civilian participation.[263]

Under current law, then, civilians can legitimately participate in certain aspects of cyberwarfare, a circumstance attributable to the increasing superannuation of the law of war. That law will eventually have to be modernized so it encompasses the various manifestations of cyberwarfare. And that process will also need to include a reassessment of the role civilians can legitimately play in cyberwarfare, as the rationale for excluding them from traditional combat operations either does not apply, or applies with less force, to cyberwarfare. This rationale existed to protect civilians from retaliatory attacks by an opposing military force. But as we saw earlier, cyberwarfare tends to eradicate distinctions between civilian and military targets; indeed, civilian infrastructure components will become a prime target in cyberwarfare.

\* \* \*

I have already explained *why* I believe countries must do this. Now I need to address *how* they can do it. While an improved strategy of the type for which I am arguing must logically be unitary in nature, that is, it must incorporate the efforts of all three constituencies into the attribution and response processes, I am dividing the "how" analysis into two sections: the first considers how to integrate military and law enforcement personnel into these processes; the second considers how, and to what extent, it is possible to incorporate civilian participation into the new, integrated military–law enforcement strategy.

### military–law enforcement integration

Integrating military and law enforcement personnel into the attribution and response processes raises distinct issues for the two broad categories of cyberattack, cyberwarfare and cybercrime/cyberterrorism. As an initial matter, it is important to note that my argument is based on integrating the efforts of the military and law enforcement constituencies, not on fusing them into a single entity. There are very good reasons to maintain the institutional separation of these entities.[264] Therefore, we are concerned only with how to achieve a specific, limited level of operational integration.

#### *cyberwarfare*

The threshold problem here is what-attribution, determining the nature of the attack. Integrating the efforts of military and law enforcement personnel into this process should not present insurmountable conceptual or practical difficulties because all we are concerned with, to this point, is identifying that

---

263  *Id.* at 194 (notes omitted). As noted above, "combatants" are members of a nation's armed forces. *See supra* note 338.
264  Aside from anything else, keeping the military separate from and subordinate to civilian authority helps ensure the survival of democracy and incorporating the military into the battle against crime and terrorism could undermine its ability to carry out its primary function of combating external threats.

there has been an attack or an attack is in progress and the nature of that attack. We can achieve an effective level of military–law enforcement integration in the "what-attribution" process and still maintain the institutional integrity of both the military and law enforcement constituencies.

Once an attack is determined to be cyberwarfare, the focus shifts to who-attribution and the need to respond. Who-attribution can be an independent inquiry or a subsidiary component of the what-attribution process. If it is initially apparent that an attack represents cyberwarfare, then who-attribution becomes an independent inquiry as it is not bound up with the process of what-attribution. If it is not initially apparent that an attack represents cyberwarfare, then who-attribution becomes a subsidiary component of the what-attribution process; here, determining the identity of the attackers is an essential component of the what-attribution process.

Integration proceeds no further in this analysis;[265] law enforcement–military integration here is necessarily limited to the attribution processes. The responsibility for responding to identified acts of cyberwarfare will continue to rest exclusively with the military;[266] to do otherwise would effectively eradicate the institutional separation between civilian and military response authority. The military therefore must continue to maintain institutional and operational control over the process of responding to external threats, however they present themselves.[267] I will later consider the extent to which civilian participation can be utilized to support the military response process.

This analysis, therefore, is concerned only with the propriety, and the practicalities, of integrating the military and law enforcement constituencies into the attribution processes for cyberwarfare. Since attribution is based upon information, it follows that this integration must focus exclusively on sharing information that may pertain to actual or potential attacks and attackers. More precisely, it must focus on law enforcement unilaterally sharing information it has lawfully collected with the military. There are at least two reasons why that is the appropriate focus of this particular integration effort. The most obvious is that the additional information provided by law enforcement can, and should, improve the military's ability to identify cyberwarfare attacks and attackers.

The perhaps less obvious reason is that this unilateral, delimited integration preserves the institutional division between civilian law enforcement and the military. If law enforcement were to be charged with affirmatively locating information relevant to identifying cyberwarfare attacks and attackers, such a charge would alter its function in impermissible ways. Law enforcement would be able to use its civil investigative authority to investigate cyberwarfare, as well as criminal activity. That, in turn, would mean law enforcement would act as a de facto agent of military authorities—scrutinizing civilian activities for purposes quite unrelated to its legitimate function of controlling criminal activity and maintaining internal order. However much we trust our military, that is a path we must not take.

---

265 But see Section IV.B.l.b, *infra*.

266 *See, e.g.,* Patience Wait, *Defense Domain, Civilian Awareness,* Gov't Computer News, Jan. 22, 2007, *available at* http://www.gcn.com/print/26_2/42958-l.html (reporting that the general in charge of Air Force's new Cyberspace Command is responsible "for creating 'cyberspace warriors,' who can react to any threats 24/7").

267 This, alone, would eliminate concerns about running afoul of the Anti-Pinkerton Act. One can argue, of course, that the Anti-Pinkerton Act should not impede integrating non-federal law enforcement into the what-attribution process for cyberwarfare because it only bars the federal government from hiring *private* security personnel. Since state and local law enforcement are not private security operatives, they presumably do not come within this prohibition. Also, the Act only prohibits the federal government's "employing" private security operatives; non-federal law enforcement officers' participation in the what-attribution process for cyberwarfare would be a function of their employment by their own, non-federal agency.

And since the military will respond only if an attack is reasonably determined to constitute cyberwarfare, the provisions of the Posse Comitatus Act should not be implicated by the law enforcement–military integration I have outlined.

So, how should this one-way information-sharing strategy work? We begin with the rather obvious premise that military personnel will be on alert for potential cyberwarfare. This premise should hold not only for personnel assigned to special "cyber commands," but rather to all military personnel who interact with cyberspace as part of their duties.[268] Personnel in both categories (but especially the latter category) should be trained to recognize the indicia of cyberwarfare attacks and report any evidence of such attacks to their superiors or the appropriate, designated agency. None of this is novel; we are simply transporting obligations military personnel have always had to the arena of cyberspace.

The novel task is conceptualizing the process by which civilian law enforcement shares information with the military. We begin with the premise that law enforcement is merely transmitting information it has collected in the routine course of its official duties; it is not gathering information specifically for the purpose of assisting the military with cyberwarfare attribution.

One issue we need to resolve is whether law enforcement should filter the information before providing it to the military in an effort to narrow its focus to likely indicia of cyberwarfare or whether it should transmit all the information it collects about every cyber-incident law enforcement officers encounter. The argument for filtering is that selective reporting reduces the risk of overwhelming the military with extraneous data. The argument against filtering is that computer systems can analyze large amounts of data, thereby reducing the possibility of overwhelming military analysts. The best approach would probably be to require both. If the circumstances of an attack warranted, law enforcement officers could initially vet the attack, using a set of criteria supplied by military personnel. If they concluded that there was a fair probability the attack was cyberwarfare, the officers would transmit the information to the military expeditiously and flag it as priority data. If, on the other hand, officers saw nothing indicating that an event implicated cyberwarfare, they would transmit information about those attacks routinely, as data to be incorporated into a more general analysis. Law enforcement agencies would presumably transmit this routine attack data with a pre-determined frequency, perhaps daily.

Admittedly, law enforcement's sharing of information in the second category with military personnel might produce concerns about the potential for eroding the partition between civilian and military authority. The information shared in the first category (likely about cyberwarfare attacks) does not violate the partition because here law enforcement is merely giving the military something to which it is legitimately entitled.

Since this information presumptively concerns warfare, it only has operational relevance to and value for the military. Sharing this information with the military therefore poses no threat to the segregation of civilian and military authority.

Logically, the same holds for the information in the second category because it is being provided not as domestic operational data, as information to be used against civilians, but as external operational data—as information the military can use in an effort to identify cyberwarfare attacks and attackers. Logic, though, should not be dispositive, given the potential for this aspect of our information-sharing endeavor to be perceived as having sinister purposes. The civilian populace might come to believe law enforcement was involved in a cabal with the military, the purpose being to spy on domestic activities for frightening, but no doubt nebulous, purposes. The best way to address this concern would be to

---

268 Arguably, this obligation to be on alert for acts of cyberwarfare could also extend to off-duty military personnel's encounters with cyberspace, in the same way an off-duty police officer who encounters criminal activity will almost certainly respond in some fashion, even if it is only to alert on-duty officers as to what is occurring. Indeed, we could encourage this type of activity by explicitly authorizing it and/or giving off-duty military personnel immunity from suit for actions they take in an effort to ascertain if a cyber-event constitutes an act of cyberwarfare. See generally Alaska Stat. § 09.65.330(a)(1) (2006) (off-duty law enforcement officer is immune from a suit for injury caused while engaging in "official duties"); Wis. Stat. § 175.40(6m)(a) (2006) (off-duty law enforcement officers may arrest a person in certain circumstances).

adopt legislation or regulations that ensure that the military's use of the second category data is limited to the purpose for which is it provided—for cyberwarfare attribution and response.[269]

## cybercrime and cyberterrorism

The analysis here is essentially a mirror image of our cyberwarfare analysis. Here, too, response authority is rigidly partitioned: civilian law enforcement has exclusive responsibility for responding to cybercrime and cyberterrorism. Given that, the only contribution the military can make to the cyber-crime/cyberterrorism *attribution* process is to assist civilian law enforcement officers with determining that an attack has occurred or is in progress; and ascertaining the nature of the attack. This assistance dynamic is the counterpoint to the dynamic analyzed above. But while the dynamics are functionally analogous, the conceptual analysis of the cybercrime/cyberterrorism assistance dynamic is more complex for at least two reasons. One is that the military's capacity to assist law enforcement is not necessarily limited to providing information about attacks. The other is that the military's assisting law enforcement with its designated function of enforcing civilian criminal law raises concerns about eroding the civilian–military authority partition that do not exist when the roles are reversed. We will begin with two implementation issues—the rationale for institutionalizing this dynamic and the nature of the information it encompasses—and then consider these conceptual questions.

It is only reasonable to assume that while they perform their constitutionally-authorized function of identifying cyberwarfare attacks and attackers, military personnel will encounter attacks that clearly are not cyberwarfare. Unless and until we parse cyberassaults into new categories, these attacks will by default constitute cybercrime or cyberterrorism. Since it is also reasonable to assume the military's ability to scan cyberspace for attacks is superior to that of civilian law enforcement, it is logical to conclude that the military will acquire information about cybercrime and cyberterrorism events that may not be available to civilian law enforcement. It would seem both logical and prudent to allow the military to share this information with civilian law enforcement because this is not information the military can act upon, and sharing it with civilian law enforcement is likely to enhance the latter's ability to identify and respond to cybercrimes and acts of cyberterrorism.

Assuming for the moment that this is an appropriate strategy, the parameters of the military's authority to transmit attack information to civilian law enforcement still needs to be resolved. Here, there seems to be no reason to filter the information according to the type of attack involved; that is, there seems to be no reason why the military could not periodically provide law enforcement with all of the unclassified information it collects concerning cyberattacks on the United States.[270] Such a transmission of data would be over-inclusive in that it would provide information about cyberwarfare, for which law enforcement has no response authority, but there seems to be no downside to allowing this as long as the information is not classified. Civilian law enforcement, after all, has neither the authority, the resources, nor the inclination to respond to cyberwarfare. And there is a good argument for allowing it: The more empirical data civilian law enforcement has about cyberwarfare attack signatures, the more effective law enforcement officers can be in identifying potential acts of cyberwarfare and sharing that

---

269    Since cyberwarfare response is the exclusive province of the military, and since the data law enforcement shares with the military cannot be used for domestic purposes, there seems to be no reason why the military cannot use information lawfully shared by the process outlined above to respond to cyberwarfare, as well as to identify it.

270    The argument for excepting classified information about cyberwarfare and non-cyberwarfare attacks is that even information in the latter category could implicate national security concerns.

Unless and until we give law enforcement officers high-level security clearances, we cannot allow the military to routinely share classified information with them. The same is also true, of course, for civilian intelligence agencies and other civilian entities that support the military and lawfully have access to classified information. *See supra* note 356. The discussion above assumes they, too, would share non-classified cyberattack information with law enforcement.

information with the military. Absent other, non-operational concerns, this seems to be an appropriate way of integrating the military and law enforcement sectors in our battle against cyberattacks.

That brings us to the first conceptual issue noted above: information-sharing is not the only type of assistance the military could at least potentially provide to law enforcement. A major challenge that law enforcement, especially non-federal law enforcement, faces in identifying and responding to cybercrime and cyberterrorism is the lack of non-personnel resources, such as hardware, software, and training for officers assigned to cybercrime/cyberterrorism units.[271] While the military cannot provide personnel,[272] it could, perhaps, alleviate this challenge by providing technical training to law enforcement officers and by donating its superfluous or out of date equipment to law enforcement. Recall that in the 1980s, Congress authorized precisely this type of assistance to improve law enforcement's ability to combat the illegal drug trade;[273] there seems, then, no doctrinal reason why the military could not provide such assistance to law enforcement for the purpose of enhancing their ability to combat cybercrime and cyberterrorism. Indeed, the argument for instituting a similar program becomes even more compelling when we note that cybercrime and cyberterrorism are analogous to the drug trade in that all three tend to encompass transborder criminal activity. The same policy considerations that justified allowing the military to provide non-personnel resources to enhance law enforcement's effectiveness in combating the drug trade consequently seem to militate in favor of allowing similar assistance in the cybercrime/cyberterrorism context.

That brings us to the second conceptual issue: the concern that letting the military assist law enforcement will erode the military–civilian law enforcement partition. This concern is not likely to be compelling with regard to the military's providing non-personnel resources; as noted above, Congress has already, and uneventfully, authorized this type of assistance in the context of a battle against a different kind of transborder crime. Now, that does not mean this issue would not be raised were this resource-support program to be instituted for civilian cybercrime and cyberterrorism units. In fact, if it were raised and if the drug war precedent did not prove dispositive, it would be necessary to analyze whether, and how, the contribution of non-personnel resources by the military could undermine the authority partition. One could credibly argue that erosion could result from law enforcement's essentially becoming indebted to the military. In this case, the postulated erosion would result not from a quid pro quo kind of indebtedness but from a shift in allegiance, in which law enforcement would begin to look to military rather than civilian authority for support. Support builds bonds between individuals, and those bonds could eventually transmute into allegiance. By that I do not mean civilian law enforcement would promptly become vassals of the military. I merely mean that institutionalizing this type of non-personnel resource assistance effort should be approached cautiously because it could have unforeseen consequences in the decades ahead.

Another argument those who oppose the non-personnel resource assistance effort could make is that the risks associated with providing assistance to combat the drug trade were much less than the risks that could ensue from providing assistance to combat cybercrime and cyberterrorism. Arguably law enforcement's efforts to combat the drug trade focused to a great extent on offshore activities and non-citizens; its efforts to combat cybercrime and cyberterrorism, on the other hand, are likely to focus to a greater extent on activity that takes place in the territorial United States and is conducted by U.S.

---

271  *See, e.g.,* Nat'l Inst. of Justice, Electronic Crime Needs Assessment for State and Local Law Enforcement 16–19 (2001), *available at* http://www.ojp.usdoj.gov/nij/pubs-sum/186276.htm.

272  Allowing the military to provide its own personnel to supplement law enforcement's resources would almost certainly violate the Posse Comitatus Act. It would also raise serious, legitimate concerns about eroding the partition between civilian and military authority.

273  *See supra* notes 293–294 and accompanying text.

citizens. Thus, theoretically, what was acceptable when law enforcement was concentrating primarily on "them" is not acceptable when law enforcement is concentrating primarily on "us." Doctrinally, this theory could be grounded in the Supreme Court's interpretation of the Fourth Amendment as applying to law enforcement activity that targets U.S. citizens and/or persons or places within the territorial United States but not applying to extraterritorial law enforcement activity directed at non-citizens.[274] Those who supported the non-personnel resource assistance effort could counter by pointing out that the effectiveness of the Fourth Amendment and similar measures in protecting citizens from over-reaching by law enforcement officers would in no way be diminished by law enforcement's relying on alternate sources of material support.

Actually, the concern that military assistance could erode the civilian–military authority partition would be more compelling with regard to the military's sharing information with civilian law enforcement. The military's providing information to law enforcement about civilian offenses (cybercrimes and cyberterrorism) could create the perception—if not the reality—that the military was spying on citizens to assist law enforcement.[275] The prospect of this perception (and reality) could doom the information assistance option unless there were a reliable way to ensure that the military's information-collecting would be conducted only for lawful military purposes. In so doing, the non-cyberwarfare data the military collected and shared with law enforcement would merely have been collected as an inadvertent byproduct of the military's carrying out its legitimate constitutional functions.

In the previous section, I suggested that the version of this issue that arises for law enforcement's sharing information with the military could be addressed by adopting statutes and/or regulations which limit the recipient's—the military's—use of data provided by law enforcement. A similar approach could work here, but it should target the provider (the military), rather than the recipient (law enforcement); statutes and other measures that bar the military from sharing any data with law enforcement except that routinely collected as an inadvertent byproduct of the military's carrying out its legitimate constitutional functions would act, in essence, as an exclusionary rule.

This approach should eliminate any incentive for the military to engage in impermissible activity in order to assist law enforcement and thereby reinforce the military–civilian authority partition; the incentive would be lacking because law enforcement could not use the information provided. Measures designed to limit law enforcement's use of data obtained from the military would not be an effective way to prevent the military from becoming a de facto agent of law enforcement because these measures would only prohibit on-record use of the data in the investigation and prosecution of cybercrimes and acts of cyberterrorism. Such an approach would be under-inclusive, as law enforcement could still use the information for strategic purposes, such as for developing initiatives or attack profiles.[276]

---

274   See, e.g., United States v. Verdugo-Urquidez, 494 U.S. 259, 266 (1990) (holding that the Fourth Amendment was intended to protect U.S. citizens against arbitrary action by their own government, not to restrain actions of the federal government against aliens outside of U.S. territory).

275   See, e.g., Posting of Bruce Schneier, Schneier on Security: Giving the U.S. Military the Power to Conduct Domestic Surveillance, http://www.schneier.com/blog/archives/2005/11/giving_the_us_m.html (Nov. 28, 2005) ("The police and the military have fundamentally different missions. The police protect citizens. The military attacks the enemy. When you start giving police powers to the military, citizens start looking like the enemy.").

If the military were to cross the line from dispassionately compiling cybercrime/cyberterrorism data as an incident of cyberwarfare monitoring to intentionally seeking out such data to assist civilian law enforcement, that would clearly violate the Posse Comitatus Act. It would also be an indication that the civilian–military partition was becoming unstable.

276   The Supreme Court long ago recognized that the exclusionary rule is ineffective in controlling police behavior "where the police either have no interest in prosecuting or are willing to forego successful prosecution in the interest of pursuing some other goal." Terry v. Ohio, 392 U.S. 1, 14 (1968).

## civilian–military–law enforcement integration

In this section, we will analyze the next step in the integration effort we are postulating: the possibility—and mechanics—of incorporating a level of civilian participation into the type of military–law enforcement integration examined above. Before we begin that analysis, however, I need to define a term that will be used in the analysis and note a premise that implicitly structures the analysis.

The term is "pure" civilian. By "pure" civilian, I mean a citizen of the United States (or of any other country that decides to implement an institutionally-integrated strategy for dealing with cyberattacks) who is neither: (1) directly employed by a branch of the military, by a military-related government agency, or by a law enforcement agency; nor (2) works as a consultant or contract employee for the military or for either type of agency. This definition also includes corporate and other artificial entities that are recognized as U.S. citizens. "Pure" civilians are completely "outside" the military and law enforcement institutional structures; under the law, they have no role in, and no responsibility for, maintaining either internal or external order.[277] The issue we analyze below is how to incorporate a level of "pure" civilian participation into the integrated military-law enforcement efforts we have already hypothesized without turning the United States into a military-police state or eroding the effectiveness of either the military or law enforcement. The goal—which may be difficult to achieve—is to use "pure" civilian efforts to enhance, but not dilute, the efficacy of either constituency.

The premise is simply that we are exploring the potential for integrating "pure" civilian participation into an integrated military–law enforcement effort of the type hypothesized above. To this point, our analysis has been based on the fundamental premise that an appropriately-circumscribed integration of these constituencies can enhance the efficacy of national efforts to address external (military) and internal (law enforcement) cyberthreats. In the sections below, we will pursue an analysis based on the secondary premise that the selective incorporation of "pure" civilian participation can further enhance the efficacy of these efforts.

One might ask why there should be any need to incorporate "pure" civilian participation into this already-integrated effort? Why not simply incorporate "pure" civilian participation into the efforts of law enforcement (only)? Additively, or alternatively, why not simply incorporate "pure" civilian participation into the efforts of the military (only)? The answers to both questions lie in the different roles, and different cultures, of the two institutions.

Integrating the efforts of "pure" civilians into the law enforcement function essentially entails orchestrating a collaboration between civilian constituencies. While law enforcement officers play an institutional role that differentiates them from "pure" civilians in their professional capacity, their status remains, at base, that of civilians.[278] Law enforcement officers work in the civilian world with civilian personnel. Their official purpose is to maintain order in civilian society, and when they are not performing their professional duties, they effectively return to "pure" civilian status.[279] As a result, there is less of an institutional and cultural gulf between civilian law enforcement officers and "pure" civilians than there is between "pure" civilians and military personnel.[280]

---

277   *See supra* Sections II–III.

278   *See, e.g.,* Judith Berkan, *Manu Dura—Official Police Department Bias Takes a Hit,* 69 Rev. Jur. U.p.R. 1267, 1274 (2000) (writing that the difference between police and the military "is that police officers are civilians and the military is not"); *see also* Robert M. Perito, Where Is the Lone Ranger When We Need Him?: America's Search for a postconflict stability force 85–86 (2004).

279   In some states, off-duty officers can make arrests for offenses committed in their presence. *See, e.g.,* State v. Brown, 672 P.2d 1268, 1269 (Wash. App. 1983). Of course, in some states civilians can make arrests under certain circumstances. *See, e.g.,* 5 Am. Jur. 2d Arrest § 56 (2006).

280   *See, e.g.,* Perito, *supra* note 371, at 85–86.

Military personnel are governed by different laws than "pure" civilians.[281] For instance, they mostly work and live in an environment that is culturally and environmentally quite distinct from the civilian culture that is the default experience of both "pure" civilians and law enforcement officers.[282] Another differentiating factor is the institutional goals military personnel are committed to achieving. Their professional role is to confront and overcome external threats to the nation-state to which they have sworn allegiance; to accomplish this, they are authorized to use methods and machineries that are not found in civilian society.[283] The activities they engage in are therefore alien to and rigidly segregated from civilian society, and civilians of all types are strictly denied access to information concerning some of these activities.

Logic and pragmatism therefore suggest we should not concentrate on integrating "pure" civilian efforts discretely into law enforcement and into the military. The institutional and cultural divide between "pure" civilians and the military would make it difficult to design and implement a standalone integration of their respective efforts. It seems the best approach is to use law enforcement as the "gateway" for incorporating a level of "pure" civilian participation into the law enforcement–military integration outlined above. This is the approach we will analyze below.

The pivotal issue in this analysis is the conceptual and doctrinal gap that separates the military and law enforcement from "pure" civilians. In the United States, this gap is the product of two established dichotomies: One is the constitutionally-mandated partitioning of civilian and military authority; the other is the de facto and de jure distinction between "pure" civilians and civilian law enforcement officers. The cumulative effect of these dichotomies is to segregate "pure" civilians from military personnel and law enforcement officers. Given that, how can we incorporate "pure" civilian efforts into the integrated law enforcement–military strategy outlined above without undermining the integrity of either or both of these dichotomies? That is, how can we do this without eroding institutionally essential distinctions between "pure" civilians and military personnel and/or law enforcement officers?[284]

Logically, there are two ways to approach this task. One is formally institutionalizing the "pure" civilian effort. This would require creating a new social institution that would serve as the conduit for "pure" civilian participation in efforts to combat cyberattacks. The other option is to proceed informally—to rely on voluntary, ad hoc participation by "pure" civilians. We will analyze each option in the sections below.

### formal

The alternatives noted above should really be labeled "more formal" and "less formal" because this alternative does not actually contemplate the creation of a "real" societal institution analogous to, say, law enforcement, education, or state government. A defining characteristic of "real" institutions is that they have an independent "presence" in society (facilities, personnel) and are the occupational focus of individuals who "belong to" that institution.[285]

There are several reasons why we cannot use a "real" societal institution as the conduit for "pure" civilian efforts against cyberattacks. One is that formally institutionalizing civilians' efforts would

---

281  *See id.*
282  *See id.*
283  *See id.*
284  For the far foreseeable future, anyway, we must retain these distinctions in order to preserve the institutional arrangement that provides the necessary baseline of protection from internal and external threats to social order. We want to incorporate a level of civilian participation into the law enforcement and military efforts, but we do not want to undermine those institutions so that we sink either into anarchy or autocracy.
285  *See, e.g.,* Michael Hechter, Karl-Dieter Opp & Reinhard Wippler, Social Institutions: Their Emergence, Maintenance and Effects 13–16 (1990).

effectively eliminate their status as "pure" civilians; they would become more or less professionalized constituents of that new institution. Such a result would defy both logic and pragmatism.

Logically, the result would be absurd; every "pure" civilian in the United States would become a (possibly recalcitrant) constituent of this new societal institution—the "pure" Civilian Cybercorps, or whatever it might be called. This result is absurd because the gravamen of a societal institution is specialization; institutions such as the military, government, and education exist to perform a specialized task that is essential for the survival of a society.[286] Integrating the entire civilian populace of a society as large as the United States into one institution would represent the antithesis of specialization, with its attendant divisions of labor. Institutionalized divisions of labor and responsibilities have become standard features of modern societies for good reason; they are effective at carrying out essential tasks. A global institution of the type outlined above would not be effective because it repudiates specialization.

Mandating participation in a new, global institution—the "pure" Civilian Cybercorps—would also require establishing governance and enforcement structures to ensure that civilians were "doing their part" to contribute to this obligatory effort. And that brings me to the second objection to this approach—the pragmatic objection. Creating and sustaining an institution such as this would require resources that simply are not available. As I noted earlier, perhaps the most significant challenge law enforcement confronts in its battle against cybercrime and cyberterrorism is a lack of resources. If we do not have the resources available to support an existing institution in its efforts to combat these threats, it is highly unlikely we could find the massive additional resources needed to create and maintain a new institutional structure.

* * *

The better path, I believe, is to create a voluntary organization along the lines I outline above in which the civilian participants' sole role is to report information about cyberevents that they have observed. This information can be transmitted to law enforcement, which passes it along to the military, or it can be sent directly to both. I suspect the best approach would be to let law enforcement serve as the conduit for transmitting information to the military except, perhaps, in what seem to be exigent circumstances. Alternatively, the organization posited above could transmit information directly to the military; it would be up to the military whether they preferred to have law enforcement vet the civilian-provided data or receive it directly.

The civilian organization should be as virtual as possible; it should consist of a web of civilians networked by e-mail and secure websites. As I noted above, the organization should provide the volunteers with at least some initial and continuing training and should provide them with a set of operating standards and cyberevent identification criteria. The role these volunteers would play in the cyberattack attribution and response effort is analogous to the role civilian aircraft spotters played in the United States during World War II: the Civil Air Patrol "enrolled civilian spotters in reconnaissance. Towers were built in coastal and border towns, and spotters were trained to recognize enemy aircraft, so as to report if any were seen."[287] The effort proved successful "almost to a fault," as in the "Plains states where many dedicated aircraft spotters took up their posts night after night ... in an area of the country that no

---

286  *See, e.g.,* Functionalism (sociology)—Wikipedia, http://en.wikipedia.org/wiki/ Functionalism_%28sociology%29 (last visited Apr. 21, 2007).

287  United States home front during World War II—Wikipedia, http://en.wikipedia.org/wiki/ Homefront-United_States-World_War_II (last visited Apr. 21, 2007).

enemy aircraft of that time could possibly hope to reach."[288] Like this effort, the voluntary organization I posed above would recruit civilians to help provide information about potential threats, although they would be virtual, rather than physical, threats.

The primary virtue of this approach is that it gives law enforcement and the military access to information they have not yet received or, in some instances, might not otherwise receive. In this way, the procedure helps to alleviate the current under-reporting of cybercrime that makes it difficult, if not impossible, for law enforcement to identify patterns and trends in cybercrime and cyberterrorism. This approach can provide a similar benefit for the military. As explained earlier, cyberwarfare, unlike its real-world counterpart, is very likely to be directed at civilian targets. As we also saw earlier, cyber-warfare is not likely to begin with a dramatic, Pearl Harbor-style attack; it is far more likely to begin with a series of probes, smaller attacks testing security on particular systems. If the participants in the voluntary organization postulated above include representatives of the corporate and other entities that comprise a nation-state's critical infrastructure, they can provide information to law enforcement and to the military about what their organization may not even realize are acts of cyberwarfare. That would markedly enhance a nation-state's attribution and response capability for this category of cyberattack.

There are at least two possible disadvantages to utilizing this approach. One is that requiring would-be volunteers to go through a vetting and training process might discourage participation. I am afraid I do not see that as a true disadvantage. If the vetting and training processes were implemented correctly, they should serve only to eliminate potential volunteers who are undesirable because they lack the responsibility, maturity, or other qualities required for acceptable participation.

The other possible disadvantage is that by recruiting civilians into a quasi-formal, law enforcement-sanctioned organization, we would almost certainly establish the participants as state agents for the purposes of applying the Fourth Amendment.[289] I see that as a necessary and inevitable consequence of implementing an approach such as this, a consequence that ensures this effort would not undermine our constitutional rights. While this would no doubt require courts to address novel issues, the applicability of the Fourth Amendment to the efforts of these civilian volunteers should not present significant difficulties. For one thing, most of the data to which they would have access would be public, not private; a cyberattacker cannot, for example, claim a Fourth Amendment expectation of privacy in his efforts to assault a corporate or other private computer system. To the extent information supplied by the civilian volunteers does incorporate proprietary and other information that can be deemed private for Fourth Amendment (or other) purposes, the sanctity of that information can in many instances be shielded by redacting it or by pseudonymizing it.

---

288   *Id.*

289   The volunteers would be acting with the purpose of assisting law enforcement and, given its cooperative relationship with the umbrella organization in which the volunteers participated, law enforcement would be deemed to have acquiesced in and/or encouraged their efforts. *See, e.g., United States v. Hall*, 142 F.3d 988, 993 (7th Cir. 1998).

routine
activities

theory

thomas j. holt

The emergence of research on various cybercrimes over the last two decades has primarily focused on the correlates of offending behaviors. These studies are particularly useful in understanding the demographic, attitudinal, and behavioral factors influencing participation in piracy, hacking, harassment, and other forms of cybercrime. However, there is less research considering the theoretical causes and correlates of cybercrime victimization. Such research is needed to understand what practices increase individual risk for various forms of victimization. Over the last decade, cybercrime scholars argued that the lifestyle-routine activities theory may be useful to account for victimization in light of its success with street crimes and delinquency (see Grabosky & Smith, 2001; Newman & Clarke, 2003).

Lifestyle-routine activities theory is the primary framework used to account for real-world victimization patterns, and argues that a motivated offender, the absence of capable guardians, and a suitable target must converge in time and space in order for crime to occur. Motivated offenders are individuals and groups who have both the inclination and ability to commit crime for various reasons (Cohen & Felson, 1979). In fact, motives vary substantially across different forms of offending. For instance, computer hackers may be motivated by the desire to acquire information, gain social status from peers, or solve a technical puzzle (Holt, 2007; Kilger, 2010). At the same time, an individual who is interested in harassing others may be motivated by anger, frustration, or the need to dominate another person (Bocij, 2004). Given the range of motives an individual may have, most researchers do not assess motives and instead focus on the other factors affecting the risk of victimization.

Similarly, a target is viewed as suitable based on its attractiveness to an offender because of a range of factors including monetary value, ease of access, or other intrinsic values (see Cohen & Felson, 1979; Lauritsen, Laub, & Sampson, 1992). The attractiveness of targets in cyberspace can vary substantially based on the interests of the offender, and may include a computer system or network, sensitive data, or an individual. For instance, a hacker may want to compromise a computer system in order to access specific information or files, or may simply want to see if that system can be penetrated (Holt, 2007). In the context of harassment, an individual may simply want to cause emotional or psychological harm to another person due to a perceived slight or a failed relationship. Thus, target suitability is related to offender motivation.

Guardians who may help to protect the target in some way can impact the relationship between motivated offenders and suitable targets. Guardians may be physical or social in nature, though it is unclear which may be more pivotal in the context of preventing criminal acts. For instance, individuals may carry pepper spray or a weapon in order to defend themselves against attack (Mustaine & Tewksbury, 2002; Schwartz, DeKeseredy, Tait, & Alvi, 2001). Physical guardians in the real world may include security cameras, barriers, lighting, and alarm systems (Cromwell & Olson, 2004). There are equivalent protective systems in cyberspace that are readily available on computer systems through antivirus software and similar programs (Mell, Kent, & Nusbaum, 2005; PandaLabs, 2007). These programs are expressly designed to reduce the likelihood of harm from hackers and malicious software by preventing certain attacks from occurring. Similarly, developing an understanding of computer technology may serve as a substantial protective factor by reducing the threat posed by more obvious forms of on-line harm, like opening attachments in e-mails from individuals you do not know. Thus, physical guardianship in on-line environments may resemble those in the real world.

In addition, social guardians can serve to reduce the likelihood of victimization by warding off attacks (Spano & Nagy, 2005). For instance, security guards in parking lots or individuals staying in a home may serve to deter offenders by raising their risk of detection (Coupe & Blake, 2006; Cromwell & Olson, 2004). Peers can also serve as guardians, though they may actually increase the risk of victimization depending upon their interests and activities. Specifically, those who are involved in crime or delinquency can actually place individuals in closer proximity to motivated offenders, and may be less likely to intervene when others are being victimized (Zhang, Welte, & Wieczorek, 2001). For instance, if your friends commit various forms of computer deviance, like hacking and downloading music or pornography, then this may increase the risk of being harassed on-line (Holt & Bossler, 2009). Presumably, delinquent friends are more likely to harass their friends and less likely to support and protect them in their on-line interactions. As a result, deviant social relationships may actually place a person in close proximity to motivated offenders and increase their risk of victimization.

This framework has been extensively used to examine the various facets of victimization in the real world, and even identification of the relationships between victims and offenders. There is, however, a great deal of contention over the utility of this framework to account for cybercrime victimization. In fact, the first article in this section discusses this issue in depth, considering the lack of temporal and physical proximity between victims and offenders in cyberspace. Yar's (2005) critical approach provides an invaluable discussion of both routine activities theory generally, and a framework to extend further research on the issue. If Yar (2005) is correct, then there should be limited empirical support for this theory across the body of literature on cybercrime victimization.

The selections following Yar (2005) give empirical assessments of routine activities theory across a variety of victimization types. Holt and Bossler (2009) provide one of the first tests of this theory to on-line harassment victimization and find that individual and peer offending have a substantive influence on the risk of harassment. Pratt, Holtfreter, and Reisig (2010) examine the influence of individual routine activities on the risk of on-line fraud victimization in a population of citizens from Florida. Finally, Reyns, Henson, and Fisher (2011) find substantive support for this theory for cyberstalking victimization in a sample of college students.

These collective works provide pertinent insights into the applicability of routine activities theory, and suggest that this framework has utility to account for the risks and correlates of cybercrime victimization. There is, however, a great deal of future research needed to improve our understanding of this theory. The initial tests presented here must be replicated across multiple populations and various forms of crime to clarify the relationship between computer use, skill, deviance, and cybercrime victimization. Furthermore, there is a need to understand the overlap between real-world routine activities and cyber activities and their roles in on-line victimization as a whole.

## discussion questions

1. How could a virtual environment make it easier for offenders to come into contact with prospective victims? For example, how could the use of Facebook or LinkedIn provide an offender with access to a population of valuable targets?

2. What on-line resources do you use on a daily basis that may actually increase your exposure to potentially motivated offenders, or increase your likelihood of victimization through disclosure of personal information?

3. What are some of the software programs that may serve a protective role in reducing the risk of cybercrime victimization? What are some of the ways that these programs may falter in protecting their user from harm?

4. People increasingly depend on social networking sites to keep in touch with others with whom they interact in the real world, as well as individuals whom they may only know in an on-line context. With that in mind, how might a person's routine use of the Internet increase their risk of victimization off-line? Could increased use of social networking sites impact real-world crime victimization like burglary or robbery?

## references

Bocij, P. (2004). *Cyberstalking: Harassment in the Internet Age and How to Protect Your Family.* Westport, CT: Praeger.

Cohen, L. E., & Felson, M. (1979). Social change and crime rate trends: A routine activity approach. *American Sociological Review, 44*, 588–608.

Coupe, T., & Blake, L. (2006). Daylight and darkness targeting strategies and the risks of being seen at residential burglaries. *Criminology, 44*, 431–464.

Cromwell, P., & Olson, J. N. (2004). *Breaking and Entering: Burglars on Burglary*. Belmont, CA: Wadsworth.

Grabosky, P., & Smith, R. (2001). Telecommunication fraud in the digital age: The convergence of technologies. In D. Wall (ed.), *Crime and the Internet* (pp. 54–75). London: Routledge.

Holt, T. J. (2007). Subcultural evolution? Examining the influence of on- and off-line experiences on deviant subcultures. *Deviant Behavior, 28*, 171–198.

Holt, T. J., & Bossler, A. M. (2009). Examining the applicability of lifestyle-routine activities theory for cybercrime victimization. *Deviant Behavior, 30*, 1–25.

Kilger, M. (2010). Social dynamics and the future of technology-driven crime. In T. J. Holt & B. Schell (eds.), *Corporate Hacking and Technology-Driven Crime: Social Dynamics and Implications* (pp. 205–227). Hershey, PA: IGI-Global.

Lauritsen, J. L., Laub, J. H., & Sampson, R. J. (1992). Conventional and delinquent activities: Implications for the prevention of violent victimization among adolescents. *Violence and Victims, 7*, 91–108.

Mell, P., Kent, K., & Nusbaum, J. (2005). *Guide to Malware Incident Prevention and Handling: Recommendations of the National Institute of Standards and Technology*. Washington, DC: National Institute of Standards and Technology.

Mustaine, E., & Tewksbury, R. (2002). Sexual assault of college women: A feminist interpretation of a routine activities analysis. *Criminal Justice Review, 27*, 89–123.

Newman, G., & Clarke, R. (2003). *Superhighway Robbery: Preventing E-Commerce Crime*. Cullompton, UK: Willan Press.

PandaLabs. (2007). Malware infections in protected systems. *Panda Labs Blog*. [Online] Available at: http://research.pandasecurity.com/blogs/images/wp_pb_malware_infections_in_protected systems.pdf

Pratt, T. C., Holtfreter, K., & Reisig, M. D. (2010). Routine online activity and Internet fraud targeting: Extending the generality of routine activity theory. *Journal of Research in Crime and Delinquency, 47*, 267–296.

Reyns, B. W., Henson, B., & Fisher, B. S. (2011). Being Pursued Online: Applying Cyberlifestyle-Routine Activities Theory to Cyberstalking Victimization. *Criminal Justice and Behavior, 11*, 1149–1169.

Schwartz, M. D., DeKeseredy, W. S., Tait, D., & Alvi, S. (2001). Male peer support and a feminist routine activities theory: Understanding sexual assault on the college campus. *Justice Quarterly, 18*, 623–649.

Spano, R., & Nagy, S. (2005). Social guardianship and social isolation: An application and extension of lifestyle/routine activities theory to rural adolescents. *Rural Sociology, 70*, 414–437.

Yar, M. (2005). The novelty of cybercrime. *European Journal of Criminology, 2*, 407–427.

Zhang, L., Welte, J. W., & Wieczorek, W. F. (2001). Deviant lifestyle and crime victimization. *Journal of Criminal Justice, 29*, 133–143.

majid yar

# an assessment in light of routine activity theory

# the novelty of "cybercrime"

The article is structured as follows. I begin by briefly addressing some of the definitional and classificatory issues raised by attempts to delimit cybercrime as a distinctive form of criminal endeavour. I then explicate the formulation of routine activity theory that is utilized in the article, and offer some general reflections on some of the pressing issues typically raised vis-a-vis the theory's explanatory ambit (in particular its relation to dispositional or motivational criminologies, and the vexed problem of the 'rationality' or otherwise of offenders' choices to engage in law-breaking behaviour). In the third section, I examine cybercrime in relation to the general ecological presuppositions of RAT, focusing specifically on whether or not the theory's explanatory dependence on *spatial and temporal convergence* is transposable to crimes commissioned in online or 'virtual' environments.

Majid Yar, "The Novelty of Cybercrime: An Assessment in Light of Routine Activity Theory," *European Journal of Criminology*, vol. 2, no. 4, pp. 407-427. Copyright © 2005 by Sage Publications. Reprinted with permission.

After considering in a more detailed manner the viability of Felson et al.'s conceptualization of 'target suitability' in relation to the presence of persons and property in virtual environments, I engage in a similar examination of issues related to 'capable guardianship'. In conclusion, I offer some comments on the extent to which cybercrimes might be deemed continuous with 'terrestrial crimes'. Substantively, I suggest that, although the core concepts of RAT are in significant degree transposable (or at least adaptable) to crimes in virtual environments, there remain some qualitative differences between virtual and terrestrial worlds that make a simple, wholesale application of its analytical framework problematic.

* * *

We can surmise that it is the supposedly novel socio-interactional features of the cyberspace environment (primarily the collapse of spatial-temporal barriers, many-to-many connectivity, and the anonymity and plasticity of online identity) that make possible new forms and patterns of illicit activity. It is in this alleged discontinuity from the socio-interactional organization of 'terrestrial crimes' that the criminological challenge of cybercrime is held to reside. I will now turn to consider whether and to what extent the routine activity approach, as a purported general theory of crime causation (Felson 2000), can embrace such novelties within its conceptual apparatus and explanatory ambit.

## delimiting the routine activity approach: situational explanation, rationality and the motivated actor

Birkbeck and LaFree (1993: 113–14) suggest that the criminological specificity of routine activity theory (RAT) can be located via Sutherland's (1947) distinction between 'dispositional' and 'situational' explanations of crime and deviance. Dispositional theories aim to answer the question of 'criminality', seeking some causal mechanism (variously social, economic, cultural, psychological or biological) that might account for why *some* individuals or groups come to possess an inclination toward law- and rule-breaking behaviour. Dispositional theories comprise the standard reference points of criminological discourse—Lombroso, Durkheim, Merton, the Chicago School, Bonger, Chambliss, and so on being 'textbook' examples.

In contrast, situational theories (including various 'opportunity' and 'social control' approaches) eschew dispositional explanations, largely on the grounds of their apparent explanatory failures—they appear recurrently unsuccessful in adequately accounting for trends and patterns of offending in terms of their nominated causes (Cohen and Felson 1979: 592, 604). Routine activity theorists 'take criminal inclination as given' (Cohen and Felson 1979: 589), supposing that there is no shortage of motivations available to all social actors for committing law-breaking acts. They do not deny that motivations can be incited by social, economic and other structural factors, but they insist that any such incitements do not furnish a *sufficient* condition for actually following through inclinations into law-breaking activity (Cohen and Felson 1979: 589, 604–5; Birkbeck and LaFree 1993: 114). Rather, the *social situations* in which actors find themselves crucially mediate decisions about whether or not they will act on their inclinations (whatever their origins). Consequently, routine activity theorists choose to 'examine the manner in which the spatio-temporal organization of social activities helps people translate their criminal inclinations into action' (Cohen and Felson 1979: 592). Social situations in which offending becomes a viable option are created by the routine activities of other social actors; in other words, the routine organizational features of everyday life create the conditions in which persons and property become available as targets for successful predation at the hands of those so motivated. For routine activity theorists, the changing organization of social activities is best placed to account for patterns, distributions, levels and trends in criminal activity. If this is the case, then the emergence of cyber-crime invites us to enquire into the routine organization of *online* activities, with the aim of discerning whether and how this 'helps people translate their criminal inclinations into action'. More broadly, it invites us to enquire whether or not the analytical schema developed by RAT—in which are postulated key variables that make up the criminogenic social situation; what Felson (1998) calls 'the chemistry for crime'—can be successfully transposed to cyber-spatial contexts, given the apparent discontinuities of such spaces vis-a-vis 'real world' settings.

Before such questions can be addressed, however, a number of extant issues relating to RAT must be tackled. The first relates to the specific formulation of the theory that is to be mobilized for present purposes. As with many other theoretical approaches RAT does not comprise a single, self-subsistent set of explanatory concepts. Rather, it can take a number of different forms, utilizing a variable conceptual apparatus and levels of analysis, depending upon the specific orientations of the criminologists who develop and mobilize it (Bennett 1991: 148). Moreover, the work of a single contributor does not remain static over time, but typically undergoes revision and development. Thus, for example, Felson has elaborated and refined his original 'chemistry for crime' over a 25-year period by introducing additional mediating variables into what is an ever-more complex framework. Here I discuss RAT in something like its 'original' formulation. This statement of the theory hypothesizes that 'criminal acts require the convergence in space and time of *likely offenders, suitable targets* and the *absence of capable guardians'* (Cohen and Felson 1979: 588, emphasis in the original). This definition has the virtue of including the 'central core of three concepts' (Bennett 1991: 148) which appear as constant features of all routine activity models.

A second issue relates to the theory's controversial attachment to presuppositions about the 'rational' character of actors' choices to engage in (or desist from) illegal activity. Routine activity approaches are generally held to be consistent with the view that actors are free to choose their courses of action, and do so on the basis of anticipatory calculation of the utility or rewards they can expect to flow from the chosen course. Felson, for example, has made explicit this presupposition (Felson 1998: 23–4; Felson 1986: 119–20), and his work has been marked by a clear convergence with 'rational choice theory' (Clarke and Felson 1993). One common objection raised in light of this commitment is the theory's potential inability to encompass crimes emanating from non-instrumental motives. Thus, for example, Miethe et al. (1987) and Bennett (1991) conclude that, although routine activity theory exhibits considerable explanatory power in relation to property offences (those oriented to material and economic gain), it is considerably weaker in respect of 'expressive' crimes, such as interpersonal violence. Similar objections can be raised from outside routine activity analysis, for example by proponents of 'cultural criminology' who highlight the neglect of emotional and affective 'seductions' that individuals experience when engaged in criminal and deviant activity (Katz 1988). I would suggest, however, that the basic difficulty here arises not so much from the attribution to actors of 'rationality' per se, but from taking such rationality to be necessarily of a limited, economic kind (Hollis 1987). It may be a mistake to view affective dispositions as inherently devoid of rationality; rather, as Archer (2000) argues, emotions can better be seen as responses to, and commentaries upon, situations that we encounter as part of our practical engagements with real-world situations. Particular emotional dispositions (such as fear, anger, boredom, excitement) are not simply random but 'reasonable' responses to the situations in which we as actors find ourselves. My point here is that, by adopting a more capacious conception of rationality (which includes aesthetic and affective dimensions), the apparent dualism between 'instrumental' and 'expressive' motivations can be significantly overcome. For the remainder of this piece I shall follow routine activity theorists in taking motivations 'as given', without, however, conceding that such motivations must necessarily be reducible to instrumental calculations of economic or material utility.

## convergence in space and time: the ecology and topology of cyberspace

At heart, routine activity theory is an *ecological* approach to crime causation, and as such the spatial (and temporal) localization of persons, objects and activities is a core presupposition of its explanatory schema. The ability of its aetiological formula (offender + target - guardian = crime) to explain and/or anticipate patterns of offending depends upon these elements converging in space and time. Routine activities, which create variable opportunity structures for successful predation, always occur in particular locations at particular times, and the spatio-temporal accessibility of targets for potential offenders is crucial in determining the possibility and likelihood of an offence being committed. As Felson (1998: 147) puts it: 'The organization of time and space is central. It … helps explain how crime occurs and what to do about it.' Thus, for example, Cohen and Felson (1979) suggest that the postwar increases in property crime rates in the United States are explicable in terms of changing routine activities such as growing female labour force participation, which takes people increasingly out of the home for regularized periods of the day, thereby increasing 'the probability that motivated offenders will converge in space and time with suitable targets in the absence of capable guardians' (1979: 593). Similarly, they argue that 'proximity to high concentrations of potential offenders' is critical in determining the likelihood of becoming a target for predation (1979: 596; see also Lynch 1987, Cohen et al. 1981 and Miethe and Meier 1990 on the positive correlation between proximity and predation). Thus, at a general level, the theory requires that targets, offenders and guardians be located in particular places, that measurable relations of spatial proximity and distance pertain between those targets and potential offenders, and that social activities be temporally ordered according to rhythms such that each of these agents is either typically present or absent at particular times. Consequently, the transposability of RAT to virtual environments requires that cyberspace exhibit a *spatio-temporal ontology* congruent with that of the 'physical world', i.e. that place, proximity, distance and temporal order be identifiable features of cyberspace. I will reflect on the spatial and temporal ontology of cyberspace in turn.

### spatiality

Discourses of cyberspace and online activity are replete with references to space and place. There are purported to exist 'portals', 'sites' complete with 'back doors', 'chat rooms', 'lobbies', 'classrooms', 'cafes', all linked together via 'superhighways', with 'mail' carrying communications between one location and another (Adams 1998: 88–9). Such talk suggests that cyberspace possesses a recognizable geography more-or-less continuous with the familiar spatial organization of the physical world to which we are accustomed. However, it has been suggested that such ways of talking are little more than handy metaphors that provide a convenient way for us to conceptualize an environment that in reality is inherently discontinuous with the non-virtual world of physical objects, locations and coordinates (Dodge and Kitchin 2001: 63). Numerous theorists and analysts of cyberspace suggest instead that received notions of place location and spatial separation are obsolete in an environment that is 'anti-spatial' (Mitchell 1995: 8). The virtual environment is seen as one in which there is 'zero distance' between its points

(Stalder 1998), such that entities and events cannot be meaningfully located in terms of spatial contiguity, proximity and separation. Everyone, everywhere and everything are always and eternally 'just a click way'. Consequently, geographical rules that act as a 'friction' or barrier to social action and interaction are broken (Dodge and Kitchin 2001: 62). If this is true, then the viability of RAT as an aetiological model for virtual crimes begins to look decidedly shaky, given the model's aforementioned dependence on spatial convergence and separation, proximity and distance, to explain the probability of offending. To take one case in point, if all places, people and objects are at 'zero distance' from all others, then how is it possible meaningfully to operationalize a criterion such as 'proximity to a pool of motivated offenders'? Despite these apparent difficulties, I would suggest that all is not lost—that we can in fact identify spatial properties in virtual environments *that at least in part* converge with those of the familiar physical environment.

Positions that claim there is no recognizable spatial topology in cyberspace may be seen to draw upon an absolute and untenable separation of virtual and non-virtual environments—they see these as two on-tologically distinct orders or experiential universes. However, there are good reasons to believe that such a separation is overdrawn, and that the relationships between these domains are characterized by both similarity and dissimilarity, convergence and divergence. I shall elaborate two distinctive ways in which cyberspace may be seen to retain a spatial geometry that remains connected to that of the 'real world'.

First, cyberspace may be best conceived not so much as a 'virtual reality', but rather as a 'real virtuality', a socio-technically generated interactional environment rooted in the 'real world' of political, economic, social and cultural relations (Castells 2002: 203). Cyberspace stands with one foot firmly planted in the 'real world', and as a consequence carries non-virtual spatialities over into its organization. This connection between virtual and non-virtual spatialities is apparent along a number of dimensions. For instance, the virtual environments (websites, chat rooms, portals, mail systems, etc.) that comprise the virtual environment are themselves physically rooted and produced in 'real space'. The distribution of capacity to generate such environments follows the geography of existing economic relations and hierarchies. Thus, for example, 50 percent of Internet domains originate in the United States, which also accounts for 83 percent of the total web pages viewed by Internet users (Castells 2002: 214, 219). Moreover, access to the virtual environment follows existing lines of social inclusion and exclusion, with Internet use being closely correlated to existing cleavages of income, education, gender, ethnicity, age and disability (Castells 2002: 247–56). Consequently, presence and absence in the virtual world translate 'real world' marginalities, which themselves are profoundly spatialized ('first world' and 'third world', 'urban' and 'rural', 'middle-class suburb' and 'urban ghetto', 'gated community' and 'high-rise estate'). In short, the online density of both potential offenders and potential targets is not neutral with respect to existing social ecologies, but translates them via the differential distribution of the resources and skills needed to be present and active in cyberspace.

A second way in which cyberspace may exhibit a spatial topology refers to the purely internal organi-zation of the information networks that it comprises. It was noted above that many commentators see the Internet and related technologically generated environments as heralding 'the death of distance' and the collapse of spatial orderings, such that all points are equally accessible from any starting point (Dodge and Kitchin 2001: 63). However, reflection on network organization reveals that *not* all 'places' are equidistant—proximity and distance have meaning when negotiating cyberspace. This will be familiar to all students and scholars who attempt to locate information, organizations and individuals via the Internet. Just because one knows, suspects or is told that a particular entity has a virtual presence on the Net, finding that entity may require widely varying expenditures of time and effort. Those domains (e.g. websites) with a higher density of connections to other domains (e.g. via 'hyperlinks') are more easily arrived at than those with relatively few. The algorithms that organize search engines prioritize sites having the highest number of links to others, thereby rendering them more proximate to the online actor. Arriving at a particular location may require one to traverse a large number of intermediate sites, thereby rendering that location relatively distant from one's point of departure; conversely, the destination may be 'only a click away'. Thus the distribution of entities in terms of the axis 'proximity-distance', and the possibility of both convergence and divergence of such entities, can be seen to have at least some purchase in cyberspace.

Despite these continuities, it should also become clear that there exist qualitative differences between the spatial organization of non-virtual and virtual worlds. Most significantly, they exhibit significantly different degrees of stability and instability in their geometries. Non-virtual spatialities are relatively stable and perdurable. Granted, they can undergo significant shifts over time: patterns of land use can and do change (as, for example, when the former industrial cores of cities are redeveloped for residential use—Zukin 1988); the sociodemographic configuration of locales is also subject to change (as with processes of 'gentrification' and 'ghettoization'—Davis 1990); the proximity of places is elastic in light of developing transport infrastructures; and so on. However, given that non-virtual spatial orderings are materialized in durable physical artefacts (buildings, roads, bridges, walls), and their social occupation and uses are patterned and institutionalized, change in their organization is likely to be incremental rather than wholesale. It is this very stability in socio-spatial orderings that permits ecological perspectives such as RAT to correlate factors such as residential propinquity with predation rates and patterns. In contrast, virtual spatialities are characterized by extreme volatility and plasticity in their configurations. It was noted above that virtual proximity and distance may be seen as the product of variable network geometries and connection densities. Yet these connections are volatile and easily transmuted—little resistance is offered by virtual architectures and topologies. Thus the distance or separation between two sites or locales can shift instantly by virtue of the simple addition of a hyperlink that provides a direct and instant path from one to the other. Similarly, virtual places and entities appear and disappear in the cyber environment with startling regularity—the average lifespan for a web page is just a couple of months (Johnston 2003); actors instantaneously appear and disappear from the environment as they log in or out of the network. Consequently, the socio-spatial organization of the virtual world is built on 'shifting sands'. This quality presents considerable difficulty for the application of routine activity analysis to cyberspace, given its presuppositions that (a) places have a relatively fixed presence and location, and (b) the presence of actors in locations is amenable to anticipation in light of regularized patterns of activity.

## temporality

The ability to locate actors and entities in particular spaces/places *at particular times* is a basic presupposition of RAT. The explanatory power of the theory depends upon routine activities exhibiting a clear temporal sequence and order (a *rhythm,* or 'regular periodicity with which events occur', and a *timing,* in which different activities are coordinated 'such as the coordination of an offender's rhythms with those of a victim'—Cohen and Felson 1979: 590). It is this temporal ordering of activities that enables potential offenders to anticipate when and where a target may be converged upon; without such anticipation, the preconditions for the commission of an offence cannot be fulfilled, nor can criminogenic situations be identified by the analyst (Felson 1998: 147–8).

The temporal structures of cyberspace, I would argue, are largely devoid of the clear temporal ordering of real-world routine activities. Cyberspace, as a *global* interactional environment, is populated by actors living in different real-world time zones, and so is populated '24/7'. Moreover, online activities span workplace and home, labour and leisure, and cannot be confined to particular, clearly delimited temporal windows (although there may be peaks and troughs in gross levels of network activity, as relatively more people in the most heavily connected time zones make use of the Internet—Dodge and Kitchin 2001: 105). Consequently, there are no *particular* points in time at which actors can be anticipated to be *generally* present or absent from the environment. From an RAT perspective, this means that rhythm and timing as structuring properties of routine activities become problematic—for offenders, for potential targets and for guardians. Given the 'disordered' nature of virtual spatio-temporalities, identifying patterns of convergence between the criminogenic elements becomes especially difficult.

Thus far, I have largely focused on the question of cyber-spatial convergence between the entities identified as necessary for the commission of an offence. Now I turn to consider the properties of those entities themselves, in order to reflect upon the relative continuity or discontinuity between their virtual and non-virtual forms. As already mentioned, the first of these elements, the 'motivated offender', is assumed rather than analysed by RAT. Therefore I shall not consider the offender further, but take the existence of motivated offenders in cyberspace as given. Instead I shall follow RAT in focusing upon the other two elements of the criminogenic formula, namely 'suitable targets' and 'capable guardians'.

* * *

## are there 'capable guardians' in cyberspace?

'Capable guardianship' furnishes the third key aetiological variable for crime causation postulated by routine activity theory. Guardianship refers to 'the capability of persons and objects to prevent crime from occurring' (Tseloni et al. 2004: 74). Guardians effect such prevention 'either by their physical presence alone or by some form of direct action' (Cohen et al. 1980: 97). Although direct intervention may well occur, routine activity theorists see the simple presence of a guardian in proximity to the potential target as a crucial deterrent. Where the guardian is a person, she/he acts as someone 'whose mere presence serves as a gentle reminder that someone is looking' (Felson 1998: 53; see also Jacobs 1961). Such guardians may be 'formal' (e.g. the police), but RAT generally places greater emphasis on the significance of 'informal' agents such as homeowners, neighbours, pedestrians and other 'ordinary citizens' going about their routine activities (Cohen and Felson 1979: 590; Felson 1998: 53). In addition to such 'social guardians', the theory also views *physical* security measures as effecting guardianship—instances include barriers, locks, alarms, and lighting on the street and within the home (Tseloni et al. 2004: 74). Taken together, the absence or presence of guardians at the point at which potential offenders and suitable targets converge in time and space is seen as critical in determining the likelihood of an offence taking place (although the importance of guardianship has been questioned by some researchers—see Miethe and Meier 1990; Massey et al. 1989).

How, then, does the concept of guardianship transpose itself into the virtual environment? The efficacy of the concept as a discriminating variable between criminogenic and non-criminogenic situations rests upon the guardian's co-presence with the potential target at the time when the motivated offender converges upon it. In terms of formal social guardianship, maintaining such co-presence is well nigh impossible, given the ease of offender mobility and the temporal irregularity of cyber-spatial activities (it would require a ubiquitous, round-the-clock police presence on the Internet). However, in this respect at least, the challenge to formal guardianship presented by cyberspace is only a more intensified version of the policing problem in the terrestrial world; as Felson (1998: 53) notes, the police 'are very unlikely to be on the spot when a crime occurs'. In cyberspace, as in the terrestrial world, it is often only when private and informal attempts at effective guardianship fail that the assistance of formal agencies is sought (Grabosky and Smith 2001: 36–7). The cyber-spatial world, like the terrestrial, is characterized by a range of such private and informal social guardians: these range from in-house network administrators and systems security staff who watch over their electronic charges, through trade organizations oriented to self-regulation, to 'ordinary online citizens' who exercise a range of informal social controls over each other's behaviour (such as the practice of 'flaming' those who breach social norms on offensive behaviour in chat rooms—Smith et al. 1997). In addition to such social guardians, cyberspace is replete with 'physical' or technological guardians, automated agents that exercise perpetual vigilance. These range from 'firewalls', intrusion detection systems and virus scanning software (Denning 1999: 353–69), to state e-communication monitoring projects such as the US government's 'Carnivore' and 'ECHELON' systems (Furnell 2002: 262–4). In sum, it would appear that RAT's concept of capable guardianship is transposable to cyberspace, even if the structural properties of the environment (such as its variable spatial and temporal topology) amplify the limitations upon establishing guardianship already apparent in the terrestrial world.

## conclusion

The impetus for this article was provided by the dispute over whether or not cybercrime ought to be considered as a new and distinctive form of criminal activity, one demanding the development of a new criminological vocabulary and conceptual apparatus. I chose to pursue this question by examining if and to what extent existing aetiologies of crime could be transposed to virtual settings. I have focused on the routine activity approach because this perspective has been repeatedly nominated as a theory capable of adaptation to cyberspace; if such adaptability (of the theory's core concepts and analytic framework) could be established, this would support the claim of *continuity* between terrestrial and virtual crimes, thereby refuting the 'novelty' thesis. If not, this would suggest *discontinuity* between crimes in virtual and non-virtual settings, thereby giving weight to claims that cybercrime is something criminologically new. I conclude that there are both significant continuities and discontinuities in the configuration of terrestrial and virtual crimes.

* * *

A more fundamental difference appears when we try to bring these concepts together in an aetiological schema. The central difficulty arises, I have suggested, from the distinctive *spatio-temporal ontologies* of virtual and non-virtual environments: whereas people, objects and activities can be clearly located within relatively fixed and ordered spatio-temporal configurations in the 'real world', such orderings appear to destabilize in the virtual world. In other words, the routine activity theory holds that the 'organization of time and space is central' for criminological explanation (Felson 1998: 148), yet the cyber-spatial environment is chronically spatio-temporally *disorganized*. The inability to transpose RAT's postulation of 'convergence in space and time' into cyberspace thereby renders problematic its straightforward explanatory application to the genesis of cybercrimes. Perhaps cybercrime represents a case not so much of 'old wine in new bottles' as of 'old wine in *no* bottles' or, alternatively, 'old wine' in bottles of varying and fluid shape. Routine activity theory (and, indeed, other ecologically oriented theories of crime causation) thus appears of limited utility in an environment that defies many of our taken-for-granted assumptions about how the socio-interactional setting of routine activities is configured.

# references

Adams, P. (1998). Network topologies and virtual place. *Annals of the Association of American Geographers 88*, 88–106.

Archer, M. (2000). *Being human: The problem of agency.* Cambridge: Cambridge University Press.

Beavon, D., Brantingham, P. L. and Brantingham, P. J. (1994). The influence of street networks on the patterning of property offenses. In R. V. Clarke (ed.) *Crime prevention studies, Vol II*, 149–63. New York: Willow Tree Press.

Bennett, R. (1991). Routine activities: A cross-national assessment of a criminological perspective. *Social Forces 70*, 147–63.

Bernburg, J. G. and Thorlindsson, T. (2001). Routine activities in social context: A closer look at the role of opportunity in deviant behavior. *Justice Quarterly 18*, 543–67.

Birkbeck, C. and LaFree, G. (1993). The situational analysis of crime and deviance. *Annual Review of Sociology 19*, 113–37.

Capeller, W. (2001). Not such a neat net: Some comments on virtual criminality. *Social & Legal Studies 10*, 229–42.

Castells, M. (2002). *The internet galaxy: Reflections on the internet, business, and society.* Oxford: Oxford University Press.

Clarke, R. and Felson, M., eds (1993). *Routine activity and rational choice.* London: Transaction Press.

*Clough, B. and Mungo, P. (1992). Approaching zero: Data crime and the computer underworld. London: Faber & Faber.*

Cohen, L. and Felson, M. (1979). Social change and crime rate trends: A routine activity approach. *American Sociological Review 44*, 588–608.

Cohen, L., Felson, M. and Land, K. (1980). Property crime rates in the United States: A macrodynamic analysis, 1947–1977; with ex ante forecasts for the mid–1980s. *American Journal of Sociology 86*, 90–118.

Cohen, L., Kluegel, J. and Land, K. (1981). Social inequality and predatory criminal victimization: An exposition and a test of a formal theory. *American Sociological Review 46*, 505–24.

Davis, M. (1990). *City of quartz: Excavating the future of Los Angeles.* London: Verso.

Denning, D. (1999). *Information warfare and security.* New York: Addison Wesley.

Dodge, M. and Kitchin, R. (2001). *Mapping cyberspace.* London: Routledge.

Felson, M. (1986). Routine activities, social controls, rational decisions and criminal outcomes. In D. Cornish and R. Clarke (eds) *The reasoning criminal.* New York: Springer Verlag.

Felson, M. (1998). *Crime and everyday life,* 2nd edn. Thousand Oaks, CA: Pine Forge Press.

Felson, M. (2000). The routine activity approach as a general social theory. In S. Simpson (ed.) *Of crime and criminality: The use of theory in everyday life.* Thousand Oaks, CA: Sage.

Felson, R. (1996). Big people hit little people: Sex differences in physical power and interpersonal violence. *Criminology 34*, 433–52.

Furnell, S. (2002). *Cybercrime: Vandalizing the information society.* London: Addison Wesley.

Grabosky, P. (2001). Virtual criminality: Old wine in new bottles? *Social & Legal Studies 10*, 243–9.

Grabosky, P. and Smith, R. (2001). Telecommunication fraud in the digital age: The convergence of technologies. In D. Wall (ed.) *Crime and the internet.* London: Routledge.

Harvey, D. (1989). *The condition of postmodernity.* Oxford: Blackwell.

Hollis, M. (1987). *The cunning of reason.* Cambridge: Cambridge University Press.

Jacobs, J. (1961). *The life and death of great American cities.* New York: Random House.

Johnston, N. (2003). Plan approved to save U.S. digital history. *Washington Post,* 15 February.

Joseph, J. (2003). Cyberstalking: An international perspective. In Y. Jewkes (ed.) *Dot.cons: Crime, deviance and identity on the internet*. Cullompton: Willan Press.

Katz, J. (1988). *The seductions of crime*. New York: Basic Books.

Leadbetter, C. (2000). *The weightless society*. New York: W. W. Norton.

Lynch, J. (1987). Routine activity and victimization at work. *Journal of Quantitative Criminology 3*, 275–82.

Massey, J., Krohn, M. and Bonati, L. (1989). Property crime and the routine activities of individuals. *Journal of Research in Crime and Delinquency 26*, 378–400.

Miethe, T. and Meier, R. (1990). Opportunity, choice and criminal victimization: A test of a theoretical model. *Journal of Research in Crime and Delinquency 27*, 243–66.

Miethe, T., Stafford, M. and Long, J. S. (1987). Social differentiation in criminal victimization: A test of routine activities/lifestyle theories. *American Sociological Review 52*, 184–94.

Mitchell, W. J. (1995). *City of bits: Space, place and the Infobahn*. Cambridge, MA: MIT Press.

Newman, G. and Clarke, R. (2002). *Etailing: New opportunities for crime, new opportunities for prevention*. Produced for the Foresight Crime Prevention Panel by the Jill Dando Institute of Crime Science, UCL; URL (consulted 13 May 2005): http://www.foresight.gov.uk/Previous_Rounds/Foresight_1999_2002/Crime_Prevention/Reports/Etailing_New_Opportunities_for_Crime_New_Opportunities_for_Prevention.html.

Newman, G. and Clarke, R. (2003). *Superhighway robbery: Preventing e-commerce crime*. Cullompton: Willan Press.

NHTCU/NOP (2002). Hi-tech crime: The impact on UK business. London: NHTCU.

Pease, K. (2001). Crime futures and foresight: Challenging criminal behaviour in the information age. In D. Wall (ed.) *Crime and the internet*. London: Routledge.

Poster, M. (1995). *The second media age*. Oxford: Polity.

Shields, R., ed. (1996). *Cultures of the internet: Virtual spaces, real histories, living bodies*. London: Sage.

Smith, C., McLaughlin, M. and Osborne, K. (1997). Conduct control on Usenet. *Journal of Computer-Mediated Communication 2*; URL (consulted 13 May 2005): http://www.ascusc.org/jcmc/vol2/issue4/smith.html.

Snyder, F. (2001). Sites of criminality and sites of governance. *Social & Legal Studies 10*, 251–6.

Stalder, F. (1998). The logic of networks: Social landscapes *vis-a-vis* the space of flows'. *Ctheory 46*; URL (consulted 13 May 2005): http://www.ctheory.net/text_file.asp?pick = 263.

Sutherland, E. (1947). *Principles of criminology*. Philadelphia: Lippincott.

Thomas, D. and Loader, B. (2000). Introduction–Cybercrime: Law enforcement, security and surveillance in the information age. In D. Thomas and B. Loader (eds) *Cybercrime: Law enforcement, security and surveillance in the information age*. London: Routledge.

Tseloni, A., Wittebrood, K., Farrell, G. and Pease, K. (2004). Burglary victimization in England and Wales, the Unites States and The Netherlands: A cross-national comparative test of routine activities and lifestyle theories. *British Journal of Criminology 44*, 66–91.

Turkle, S. (1995). *Life on the screen: Identity in the age of the internet*. New York: Simon & Schuster.

Wall, D. (2001). Cybercrimes and the internet. In D. Wall (ed.) *Crime and the internet*. London: Routledge.

Webster, F. (2002). *Theories of the information society*, 2nd edn. London: Routledge.

Zukin, S. (1988). *Loft living: Culture and capital in urban change*. London: Radius.

thomas j. holt
and
adam m. bossler

examining

# applicability

of
lifestyle-

the

routine

## activities theory for cybercrime victimization

Yar (2005) recently argued that virtual environments are spatially and temporally disconnected, limiting the "wholesale application" of the basic theoretical constructs of this theory (409). Yar (2005) argued that the temporal structure of cyberspace is disorganized, as it is active at all times around the world, although individuals may connect and disconnect rapidly and web pages come and go in relatively short periods of time. Yar (2005) therefore concludes that the nature of cyberspace limits the potential for the lifestyle-routine activities of victims to create social situations that enable motivated offenders to prey upon property or persons (412). Without any empirical tests, however, it is unclear if this is a premature conclusion or a valid argument.

Thus, a need exists to assess whether LRAT can account for cybercrime victimization. This

Thomas J. Holt & Adam M. Bossler, "Examining the Applicability of Lifestyle-Routine Activities Theory for Cybercrime Victimization," *Deviant Behavior*, vol. 30, no. 1, pp. 1-25. Copyright © 2009 by Taylor & Francis Group LLC. Reprinted with permission.

exploratory study will attempt to address this significant gap in the research literature in two ways. First, we will examine whether measures of lifestyle-routine activities can account for experiences with one form of cybercrime victimization, on-line harassment. Second, we explore the relationship between involvement in computer crime and computer victimization to consider the potential reciprocal relationship. The findings will benefit computer crime researchers and the larger literature on LRAT by providing an initial empirical assessment of this theory. We conclude with directions for future theoretical research.

## applying lifestyle-routine activities to cybercrime

Some researchers argue cyberstalking is distinct from off-line stalking in that perpetrators can target and harass their victims in unique ways and need not come into physical contact with the victim. Both offenses, however, produce fear and concern in the victims, who are primarily female (Bocij 2004). As a consequence, cyberstalking and real-world stalking share some similarities and are related offenses (see Bocij 2004; Wall 2001). In turn, it is possible that the findings identified in previous research on real-world stalking may be applied to virtual environments.

Studies using LRAT have identified a number of risk factors for off-line stalking, particularly using college samples with a specific focus on women (Bjerregaard 2000; Logan et al. 2000; Fisher et al. 2002; Tjaden and Thoenees 1998). Women experienced greater risk of stalking victimization than males due to greater exposure and proximity to potential offenders on a regular basis in classes, dorms, parties, and bars (Fisher et al. 2002; Logan et al. 2000; Tjaden and Thoenees 1998). Younger women and those who frequently date or are in intimate relationships may be more attractive targets for stalkers (Fisher et al. 2002; Tjaden and Thoenees 1998). A potential stalker may also easily target individuals that they have an existing emotional connection with, or knowledge of his or her schedule (Fisher et al. 2002). Schwartz and Pitts (1995) found that women are also at a higher risk because of the large presence of males that support or condone sexual violence, creating a ''rape culture'' (12). Additionally, women whose male friends got females drunk for the purposes of sexual relationships were more likely to be sexually victimized.

These characteristics may hold true for on-line harassment considering that those who spend a great deal of time chatting with others on-line may also develop intense emotional connections to another, despite the physical distance separating them (see Bocij 2004; Finn 2004). Individuals, especially females, may increase their chances of coming in contact with potential harassers by being interested in computers and regularly using computer-mediated communications such as chatrooms or social networking sites to connect with others (Finn 2004). These websites allow individuals to share pictures and personal information with others, exposing their potential as a target to would-be harassers (Patchin and Hinduja 2007).

Furthermore, the gendered nature of on-line communications may affect the risk of victimization. Research suggests that on-line communications are masculine in nature, which complicates the process of communicating. Exchanges between users on-line may take an aggressive adversarial tone where individuals attempt to dominate one another through linguistic conflict (see Gilboa 1996; Herring 1999). This masculine exchange is different from female communication patterns that utilize polite communications and gendered language that lead women to be ignored, criticized, or harassed by male users (Herring 1999; Taylor 2003). For example, women who are interested in technology often report a high degree of sexual harassment or hostility from others on-line (Herring 1999; Taylor 2003). Thus, gender could affect who is targeted for on-line harassment. Knowledge of computer systems may also play a role in target attractiveness, as a skilled computer user may be better prepared to deal with threats on-line.

Some behaviors individuals engage in, however, are also deviant acts that expose the victim to a larger population of offenders (Sampson and Laurtisen 1990). For example, women who engage in criminal or deviant behavior, including drinking and drug use, are at a greater risk of real-world stalking behaviors (Fisher et al. 2002; Mustaine and Tewksbury 1998) and sexual assaults (Schwartz and Pitts 1995). Little research has explored the relationship between on-line deviance and victimization, and Yar (2005) provided no assessment of this relationship in his critique. Research on computer hackers suggests that they often experience harassment and other forms of focused computer attack at the hands of others involved in this deviant subculture (Holt 2007; Jordan and Taylor 1998; Taylor 2003). Gilboa (1996) and Taylor (2003) also found that female computer hackers received a great deal of harassment from male hackers, over and above expected levels of abusive remarks. Thus, involvement in computer crime and deviance may increase exposure to motivated offenders, leading to a higher likelihood of victimization.

Finally, physical and social guardianship factors have mixed effects on the risk of real-world stalking victimization (Fisher et al. 2002). Physical guardianship measures, such as carrying a knife or mace, are correlated with the risk of stalking, although this may be an artifact of cross-sectional research design (Fisher et al. 2002; Mustaine and Tewksbury 1998). Living alone does appear to increase the risk of victimization, as a lack of social guardians may increase an offender's ability to gain easy, immediate access to their target (Fisher et al. 2002).

The role of guardianship, both physical and social, for on-line harassment is even less clear, as few have examined this issue empirically. For example, a range of computer programs (e.g., anti-virus programs, firewalls) have been designed to act as physical guardians to decrease the threat of system intrusions by viruses and malicious software; yet they are not meant to deal with threatening communications. Ownership and regular updating of protective software may reduce the likelihood of victimization because the individual is more cognizant of threats and risky behaviors on-line. Similarly, social guardians may also play a role in on-line harassment, particularly when a person's peers are involved in computer crime and deviance (Yar 2005:423). In the real world, spending time with delinquents or criminals increases a person's exposure to motivated offenders and may reduce the likelihood they may intervene when a person is being victimized (Zhang et al. 2001). The possible anonymity afforded by virtual environments may increase the likelihood that an individual will harass his or her friends while on-line without fear of reprisal (see Furnell 2002). Thus, peer involvement in computer-based deviance may increase a person's likelihood of victimization while on-line.

## the present study

The above review illustrates that there are several potential linkages between LRAT and cybercrime victimization. This study provides an initial analysis of hypotheses derived from LRAT to explore its capacity to explain on-line harassment. Specifically, we consider the relationship between measures of routine computer use, including time spent interacting with others on-line and an individual's knowledge of computers, and the risk of being harassed while on-line. Although Yar (2005) does not discuss the relationship between one's own involvement in computer deviance and victimization, we explore this important relationship. This study also examines the role of social guardianship via peer involvement in computer crime and physical guardianship through computer-based protective software such as firewalls. The effect of target suitability is assessed using demographic characteristics such as gender and age.

## methods

This analysis utilizes data from a self-report survey administered to 788 college students enrolled in 10 courses, 5 of which allowed students from every college to enroll, offered on a southeastern university campus between August and October 2006. The sample was 57% female and predominantly white (77.9%), comparable to the larger university population (52.5% female; 75% white). This purposive sample was developed because of college students' involvement in and knowledge of risky behavior regarding computers and other technological devices (see Skinner and Fream 1997; Higgins 2005) as well as their increased risk of sexual victimization and stalking (Fisher et al. 2002).

* * *

## dependent variable

Respondents were asked how many times within the last 12 months have they been the victim of someone harassing them in a chatroom, IRC, or Instant Message chat (options being never, 1–2 times, 3–5 times, 6–9 times, and 10 or more times).[1] Because of limited variation in the responses and skewness, the measure was collapsed into a dichotomous measure (0 = no victimization; 1 = victimization) and logistic regression was employed. A total of 18.9% of the respondents reported experiencing harassment on-line at some point within the last year, reflecting similar statistics from existing research (see Finn 2004) (Table 1).[2]

---

1 There are several venues for real time communication on-line, including chatrooms, instant messaging, and Internet Relay Chat (IRC), although there are distinct differences across these outlets (Taylor et al. 2006). For example, chatrooms are often Web-based and allow groups of people to communicate simultaneously. All messages, however, can be seen by any person logged into the chat room. Alternatively, instant messaging services run through stand alone software programs like AIM or Yahoo and send messages directly to a single individual rather than groups. Finally, IRC operates on a separate portion of the Internet and special software is needed to access the system. Individuals must then log in to category-based channels, such as sports or movies. IRC provides group-based chat functions much like chatrooms, although private messages can also be created in the same fashion as instant messaging services (see Taylor et al. 2006).

2 Of the 578 cases analyzed, 13.7% reported being victimized 1–2 times, 4% reported 3–5 times, .5% ($n = 3$) reported being victimized 6–9 times, and .7% ($n = 4$) reported 10 or more victimizations. In our initial analyses, we collapsed the last three categories into one category (three or more) because of the small $n$ in these categories and created a three-point ordinal measure. We then ran ordered logistic regression models. Because of a large number of independent variables that are not dichotomous and only 30 respondents reporting three or more victimizations, 66.7% of the cells had zero frequencies. In order to address this empty cell issue, but not wanting to lose variation in our independent variables, we collapsed the dependent variable into two categories (0 = non-victimization; 1 = victimization) and ran logistic regression models. The logistic regression models (as presented in the tables) are substantively similar to the ordered logistic regression models. Additionally, we would not have been able to partition the ordered logistic regression models by sex because of the small number of males who have been victimized and the large number of independent variables. Tobit regressions were not performed because our dependent variable consisted of a single ordinal item that can be examined via ordered logistic regression. Once the dependent variable was collapsed into a dichotomous measure, and 18.9% of the sample fell into one category, special forms of regression such as tobit or rare-case logistic regression were not necessary because logistic regression can adequately handle this distribution.

Table 1.   Sample Descriptives (n = 578)

| | Mean | Std. dev | Min | Max. |
|---|---|---|---|---|
| Dependent variable | | | | |
| On-line harassment | .189 | .392 | 0 | 1 |
| Computer | | | | |
| Ownership | .137 | .344 | 0 | 1 |
| Dial-up | .048 | .215 | 0 | 1 |
| T-1 | .076 | .265 | 0 | 1 |
| Computer use | | | | |
| Skill level | .675 | .569 | 0 | 2 |
| Hrs work/school | 1.52 | 1.36 | 0 | 4 |
| Hrs non-wrk/school | 1.59 | 1.37 | 0 | 4 |
| Shopping | 1.26 | 1.10 | 0 | 5 |
| Video games | .792 | 1.23 | 0 | 5 |
| E-mail | 2.78 | 1.28 | 0 | 5 |
| Chatrooms | 1.91 | 1.75 | 0 | 5 |
| Programming | .374 | .774 | 0 | 5 |
| Myspace | .152 | .360 | 0 | 1 |
| Computer deviance | .411 | .531 | 0 | 3 |
| Pirating software | .332 | .759 | 0 | 3 |
| Pirating media | 1.03 | 1.20 | 0 | 3 |
| Pornography | .548 | 1.04 | 0 | 3 |
| Hacking | .185 | .500 | 0 | 3 |
| Guardians | | | | |
| Friends deviance | .725 | .603 | 0 | 3 |
| Anti-virus | .874 | .332 | 0 | 1 |
| Spybot software | .301 | .459 | 0 | 1 |
| Ad-aware software | .351 | .478 | 0 | 1 |
| Microsoft Update | .614 | .487 | 0 | 1 |
| Security Center | .133 | .340 | 0 | 1 |
| Software firewall | .517 | .500 | 0 | 1 |
| Hardware firewall | .405 | .491 | 0 | 1 |
| Demographics | | | | |
| Female | .576 | .495 | 0 | 1 |
| African American | .107 | .310 | 0 | 1 |
| Other | .111 | .314 | 0 | 1 |
| Age | .841 | .884 | 0 | 3 |
| Employment | .820 | .602 | 0 | 2 |

## independent variables

Multiple measures of respondents' computer use for work, school, and personal interests were included in the instrument to assess potential exposure to motivated offenders. Respondents were asked who owned the computer *(ownership)* that they used most often (0 = you/family; /family; 1 = other, including friends, school, and employer). Two dummy measures were included to assess Internet connection speed *(Dial-up* and *T-1 or higher, DSL/Cable Modem* being the comparison group), thereby assessing their ability to participate more fully in chat-rooms, Web-forums, and other interactive social networking sites.

A self-assessment item was included to measure the respondents' knowledge, skill, and computer use *(skill level)*. This three category index was based on general categories of computer proficiency: (1) I can surf the 'net, se common software, but not fix my own computer (normal); (2) I can use a variety of software and fix some computer problems I have (intermediate); and (3) I can use Linux, most software, and fix most computer problems I have (advanced) (Rogers 2001). Thirty-seven percent (37.7%) of the respondents assessed their skill level as normal, whereas 57.1 % and 5.2% assessed their skill level as intermediate and advanced, respectively.[3]

To directly assess the amount of time they spend using a computer daily, respondents were asked to indicate how many hours per week in the last year have they spent on a computer for both work or school *(Hrs. work/school)* and also outside of work or school *(Hrs. non-work/school)*, with options being less than 5 hours, 5–10 hours, 11–15 hours, 16–20 hours, and 21 or more hours. The frequency distribution of these two measures appear similar, although they are not highly correlated (Spearman = .259).[4] Therefore, they are measuring two distinct aspects of how computer usage is integrated into their daily routines.

To specifically measure *how* they spend their time on the computer, respondents were also asked to indicate how much time they spent each week on average over the past six months for each of the following activities: shopping/going to auction sites *(shopping)*, playing video games *(video games)*, checking e-mail *(e-mail)*, using chatrooms/IRC/IM *(chatrooms)*, and programming *(programming)*, with options being never, less than one hour, 1–2 hours, 3–5 hours, 6–9 hours, and 10 or more hours. The use of popular social networking websites *(Myspace)* to share personal information was measured with the following question "I generally avoid using websites like Facebook, Myspace, and classmates. com" (0 = no; 1 = yes).

To explore the connection between virtual offending and victimization, we created a computer deviance scale *(Computer dev.)* from six questions that ask respondents to indicate how often (options being never, 1–2 times, 3–5 times, 6 or more times) they have either used their computer resources or another person's to: (1) knowingly use, make, or give another person a "pirated" copy of commercially sold computer software; (2) knowingly use, make, or give to another person "pirated" media (music, television show, or movie); (3) look at pornographic or obscene material; (4) guess another's password to get into his or her computer accounts or files; (5) access another's computer account or files without his or her knowledge or permission to look at information or files; and (6) add, delete, change, or print any information in another's computer files without the owner's knowledge or permission (Rogers 2001; Skinner and Fream 1997). The responses were averaged, creating a scale ranging from 0 to 3 with satisfactory reliability (alpha = .7223). It should be noted that the data set does not include a specific measure on whether or not the respondent has himself or herself harassed someone on-line, meaning that we cannot directly assess the link between on-line harassment offending and victimization. The scale, however, is reliable, has face validity, and includes important types of computer deviance.

Capable guardianship was assessed using multiple direct and indirect measures in keeping with traditional assessments of LRAT (see Cohen and Felson 1979). To assess social guardianship, respondents

---

3 A fourth category was provided for this question, stating "I am afraid of computers and don't use them unless I absolutely have to." Only one student in the data set and no students in the 578 cases analyzed indicated they fell into this category, indicating that this sample is relatively computer literate.

4 For the measure assessing how many hours per week the respondents spend on a computer for work or school, the respondents reported that 26.6% spent less than 5 hours, 32.7% spent 510 hours, 17.5% were on the computer 1115 hours, 8.5% reported being on the computer 1620 hours, and 14.7% reported 21 hours or more. Regarding the number of hours on a computer outside of work or school, 24.6% reported being on a computer less than 5 hours, 33.2% reported 510 hours, 16.4% spent 1115 hours, 10.2% reported 1620 hours, and 15.6% reported 21 or more hours.

were asked to assess how many of their friends committed any of the computer deviant acts *(Friends deviance)* that were utilized to create the computer deviance scale (options being: 0 = none of them; 1 = very few of them; 2 = about half of them; 3 = more than half of them).[5] The responses were added and divided by six, creating a reliable scale (alpha = .7898). We measured physical guardianship by asking respondents whether or not (0 = no;1 = yes) they own and update their anti-virus *(Anti-virus)*, spybot *(Spybot software)*, and ad-aware software *(Ad-aware software)*, as well as Microsoft Update *(Microsoft Update)*, AOL or another Internet Service Providers' Security Center *(Security Center)*, and any software *(Software firewall)* and hardware *(Hardware firewall)* firewalls.[6]

Finally, we examine whether sex, race, age, and employment affect the risk of on-line harassment. *Sex* is a dichotomous measure (0 = male; 1 = female). We include two dummy measures for race *(African American* and *other;* white being the comparison group).[7] Age is a four-point ordinal scale (0 = 19 and under; 1 = 20–21; 2 = 22–25, 3 = 26 and up) whereas *employment status* is measured as a three-point ordinal scale (0 = unemployed; 1 = part-time/temp; 2 = full time).

## findings

We estimated logistic regression models with on-line harassment victimization as the dependent variable (see Table 2).[8] The analysis (see Model 1) indicates that most measures of routine activities theory do not affect the odds of being harassed on-line. Neither owning a computer nor the speed of one's Internet connection increases the odds of being harassed. Additionally, being more computer literate and having more computer skills does not act as a protective factor.[9] Most of the respondent's general computer use and activities, including shopping, playing video games, or checking email, do not have a significant impact.

Instead, the number of hours an individual spends in chatrooms, IRC, and IM and their involvement in computer deviance has a significant impact on their risk of victimization. These findings illustrate that simply spending more time on the computer does not increase victimization risks, nor does spending

---

5   The original survey question also included an option of "all of them." Because of the small number of respondents who reported all of their friends pirated software or committed any of the "hacker-like" behaviors, "all of them" were combined with "more than half." All models were also run with a scale created from the non-recategorized questions; these models were substantively similar to the results in Tables 2 and 3.

6   These measures do not create a reliable scale (alpha = .5053). We ran additional analyses for the full sample and for each of the subsamples with the scale included instead of the seven separate measures. The scale was not significantly related to on-line harassment. Therefore we included the seven separate measures instead of incorporating an unreliable scale.

7   Respondents were asked to identify themselves as white, African American, Hispanic, Asian, or another racial group. Asians, Hispanics, and other race categories only comprise 5.2%, 2.8%, and 3.1% of the respective sample. The original models analyzed included separate dummy measures for each group; however, no race measure was significant. Thus, these race groups were combined into one category to simplify the model. This combination of groups did not affect any results.

8   Multicollinearity was not an issue for the analysis using the full sample (*n* = 578 cases) or for the analyses partitioned by sex. No VIF was over 10 and no tolerance level was below .2. The two measures with the lowest tolerance levels and highest VIFs are the computer deviance scale (tolerance of .513 and VIF of 1.951) and the friends' computer deviance scale (tolerance of .534 and VIF of 1.874). The issue was slightly worse for the male sample analysis (computer deviance scale had tolerance of .497 and VIF of 2.012 and friends' computer deviance scale had tolerance of .512 and VIF of 1.954), but these scores do not raise concerns.

9   To further examine whether skill level is related to on-line harassment, we also ran models using dummy measures assessing whether they have used and can operate Windows 95/98, Windows NT/2000, Windows XP, Macintosh, UNIX, and Linux (adapted from Rogers 2001). We ran zero-order models and full models (including and excluding the skill level measure) for the full sample and the male and female subsamples. In no model did the ability to run a certain program affect on-line harassment, nor did the inclusion of these measures affect any of the results presented in the analyses section. Additionally, the six dummy measures do not create a reliable scale (alpha = .5424) and cannot be used as a measure of computer skill.

Table 2. Logistic Regression Models Predicting Victimization of On-Line Harassment

| | Harassment | | | | | |
|---|---|---|---|---|---|---|
| | Model 1 | | | Model 2 | | |
| | B | Std. error | Odds ratio | B | Std. error | Odds ratio |
| Computer | | | | | | |
| Ownership | —.229 | (.388) | .795 | —.209 | (.391) | .811 |
| Dial-up | .469 | (.535) | 1.599 | .481 | (.539) | 1.618 |
| T-1 | .049 | (.452) | 1.050 | .036 | (.454) | 1.036 |
| Computer use | | | | | | |
| Skill level | .132 | (.235) | 1.141 | .189 | (.241) | 1.208 |
| Hrs work/school | .052 | (.093) | 1.053 | .057 | (.094) | 1.058 |
| Hrs non-wrk/school | —.106 | (.103) | .899 | —.099 | (.103) | .906 |
| Shopping | .083 | (.113) | 1.086 | .083 | (.115) | 1.087 |
| Video games | —.023 | (.106) | .977 | —.020 | (.108) | .980 |
| E-mail | —.048 | (.108) | .953 | —.052 | (.109) | .950 |
| Chatrooms | .247** | (.079) | 1.281 | .257*** | (.080) | 1.293 |
| Programming | —.097 | (.162) | .908 | —.115 | (.164) | .891 |
| Myspace | —.327 | (.461) | .721 | —.344 | (.468) | .709 |
| Computer deviance | .576* | (.269) | 1.779 | — | — | — |
| Pirating software | — | — | — | —.220 | (.184) | .803 |
| Pirating media | — | — | — | .091 | (.114) | 1.096 |
| Pornography | — | — | — | .081 | (.145) | 1.084 |
| Hacking | — | — | — | .603* | (.236) | 1.828 |
| Guardians | | | | | | |
| Friends deviance | .633** | (.244) | 1.884 | .635** | (.247) | 1.887 |
| Anti-virus | — .081 | (.356) | .922 | —.006 | (.368) | .994 |
| Spybot software | —.040 | (.273) | .961 | —.002 | (.274) | .998 |
| Ad-aware software | — .298 | (.266) | .742 | —.288 | (.268) | .750 |
| Microsoft Update | .161 | (.260) | 1.175 | .179 | (.262) | 1.196 |
| Security Center | .439 | (.319) | 1.551 | .461 | (.321) | 1.586 |
| Software firewall | — .266 | (.248) | .767 | —.243 | (.249) | .784 |
| Hardware firewall | .071 | (.252) | 1.074 | .074 | (.252) | 1.077 |
| Demographics | | | | | | |
| Female | 1.012*** | (.294) | 2.751 | .900** | (.324) | 2.460 |
| African American | .522 | (.390) | 1.686 | .531 | (.391) | 1.701 |
| Other | .046 | (.384) | 1.047 | .063 | (.388) | 1.065 |
| Age | — .207 | (.160) | .813 | —.181 | (.164) | .834 |
| Employment | .288 | (.204) | 1.334 | .296 | (.206) | 1.345 |
| Constant | —3.329*** | (.576) | .036 | —3.410*** | (.589) | .033 |
| **Pseudo R²** | .179 | | | .190 | | |

more time on interactive websites.[10] This suggests that general exposure to others via the Internet does

---

10   To further examine this issue, we ran all full models without the specific computer activity measures (shopping, video game, e-mail, chatrooms, and programming) to further assess whether a relationship between general hours on the computer and cyberspace harassment victimization exists. We also ran models including only one of the general hours on the computer measures. We believed that this would provide the "general hours on the computer" measure the best opportunity to be statistically significant. In no model was a significant relationship between general hours on the computer (for work and school and outside of work and school) and chatroom victimization found.

not increase victimization. Rather, one must spend more time with others in a specific context to influence the risk of on-line harassment.

The model also illustrates the connection between involvement in computer deviance and virtual victimization. Following findings from studies of traditional crime, individuals who commit computer deviance are also more likely to be victimized themselves. If the computer deviance measure is separated into its basic components of pirating software, pirating media, viewing pornography, and hacking,[11] only pirating media (B = .254, *p* = .003) and hacking (B = .787, p < .001) have zero-order effects on cyberspace harassment (results not shown). Much of the relationship between computer deviance and on-line harassment can be explained by the respondent's participation in hacking (B = .603), as this is the only computer deviance measure significant in the full model (Table 2: Model 2). This may be a direct result of the risks associated with becoming a computer hacker because hacking is a skill gained through experimenting with computers in a way that can damage or destroy computer systems (Taylor 2003). Many hackers communicate and learn from others in on-line environments that can be quite hostile (see Holt 2007). In turn, hackers report a range of victimization experiences, especially harassment from others on-line (Holt 2007; Jordan and Taylor 1998; Taylor 2003). Thus, computer crime and victimization mirror some relationships to real-world offending despite existing debate on the nature of cybercrime (see Wall 2001).

Physical computer guardianship, including firewalls and anti-virus programs, did not reduce the odds of being harassed while on-line. We theorized that these programs are not meant for this express purpose. They did not appear, however, to act as indirect measures of "general computer capable guardians." In congruence with the previous finding that one must spend time in a specific context (i.e., chatrooms, IRC, IM) to increase the risk of on-line harassment, knowing whether or not that person takes precautions to protect himself or herself in general on the computer does not predict victimization of a specific type of computer crime.

At the same time, social guardianship influenced harassment victimization. Having friends involved in computer-based deviance increased the odds of being harassed, suggesting that these respondents exposed themselves to motivated offenders and minimized the number of individuals who could assist if an individual is being harassed. As a result, social guardianship may be as important for on-line harassment as it is for off-line harassment (Fisher et al. 2002).

Finally, our model indicates that race, age, and employment do not appear to act as indicators of target attractiveness for online harassment. At the same time, being female increases one's odds of being harassed on-line by 2.751. Whereas only 13.5% of the males had been victimized, almost a quarter (22.8%) of the females reported being harassed on-line within the last year. Of interest is the gender odds ratio increase from a zero-order model (results not shown on table; b = .642**, std. error = .228, odds ratio = 1.900) to the full model (Model 1 = 2.751; Model 2 = 2.460). If the odds ratio had decreased, this could be interpreted as the relationship between sex and harassment victimization being mediated or explained by differing computer routines and precautions (i.e., software, deviant friends). The observed increase in the odds ratio from the zero-order model to the full model indicates that simply being female dramatically increases their status as a suitable target for harassment.

---

11 Pirating software and media are not included together because they create an unreliable scale (a = .5681). Furthermore, pirating software and media do not predict victimization similarly. The three hacking items do create a reliable scale (alpha = .8585).

## gender differences in harassment

In light of previous research exploring the interaction between gender, lifestyle choices, and routine activities (see Schwartz and Pitts 1995), we explored how this interaction affects on-line harassment by partitioning the model by sex (see Daly and Maher 1998 for discussion on problems of treating gender as dichotomous measure). Table 3 illustrates that many of the daily activities and precautions do not predict victimization rates for males or females, meaning that LRAT does not appear more suitable in explaining one sex's victimization over the other beyond the finding that females are more suitable targets. For both sexes, spending more time in a specific on-line setting (i.e., chatrooms, IRC or IM) increased the odds of being harassed. The same routine behaviors and lifestyle choices, however, are not significant in both models. The models indicate that males who use dial-up are more at risk to be harassed whereas females might be less at risk, thus making dial-up an unusual risk factor for one sex and a protective factor for another. Additionally, it would appear that females are more at risk to be harassed if they commit computer deviance or have friends who do the same, replicating the traditional non-computer literature (Schwartz and Pitts 1995).

Z-tests comparing regression coefficients do not support these conclusions. There is no statistical difference between the male and female models regarding Internet speed or the impact of friends' deviance. In fact, the only significant coefficient difference is *skill level*. Possessing more computer skills is a stronger protective factor for males than females. Gendered communication patterns may make women more likely to experience sexual harassment or hostile treatment (Herring 1999; Taylor 2003). Research on the computer hacker subculture found that females are more likely to be harassed because of their gender (Gilboa 1996; Taylor 2003). It should be noted that although the z-test indicates a significant difference between the two models, *skill level* is not significant in either model. Thus, the relationship between skill level and on-line harassment is tenuous.[12]

\* \* \*

First, most measures of routine computer use and physical guardianship had little influence on the likelihood of being harassed while chatting on-line. Regular use of chatrooms and other forms of computer-mediated communications were associated with increased victimization risk, possibly by increasing exposure to motivated offenders. This finding parallels LRAT research that reveals that simply leaving one's house is not the essential risk factor in explaining victimization; it is where that person goes and what they do (Mustaine and Tewskbury 1998). Similarly, simply owning a computer and

---

12   The pseudo R-square value for the male model (.316) is greater than the female (.207) and full models (.179). It must be noted that the pseudo R-squares presented are Nagelkerke R squares. If Cox and Snell R squares were presented, the pseudo R-squares for the two models would be more comparable (male = .172; female = .136). Although the z-tests only showed a significant difference between skill level, several measures [ownership, computer speed (dial-up and T-1), and race (African American and other)] were larger in one model over the other, but were not found to be significant across models because of large standard errors. To examine whether the inclusion of these measures explains the disparity, we ran additional models excluding them. These analyses illustrated that much of the difference can be explained by the three types of variables listed earlier. When computer speed is excluded, the male model has a Nagelkerke R-square of .290 and a Cox and Snell R-square of .159. The female model's Nagelkerke R-square is .206 with a Cox and Snell of .136. When computer speed and computer ownership are excluded, the male model's Nagelkerke R-square drops to .250 and the Cox and Snell is .137. The female model's Nagelkerke and Cox and Snell remain stable at .205 and .135, respectively. Finally, when all three categories of variables are excluded, the Nagelkerke for the male model continues to drop to .233 with a Cox and Snell of .127. The female model's Cox and Snell is actually larger than that of the males (.130) and the Nagelkerke only drops to .198. As a result, much of the disparity in pseudo R-squares can be explained by the decision to provide Nagelkerke R-squares and that the measures of computer speed, ownership, and race helped explain a small number of male victimizations and not female victimizations, though they are not significant across models.

Table 3. Logistic Regression Models Predicting On-Line Harassment for Male and Female Subsamples

| | Male and Female Subsamples | | | | | | |
|---|---|---|---|---|---|---|---|
| | Male (n = 245) | | | Female (n = 333) | | | |
| | | Std. | Odds | | Std. | Odds | Z |
| | B | error | ratio | B | error | ratio | score |
| Computer | | | | | | | |
| Ownership | —7.208 | (17.073) | .001 | .273 | (.437) | 1.314 | —.44 |
| Dial-up | 2.032* | (.975) | 7.629 | —.179 | (.705) | .836 | 1.84 |
| T-1 | .318 | (.852) | 1.374 | —.149 | (.597) | .862 | .45 |
| Computer use | | | | | | | |
| Skill level | —.757 | (.492) | .469 | .448 | (.296) | 1.565 | —2.10 |
| Hrs work/ school | .285 | (.171) | 1.330 | —.080 | (.124) | .923 | 1.73 |
| Hrs non-wrk/ school | .093 | (.187) | 1.098 | —.215 | (.134) | .806 | 1.34 |
| Shopping | .001 | (.225) | 1.001 | .136 | (.142) | 1.146 | —.51 |
| Video games | .104 | (.159) | 1.109 | —.072 | (.163) | .930 | .77 |
| E-mail | —.328 | (.239) | .720 | .065 | (.135) | 1.067 | —1.43 |
| Chatrooms | .398* | (.156) | 1.489 | .212* | (.100) | 1.236 | 1.00 |
| Programming | .137 | (.268) | 1.147 | —.253 | (.217) | .777 | 1.13 |
| Myspace | —.513 | (.835) | .598 | —.262 | (.625) | .769 | —.24 |
| Computer deviance | .255 | (.428) | 1.290 | 1.026* | (.442) | 2.789 | —1.25 |
| Guardians | | | | | | | |
| Friends deviance | .502 | (.423) | 1.652 | .723* | (.349) | 2.061 | —.40 |
| Anti-virus | —.105 | (.750) | .900 | —.294 | (.467) | .745 | .21 |
| Spybot | —.123 | (.493) | .884 | —.189 | (.369) | .828 | .11 |
| Ad-aware | .445 | (.536) | 1.560 | —.703 | (.366) | .495 | 1.77 |
| Microsoft Update | .113 | (.529) | 1.120 | .197 | (.323) | 1.217 | —.14 |
| Security Center | .409 | (.671) | 1.506 | .602 | (.398) | 1.826 | —.25 |
| Software firewall | —.316 | (.479) | .729 | —.273 | (.314) | .761 | —.08 |
| Hardware firewall | .076 | (.465) | 1.079 | .016 | (.322) | 1.016 | .11 |
| Demographics | | | | | | | |
| African American | .301 | (.809) | 1.351 | .477 | (.472) | 1.612 | —.19 |
| Other | —1.134 | (1.108) | .322 | .417 | (.449) | 1.517 | —1.30 |
| Age | —.066 | (.293) | .936 | —.372 | (.217) | .689 | .84 |
| Employment | .514 | (.392) | 1.671 | .244 | (.272) | 1.277 | .57 |
| Constant | —3.222** | (1.118) | .040 | —2.235*** | (.664) | .107 | |
| Pseudo $R^2$ | .316 | | | .207 | | | |

spending time on the Internet may not increase on-line harassment; instead, involvement in a specific setting may be required.

Second, committing computer-based deviance increases one's risk of on-line victimization, mirroring previous research that has identified an association between real-world delinquent behavior and victimization (Sampson and Lauritsen 1990; Zhang et al. 2001). Such a relationship has not been identified in previous examinations of computer criminality. Engaging in deviant lifestyles on-line may expose individuals to offenders, thereby increasing their risk of victimization. Additionally, respondents who had friends who committed computer deviance were also more at risk for harassment because of being in closer proximity to motivated offenders and by decreasing social guardianship.

Third, our findings illustrate the need for gender to be included in the important discussion on the applicability of LRAT to cybercrime victimization, especially on-line harassment. Females were more likely to be victimized because of being viewed as attractive targets, not because of computer-related behavior and/or precautions. Women with strong computer skills may also be more likely to be victimized possibly as a consequence of the gendered nature of cyberspace and differences in communication patterns that may lead women to be easily identified on-line and perceived as suitable targets for harassment (Taylor 2003).

Taken as a whole, the findings could be interpreted as a validation of Yar's (2005) critique that cyberspace does not allow for the critical physical intersection of victims and offenders. This conclusion, however, would overlook our three crucial findings. Because Yar (2005) did not address the link between on-line deviant behavior and victimization risk identified in previous LRAT research, we are not prepared to dismiss the value of LRAT for cybercrime. Yar's (2005) critique might also be applied too generally to cybercrime. Previous LRAT research has shown that daily routines do not predict all types of victimization equally; this can be the case even *within* the same crime category. For example, Mustaine and Tewsbury (1998) found that the predictors of larceny theft victimization differed regarding whether they were studying larceny theft over or under $50. Similarly, LRAT and its risk factors will probably not apply to cybercrime generally nor entire cybercrime typologies (e.g., Wall 2001). Instead, LRAT will probably have its greatest success in applying to cybercrime when specific cybercrimes, such as credit card theft and malicious software infection, are examined.

\* \* \*

Finally, this exploratory analysis highlights the need for future research exploring cybercrime victimization to refine the measures of routine computer use. Until recently, LRAT testing has primarily relied on demographic variables as proxy measures for risky behaviors (Mustaine and Tewksbury 1998). Although our test did not rely on demographic proxies, many of our measures of routine computer usage (i.e., number of hours in chatrooms, e-mail, etc.) could be considered proxy measures with limited response categories. Our measures of routine computer usage captured how much time respondents spent performing certain activities, but did not capture what they were actually doing in these domains, with whom they were interacting, or when. Considering how the dynamics in specific settings can affect the probability of victimization, future research examining the intricacies of on-line use could help explain how this realm brings motivated offenders and suitable targets together without capable guardianship.

## references

Bjerregaard, Beth. 2000. "An Empirical Study of Stalking Victimization." *Violence and Victims* 15:389–406.

Bocij, Paul. 2004. *Cyberstalking: Harassment in the Internet Age and How to Protect Your Family.* Westport, CT: Praeger.

Cohen, Lawrence E. and Marcus Felson. 1979. "Social Change and Crime Rate Trends: A Routine Activity Approach." *American Sociological Review* 44:588–608.

Computer Security Institute. 2007. "Computer Crime and Security Survey." Retrieved June 3, 2007, from (http://www.cybercrime.gov/FBI2006.pdf).

Daly, Kathleen and Lisa Maher. 1998. *Criminology at the Crossroads: Feminist Readings in Crime and Justice.* Oxford: Oxford University Press.

Finkelhor, David, Kimberly J. Mitchell, and Janice Wolak. 2000. *Online Victimization: A Report on the Nation's Youth.* Washington, DC: National Center for Missing and Exploited Children.

Finn, Jerry. 2004. "A Survey of Online Harassment at a University Campus." *Journal of Interpersonal Violence* 19(4):468–483.

Fisher, Bonnie S., Francis T. Cullen, and Michael G. Turner. 2002. "Being Pursued: Stalking Victimization in a National Study of College Women." *Criminology and Public Policy* 1(2):257–308.

Furnell, Steven. 2002. *Cybercrime: Vandalizing the Information Society.* Boston, MA: Addison-Wesley.

Gilboa, N. 1996. "Elites, Lamers, Narcs and Whores: Exploring the Computer Underground." Pp. 98–113. In *Wired Women: Gender and New Realities in Cyberspace,* edited by L. Cherny and E. R. Weise. Seattle, WA: Seal Press.

Grabosky, Peter N. 2001. "Virtual Criminality: Old Wine in New Bottles?" *Social and Legal Studies* 10:243–249.

Grabosky P. N. and Smith R. 2001. "Telecommunication Fraud in the Digital Age: The Convergence of Technologies." Pp. 29–43. In *Crime and the Internet,* edited by D. Wall. New York: Routledge.

Herring, S. C. 1999. "The Rhetorical Dynamics of Gender Harassment Online." *The Information Society* 15(3):151–167.

Higgins, George E. 2005. "Can Low Self-Control Help with the Understanding of the Software Piracy Problem?" *Deviant Behavior* 26(1):1–24.

Holt, Thomas J. 2007. "Subcultural Evolution? Examining the Influence of On- and Off-Line Experiences on Deviant Subcultures." *Deviant Behavior* 28(2):171–198.

Internet Crime Complaint Center. 2007. "Internet Crime Report." Retrieved on April 25, 2007 from (http://www.ic3.gov/media/annual-report/2006_IC3Report.pdf).

Jensen, Gary F. and David Brownfield. 1986. "Gender, Lifestyles, and Victimization: Beyond Routine Activity." *Violence and Victims* 1:85–99.

Jordan, Tim and Paul Taylor. 1998. "A Sociology of Hackers." *The Sociological Review* 46(4): 757–780.

Lauritsen, Janet L., John H. Laub, and Robert J. Sampson. 1992. "Conventional and Delinquent Activities: Implications for the Prevention of Violent Victimization among Adolescents." *Violence and Victims* 7:91–108.

Logan, T. K., Carl Leukefeld, and Robert Walker. 2000. "Stalking as a Variant of Intimate Violence: Implications from a Young Adult Sample." *Violence and Victims* 15:91–111.

Miethe, Terance D. and Robert F. Meier. 1994. *Crime and Its Social Context: Toward an Integrated Theory of Offenders, Victims, and Situations.* Albany: SUNY Press.

Mustaine, Elizabeth Ehrhardt, and Richard Tewksbury. 1998. "Predicting Risk of Larceny Theft Victimization: A Routine Activity Analysis Using Refined Lifestyle Measures." *Criminology* 36:829–857.

Newman, Grame and Ronald Clarke. 2003. *Superhighway Robbery: Preventing E-Commerce Crime.* Cullompton, UK: Willan Press.

Osgood, D. Wayne, Janet K. Wilson, Patrick M. O'Malley, Jerald G. Bachman, and Lloyd D. Johnston. 1996. "Routine Activities and Individual Deviant Behavior." *American Sociological Review* 61(4):635–655.

Patchin, Justin and Sameer Hinduja. 2007. "What Kids Do on MySpace." *Technology and Learning* 27(7):7.

Pease, K. 2001. "Crime Futures and Foresight: Challenging Criminal Behavior in the Information Age." Pp. 18–28. In *Crime and the Internet,* edited by D. Wall. New York: Routledge.

Rogers, Marcus K. 2001. *A Social Learning Theory and Moral Disengagement Analysis of Criminal Computer Behavior: An Exploratory Study.* Unpublished doctoral dissertation. Manitoba University, Canada.

Sampson, Robert J. and Janet L. Lauritsen. 1990. "Deviant Lifestyles, Proximity to Crime, and the Offender-Victim Link in Personal Violence." *Journal of Research in Crime and Delinquency* 27:110–139.

Schwartz, Martin D. and Victoria L. Pitts. 1995. "Exploring a Feminist Routine Activities Approach to Explaining Sexual Assault." *Justice Quarterly* 12:9–31.

Skinner, William F. and Anne M. Fream. 1997. "A Social Learning Theory Analysis of Computer Crime among College Students." *Journal of Research in Crime and Delinquency* 34(4):495–518.

Taylor, Paul A. 2003. "Maestros or Misogynists? Gender and the Social Construction of Hacking." Pp. 126–146. In *Dot.cons: Crime, Deviance and Identity on the Internet,* edited by Y. Jewkes. Portland, OR: Willan Publishing.

Taylor, Robert W. Tory J. Caeti, D. Kall Loper, Eric J. Fritsch, and John Lieder bach. 2006. *Digital Crime and Digital Terrorism.* Upper Saddle River, NJ: Pearson Prentice Hall.

Tjaden, Patricia and Nancy Thoenees. 1998. *Stalking in America: Findings from the National Violence Against Women Survey.* US Department of Justice, Office of Justice Programs. Washington, DC: US Government Printing Office.

Wall, D. S. 2001. "Cybercrimes and the Internet." Pp. 1–17. In *Crime and the Internet,* edited by D. S. Wall. New York: Routledge.

Yar, Majid. 2005. "The Novelty of 'Cybercrime': An Assessment in Light of Routine Activity Theory." *European Journal of Criminology* 2(4):407–427.

Zhang, Lening, John W. Welte, and William F. Wiecxorek. 2001. "Deviant Lifestyle and Crime Victimization." *Journal of Criminal Justice* 29:133–143.

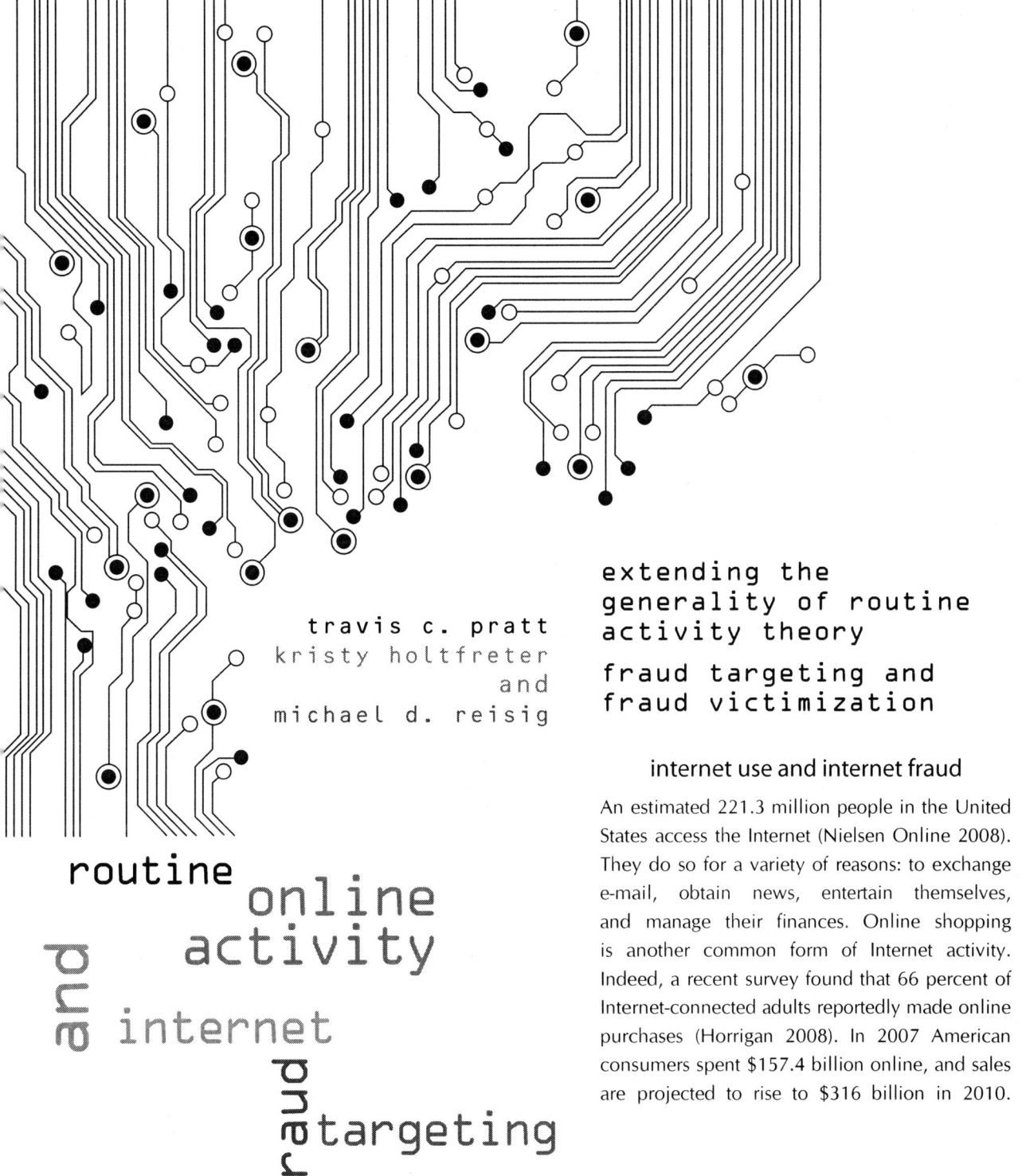

travis c. pratt
kristy holtfreter
and
michael d. reisig

extending the
generality of routine
activity theory

fraud targeting and
fraud victimization

### internet use and internet fraud

An estimated 221.3 million people in the United States access the Internet (Nielsen Online 2008). They do so for a variety of reasons: to exchange e-mail, obtain news, entertain themselves, and manage their finances. Online shopping is another common form of Internet activity. Indeed, a recent survey found that 66 percent of Internet-connected adults reportedly made online purchases (Horrigan 2008). In 2007 American consumers spent $157.4 billion online, and sales are projected to rise to $316 billion in 2010.

routine online activity and internet fraud targeting

Online shopping has become so prevalent that this form of spending now accounts for 12 percent of total retail sales (U.S. Census Bureau 2008).

Despite the growth in e-commerce, studies show that a majority of online consumers believe the risks associated with Internet use are far from benign. For example, a recent IBM-sponsored survey found that approximately 70 percent of Internet users reported that they believe they are more likely to be the victim of a cybercrime than a physical crime (Criminal Law Reporter 2006). What is more, a large number of Internet users perceive the risks associated with using their credit card to make an online purchase to outweigh the benefits (i.e., convenience; Bhatnagar, Misra, and Rao 2000; Horrigan 2008).

Chief among consumers' concerns about online victimization is theft, especially credit card theft—a fear that may not be unfounded (Reisig, Pratt, and Holtfreter 2009). As stated previously, nearly one third of the adult population in the United States reports that they have been targeted by perpetrators of consumer fraud, with nearly one in nine people reporting having been victimized in the past year (Anderson 2004). Extrapolating this percentage to the 221 million Internet users would translate into nearly 25 million fraud victims—roughly 18 times the number of murder, rape, armed robbery, and aggravated assault victims combined (U.S. Department of Justice 2008). Given the financial importance of fraud victimization and its relevance to such a large portion of the online population, it is important to understand the nature of this form of criminal victimization.

\* \* \*

## routine activity theory and fraud targeting

The diversity of methods used by fraud perpetrators to make contact with potential victims has made the prediction of fraud targeting a difficult undertaking. Despite theoretical advances, much of the empirical literature in criminology has focused solely on identifying sociodemographic correlates of fraud targeting and victimization (e.g., age, gender, marital status, and socioeconomic status).[1] As such, with regard to routine online activities, some consistent sociodemographic differences between online shoppers and nonshoppers have been observed. Online shoppers tend to be relatively well educated and occupy higher income brackets (Farag et al. 2006; Ratchford, Talukadar, and Lee 2001; Soopramanien and Robertson 2007; Stranahan and Kosiel 2007; Swinyard and Smith 2003). Several studies also show that males are more likely to make purchases online (Chang and Samuel 2004; Farag et al. 2006; Korgaonkar and Wolin 2002; Soopramanien and Robertson 2007). Research findings regarding the differential use of online shopping across age and racial/ethnic groups are far less conclusive (Chang and Samuel 2004; Sorce, Perotti, and Widrick 2005; Stranahan and Kosiel 2007). In addition, studies that focus on time spent online, generally speaking, reveal differential patterns of Internet usage across social groups. For example, research shows that higher income and better educated Internet users spend more time online (Korgaonkar and Wolin 1999), as do men (Fallows 2005; Nielsen Online 2008).

Although this research is certainly useful for marketing purposes, such a focus is problematic since empirical evidence suggests that fraud perpetrators target consumers from all backgrounds (Holtfreter et al. 2006) and that fraud victimization cannot be consistently predicted with only sociodemographic

---

1 Noteworthy exceptions include recent studies on identity theft, a form of fraud victimization that may or may not involve technology (McNally and Newman 2008). For example, Copes and Vieraitis's (2008) interviews of 59 convicted identity thieves indicated that offenders perceived little risks of being apprehended. Additionally, Pontell, Brown, and Tosouni's (2008) analysis of identity theft complaint data revealed important details about the nature of victim–offender relationships: namely, the majority of victims had some personal connection to the offender. Although neither of these studies included measures of routine online activities, they have important implications for situational crime prevention, confirming that Clarke's (1997) opportunity-reducing strategies can be applied to a variety of fraud victimization contexts.

variables (Holtfreter et al. 2008; Titus, Heinzelmann, and Boyle 1995). A theoretical understanding of fraud targeting/victimization is therefore necessary if we are to fully understand the nature of crime in this context. In this study we therefore draw upon theoretical discussions regarding criminal victimization in general, as well as the fraud-specific literature rooted in routine activity theory and situational crime prevention (Newman and Clarke 2003).

Cohen and Felson (1979) argued that structural changes in aggregate routines can influence the convergence in time and space of motivated offenders and suitable targets in the absence of capable guardians. The theory, which assumes a constant supply of motivated offenders, focuses on the behaviors, activities, and situational contexts that place would-be targets at risk for victimization. In the study of street crime victimization, routine activity theory has informed public policy, particularly with the development of situational crime prevention strategies intended to increase guardianship (Clarke 1995). Early applications of this model focused on revealing "profiles" of likely victims of violence, such as young, minority males. Taking this logic a step further, Clarke (1999) broadened our understanding of nonviolent crime targeting on "hot" products (i.e., those most likely to be selected by thieves).

Recent studies of street crime have focused on theoretically based indicators of routines and lifestyles that may increase victimization risk for certain individuals. In the street crime context, research by Stewart, Schreck, and colleagues has revealed that deviant lifestyles involving various illegal behaviors (e.g., prostitution and drug use) increase exposure to motivated offenders, thereby elevating the odds of violent victimization (see e.g., Schreck and Fisher 2004; Schreck, Stewart, and Fisher 2006; Schreck, Wright, and Miller 2002; Stewart, Elifson, and Sterk 2004). The applicability of traditional indicators of routine activities (e.g., deviant lifestyles) has been called into question in the consumer fraud context, however, since individuals are typically targeted by fraudsters during the course of routine, nondeviant behaviors and day-to-day lifestyle choices (Holtfreter et al. 2008). Put simply, the types of routine behaviors that could be considered "risky" shift when considering fraud targeting (i.e., from deviant to nondeviant behaviors), and such behaviors may be specific to the context under consideration (e.g., cyberspace).

Accordingly, Cohen and Felson (1979:591) noted long ago that "technological advances designed for legitimate purposes" can influence the nature of criminal victimization. Among these potential changes, Cohen and Felson (1979:599) pointed to "changes in the sales of consumer goods" as a contributing factor to increased criminal opportunities. The penetration of the Internet into consumer lifestyles represents a key structural change that is relevant to a routine activity explanation of fraud targeting. Approximately 88 percent of American households have online access (Parks Associates 2008). This is a considerable increase from U.S. census estimates of 50 percent in 2001 and 18 percent in 1997 (Day, Janus, and Davis 2005). Evidence suggests that consumers are increasingly willing to buy online, but Internet use (e.g., purchasing from Web sites and time spent online) varies across consumers from different walks of life. Direct-to-consumer marketing communication channels such as the Internet provide cost- and time-efficient options, but may create unguarded exposure to fraudsters (Lin 2006). As Cohen and Felson (1979) predicted, fraudsters feed upon the legal activities (e.g., modes of commerce reflecting unguarded exposure) of everyday life to target potential victims (Langenderfer and Shimp 2001; Shover, Coffey, and Hobbs 2003; Shover, Coffey, and Sanders 2004).

As Newman and Clarke (2003:78) argue, the Internet, and online shopping in particular, presents multiple opportunities for fraud targeting and victimization. In fact, while tangible items (e.g., electronics) were once "hot products," the transformations associated with e-commerce crime, particularly information storage and transmission, has created very lucrative targets. Indeed, because retailer databases containing attractive consumer information (e.g., names, addresses, passwords, credit/debit card and/or bank account details) fit the characteristics Clarke (1999) refers to as C.R.A.V.E.D., they have become a coveted target for cyber fraudsters (Newman and Clarke 2003). Although routine activity theory predicts that more time spent away from home will increase victimization risk in other contexts (e.g., burglary of an unguarded residence), this proposition is less applicable to Internet fraud targeting, given that consumers often engage in routine online activities (e.g., shopping on Web sites) while in the safe confines of their own homes. What this means is that in the fraud victimization context, staying home and spending time (and money) online exposes potential targets for victimization.[2]

## current focus

The current study addresses two issues. First, guided by prior marketing and consumer research, we investigate the extent to which sociodemographic characteristics explain routine online activities, such as purchasing goods from an Internet Web site. Second, we assess whether routine online activities significantly increase the odds of Internet fraud targeting, net of consumer attributes (e.g., age, race, and income). Routine activity theory suggests that online activities reflect greater unguarded exposure to potential motivated offenders. Because we are able to directly measure online activities, we hypothesize that the effects of consumer attributes on Internet fraud targeting are, comparatively speaking, far less salient. We carry out our objectives using data from a telephone survey of adult consumers conducted in the state of Florida.

## method

### participants

Data for this study come from a telephone survey of 1,000 adults in the state of Florida. The survey was conducted over a five-week period, from December 21, 2004 to January 25, 2005. The sample was generated using the Mitofski-Waksberg procedure, which is a form of random digit dialing commonly used to produce equal probability samples of households with working telephones (see Waksberg 1978 for details). The surveys were administered by trained interviewers employed by a reputable private research firm.[3] Several steps were taken to ensure that reasonable response and completion rates were achieved.[4] The response rate was 43.6 percent.[5] Cases of unknown eligibility (e.g., busy signals) and

---

2   A key distinction is that the concept of "place" in offline crime typically refers to a small area, such as a street (see Eck and Weisburd 1995). In a street crime context, offenders may select victims based on situational characteristics of the place (e.g., proximity to a suitable target). In comparison, the Internet is a virtual place, not bound by the geographical and spatial constraints inherent in street crime (Wall 2007a; Yar 2006). Online, the problem of physical proximity to suitable targets is neutralized (Newman and Clarke 2003). This unique context therefore provides a vast array of criminal opportunities for motivated offenders.

3   Of the completed interviews, 10 percent were selected randomly and called back by supervisors and asked verification questions. Doing so helped minimize interviewer error.

4   Among the steps taken to ensure data quality included contacting refusals 10 days after the initial contact to encourage participation, using a 10-callback rule prior to substituting records of unknown eligibility, and using the Data-Tel predictive dialer to pass screened calls on to an operator to determine the appropriate disposition code or action.

5   The response rate for this project compares favorably to studies assessing response rates for telephone interviews. A recent analysis of 80 telephone surveys using random digit dialing conducted over a five-year period (from 2000 to 2004) by the University of Florida's Survey Research Center revealed a modal response rate of 25 percent (McCarty et al. 2006). Less than optimal response rates for telephone surveys have become increasingly common nationwide over the past 25 years (Curtin, Presser, and Singer, 2005). Available evidence demonstrates, however, that traditional telephone survey methodologies that achieve modest response rates (e.g., 27 percent) yield samples that are equally representative in terms of demographic and lifestyle characteristics when compared to more rigorous telephone survey strategies (e.g., use of

known ineligibility (e.g., fax machines) were not included in the response rate (American Association for Public Opinion Research 2004). The completion rate was 95 percent for those persons beginning the survey.[6] Each survey took approximately 12 minutes to administer. After imputing missing responses, we had complete information for 922 participants.[7]

When compared to population estimates from the 2000 decennial census, the sample used in the present study approximates the target population across several demographic variables. Nevertheless, individuals who received bachelor's and graduate/professional degrees (35.9 percent in the sample compared to 22.4 percent in the population) and people 65 years and older (43 percent in the sample compared to 23.6 percent in the population) are overrepresented in the sample. The sample consists of a smaller proportion of individuals who have never married (13.4 percent in the sample compared to 23.8 percent in the population) and people between the ages of 20 and 34 years (11.4 percent in the sample compared to 25.2 percent in the population) than reported in the 2000 census.[8] Despite these differences, the sample used in the present study is representative of the adult population in the state of Florida along several demographic characteristics (e.g., annual household income, middle age groups, high school graduates, and those with some college).[9]

## dependent variable

*Internet fraud targeting.* A series of questions were used to determine whether participants were targeted by fraud perpetrators via the Internet. First, survey respondents were asked whether "there ever was a time you felt you were the subject of a consumer fraud attempt?" Next, participants were asked when the attempt took place. Because memory decay bias was a concern, cases that occurred within one year of the interview were selected. Participants who reported that they had been targeted within the past year were read a list of 13 items describing common fraud schemes (e.g., "an investment deal that turned out to be phony" and "agreed to buy a product or service for a certain price but was later charged a lot more"). An open-ended response was administered to respondents who did not select an item from the list. Open-ended responses were carefully screened to ensure that these experiences actually reflected consumer fraud (see Titus 2001). Using these 16 survey items, we determined that 15.18 percent of participants were recent targets of consumer fraud. Finally, respondents were asked how they first learned about the fraud attempt. Three of the options included in the survey were Internet related: (1) through an Internet auction site, (2) from an Internet Web site (other than an auction site), and (3) from an email. Targeting experiences that initially took place via these three online avenues

financial incentives to increase participation and sending pre-interview letters to selected participants) that yield higher response rates (e.g., 51 percent; Pew Research Center 2004).

6    The completion rate achieved in this study is higher than the national average (see Weisberg, Krosnick, and Bowen 1989).

7    Missing survey data were handled using the similar response pattern imputation (SRPI) available in PRELIS version 2.30 (Joreskog and Sorbom 1996). Extant research has demonstrated that SRPI is a more reliable data imputation procedure than alternative methods, such as mean imputation and listwise deletion (Gmel 2001).

8    Landline-only telephone surveys have been found to generate samples that do not accurately represent young adults. One explanation for this outcome is that young adults are more likely to rely on cell phones and computers for their telecommunications needs. Older adults tend to rely more on landline telephones. A recent study that compared landline-only samples to mixed samples (i.e., both landline and cell-only sampling frames) produced population estimates nearly identical to those observed using only a landline sample (Keeter et al. 2007).

9    Despite the response rate and the overrepresentation of older, white, married, and better-educated respondents, which may indicate that the probability of selection differed across various groups of potential respondents, we did not employ sample weights in the regression analyses. While sample weights are useful for providing accurate univariate descriptions of variables, they are inappropriate in a multivariate context because they may bias the parameter estimates either upward or downward in the direction of the sample weights themselves rather than the values of the variables being weighted (see, e.g., Hanushek and Jackson 1977; Tabachnick and Fidell 2001).

were selected and included in the outcome measure. Approximately 3 percent of the sample reported that they were targeted by perpetrators of consumer fraud via the Internet during the year leading up to the survey. Internet fraud targeting is a binary variable (1 = yes, 0 = no).

## independent variables

*Routine online activity.* Two key variables of interest were used to measure respondents' routine online activity. For the first variable, hours spent online, participants were first administered a screening question. Specifically, respondents were asked whether they "ever go online to access to Internet or World Wide Web or send and receive email?" If they responded "yes," they were then asked "how many hours each week would you say you spend on the Internet?" The mean number of hours spent online each week was 6.51 *(SD* = 11.24), comparable to the 8 hours per week reported in a national survey (Harris Poll 2005). The second variable, Internet Web site purchase, captured whether participants had purchased something from an Internet Web site during the year prior to the survey (1 = yes, 0 = no). Nearly 45 percent of respondents indicated that they had recently made such a purchase.

*Personal characteristics.* Nine sociodemographic variables were included in the multivariate analyses: age (respondent's age in years), education (1 = some grade school, 2 = some high school, 3 = high school graduate [or equivalency], 4 = technical or vocational school, 5 = some college, 6 = college graduate, and 7 = graduate/professional degree), income (1 = less than $20,000, 2 = $20,000 to $40,000, 3 = $40,001 to $60,000, 4 = $60,001 to $80,000, 5 = $80,001 to $100,000, and 6 = more than $100,000), retired (1 = yes), homeowner (1 = yes), male (1 = yes), married (1 = yes), black (1 = yes), and Latino (1 = yes). Descriptive statistics for the variables used in the current study are provided in Table 1.

\* \* \*

Table 1.   Descriptive Statistics (*N* = 922)

| Variables | *M* | *SD* |
|---|---|---|
| Internet fraud targeting (1 = targeted online in the past year, 0 = otherwise) | 0.03 | 0.16 |
| Hours spent online (number of hours spent online each week) | 6.51 | 11.24 |
| Internet Web site purchase (1 = purchased something online in the past year, 0 = otherwise) | 0.45 | 0.50 |
| Age (respondents' age in years) | 57.38 | 18.43 |
| Education (1 = some grade school to 7 = graduate or professional degree) | 4.63 | 1.56 |
| Income (1 = less than $20,000 to 6 = $100,000 or more) | 3.13 | 1.51 |
| Retired (1 = retired respondent, 0 = otherwise) | 0.43 | 0.50 |
| Homeowner (1 = respondent owns home, 0 = otherwise) | 0.83 | 0.37 |
| Male (1 = male respondent, 0 = female respondent) | 0.45 | 0.50 |
| Married (1 = married respondent, 0 = otherwise) | 0.59 | 0.49 |
| Black (1 = African-American respondent, 0 = otherwise) | 0.09 | 0.29 |
| Latino (1 = Latino respondent, 0 = otherwise) | 0.09 | 0.29 |

To determine whether routine online activity and personal attributes are empirically linked to Internet fraud targeting, three logistic regression models are presented in Table 3. Model 1 features the nine sociodemographic variables used in Table 2. Only two variables—age and education—are associated with Internet fraud targeting. Younger and more educated individuals are significantly more likely to be targets of consumer fraud via the Internet. In model 2, Internet fraud targeting was regressed onto the two routine online activity variables. Note that we apply a square-root transformation to the hours spent online variable to reduce the skew that resulted from a few individuals who reported that they spend a considerable amount of time online each week ($M = 2.27$, $SD = 1.54$).[10] When compared to model 1, model 2 provides a good fit to the data as indicated by McFadden's $R^2$. Both of the covariates included in the logistic regression equation were statistically significant. Making a purchase from a Web site has a substantial effect on Internet fraud targeting. More specifically, buying something from a Web site increases the odds of Internet fraud targeting by 377 percent. Thus far, the results from the first two models in Table 3 indicate that routine online activity is more important in explaining Internet fraud targeting relative to consumer attributes.

A saturated model that included both personal characteristics and routine online activity variables is featured on the right-hand side of Table 3.[11] The effects of age and education failed to reach statistical significance ($p = .13$ and $.21$, respectively) when the two routine online activity variables were included in the model, suggesting that the effect of education and age on Internet fraud targeting is fully explained by the number of hours consumers spend online and whether they make purchases from Internet Web sites. The effect of making online purchases on Internet fraud targeting persisted in model 3. Under this model specification, those who make purchases from Web sites increase the odds that they will be targeted by cyber-fraudsters by 290 percent. The effect of hours spent online on Internet fraud targeting was also positive and statistically significant ($p < .05$, one-tailed test).

## discussion

Internet fraud, like victimization for many other types of crime, affects a large portion of the population. Furthermore, it is reasonable to expect fraud victimization rates to continue to increase as opportunities for online activity (both legal and illegal) expand and as a greater portion of the population feels comfortable performing all manner of tasks online. Indeed, rates of Internet use in general have been increasing steadily over the years, and online economic activity has increased accordingly (U.S. Census Bureau 2008; U.S. Department of Commerce 2008). Given the capacity of Internet fraud to affect so many lives, the purpose of the present study was to gain a better theoretical and empirical understanding of this form of criminal victimization—in particular, to uncover the key factors that predict fraud targeting online.

First, the previous empirical work on fraud targeting, which has relied almost exclusively on correlating respondents' sociodemographic characteristics with various dimensions of experiences with fraudsters (see Holtfreter et al. 2008), has failed to fully capture the nature of this form of criminal victimization. In short, when it comes to understanding why certain people are targeted by fraud perpetrators, it is simply not enough to focus on demographics while ignoring criminologically informed

---

10  Prior to reexpressing the distribution, a constant term ($+1$) was added to the scores to eliminate zero values.

11  The variance inflation factors (VIF) scores for model 3 are below 2.5, and none of the condition indices exceed 20. These diagnostics confirm that harmful collinearity is not cause for concern.

Table 2.  Internet Fraud Targeting Logistic Regression Models (N — 922)

| | Model 1 | | | | Model 2 | | | | Model 3 | | | |
|---|---|---|---|---|---|---|---|---|---|---|---|---|
| Variables | b | SE | exp(b) | z Test | b | SE | exp(b) | z Test | b | SE | exp(b) | z Test |
| Constant | -3.94 | 1.31 | — | -3.01** | -5.21 | 0.54 | — | -9.73** | -4.91 | 1.48 | — | -3.31** |
| Hours spent online[3] | — | — | — | | 0.21 | 0.10 | 1.24 | 2.19* | 0.19 | 0.10 | 1.21 | 1.86+ |
| Internet Web site purchase | — | — | — | | 1.56 | 0.58 | 4.77 | 2.71** | 1.36 | 0.66 | 3.90 | 2.06* |
| Age | -0.04 | 0.02 | 0.96 | -2.13* | — | — | — | | -0.03 | 0.02 | 0.97 | -1.53 |
| Education | 0.33 | 0.15 | 1.39 | 2.21* | — | — | — | | 0.19 | 0.15 | 1.20 | 1.26 |
| Income | 0.02 | 0.17 | 1.02 | 0.11 | — | — | — | | -0.05 | 0.18 | 0.95 | 0.30 |
| Retired | 0.37 | 0.84 | 1.44 | 0.44 | — | — | — | | 0.54 | 0.75 | 1.71 | 0.72 |
| Homeowner | 0.16 | 0.63 | 1.18 | 0.26 | — | — | — | | 0.02 | 0.63 | 1.02 | 0.04 |
| Male | 0.56 | 0.42 | 1.75 | 1.33 | — | — | — | | 0.51 | 0.44 | 1.66 | 1.16 |
| Married | 0.20 | 0.43 | 1.23 | 0.47 | — | — | — | | 0.17 | 0.45 | 1.19 | 0.38 |
| Black | 0.26 | 0.69 | 1.30 | 0.38 | — | — | — | | 0.49 | 0.70 | 1.62 | 0.69 |
| Latino | -0.49 | 0.70 | 0.61 | -0.70 | — | — | — | | -0.59 | 0.73 | 0.56 | 0.80 |
| | Model $X^2$ = 45.05** | | | | Model $X^2$ = 17.23** | | | | Model $X^2$ = 51.27** | | | |
| | McFadden's $R^2$ = .06 | | | | McFadden's $R^2$ = .09 | | | | McFadden's $R^2$ = .11 | | | |

indicators of the routine online activities that put people at risk for victimization. To be sure, the effects of all of our measured sociodemographic characteristics on fraud targeting were fully mediated by the variables measuring respondents' routine online activities. Assumptions that rely on inferences about the relationships between demographic characteristics and fraud targeting are therefore fundamentally misplaced. Instead, understanding the problem of fraud targeting requires an appreciation of how online exposure shapes the opportunity structure for victimization in this context.

Second, and relatedly, routine activity theory and situational crime prevention provide an excellent framework for informing the study of this area of crime targeting. The routine activity perspective (Cohen and Felson 1979; Cohen, Kluegel, and Land 1981; see also Hindelang, Gottfredson, and Garafolo 1978) has been a staple of the criminal victimization literature in general for nearly three decades now (Pratt and Cullen 2005). It has been applied most often to the explanation of violent victimization (Belknap 1987; Dugan and Apel 2005; Dugan, Nagin, and Rosenfeld 2003; Gottfredson 1981; Jensen and Brownfield 1986; Kennedy and Forde 1990; Messner and Tardiff 1987; Miethe and Meier 1994; Mitchell and Finkelhor 2001; Rodgers and Roberts 1995; Sampson 1987; Sampson and Lauritsen 1990; Sampson and Wooldredge 1987).

\* \* \*

## funding

The authors disclosed receipt of the following financial support for the research and/or authorship of this article:

The authors thank the State of Florida, Office of the Attorney General, for their financial support of this study.

## references

American Association for Public Opinion Research. 2004. *Standard Definitions: Final Dispositions of Case Codes and Outcome Rates for Surveys.* Ann Arbor, MI: Author.

Anderson, Keith B. 2004. *Consumer Fraud in the United States: An FTC Survey.* Washington, DC: Federal Trade Commission.

Belknap, Joanne. 1987. "Routine Activity Theory and the Risk of Rape: Analyzing Ten Years of National Crime Survey Data." *Criminal Justice Policy Review* 2:337–56.

Belsley, David A., Edwin Kuh, and Roy E. Welsch. 1980. *Regression Diagnostics.* New York: John Wiley.

Berg, Sara. 2008. "Preventing Identity Theft through Information Technology." Pp. 151–67 in *Perspectives on Identity Theft,* edited by M. M. McNally and G. R. Newman. Monsey, NY: Criminal Justice Press.

Bhatnagar, Amit, Sanjog Misra, and H. Raghav Rao. 2000. "On Risk, Convenience, and Internet Shopping Behavior: Why Some Consumers Are Online Shoppers While Others Are Not." *Communications of the Association for Computing Machinery* 33:98–105.

Budd, Tracey. 1999. *Burglary of Domestic Dwellings: Findings from the British Crime Survey.* London: Home Office Statistical Bulletin.

Burns, Ronald G., Keith H. Whitworth, and Carol Y. Thompson. 2004. "Assessing Law Enforcement Preparedness to Address Internet Fraud." *Journal of Criminal Justice* 32:477–93.

Chang, Joshua and Nicholas Samuel. 2004. "Internet Shopper Demographics and Buying Behavior in Australia." *Journal of American Academy of Business* 5:171–76.

Clarke, Ronald V. 1995. "Situational Crime Prevention." Pp. 91–150 in *Building a Safer Society: Strategic Approaches to Crime Prevention,* edited by M. Tonry and D. P. Farrington. Chicago: University of Chicago Press.

Clarke, Ronald V. 1997. *Situational Crime Prevention: Successful Case Studies.* 2nd ed. Albany, NY: Harrow & Heston.

Clarke, RonaldV. 1999. *Hot Products: Understanding, Anticipating, and Reducing Demand for Stolen Goods* (Police Research Series, Paper 112). London: Home Office.

Clarke, Ronald V. and David Weisburd. 1994. "Diffusion of Crime Control Benefits: Observations on the Reverse of Displacement." Pp. 165–83 in *Crime Prevention Studies.* Vol. 2, edited by R. V. Clarke. Monsey, NY: Criminal Justice Press.

Cohen, Lawrence E. and Marcus Felson. 1979. "Social Change and Crime Rate Trends: A Routine Activity Approach." *American Sociological Review* 52:170–83.

Cohen, Lawrence E., Marcus Felson, and Kenneth C. Land. 1980. "Property Crime Rates in the United States: A Macrodynamic Analysis, 1947–1977, with Ex Ante Forecasts for the Mid-1980s." *American Journal of Sociology* 86:90–117.

Cohen, Lawrence E., James R. Kluegel, and Kenneth C. Land. 1981. "Social Inequality and Predatory Criminal Victimization: An Exposition and Test of a Formal Theory." *American Sociological Review* 46:505–24.

Copes, Heath and Lynne Vieraitis. 2008. "The Risks, Rewards, and Strategies of Stealing Identities." Pp. 87–110 in *Perspectives on Identity Theft. Crime Prevention Studies.* Vol. 23, edited by M. McNally and G. R. Newman. Monsey, NY: Criminal Justice Press.

Criminal Law Reporter. 2006. "More Americans Fear Cybercrime than Physical Crime, According to IBM Study." *Criminal Law Reporter* 78:725.

Curtin, Richard, Stanley Presser, and Eleanor Singer. 2005. "Changes in Telephone Survey Nonresponse over the Past Quarter Century." *Public Opinion Quarterly* 69:87–98.

Day, Jennifer C., Alex Janus, and Jessica Davis. 2005. *Computer and Internet Use in the United States.* Washington, DC: U.S. Census Bureau.

Dugan, Laura and Robert Apel. 2005. "The Differential Risk of Retaliation by Relational Distance: A More General Model of Violent Victimization." *Criminology* 43:697–728.

Dugan, Laura, Daniel S. Nagin, and Richard Rosenfeld. 2003. "Exposure Reduction or Retaliation? The Effects of Domestic Violence Resources on Intimate-Partner Homicide." *Law and Society Review* 37:169–98.

Eck, John E. and David Weisburd. 1995. "Crime Places in Crime Theory." Pp. 1–33 in *Crime and Place, Crime Prevention Studies.* Vol. 4, edited by J. E. Eck and D. Weisburd. Monsey, NY: Criminal Justice Press.

Fallows, Deborah. 2005. *How Women and Men Use the Internet.* Washington, DC: Pew Internet and American Life Project.

Farag, Sendg, Jesse Weltevreden, Ton Van Rietbergen, Marty Dijst, and Frank Van Ort. 2006. "E-Shopping in the Netherlands: Does Geography Matter?" *Environment and Planning B: Planning and Design* 33:59–74.

Fattah, Ezzat. 1993. "The Rational Choice/Opportunity Perspectives as a Vehicle for Integrating Criminological and Victimological Theories." Pp. 225–58 in *Routine Activity and Rational Choice,* edited by R. Clarke and M. Felson. New York: Transaction.

Federal Bureau of Investigation. 2001. Press release: Internet fraud investigation "operation cyber loss." Retrieved http://www.fbi.gov/pressrel/pressrel01/ifcc052301.htm.

Federal Trade Commission. 2006. *Consumer Fraud and Identity Theft Complaint Data*. Washington, DC: Author.

Felson, Marcus. 1986. "Linking Criminal Choices, Routine Activities, Informal Social Control, and Criminal Outcomes." Pp. 119–28 in *The Reasoning Criminal: Rational Choice Perspective on Offending,* edited by D. B. Cornish and R. V. Clarke. New York/Berlin: Springer-Verlag.

Ferraro, Monique Mattei, Eoghan Casey, and Michael McGrath. 2004. *Investigating Child Exploitation and Pornography*. San Diego, CA: Academic Press.

Finkelhor, David, Kimberly J. Mitchell, and Janis Wolak. 2000. *Online Victimization: A Report on the Nation's Youth*. Washington DC: Office of Juvenile Justice and Delinquency Prevention.

Fletcher, Nigel. 2007. "Challenges for Regulating Fraud in Cyberspace." *Journal of Financial Crime* 14:190–207.

Fox, John. 1991. *Regression Diagnostics*. Newbury Park, CA: Sage.

Gardner, William, Edward Mulvey, and Esther Shaw. 1995. "Regression Analysis of Counts and Rates: Poisson, Overdispersed Poisson, and Negative Binomial Models." *Psychological Bulletin* 118:392–404.

Gelber, Alexandra. 2006. "Federal Jurisdiction in Child Pornography Cases." *United States Attorney's Bulletin* 54(7):3–7.

Gmel, Gerhard. 2001. "Imputation of Missing Values in the Case of Multiple Item Instrument Measuring Alcohol Consumption." *Statistics in Medicine* 20:2369–81.

Gottfredson, Michael R. 1981. "On the Etiology of Criminal Victimization." *Journal of Criminal Law and Criminology* 72:714–26.

Grabowsky, Peter N. and Russell G. Smith. 1998. *Crime in the Digital Age: Controlling Telecommunications and Cyberspace Illegalities*. New Brunswick, NJ: Transaction Publishers.

Grazioli, Stefano and Sirkka L. Jarvenpaa. 2001. "Deceived: Under Target Online." *Communications of the ACM* 46:196–205.

Hanushek, Eric A. and John E. Jackson. 1977. *Statistical Methods for Social Scientists*. San Diego, CA: Academic Press.

Harris Poll. 2005. "Almost Three-Quarters of All American Adults Go Online. Harris Interactive Poll." Retrieved March 5, 2010 (http://www.harrisinteractive.com/harris_poll/index.asp?PID=569).

Hesseling, Rene B. P. 1995. "Displacement: A Review of the Literature." Pp. 197–230 in *Crime Prevention Studies*. Vol. 3, edited by R. V. Clarke. Monsey, NY: Criminal Justice Press.

Hindelang, Michael J., Michael R. Gottfredson, and James Garafolo. 1978. *Victims of Personal Crime*. Cambridge, MA: Ballinger.

Holtfreter, Kristy, Michael D. Reisig, and Thomas G. Blomberg. 2006. "Consumer Fraud Victimization in Florida: An Empirical Study." *St. Thomas Law Review* 18:761–89.

Holtfreter, Kristy, Michael D. Reisig, and Travis C. Pratt. 2008. "Low Self-control, Routine Activities, and Fraud Victimization." *Criminology* 46:189–220.

Holtfreter, Kristy, Michael D. Reisig, Nicole Leeper Piquero, and Alex R. Piquero. 2010. "Low Self-Control and Fraud: Offending, Victimization, and Their Overlap." *Criminal Justice and Behavior* 37:188–203.

Horrigan, John B. (2008). *Online Shopping*. Washington, DC: Pew Internet & American Life Project.

Internet Crime Complaint Center. 2006. *Internet Crime Report*. Washington, DC: The National White Collar Crime Center and the Federal Bureau of Investigation.

Jensen, Gary F. and David Brownfield. 1986. "Gender, Lifestyles, and Victimization: Beyond Routine Activity." *Violence and Victims* 1:85–99.

Johnson, Shane D., Wim Bernasco, Kate Bowers, Henk Elffers, Jerry Ratcliffe, George Rengert, and Michael Townsley. 2007. "Space-time Patterns of Risk: A Cross-national Assessment of Residential Burglary Victimization." *Journal of Quantitative Criminology* 23:201–19.

Jöreskog, Karl G. and Dag Sorbom. 1996. *PRELIS 2: User's Reference Guide.* Chicago: Scientific Software International.

Keeter, Scott, Courtney Kennedy, April Clark, Trevor Tompson, and Mike Mokrzycki. 2007. "What's Missing from National Landline RDD Surveys? The Impact of the Growing Cell-only Population." *Public Opinion Quarterly* 71:772–92.

Kennedy, Leslie W. and David R. Forde. 1990. "Routine Activities and Crime: An Analysis of Victimization in Canada." *Criminology* 28:137–52.

Korgaonkar, Pradeep K. and Lori D. Wolin. 1999. "A Multivariate Analysis of Web Usage." *Journal of Advertising Research* 39:53–68.

Korgaonkar, Pradeep and Lori D. Wolin. 2002. "Web Usage, Advertising, and Shopping: Relationship Patterns." *Internet Research* 12:191–204.

Land, Kenneth C., Patricia McCall, and Daniel S. Nagin. 1996. "A Comparison of Poisson, Negative Binomial, and Semiparametric Mixed Poisson Regression Models." *Sociological Methods and Research* 24:387–442.

Langenderfer, Jeff and Terrance A. Shimp. 2001. "Consumer Vulnerability to Scams, Swindles, and Fraud: A New Theory of Visceral Influences on Persuasion." *Psychology and Marketing* 18:763–83.

Lauritsen, Janet L. 2001. "The Social Ecology of Violent Victimization: Individual and Contextual Effects in the NCVS." *Journal of Quantitative Criminology* 17:3–32.

Levi, Michael. 1998. "Organizing Plastic Fraud: Enterprise Criminals and the Sidestepping of Fraud Prevention." *The Howard Journal* 37:423–38.

Levi, Michael and David S. Wall. 2004. "Technologies, Security, and Privacy in the Post-9/11 European Information Society." *Journal of Law and Society* 31: 194–220.

Licht, Mark H. 1995. "Multiple Regression and Correlation." Pp. 19–64 in *Reading and Understanding Multivariate Statistics,* edited by L. Grimm and P. Yarnold. Washington, DC: American Psychological Association.

Lin, Carolyn A. 2006. "Interactive Media Technology and Electronic Shopping." Pp. 203–22 in *Communication Technology and Social Change: Theory and Implications,* edited by C. A. Lin and D. J. Atkin. New York: Routledge.

Long, J. Scott and Jeremy Freese. 2006. *Regression Models for Categorical Dependent Variables Using Stata.* 2nd ed. College Station, TX: Stata Press.

McCarty, Christopher, Mark House, Jeffrey Harman, and Scott Richards. 2006. "Effort in Phone Survey Response Rates: The Effects of Vendor and Client-controlled Factors." *Field Methods* 18:172–88.

McNally, Megan M. and Graeme R. Newman. 2008. *Perspectives on Identity Theft. Crime Prevention Studies.* Vol. 23. Monsey, NY: Criminal Justice Press.

Messner, Steven F. and Kenneth Tardiff. 1987. "The Social Ecology of Urban Homicide: An Application of the 'Routine Activities' Approach." *Criminology* 23:241–67.

Miethe, Terance and Robert F. Meier. 1994. *Crime and Its Social Context: Toward an Integrated Theory of Offenders, Victims, and Situations.* Albany: State University of New York Press.

Mitchell, Kimberly J. and David Finkelhor. 2001. "Risk of Crime Victimization Among Youth Exposed to Domestic Violence." *Journal of Interpersonal Violence* 16:944–64.

Moore, Elizabeth and Michael Mills. 1990. "The Neglected Victims and Unexamined Costs of White-collar Crime." *Crime and Delinquency* 36:408–18.

Newman, Graeme R. 2008. "Identity Theft and Opportunity." Pp. 9–31 in *Perspectives on Identity Theft. Crime Prevention Studies*. Vol. 23, edited by M. M. McNally and G. R. Newman. Monsey, NY: Criminal Justice Press.

Newman, Graeme R. and Ronald V. Clarke. 2003. *Superhighway Robbery: Preventing E-Commerce Crime*. Devon, UK: Willan Publishing.

Nielsen Online. 2008. *Nielsen Online Reports Topline U.S. data for March 2008*. New York: Nielsen Company.

Parks Associates. 2008. *Only One in Five Households Has Never Used E-Mail*. Dallas, TX: Parks Associates.

Pew Research Center. 2004. *Survey Experiment Shows Polls Face Growing Resistance, but Still Representative*. Washington, DC: Pew Research Center.

Piquero, Alex R., John MacDonald, Adam Dobrin, Leah E. Daigle, and Francis T. Cullen. 2005. "Self-control, Violent Offending, and Homicide Victimization: Assessing the General Theory of Crime." *Journal of Quantitative Criminology* 21:55–71.

Pontell, Henry N., Gregory C. Brown, and Anastasia Tosouni. 2008. "Stolen Identities: A Victim Survey." Pp. 57–85 in *Perspectives on Identity Theft. Crime Prevention Studies*. Vol. 23, edited by M. M. McNally and G. R. Newman. Monsey, NY: Criminal Justice Press.

Pratt, Travis C. 2009. *Addicted to Incarceration: Corrections Policy and the Politics of Misinformation in the United States*. Thousand Oaks, CA: Sage.

Pratt, Travis C. and Francis T. Cullen. 2005. "Assessing Macro-level Predictors and Theories of Crime: A Meta-analysis." *Crime and Justice: A Review of Research* 32:373–450.

Ratchford, Brian T., Debabrata Talukadar, and Myung-Soo Lee. 2001. "A Model of Consumer Choice of the Internet as an Information Source." *International Journal of Electronic Commerce* 5:7–21.

Reisig, Michael D., Travis C. Pratt, and Kristy Holtfreter. 2009. "Perceived Risk of Internet Theft Victimization: Examining the Effects of Social Vulnerability and Impulsivity." *Criminal Justice & Behavior* 36:369–84.

Rodgers, Karen and Georgia Roberts. 1995. "Women's Non-spousal Multiple Victimization: A Test of the Routine Activities Theory." *Canadian Journal of Criminology* 37:363–91.

Sampson, Robert J. 1987. "Personal Violence by Strangers: An Extension and Test of the Opportunity Model of Predatory Victimization." *Journal of Criminal Law and Criminology* 78:327–56.

Sampson, Robert J. and Janet L. Lauritsen. 1990. "Deviant Lifestyles, Proximity to Crime, and the Offender-Victim Link in Personal Violence." *Journal of Research in Crime and Delinquency* 27:110–39.

Sampson, Robert J. and John D. Wooldredge. 1987. "Linking the Micro- and Macro-level Dimensions of Lifestyle-Routine Activity and Opportunity Models of Predatory Victimization." *Journal of Quantitative Criminology* 3:371–93.

Schreck, Christopher J. and Bonnie S. Fisher. 2004. "Specifying the Influence of Family and Peers on Violent Victimization: Extending Routine Activities and Lifestyles Theories." *Journal of Interpersonal Violence* 19:1021–41.

Schreck, Christopher J., Eric A. Stewart, and Bonnie S. Fisher. 2006. "Self-control, Victimization, and the Influence on Risky Lifestyles: A Longitudinal Analysis Using Panel Data." *Journal of Quantitative Criminology* 22:319–40.

Schreck, Christopher J., Richard A. Wright, and J. Mitchell Miller. 2002. "A Study of Individual and Situational Antecedents of Violent Victimization." *Justice Quarterly* 19:159–80.

Shover, Neal, Glenn S. Coffey, and Dick Hobbs. 2003. "Crime on the Line: Telemarketing Fraud and the Changing Nature of Professional Crime." *British Journal of Criminology* 43:489–505.

Shover, Neal, Glenn S. Coffey, and Clinton R. Sanders. 2004. "Dialing for Dollars: Opportunities, Justifications, and Telemarketing Fraud." *Qualitative Sociology* 27:59–75.

Soopramanien, Didier and Alastair Robertson. 2007. "Adoption and Usage of Online Shopping: An Empirical Analysis of the Characteristics of 'Buyers,' 'Browsers' and 'Non-Internet shoppers.'" *Journal of Retailing and Consumer Services* 14:73–82.

Sorce, Patricia, Victor Perotti, and Stanley Widrick. 2005. "Attitude and Age Differences in Online Buying." *International Journal of Retail and Distribution Management* 33:122–32.

Stewart, Eric A., Kirk W. Elifson, and Claire E. Sterk. 2004. "Integrating the General Theory of Crime into an Explanation of Violent Victimization among Female Offenders." *Justice Quarterly* 21:159–81.

Stranahan, Harriet and Dorota Kosiel. 2007. "E-Tail Spending Patterns and the Importance of Online Store Familiarity." *Internet Research* 4:421–34.

Swinyard, William R. and Scott Smith. 2003. "Why People (Don't) Shop Online: A Lifestyle Study of the Internet Consumer." *Psychology and Marketing* 20: 567–97.

Tabachnick, Barbara G. and Linda S. Fidell. 2001. *Using Multivariate Statistics*. 4th ed. Boston: Allyn and Bacon.

Titus, Richard. 2001. "Personal Fraud and Its Victims." Pp. 57–74 in *Crimes of Privilege: Readings in White-Collar Crime,* edited by N. Shover and J. P. Wright. Oxford, UK: Oxford University Press.

Titus, Richard, Fred Heinzelmann, and John Boyle. 1995. "Victimization of Persons by Fraud." *Crime and Delinquency* 41:54–72.

U.S. Census Bureau. 2008. *Projected Online Retail Sales*. Washington, DC: U.S. Census Bureau, Housing and Household Economic Statistics Division.

U.S. Department of Commerce. 2008. *U.S. Census Bureau News: Quarterly Retail E-Commerce Sales, 4th Quarter 2007*. Washington, DC: U.S. Department of Commerce.

U.S. Department of Justice. 2008. *Crime in the United States, 2006*. Washington, DC: U.S. Department of Justice.

Waksberg, Joseph. 1978. "Sampling Methods for Random Digit Dialing." *Journal of the American Statistical Association* 73:40–6.

Wall, David S. 2005. "The Internet as a Conduit for Criminals." Pp. 77–98 in *Information Technology and the Criminal Justice System,* edited by A. Pattavina. Thousand Oaks, CA: Sage.

Wall, David S. 2007a. *Cybercrime: The Transformation of Crime in the Information Age*. Cambridge, UK: Polity.

Wall, David S. 2007b. "Policing Cybercrimes: Situating the Public Police in Networks of Security within Cyberspace." *Police Practice and Research* 8:183–205.

Weisberg, Herbert, John Krosnick, and Bruce Bowen. 1989. *An Introduction to Survey Research and Data Analysis*. Glenview, IL: Scott Foresman.

Weisburd, David, Laura A. Wyckoff, Justin Ready, John E. Eck, Joshua C. Hinkle, and Frank Gajweski. 2006. "Does Crime Just Move Around the Corner? A Controlled Study of Spatial Displacement and Diffusion of Crime Control Benefits." *Criminology* 44:549–92.

Willison, Robert. 2008. "Applying Situational Crime Prevention to the Information Systems Security Context." Pp. 169–92 in *Perspectives on Identity Theft. Crime Prevention Studies*. Vol. 23, edited by M. M. McNally and G. R. Newman. Monsey, NY: Criminal Justice Press.

Wilson, Debbie, Alison Patterson, Gemma Powell, and Rachelle Hembury. 2006. "Fraud and Technology Crimes: Findings from the 2003/04 British Crime Survey, the 2004 Offending, Crime and Justice

Survey and Administrative Sources. Online Report 9/06." London: Research, Development and Statistics Directorate, Home Office. Retrieved March 5, 2010 (http://www.homeoffice.gov.uk/rds/offending_survey.html).

Wortley, Richard and Stephen Smallbone. 2006. "Applying Situational Principles to Sexual Offenses against Children." Pp. 7–35 in *Situational Prevention of Child Sexual Abuse. Crime Prevention Studies*. Vol. 19, edited by R. Wortley and S. Smallbone. Monsey, NY: Criminal Justice Press.

Yar, Majid. 2006. *Cybercrime and Society*. Thousand Oaks, CA: Sage.

bradford w. reyns
billy henson
and
bonnie s. fisher

pursued being online

# applying cyberlifestyle-routine activities theory to cyberstalking victimization

Researchers have examined different aspects of cybervictimization (e.g., online fraud, online harassment, sexual solicitation, cyberstalking), mostly with an eye toward describing and estimating the prevalence and incidence of victimization (e.g., Finkelhor, Mitchell, & Wolak, 2000; Finn, 2004; Nhan, Kinkade, & Burns, 2009; Spitzberg & Hoobler, 2002; Wolak, Mitchell, & Finkelhor, 2007). A limited number of researchers have attempted to utilize the lifestyle-routine activities perspective to explain opportunities for online victimization (Bossler & Holt, 2009; Choi, 2008; Holt & Bossler, 2009; Holtfreter et al., 2008; Marcum, Higgins, & Ricketts, 2010; Pratt et al., 2010). Thus far, however, the issue of separation in time and space between the victim and offender and how this divergence affects the opportunity structure for online victimization has not been addressed theoretically. Adapting lifestyle-routine activities theory to take into account the spatial and temporal divergence between victims and offenders in cyberspace environments has implications not only for the theory itself but also for the operationalization and measurement of the key lifestyle-routine activities concepts. The current study addresses these theoretical and empirical shortfalls by examining online lifestyles and routine activities that might create opportunities that can put individuals at risk for a particular type of cybervictimization—cyberstalking.

* * *

## circumstances that create opportunities for victimization

An intersection in time and space of potential victims and offenders may not be all that is necessary to create an opportunity for victimization within a cyberspace environment. In testing lifestyle-routine activities theory, researchers have identified exposure to motivated offenders, proximity to motivated offenders, target attractiveness, and guardianship as key causal mechanisms in explaining opportunities for victimization. All else equal, greater exposure to motivated offenders, greater proximity to motivated offenders, and greater target attractiveness are hypothesized to increase risks for victimization. Guardianship, on the other hand, acts as a buffer against victimization by disrupting criminal opportunity structures, thereby decreasing likelihood of victimization. These theoretical propositions have received strong empirical support in accounting for a variety of types of personal and property victimization across different samples (e.g., Cohen, Felson, & Land, 1980; Cohen, Kluegel, & Land, 1981; Fisher, Daigle, & Cullen, 2010; Fisher, et al., 1998; Holtfreter et al., 2008; Miethe & Meier, 1990; Mustaine & Tewkesbury, 1999; Pratt et al., 2010; Schreck & Fisher, 2004; Schreck, Wright, & Miller, 2002; Spano & Freilich, 2009; Wilcox Rountree et al., 1994).

* * *

## cyberstalking victimization

Cyberstalking can be defined as the repeated pursuit of an individual using electronic or Internet-capable devices (Reyns, Henson, & Fisher, in press). A number of online behaviors on the part of the offender can be considered cyberstalking. According to the National Crime Victimization Study stalking supplement, these behaviors include harassment or threats via e-mail, instant messenger, chat rooms, message or bulletin boards, or other Internet sites (Baum, Catalano, Rand, & Rose, 2009). Cyberstalkers can also use electronic devices to monitor their victims, such as cameras, listening devices, computer programs, and Global Positioning System. Although there is by no means a widely agreed-upon definition of cyberstalking, the above definition is compatible with most of the extant research on the topic, emphasizing repeated pursuit behaviors by electronic means (D'Ovidio & Doyle, 2003; Finkelhor et al., 2000; Finn, 2004; Holt & Bossler, 2009; Jerin & Dolinsky, 2001; Marcum et al., 2010; Sheridan & Grant, 2007; Spitzberg & Hoobler, 2002).

Despite the apparent interest in the topic of cyberstalking victimization by researchers (e.g., Parsons-Pollard & Moriarty, 2008; Pittaro, 2007; Reyns, 2010; Roberts, 2008) and government officials (Ashcroft, 2001; Reno, 1999), few empirical assessments of this type of victimization have been undertaken (Parsons-Pollard & Moriarty, 2009). The studies that have examined cyberstalking victimization suggest that it is a potentially widespread event that is worthy of further study. For instance, Reyns et al. (in press) estimated the lifetime prevalence of cyberstalking victimization among a sample of college undergraduates in the Midwest to be 40.8%, with more than 46% of the women and more than 32% of the men experiencing online pursuit behaviors. Earlier studies of cyberstalking support the finding that this type of victimization is experienced by a significant portion of individuals (e.g., Alexy, Burgess, Baker, & Smoyak, 2005; Baum et al., 2009; D'Ovidio & Doyle, 2003; Fisher et al., 2002; Jerin & Dolinsky, 2001; Sheridan & Grant, 2007; Spitzberg & Hoobler, 2002). For example, in the stalking supplement to the National Crime Victimization Study, it was reported that among victims of stalking, 26% also experienced some form of cyberstalking as part of the pursuit behaviors of the offender (Baum et al., 2009).

Although a handful of research studies have been published estimating the extent of cyberstalking victimization, few have examined the factors that increase or decrease individuals' risk for victimization. Explanations of why individuals are at risk have not, for the most part, advanced beyond descriptive demographic characteristics (e.g., sex, race, relationship status), and most studies of cyberstalking are lacking a theoretical framework. Investigating risk factors grounded in the lifestyles and routine activities of individuals that incorporate a theoretical framework allows for hypothesis testing that would advance understanding of why individuals are at risk of cyberstalking. This type of analysis also may provide insights into designing evidence-based situational crime prevention initiatives that are tailored to cyberstalking victimization. The current study addresses these theoretical and empirical limitations in the previous research in two ways. First, the current study incorporates our cyberlifestyle-routine activities theory to guide hypothesis testing and operationalization of all of the core theoretical concepts (i.e., exposure, proximity, target attractiveness, and guardianship). Second, it examines online lifestyles and routine activities within this cyberlifestyle-routine activity framework that may create online opportunities for individuals at risk for cyberstalking victimization. By addressing these issues, the current study will both expand lifestyle-routine activities theory beyond traditional conceptions of place and improve measurement of the key theoretical concepts in cyberspace environments so measures are tailored to the development of cyberstalking victimization opportunities and grounded in the cyberlifestyle-routine activities theory.

* * *

# method

## procedure

Data were collected in spring of 2009, via a self-report victimization survey, from a simple random sample of undergraduate college students at a large urban university in the Midwest. The university registrar's office provided the sampling frame that included students between 18 and 24 years old who were enrolled full-time during the spring term of 2009. Anticipating a low response rate due to the nature of web-based surveys (see Couper, 2000) and the youthful population under study, 10,000 students were randomly chosen for inclusion in the sample, which is approximately one third of the undergraduate student body. To help encourage students' participation, the registrar's office sent e-mail invitations to the selected students asking them to participate in the survey. Three waves of e-mails were sent to students' school-issued e-mail accounts at approximately 3-week intervals. Per Dillman's (2007) tailored-design method, the language of the invitation e-mails varied slightly across waves in an effort to elicit a higher rate of participation.

## participants

As is the case with most web-based surveys, the response rate for the current study is difficult to calculate because it is not possible to determine how many of the 10,000 invitations that were sent out were actually received, opened, or read by the selected students. A conservative estimate of the response rate can be calculated based on the total number of surveys completed and the total number of e-mail invitations sent. This produces a response rate of 13.1%.[1] A less conservative estimate can be calculated based on the number of students who clicked on the web link to the informed consent form that was embedded in the e-mail invitation. This group of 1,951 students completed 1,310 surveys, resulting in a response rate of 67.1%. After cases containing a substantial amount of missing data were deleted, the final sample size included 974 students. If only those participants who began the survey, meaning they answered the first question ($n = 1,268$), were considered, the response rate based on the final sample would be 76.8% (see Pratt et al., 2010).

The final sample of students possesses the following characteristics: 61% female, 86% White, with a mean age of 20 years. The undergraduate population of students who were eligible for inclusion in the sample was 48.7% female, 80.3% White, with a mean age of 21 years. Since enrollment changes daily, these population characteristics represent the pool of eligible students as of May 18, 2009. The overall undergraduate student body for the 2008–2009 academic year was 53% female and 77% White, so the sample is slightly heavy on females and Whites compared to their representation in the undergraduate population. Statistics related to the age of the undergraduate student body for the 2008–2009 academic year were not available.

## measures

Our adapted cyberlifestyle-routine activities theory guided the development of variables used in the multivariate analysis to identify risk factors for cyberstalking victimization. Descriptive statistics for each victimization, lifestyle-routine activity, and control variable are presented in Table 1.

## dependent variables

*Cyberstalking victimization.* Cyberstalking is defined as the repeated pursuit of an individual using electronic or Internet-capable devices. A respondent was coded as a cyberstalking victim if he or she had been (a) repeatedly contacted online after asking the person to stop, (b) repeatedly harassed online, (c) the recipient of repeated and unwanted sexual advances, or (d) repeatedly threatened with violence while online. Respondents were asked whether they had ever experienced any of these online pursuit behaviors. These four items were used to create a fifth dependent variable that measured whether the respondent experienced one or more of these behaviors on two or more occasions. As Table 1 illustrates, 41% of respondents have experienced a form of cyberstalking at some point in their lives, with unwanted contact (23%) and harassment (20%) being the most frequently experienced types of pursuit behaviors, followed by unwanted sexual advances (14%) and threats of violence (4%).

---

1   By conventional standards, a response rate of 13.1% is low, but recent research suggests that it is not surprising given the mode of administration and the population under study. For instance, Dillman et al. (2009) compared response rates of mixed-mode surveys and reported that response rates varied widely across modes of administration. In this study, mail surveys produced the highest response rates at 75%, and web surveys yielded the lowest at 12.7%. Similar studies of comparable populations have produced rates of participation similar to those in the current study (e.g., Hilinski, 2009; Nobles, Fox, Piquero, & Piquero, 2009; Patton, Nobles, & Fox, 2010).

Table 1. Variables, Scales, and Descriptive Statistics

| Variable | Scale | M | SD | Minimum | Maximum | n | Cronbach's a |
|---|---|---|---|---|---|---|---|
| Dependent variable | | | | | | | |
| Unwanted contact | (0 = no, 1 = yes) | 0.23 | 0.42 | 0 | 1 | 974 | |
| Harassment | (0 = no, 1 = yes) | 0.20 | 0.40 | 0 | 1 | 964 | |
| Sexual advances | (0 = no, 1 = yes) | 0.14 | 0.34 | 0 | 1 | 953 | |
| Threats of violence | (0 = no, 1 = yes) | 0.04 | 0.20 | 0 | 1 | 942 | |
| Cyberstalking victimization | (0 = no, 1 = yes) | 0.41 | 0.49 | 0 | 1 | 974 | |
| Independent variable | | | | | | | |
| Online exposure | | | | | | | |
| Time spent online | (Number of hours per day) | 3.93 | 2.63 | 1 | 16 | 974 | |
| Number of social networks | (Number of online social network accounts) | 2.56 | 1.65 | 1 | 15 | 974 | |
| Number of updates to social network | (Number of updates to social networks per day) | 2.25 | 3.77 | 0 | 25 | 974 | |
| Number of photos online | (Natural log of the number of photos posted) | 5.14 | 1.34 | 0 | 8.52 | 974 | |
| Use AOL Instant Messenger | (0 = no, 1 = yes) | 0.35 | 0.47 | 0 | 1 | 974 | |
| Online proximity | | | | | | | |
| Add stranger | (0 = no, 1 = yes) | 0.77 | 0.44 | 0 | 1 | 974 | |
| Number of friends | (Natural log of the number of friends online) | 5.87 | 0.84 | 1.95 | 8.52 | 974 | |
| Friend service | (0 = no, 1 = yes) | 0.03 | 0.17 | 0 | 1 | 974 | |
| Online guardianship | | | | | | | |
| Profile(s) set to private | (0 = no, 1 = yes) | 0.82 | 0.37 | 0 | 1 | 974 | |
| Use profile tracker | (0 = no, 1 = yes) | 0.11 | 0.32 | 0 | 1 | 974 | |
| Deviant peers | (Mean level of peer deviance) | 2.09 | 1.52 | 0 | 10 | 974 | .80 |
| Online target attractiveness | | | | | | | |
| Composite measure | (Mean level of target attractiveness) | 0.58 | 0.23 | 0 | 1 | 974 | .71 |
| Gender | (0 = male, 1 = female) | 0.61 | 0.48 | 0 | 1 | 974 | |
| Relationship status | (0 = single, 1 = nonsingle) | 0.57 | 0.49 | 0 | 1 | 974 | |
| Sexual orientation | (0 = heterosexual, 1 = other) | 0.06 | 0.23 | 0 | 1 | 974 | |
| Online deviance | (Mean level of online deviance) | 0.19 | 0.15 | 0 | 1 | 974 | .68 |
| Control variables | | | | | | | |
| Age | (0 = younger than 21 years, 1 = 21 and older) | 0.38 | 0.48 | 0 | 1 | 974 | |
| Non-White | (0 = White, 1 = non-White) | 0.13 | 0.33 | 0 | 1 | 974 | |
| Offline risky activities | (Mean level of offline risk) | 11.61 | 12.65 | 0 | 75 | 974 | .67 |

## independent variables

*Online exposure to motivated offenders.* Exposure to motivated offenders online is hypothesized to increase students' likelihood of victimization. For crimes taking place in a physical environment, exposure has been operationalized with variables measuring time spent outside the home, time spent outside the home at night, propensity to be in at-risk environments (e.g., drinking establishments), and the like.

With respect to cyberspace environments, these indicators of exposure are unlikely to increase one's likelihood of victimization because they are indicators of exposure in physical space, not cyberspace. However, the concept of exposure can be adapted to reflect online exposure to motivated offenders.

To capture the online context of exposure to likely or motivated offenders, the current study incorporates five aspects of exposure: (a) amount of time spent online each day, (b) number of online social networks owned by the respondent, (c) the number of times each day the respondent updates his or her online social network accounts, (d) the number of photos the respondent has posted online, and (e) whether the respondent uses AOL Instant Messenger. The distribution of the number of photos measure was highly skewed, with a few respondents reporting to have 10,000 photos. As a result, the natural log of the measure is being used in the following analyses. Each of these measures represents a degree of online exposure to motivated offenders that might facilitate the creation of opportunities for cyberstalking victimization according to the cyberlifestyle-routine activities theory.

As Table 1 illustrates, based on the current measures of exposure, this sample of college students is connected to the Internet in a number of ways, indicating a high level of exposure. For instance, the average student in the sample is online for about 4 hours every day, and approximately 35% of the students use AOL Instant Messenger to stay connected with others.

*Online proximity to motivated offenders.* Proximity to motivated offenders represents the actual physical proximity of potential victims to likely offenders. However, crimes taking place within online networks do not necessarily have to involve physical or temporal proximity between the victim and the offender. Within a system such as the Internet, victims and offenders can come into virtual proximity to one another. For example, chat rooms bring together users from various physical locations (e.g., different cities, states, or countries) to participate in real-time communication within the same online forum. Were it not for the chat room, it is unlikely that these Internet users would have any interaction with one another, so participating in such a forum may reflect online proximity to motivated offenders.

In the current study, online proximity to motivated offenders is measured with three variables: (a) whether the respondent allows other Internet users whom he or she does not know (i.e., strangers) to access his or her online social networks, which may include personal information (e.g., contact information, photos, interests); (b) the number of "friends" that the respondent has across all of his or her online social networks; and (c) whether the respondent has ever utilized an online service designed to assist him or her in acquiring friends for his or her online social network. As with the number of photos measure, the distribution of the number of friends measure was highly skewed, with a few respondents reporting to have 5,000 friends. As a result, the natural log of the measure is being used in the following analyses.

*Online guardianship.* Prior personal victimization research has typically focused on two dimensions of guardianship: physical guardianship and social guardianship (e.g., Mustaine & Tewksbury, 1998; Newman, 1996; Sampson & Wooldredge, 1987; Tewksbury & Mustaine, 2003; Wilcox Rountree & Land, 1996). Physical guardianship often involves target hardening, such as locking doors, erecting barriers (e.g., fences), and implementing police patrols. In online environments, the physical component of guardianship has been operationalized by measuring the presence of firewalls and security programs (Choi, 2008; Holt & Bossler, 2009). However, with respect to the crime of cyberstalking, these protections are unlikely to be effective as they are designed to defend against outside threats to the computer and/or software and not protect the user against potentially unwanted communications.

Physical guardianship in cyberspace is captured in the current study with two variables: (a) whether the respondent has his or her online social network or blog set to limited access so only approved parties can view profiles/information and (b) whether the respondent utilizes an online profile tracker to view who has visited his or her social network or blog, when it was visited, and where the visitors are from. These measures are appropriate indicators of online guardianship in the current context because they might affect opportunities for cyberstalking victimization through self-guardianship. Statistics presented in Table 1 highlight the propensity toward self-guardianship among members of the sample (i.e., most students have their online social networks set to limited access).

Social guardianship indicates the presence of others who, by their presence or degree of guardianship responsibility, may discourage crimes from taking place (Felson, 1995). In terms of online/network environments, social guardianship has been measured with indicators of the victim's online peers. For instance, Holt and Bossler (2009) operationalized a lack of social guardianship with a measure of online peer deviance. In the current study, ineffective social guardianship is similarly measured with a single variable indicating how likely the respondent believes it is that a friend will use the information he or she has posted online to harass, stalk, or threaten him or her (on a scale from 1 to 10). This variable measures a lack of guardianship online, with deviant peers (i.e., those perceived to have the potential to harass, stalk, or threaten the respondent) being less likely to serve as capable guardians.

*Online target attractiveness.* Target attractiveness has been described as "the material or symbolic desirability of persons or property targets to potential offenders, as well as the perceived inertia of a target against illegal treatment" (Cohen et al., 1981, p. 508). In other words, certain targets may be more attractive to a potential offender if they have some value to the offender (e.g., they are valuable or enjoyable) or if they are easy targets (e.g., small-sized items are easier to shoplift, a young or elderly person may not have the ability to resist an attack) (Clarke, 1999). In the case of online victimization, certain information might facilitate the offender's pursuit of the victim (e.g., e-mail addresses, instant messenger IDs) or make the individual a more desirable target (e.g., posting relationship status, photos, sexual orientation), thereby increasing an individual's attractiveness as a target.

Nine measures of target attractiveness based on the type of information the respondents posted are utilized: (a) full name, (b) relationship status, (c) sexual orientation, (d) instant messenger ID, (e) e-mail address, (f) addresses for other social network/blog sites, (g) interests and/or activities, (h) photos of themselves, and (i) videos of themselves. A single composite measure of the respondent's target attractiveness was created by averaging these nine survey items (Cronbach's alpha = .71). As illustrated in Table 1, based on this composite measure of online target attractiveness, the average respondent presents a moderately attractive target to potential offenders. The respondent's gender, relationship status, and sexual orientation are also used as measures of target attractiveness in the current analysis.

*Online/electronic deviant lifestyle.* A large body of criminological research has identified participation in deviant activities or lifestyles as a risk factor for a variety of types of victimization (e.g., Henson, Wilcox, Reyns, & Cullen, 2010; Jensen & Brownfield, 1986; Lauritsen, Laub, & Sampson, 1992; Lauritsen, Sampson, & Laub, 1991; Sampson & Lauritsen, 1990), including cybervictimization (e.g., Choi, 2008; Holt & Bossler, 2009). Engaging in deviant lifestyles or routine activities is hypothesized to increase one's exposure and proximity to motivated offenders (i.e., other deviants) and place the individual in situations conducive to victimization (e.g., lack of capable guardianship).

For this study, an online deviant lifestyle is measured with eight items representing different deviant acts that the respondent had previously engaged in, including whether the respondent had (a) repeatedly contacted or attempted to contact someone online after the person asked/told the respondent to stop, (b) repeatedly harassed or annoyed someone online after the person asked/told the respondent to stop,

(c) repeatedly made unwanted sexual advances toward someone, (d) repeatedly spoken to someone in a violent manner or threatened to physically harm him or her online after he or she asked/told the respondent to stop, (e) attempted to hack into someone's online social network account, (f) downloaded music or movies illegally, (g) sent sexually explicit images to someone online or through text messaging, and (h) received sexually explicit images from someone online or through text messaging. A measure of the respondent's mean online deviance was created (Cronbach's alpha = .68).

## control variables

*Demographics.* Research has consistently identified certain demographic characteristics as potentially important correlates of stalking victimization. For example, with their discussion of the National Violence Against Women Survey, Tjaden and Thoennes (1998) reported that females were more than three times as likely as males to be victims of stalking. Furthermore, Basile, Swahn, Chen, and Saltzman (2006) found that younger individuals had much higher odds of experiencing stalking victimization than older individuals. As has been the case in previous research, the effects of race (White/non-White) and age (in years) will be controlled for in the current analysis.

*Offline risky activities.* Participation in what are considered risky activities (e.g., drinking heavily, frequently attending parties) has been identified as a well-known correlate of college student victimization (e.g., Fisher et al., 1998; Mustaine & Tewksbury, 1998). However, the relationship between these types of activities and online victimization has thus far not been explored empirically by researchers. Therefore, a measure of risky offline activities was created as a control variable in the current study based on the summed responses to three survey items measuring the respondent's (a) alcohol consumption, (b) frequency of party attendance, and (c) bar and night club patronage (Cronbach's alpha = .67).

## analysis

Given the dichotomous nature of the dependent variables, binary logistic regression is an appropriate statistical technique for examining the relationships between online lifestyles and routine activities and cyberstalking victimization. Logistic regression models were estimated for each of the four types of pursuit behaviors constituting cyberstalking victimization—unwanted contact, harassment, sexual advances, and threats of violence—as well as for the overall cyberstalking victimization measure.

Prior to modeling these relationships, the possibility of multicollinearity between the independent variables was explored. The resulting tolerance statistics indicate that multicollinearity is not a statistical issue with the independent variables used in this analysis.[2] Relationships are considered statistically significant at the .05 alpha level of significance.

## results

### online exposure

As Table 2 illustrates, the online exposure variables did not produce consistent effects across the types of pursuit behaviors. However, four of these variables are associated with statistically significant increases in likelihood of victimization. For instance, the number of photos posted on an online social network is

---

2   According to Menard (2010), tolerance statistic values less than 0.2 are cause to be concerned about multicollinearity among the independent variables. In the current study, tolerance was estimated for these variables, and the values for these statistics range between 0.6 and 0.9. These are well within the acceptable range, indicating that multicollinearity is not a statistical threat to the results of the current study.

Table 2.  Binary Logistic Regression Coefficients, Standard Errors, and Exponentiated Coefficients for Cyberstalking Victimization

| Variable | Model 1: Unwanted Contact | | | Model 2: Harassment | | | Model 3: Sexual Advances | | | Model 4: Threats of Violence | | | Model 5: Cyberstalking | | |
|---|---|---|---|---|---|---|---|---|---|---|---|---|---|---|---|
| | Coefficient | SE | Exp(B) | Coefficient | SE | Exp(B) | Coefficient | SE | Exp(B) | Coefficient | SE | Exp(B) | Coefficient | SE | Exp(B) |
| Exposure | | | | | | | | | | | | | | | |
| Time online | 0.03 | 0.03 | 1.03 | −0.01 | 0.03 | 0.98 | −0.03 | 0.04 | 0.97 | 0.07 | 0.05 | 1.07 | −0.02 | 0.03 | 0.98 |
| Number social networks | 0.09 | 0.05 | 1.10 | 0.08 | 0.05 | 1.09 | 0.07 | 0.06 | 1.07 | 0.07 | 0.08 | 1.07 | 0.13** | 0.05 | 1.14 |
| Number social network updates | 0.003 | 0.02 | 1.00 | 0.02 | 0.02 | 1.02 | 0.06** | 0.02 | 1.06 | −0.04 | 0.05 | 0.96 | 0.03 | 0.02 | 1.04 |
| Photos on social network (ln) | −0.08 | 0.07 | 0.92 | 0.18* | 0.08 | 1.20 | −0.07 | 0.09 | 0.93 | 0.15 | 0.15 | 1.16 | 0.10 | 0.07 | 1.11 |
| AOL Instant Messenger | 0.06 | 0.18 | 1.06 | 0.03 | 0.19 | 1.04 | 0.05 | 0.23 | 1.06 | 0.13 | 0.37 | 1.15 | 0.38* | 0.16 | 1.46 |
| Proximity | | | | | | | | | | | | | | | |
| Add stranger | 0.75*** | 0.21 | 2.12 | 0.86*** | 0.23 | 2.37 | 0.88** | 0.29 | 2.41 | 0.28 | 0.43 | 1.33 | 0.94*** | 0.18 | 2.56 |
| Friends on social network (ln) | 0.004 | 0.12 | 1.00 | −0.19 | 0.13 | 0.82 | 0.18 | 0.16 | 1.20 | −0.43 | 0.23 | 0.65 | −0.09 | 0.11 | 0.90 |
| Friend service | 0.15 | 0.41 | 1.16 | −0.34 | 0.45 | 0.96 | 0.53 | 0.46 | 1.70 | 0.44 | 0.76 | 1.56 | 0.17 | 0.42 | 1.19 |
| Guardianship | | | | | | | | | | | | | | | |
| Social network private | 0.31 | 0.23 | 1.36 | 0.10 | 0.24 | 1.11 | 0.15 | 0.29 | 1.17 | 0.44 | 0.49 | 1.56 | 0.28 | 0.21 | 1.32 |
| Profile tracker | 0.64** | 0.23 | 1.90 | −0.01 | 0.26 | 0.99 | 0.52 | 0.28 | 1.69 | 1.04** | 0.43 | 2.82 | 0.59** | 0.24 | 1.81 |
| Deviant peers | 0.19*** | 0.05 | 1.22 | 0.21*** | 0.05 | 1.23 | 0.20*** | 0.05 | 1.22 | 0.15 | 0.09 | 1.16 | 0.25*** | 0.05 | 1.28 |
| Target attractiveness | | | | | | | | | | | | | | | |
| Composite measure | 0.28 | 0.41 | 1.32 | 0.29 | 0.42 | 1.34 | 0.19 | 0.53 | 1.21 | −0.49 | 0.75 | 0.61 | 0.28 | 0.35 | 1.32 |
| Gender | 0.73*** | 0.19 | 2.07 | 0.82*** | 0.20 | 2.28 | 1.21*** | 0.26 | 3.36 | −0.58 | 0.37 | 0.56 | 0.58*** | 0.17 | 1.79 |
| Relationship status | 0.38* | 0.17 | 1.47 | −0.12 | 0.18 | 0.88 | 0.19 | 0.22 | 1.21 | 0.16 | 0.35 | 1.17 | 0.11 | 0.15 | 1.12 |
| Sexual orientation | 0.54 | 0.32 | 1.73 | −0.15 | 0.35 | 0.85 | 0.65 | 0.37 | 1.91 | 0.26 | 0.59 | 1.29 | 0.33 | 0.32 | 1.39 |
| Online deviance | 1.85*** | 0.54 | 6.38 | 2.37*** | 0.56 | 10.78 | 2.76*** | 0.63 | 15.81 | 2.50** | 0.98 | 12.21 | 2.67*** | 0.53 | 14.42 |
| Controls | | | | | | | | | | | | | | | |
| Age | −0.24 | 0.17 | 0.78 | −0.28 | 0.18 | 0.75 | 0.21 | 0.22 | 1.23 | −0.27 | 0.35 | 0.76 | −0.13 | 0.15 | 0.87 |
| Non-White | 0.32 | 0.24 | 1.38 | −0.03 | 0.27 | 0.97 | −0.036 | 0.33 | 0.70 | −0.57 | 0.59 | 0.56 | 0.26 | 0.24 | 1.30 |
| Offline risky activities | −0.002 | 0.01 | 0.99 | −0.01* | 0.01 | 0.98 | 0.01 | 0.01 | 1.01 | 0.01 | 0.01 | 1.00 | −0.004 | 0.01 | 0.99 |
| Constant | −3.82 | 0.66 | 0.02 | −3.45*** | 0.68 | 0.03 | −6.06*** | 0.89 | 0.002 | −2.90** | 1.20 | 0.05 | −3.39*** | 0.60 | 0.03 |
| −2 log likelihood | 928.48 | | | 868.64 | | | 639.27 | | | 302.68 | | | 1114.24 | | |
| Model $\chi^2$ | 129.18*** | | | 104.93*** | | | 127.41*** | | | 34.53** | | | 202.55*** | | |
| Nagelkerke $R^2$ | 0.19 | | | 0.16 | | | 0.22 | | | 0.12 | | | 0.25 | | |
| n | 974 | | | 964 | | | 953 | | | 942 | | | 974 | | |

*$p < .05$. **$p < .01$. ***$p < .001$.

being pursued online

113

a significant and positive predictor of online harassment. The number of daily social network updates is associated with a modest increase in odds of receiving unwanted sexual advances while online, and the number of social networking accounts that a respondent has opened as well as the use of AOL Instant Messenger are predictive of increased likelihood of cyberstalking victimization. None of the other online exposure variables produced statistically significant effects on odds of victimization.

## online proximity

As reported in Table 2, of the three online proximity variables, only one is significantly related to victimization. That is, allowing strangers to access personal online information (i.e., adding strangers as friends to online social networks) is predictive of unwanted contact, harassment, sexual advances, and overall cyberstalking victimization. In each model, the odds of victimization are more than doubled for those who allow strangers to access their online profiles.

## online guardianship

According to Table 2, two of the three online guardianship measures—use of an online profile tracker and online peer deviance—are positive predictors of victimization. Online profile trackers are designed to monitor social network activity so that the user can keep an eye on who is viewing his or her personal information and take preventive measures if troubling patterns develop. This is essentially a form of self-guardianship, but the variable performs contrary to expectations, with those using profile trackers having increased odds of victimization for unwanted contact, threats, and cyberstalking. A possible explanation for this effect is that those who experienced problems online decided to adopt profile trackers to keep themselves safe in the future. The second variable, online peer deviance, increased likelihood of victimization for four of the five victimization variables. Those students who believed that their online friends might harass, threaten, or stalk them using the information that they have posted online are indeed more likely to have such experiences. Although the effects are modest, those with deviant peers online (indicating a lack of capable guardianship) are more likely to experience unwanted contact, harassment, sexual advances, and overall cyberstalking while online.

## online target attractiveness

As Table 2 indicates, gender and relationship status are both significant predictors of online pursuit, whereas the composite target attractiveness measure and sexual orientation are not significantly related to any of the five cyberstalking victimization variables. Consistent with prior victimization research, being female doubles victimization risk for both unwanted contact and harassment victimization, triples the risk for sexual advances, and increases overall cyberstalking victimization odds 1.8 times.

## online deviance

The online deviance measure stands out as the strongest and most consistent predictor of cyberstalking victimization across models. Table 2 illustrates that higher mean online deviance increases odds of unwanted contact more than 6 times, harassment more than 10 times, sexual advances more than 15 times, threats more than 12 times, and overall cyberstalking more than 14 times. Therefore, consistent with previous work examining the link between offending and victimization, these results not only highlight the link between deviance and victimization but also demonstrate support for this relationship in online environments.

# discussion and conclusions

The results of the current study provide support for the ability of the cyberlifestyle-routine activities theory to explain cyberstalking victimization. Although measures of each theoretical concept were significantly related to various forms of cyberstalking victimization (e.g., repeated contact, unwanted sexual advances), the strength of these relationships varied across the dependent variables (i.e., pursuit behaviors). Online exposure and proximity proved to have the weakest relationships with victimization, with measures being significantly related to only a couple of measures of cyberstalking. Online target attractiveness and guardianship had moderate effects on cyberstalking, with at least one measure of each concept being significantly related to every form of victimization. Finally, online deviance had the strongest effect on all forms of victimization, being significantly related to every form of cyberstalking victimization.

A few of these variable effects warrant further discussion. First, online exposure to offenders—which was shown by Marcum (2009) to have a significant effect on online victimization—proved to be one of the weakest predictors of cyberstalking in the current study. Although this variation could be the result of different methods of operationalization, it is also possible that the introduction of online proximity and target attractiveness measures mediated some of the effect of online exposure. Second, there is a significant and positive relationship between one of the measures of guardianship—use of a profile tracker—and several measures of cyberstalking victimization. On its surface, this finding seems to indicate that self-protective measures can be harmful. As previously mentioned, however, this may be the result of a temporal order issue (i.e., individuals may use the profile tracker after experiencing online victimization). Further research is needed to specify the temporal ordering of this relationship. Third, the composite measure of target attractiveness was not significantly related to any of the cyberstalking pursuit behaviors. This is counter to expectations, as a more attractive target is expected to increase one's chances of victimization.

Consequently, it has not been clearly established in the existing lifestyle-routine activities literature which (if any) of these theoretical concepts is more important in explaining victimization, and as a result, these measures should not be considered separately. Does guardianship matter more than target attractiveness? Does proximity matter more than exposure? In the current study, the answers to both questions appear to be yes, but clearly more research is needed to clarify the role of these theoretical concepts in different types of victimization.

Taken as a whole, the results of the current study suggest that the lifestyle-routine activity perspective can be successfully adapted to cyberspace to explain online forms of victimization. In this case, the cyberstalking victimization of college students appears to be a function of decisions and online behaviors that facilitate the intersection of the victim and the offender within cyberspace: specifically, behaviors that bring motivated offenders into closer virtual proximity with the victim (i.e., adding strangers as friends), participating in deviant activities while online (i.e., hacking, harassing others), and associating with deviant peers while online (indicating a lack of capable guardianship online).

# references

Alexy, E. M., Burgess, A. W., Baker, T., & Smoyak, S. A. (2005). Perceptions of cyberstalking among college students. *Brief Treatment and Crisis Intervention, 5,* 279–289.

Ashcroft, J. (2001). *Stalking and domestic violence: Report to Congress.* Washington, DC: U.S. Department of Justice.

Basile, K. C., Swahn, M. H., Chen, J., & Saltzman, L. E. (2006). Stalking in the United States: Recent national prevalence estimates. *American Journal of Preventive Medicine, 31,* 172–175. Baum, K., Catalano, S., Rand, M., & Rose, K. (2009). *Stalking victimization in the United States.* Washington, DC: U.S. Department of Justice.

Bossler, A. M., & Holt, T. J. (2009). On-line activities, guardianship, and malware infection: An examination of routine activities theory. *International Journal of Cyber Criminology, 3,* 400–420.

Brantingham, P., & Brantingham, P. (1995). Crime generators and crime attractors. *European Journal on Criminal Policy & Research, 3,* 5–26.

Buhi, E. R., Clayton, H., & Surrency, H. H. (2009). Stalking victimization among college women and subsequent help-seeking behaviors. *Journal of American College Health, 57,* 419–425.

Cass, A. I. (2007). Routine activities and sexual assault: An analysis of individual- and school-level factors. *Violence and Victims, 22,* 350–366.

Choi, K. (2008). Computer crime victimization and integrated theory: An empirical assessment. *International Journal of Cyber Criminology, 2,* 308–333.

Clarke, R. V. (1999). *Hot products: Understanding, anticipating and reducing demand for stolen goods.* London, UK: Home Office.

Cohen, L. E., & Felson, M. (1979). Social change and crime rate trends: A routine activity approach. *American Sociological Review, 44,* 588–608.

Cohen, L. E., Felson, M., & Land, K. C. (1980). Property crime rates in the United States: A macrodynamic analysis, 1947–1977 with ex ante forecasts for the mid-1980s. *American Journal of Sociology, 86,* 90–118.

Cohen, L. E., Kluegel, J. R., & Land, K. C. (1981). Social inequality and predatory criminal victimization: An exposition and test of a formal theory. *American Sociological Review, 46,* 505–524.

Couper, M. P. (2000). Web surveys: A review of issues and approaches. *Public Opinion Quarterly, 64,* 464–494.

Dillman, D. A. (2007). *Mail and Internet surveys: The tailored design method.* Hoboken, NJ: John Wiley.

Dillman, D. A., Phelps, G., Tortora, R., Swift, K., Kohrell, J., Berck, J., & Messer, B. L. (2009). Response rate and measurement differences in mixed-mode surveys using mail, telephone, interactive voice response (IVR) and the Internet. *Social Science Research, 38,* 1–18.

D'Ovidio, R., & Doyle, J. (2003). A study on cyberstalking: Understanding investigative hurdles. *FBI Law Enforcement Bulletin, 73,* 10–17.

Eck, J. E., & Clarke, R. V. (2003). *Classifying common police problems: A routine activity approach* (Crime Prevention Studies, Vol. 16, pp. 7–39). Monsey, NY: Criminal Justice Press.

Eck, J. E., & Weisburd, D. (1995). *Crime and place.* Monsey, NY: Criminal Justice Press.

Felson, M. (1995). Those who discourage crime. In J. E. Eck & D. Weisburd (Eds.), *Crime and place* (Crime Prevention Studies, Vol. 4, pp. 53–66). Monsey, NY: Criminal Justice Press.

Felson, M. (1998). *Crime and everyday life* (2nd ed.). Thousand Oaks, CA: Sage.

Felson, M. (2002). *Crime and everyday life* (3rd ed.). Thousand Oaks, CA: Sage.

Finkelhor, D., Mitchell, K. J., & Wolak, J. (2000). *Online victimization: A report on the nation's youth.* Washington, DC: U.S. Department of Justice.

Finn, J. (2004). A survey of online harassment at a university campus. *Journal of Interpersonal Violence, 19,* 468–483.

Fisher, B. S. (1995). *Crime and fear on campus. Annals of the American Academy of Political and Social Science, 539,* 85.

Fisher, B. S., Cullen, F. T., & Turner, M. G. (2002). Being pursued: Stalking victimization in a national study of college women. *Criminology & Public Policy, 1,* 257–308.

Fisher, B. S., Daigle, L. E., & Cullen, F. T. (2010). *Unsafe in the ivory tower: The sexual victimization of college women.* Thousand Oaks, CA: Sage.

Fisher, B. S., Sloan, J. J., Cullen, F. T., & Lu, C. (1998). Crime in the ivory tower: Level and sources of student victimization. *Criminology, 36,* 671–710.

Garofalo, J. (1987). Reassessing the lifestyle model of criminal victimization. In M. R. Gottfredson & T. Hirschi (Eds.), *Positive criminology* (pp. 23–42). Newbury Park, CA: Sage.

Grabosky, P. N. (2001). Virtual criminology: Old wine in new bottles? *Social and Legal Studies, 10,* 243–249.

Henson, B., Wilcox, P., Reyns, B. W., & Cullen, F. T. (2010). Gender, adolescent lifestyles, and violent victimization: Implications for routine activity theory. *Victims and Offenders, 5,* 1–26.

Hilinski, C. M. (2009). Fear of crime among college students: A test of the shadow of sexual assault hypothesis. *American Journal of Criminal Justice, 34,* 84–102.

Hindelang, M. J., Gottfredson, M. R., & Garofalo, J. (1978). *Victims of personal crime: An empirical foundation for a theory of personal victimization.* Cambridge, MA: Ballinger.

Holt, T. J., & Bossler, A. M. (2009). Examining the applicability of lifestyle-routine activities theory for cybercrime victimization. *Deviant Behavior, 30,* 1–25.

Holtfreter, K., Reisig, M. D., & Pratt, T. C. (2008). Low self-control, routine activities, and fraud victimization. *Criminology, 46,* 189–220.

Jensen, G. F., & Brownfield, D. (1986). Gender, lifestyles, and victimization: Beyond routine activity. *Violence and Victims, 1,* 85–99.

Jerin, R., & Dolinsky, B. (2001). You've got mail! You don't want it: Cyber-victimization and on-line dating. *Journal of Criminal Justice and Popular Culture, 9,* 15–21.

Jordan, C. E., Wilcox, P., & Pritchard, A. J. (2007). Stalking acknowledgement and reporting among college women experiencing intrusive behaviors: Implications for the emergence of a "classic stalking case." *Journal of Criminal Justice, 35,* 556–569.

Lauritsen, J. L., Laub, J. H., & Sampson, R. J. (1992). Conventional and delinquent activities: Implications for the prevention of violent victimization among adolescents. *Violence and Victims, 7,* 91–108.

Lauritsen, J. L., Sampson, R. J., & Laub, J. H. (1991). The link between offending and victimization among adolescents. *Criminology, 29,* 265–292.

Marcum, C. D. (2009). *Adolescent online victimization: A test of routine activities theory.* El Paso, TX: LFB Scholarly.

Marcum, C. D., Higgins, G. E., & Ricketts, M. L. (2010). Potential factors of online victimization of youth: An examination of adolescent online behaviors utilizing routine activity theory. *Deviant Behavior, 31,* 381–410.

Menard, S. (2010). *Logistic regression: From introductory to advanced concepts and applications.* Thousand Oaks, CA: Sage.

Miethe, T. D., & Meier, R. F. (1990). Opportunity, choice, and criminal victimization: A test of a theoretical model. *Journal of Research in Crime and Delinquency, 27,* 243–266.

Mustaine, E. E., & Tewksbury, R. (1998). Predicting risks of larceny theft victimization: A routine activity analysis using refined lifestyles measures. *Criminology, 36,* 829–858.

Mustaine, E. E., & Tewksbury, R. (1999). A routine activity theory explanation for women's stalking victimizations. *Violence Against Women, 5,* 43–62.

Mustaine, E. E., & Tewksbury, R. (2002). Sexual assault of college women: A feminist interpretation of a routine activities analysis. *Criminal Justice Review, 27,* 89–123.

Newman, O. (1996). *Creating defensible space.* Washington, DC: U.S. Department of Housing and Urban Development.

Nhan, J., Kinkade, P., & Burns, R. (2009). Finding a pot of gold at the end of an Internet rainbow: Further examination of fraudulent email solicitation. *International Journal of Cyber Criminology, 3,* 452–475.

Nobles, M. R., Fox, K. A., Piquero, N., & Piquero, A. R. (2009). Career dimensions of stalking victimization and perpetration. *Justice Quarterly, 26,* 476–503.

Parsons-Pollard, N., & Moriarty, L. J. (2008). Cyberstalking: What's the big deal? In L. J. Moriarty (Ed.), *Controversies in Victimology* (2nd ed., pp. 1031–13). Cincinnati, OH: Anderson.

Parsons-Pollard, N., & Moriarty, L. J. (2009). Cyberstalking: Utilizing what we do know. *Victims and Offenders, 4,* 435–441.

Patton, C. L., Nobles, M. R., & Fox, K. A. (2010). Look who's stalking: Obsessive pursuit and attachment theory. *Journal of Criminal Justice, 38,* 282–290.

Pittaro, M. L. (2007). Cyber stalking: An analysis of online harassment and intimidation. *International Journal of Cyber Criminology, 1,* 180–197.

Pratt, T. C., Holtfreter, K., & Reisig, M. D. (2010). Routine online activity and Internet fraud targeting: Extending the generality of routine activity theory. *Journal of Research in Crime and Delinquency, 47,* 267–296.

Reno, J. (1999). *Cyberstalking: A new challenge for law enforcement and industry.* Washington, DC: U.S. Department of Justice. Retrieved from http://www.justice.gov/criminal/cybercrime/cyberstalking.htm.

Reyns, B. W. (2010). A situational crime prevention approach to cyberstalking victimization: Preventive tactics for Internet users and online place managers. *Crime Prevention and Community Safety, 12,* 99–118.

Reyns, B. W., Henson, B., & Fisher, B. S. (in press). Stalking in the twilight zone: Extent of cyberstalking victimization and offending among college students. *Deviant Behavior.* DOI 10.1080/01639625.2010.538364

Roberts, L. (2008). Jurisdictional and definitional concerns with computer-mediated interpersonal crimes: An analysis on cyber stalking. *International Journal of Cyber Criminology, 2,* 271–285.

Sampson, R. J., & Lauritsen, J. L. (1990). Deviant lifestyles, proximity to crime, and the offender-victim link in personal violence. *Journal of Research in Crime and Delinquency, 27,* 110–139.

Sampson, R. J., & Wooldredge, J. (1987). Linking the micro- and macro-level dimensions of lifestyle-routine activity and opportunity models of predatory victimization. *Journal of Quantitative Criminology, 3,* 371–393.

Schreck, C. J., & Fisher, B. S. (2004). Specifying the influence of family and peers on violent victimization: Extending routine activities and lifestyles theories. *Journal of Interpersonal Violence, 19,* 1021–1041.

Schreck, C. J., Wright, R. A., & Miller, J. M. (2002). A study of individual and situational antecedents of violent victimization. *Justice Quarterly, 19,* 159–180.

Schwartz, M. D., & Pitts, V. L. (1995). Exploring a feminist routine activities approach to explaining sexual assault. *Justice Quarterly, 12,* 9–31.

Shaw, C. R., & McKay, H. D. (1942). *Juvenile delinquency and urban areas.* Chicago, IL: University of Chicago Press.

Sheridan, L. P., & Grant, T. (2007). Is cyberstalking different? *Psychology, Crime & Law, 13,* 627–640.

Sherman, L. S., Gartin, P. R., & Buerger, M. E. (1989). Hot spots of predatory crime: Routine activities and the criminology of place. *Criminology, 27,* 27–55.

Spano, R., & Freilich, J. D. (2009). An assessment of the empirical validity and conceptualization of individual level multi-variate studies of lifestyle/routine activities theory published from 1995 to 2005. *Journal of Criminal Justice, 37,* 305–314.

Spitzberg, B. H., & Hoobler, G. (2002). Cyberstalking and the technologies of interpersonal terrorism. *New Media & Society, 4,* 71–92.

Tewksbury, R., & Mustaine, E. E. (2003). College students' lifestyles and self-protective behaviors: Further considerations of the guardianship concept in routine activity theory. *Criminal Justice and Behavior, 30,* 302–327.

Tillyer, M. S., & Eck, J. E. (2009). Routine activities. In J. M. Miller (Ed.), *21st century criminology: A reference handbook* (pp. 279–287). Thousand Oaks, CA: Sage.

Tjaden, P., & Thoennes, N. (1998). *Stalking in America: Findings from the National Violence Against Women Survey.* Washington, DC: U.S. Department of Justice, Bureau of Justice Statistics.

Wilcox Rountree, P., & Land, K. C. (1996). Burglary victimization, perceptions of crime risk, and routine activities: A multilevel analysis across Seattle neighborhoods and census tracts. *Journal of Research in Crime and Delinquency, 33,* 147–180.

Wilcox Rountree, P., Land, K. C., & Miethe, T. D. (1994). Macro-micro integration in the study of victimization: A hierarchical logistic model analysis across Seattle neighborhoods. *Criminology, 32,* 387–414.

Wolak, J., Mitchell, K. J., & Finkelhor, D. (2007). Does online harassment constitute cyberbullying? An exploration of online harassment by known peers and online-only contacts. *Journal of Adolescent Health, 41,* S52–S58.

Yar, M. (2005). The novelty of "cybercrime": An assessment in light of routine activity theory. *European Journal of Criminology, 2,* 407–427.

Learning

Social

and

Self-
Control

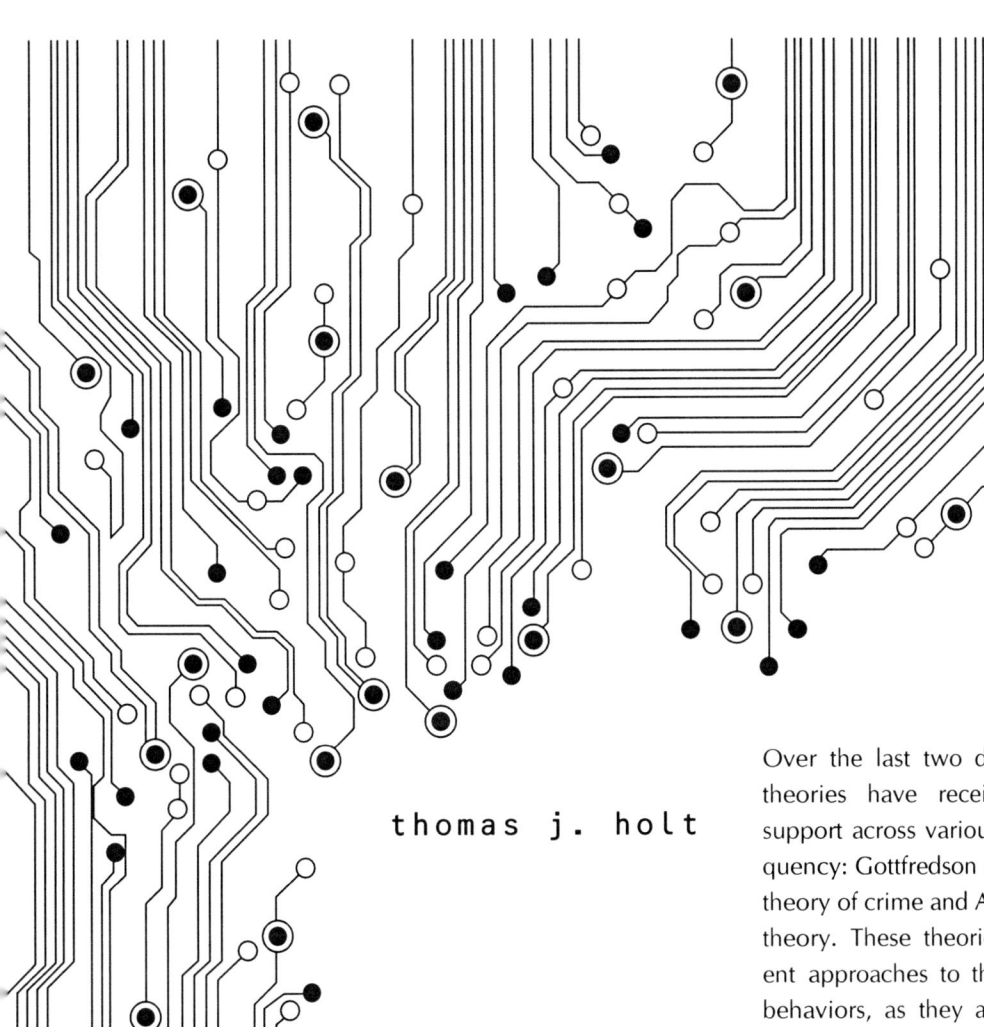

thomas j. holt

Over the last two decades, two criminological theories have received substantive empirical support across various forms of crime and delinquency: Gottfredson and Hirschi's (1990) general theory of crime and Akers's (1998) social learning theory. These theories take substantively different approaches to the explanation of offending behaviors, as they are generated from separate theoretical constructs. Despite this difference, most research has found that components of each theory are significant when they are included in an analysis, suggesting that they have utility in accounting for criminality (Pratt & Cullen, 2000; Pratt et al., 2009). In fact, both of these theories have been used with some success to account for various forms of cybercrime (Bossler & Burruss, 2010; Buzzell, Foss, & Middleton, 2006; Hinduja & Ingram, 2008; Higgins, 2005; Higgins, Fell, & Wilson, 2006; Holt, Bossler, & Burruss, 2010; Ingram & Hinduja, 2008; Morris & Higgins, 2010; Skinner & Fream, 1997). This has led to some confusion, since these concepts may either be integrated together for theoretical harmony (Akers, 2008), or held separate due to differences in their explanatory variables (Gottfredson & Hirschi, 1990; Hirschi, 1989). In order to understand and consider the value of these theories, each will be discussed in detail.

To begin, one of the most significant and consistently identified correlates of both juvenile and adult offending is the relationship to individuals engaged in crime. The link between having friends or family involved in criminality and personal participation in offending has led to a substantive body of research and theory to account for this relationship. In fact, Sutherland (1947) developed one of the first such theories, which argued that crime is a learned behavior acquired through associations with intimate others. This theory, called differential association, centered on the notion that the time individuals spend with others who engage in criminal or deviant behaviors will have a direct influence on the likelihood that individuals will accept definitions supportive of offending as a whole. In turn, those with a greater proportion of definitions that favor offending will be more likely to engage in crime.

While Sutherland's (1947) theory provided an initial framework to consider crime as a social phenomenon, additional research was needed to clarify the mechanisms of the learning process that leads to offending behaviors. Thus, Ron Akers (1998) expanded upon Sutherland's theory by combining tenets of differential association with the psychological principals of social rewards and punishments for behavior. In fact, Akers's (1998) social learning theory is based on four variables: differential association, definitions, differential reinforcement, and imitation. These components interact through a dynamic process with a significant influence on behavior.

The social learning process begins with the relationships individuals have with deviants and nondeviants, or differential association (Akers, 1998). The relationships people have with others vary, though the most influential relationships are those that involve intimates such as family and friends. Friendships and social bonds provide individuals with a model for deviant or nondeviant behavior, depending on the differential associations they have toward groups involved in deviant behavior (Akers, 1998; Akers & Lee, 1996; Lee, Akers, & Borg, 2004).

Differential associations with deviant peers provide definitions for behavior that affect a person's attitude toward and perception of offending, especially justifications that neutralize the negative consequences of deviance (Akers, 1998). Those individuals who have a greater proportion of neutralizing definitions or beliefs supportive of deviant behavior will be more likely to engage in such activities (Akers & Jensen, 2006; Akers & Lee, 1996; Lee, Akers, & Borg, 2004).

The acceptance of definitions supportive of offending are critical to justify and foster behavior, though the impact of social reinforcements and punishments shape present and future action. In particular, social learning theory recognizes that the way behavior is reinforced or punished will have a substantive affect on activities over time through concepts from Skinner's (1953) theory of operant conditioning. Reinforcements for behavior can be positive in nature, such as praise from peers, or negative, through the removal of unpleasant stimuli. At the same time, deviant behavior can also lead to punishments which can also be positive or negative. For instance, a positive punishment involves the addition of something undesirable, such as being grounded or arrested. Negative punishments are those where something that a person desires is removed, such as being unable to go out or watch television.

Finally, imitation plays a critical role in social learning, as an individual may engage in crime after watching someone else engage in such an act (Akers, 1998). As behaviors are repeated over time, the initial influence of imitation decreases relative to the role of differential reinforcements and definitions that favor offending. Several studies have found strong effects for imitation (Boering, Shehan, & Akers, 1991; Spear & Akers, 1988). These measures are often absent in tests, however, because of their narrow role in the learning process and an empirical overlap with differential association (Akers & Lee, 1996; Lee et al., 2004).

Social learning theory is one of the most commonly tested theories to account for various forms of crime (Pratt et al., 2009), and holds particular value for cybercrimes. This is most likely due to the fact that individuals must "learn not only how to operate a highly technical piece of equipment but also specific procedures, programming, and techniques for using the computer illegally" (Skinner & Fream, 1997:498). While computer technology has become extremely user-friendly, individuals still must learn the basic dynamics of computer use and abuse from others, especially for music piracy (Higgins, 2005; Higgins & Wilson, 2006), and computer hacking (Bossler & Burruss, 2010; Holt, 2007).

There is substantive support for various aspects of the social learning process with multiple forms of cybercrime. Many studies have identified a strong relationship between deviant peer relationships and cybercrime (e.g., Higgins, 2005; Skinner & Fream, 1997). There is also a strong connection between deviant peers and the acceptance of definitions that support or neutralize involvement in piracy (Higgins, 2005; Ingram & Hinduja, 2008), and hacking (Holt, 2007). There is also limited support for the role of differential reinforcement in cybercrime offending, since Skinner and Fream (1997) found that punishments that were more severe for involvement in cybercrime were correlated with reduced participation in hacking activities. The effects of imitation on cybercrime vary based on the type of cybercrime committed. Imitation of family members influenced piracy, while teacher encouragement and participation in electronic bulletin boards increased the likelihood of guessing passwords and other deviant acts (Skinner & Fream, 1997).

While there is substantive support for social learning theory, there is an equally large body of research investigating one of the most parsimonious and highly tested criminological theories of the last two decades: Gottfredson and Hirschi's (1990) general theory of crime. This theory argues that most crimes are relatively simple to perform, and provide offenders with immediate gratification through cash or a release of aggression. In addition, offenders tend to have certain behavioral and attitudinal characteristics. Specifically, criminals tend to be impulsive, insensitive, and give little consideration to the future. They act on the spur of the moment, and as a result give little thought to the consequences of their actions. In fact, they usually fail in school, and engage in a variety of risky behaviors such as smoking, drug use, gambling, and unprotected sex. Finally, these behavior patterns persist over time, such that juvenile delinquents frequently become adult offenders.

Based on these factors, Gottfredson and Hirschi argue that criminal behavior is a consequence of one's level of self-control, or the ability to constrain individual behavior through internal regulation. The authors argue that self-control is formed in childhood through parental child-rearing techniques. Since deviant and delinquent behavior begins at an early age, the roots of self-control must stem from the ability of parents to instill in their child a sense of restraint. Parents who consistently monitor their child's behavior, recognize when they behave inappropriately, and punish those behaviors are able to demonstrate what constitutes appropriate and acceptable behavior. Over time, the child will internalize the ability to regulate or control their own behavior, and manifest self-control. At the same time, those parents who fail to regulate inappropriate behavior will produce children with low self-control who have difficulty controlling their actions later.

Since its development, low self-control has consistently been linked to various forms of crime and deviance, ranging from student cheating to more serious street crime (Gibson & Wright, 2001; Grasmick, Tittle, Bursik, & Arneklev, 1993; Piquero & Tibbetts, 1996) and is considered one of the strongest correlates of crime generally (Pratt & Cullen, 2000). Low self-control has been found to predict viewing on-line pornography (see Buzzell et al., 2006), and various forms of piracy (Higgins, 2005;

Higgins et al., 2006; Higgins & Wilson, 2006; Hinduja & Ingram, 2008). Thus, self-control appears to have some value in explaining individual participation for a wide variety of cybercrimes.

In light of the substantive body of research that has emerged supporting each of these theories, it is imperative to assess their value to account for involvement in cybercrimes. There is, however, a substantive literature around these theories, making it difficult to provide a fully comprehensive examination of this literature here. Instead, this section includes three articles that provide either initial tests or unique extensions of these two theories. Thus, interested researchers and readers should seek out the various works cited throughout this section to expand their knowledge of these issues.

The first article in this section by Skinner and Fream (1997) provides a seminal test of a pure social learning model with a college sample. This study assesses the relationship between all four variables of the social learning process and multiple forms of cybercrime offending. Their findings, which provide support for the relationship between social learning and cybercrime, are commonly cited, and their measures serve as the basis for multiple subsequent studies.

The second paper by Wolfe and Higgins (2009) provides an analysis of the factors that predict having relationships with individuals who engage in digital piracy. This study provides a mixed model of elements from social learning theory with measures for self-control to consider how these theories operate in the same statistical test. The findings indicate that self-control is significantly associated with peers who engage in piracy, though the inclusion of definitions favorable to piracy ameliorates this relationship. As a consequence, this study illustrates the influence of both theories in the prediction of cybercrime and peer associations.

The final paper in this series (Bossler & Holt, 2010) considers the influence of self-control as a predictor for cybercrime victimization. While Gottfredson and Hirschi's (1990) general theory of crime was initially developed to account for offending, recent research has combined this framework with routine activities theory to argue that those with low self-control are likely to be exposed to others who are likely to engage in crime (Schreck, Wright, & Miller, 2002). As a result, this increases individual proximity to offenders and increases the risk of victimization from a routine activities standpoint (Schreck et al., 2002). The analyses of Bossler and Holt (2010) provide an initial assessment of the value of this framework to account for multiple forms of cybercrime victimization. In turn, they find that it is a weak predictor for some forms of victimization, though this relationship disappears when accounting for individual and peer offending.

These papers generally illustrate the substantive theoretical value of both social learning theory and self-control, though they do not provide conceptual clarity on how to combine these models. It is clear that both factors matter in accounting for cybercrime offending, though it is not evident whether self-control is a less significant predictor than differential associations and acceptance of definitions for offending. In addition, most tests of social learning theory for cybercrimes only assess measures of differential association and definitions, limiting our understanding of the influence of imitation and differential reinforcement on the social learning process generally (Higgins, 2005; Higgins et al., 2006, 2007; Higgins & Wilson, 2006).

With regard to the general theory of crime, it is not clear if low self-control can account for all forms of cybercrime offending. More technical offenses, like the creation of malicious software or complex hacks, require a great deal of persistence and complex thought (Bossler & Burruss, 2010; Holt & Kilger, 2008). As a result, these offenders may actually have higher levels of self-control, despite their involvement in cybercrime. Similarly, the weak findings of Bossler and Holt (2010) require substantive future investigation to understand what role the general theory of crime plays for certain forms of cybercrime victimization. Thus, there is a substantial body of research that must be developed to understand the relationship between self-control, social learning theory, and cybercrime.

## discussion questions

1. What are some of the ways that individuals may identify deviant peers in a virtual environment? How might offending tactics and strategies be shared on-line? Think carefully about all the various forms of on-line media that could be used to explain the process of various forms of cybercrime on-line.

2. Do you think that deviant peer relationships in virtual environments can have a greater influence on criminality than those in the real world? What, if any, differences can be observed between friendships in on- and off-line spaces, and how might they differentially impact willingness to engage in cybercrime?

3. If self-control leads individuals to act impulsively and immediately act upon opportunities to offend, are there any forms of cybercrime that may not be explained by this theory? For instance, could computer hacking or e-mail-based fraud be successfully performed by a shortsighted and impatient offender?

4. Why might an individual with low self-control have a more difficult time protecting him- or herself in cyberspace? For instance, would someone with low self-control use different passwords, or engage in more risky information sharing in social networking sites than their peers with higher levels of self-control?

## references

Akers, R. L. (1998). *Social Learning and Social Structure: A General Theory of Crime and Deviance.* Boston: Northeastern University Press.

Akers, R. L. (2008). Self-control and social learning theory. In E. Goode (ed.), *Out of Control: Assessing the General Theory of Crime* (pp.77–89). Stanford, CA: Stanford University Press.

Akers, R. L., & Jensen, G. F. (2006). The empirical status of social learning theory of crime and deviance: The past, present, and future. In F. T. Cullen, J. P. Wright, & K. R. Blevins (eds.), *Taking Stock: The Status of Criminological Theory* (pp. 37–76). New Brunswick, NJ: Transaction Publishers.

Akers, R. L., & Lee, G. (1996). A longitudinal test of social learning theory: Adolescent smoking. *Journal of Drug Issues, 26,* 317–343.

Boeringer, S., Shehan, C. L., & Akers, R. L. (1991). Social contexts and sexual learning in sexual coercion and aggression: Assessing the contribution of fraternity membership. *Family Relations, 40,* 558–564.

Bossler, A. M., and Burruss, G.W. (2011). The general theory of crime and computer hacking: Low self-control hackers? In T. J. Holt & B. H. Schell (eds.), *Corporate Hacking and Technology-Driven Crime: Social Dynamics and Implications* (pp. 38–67). Hershey, PA: IGI Global.

Bossler, A. M., & Holt, T. J. (2010). The effect of self-control on victimization in the cyberworld. *Journal of Criminal Justice, 38,* 227–236.

Buzzell, T., Foss, D., & Middleton, Z. (2006). Explaining use of online pornography: A test of self-control theory and opportunities for deviance. *Journal of Criminal Justice and Popular Culture, 13,* 96–116.

Gibson, C., & Wright, J. (2001). Low self-control and coworker delinquency: A research note. *Journal of Criminal Justice, 29,* 483–492.

Gottfredson, M. R., & Hirschi, T. (1990). *A General Theory of Crime*. Stanford, CA: Stanford University Press.

Grasmick, H. G., Tittle, C. R., Bursik, R. J., & Arneklev, B. J. (1993). Testing the core empirical implications of Gottfredson and Hirschi's general theory of crime. *Journal of Research on Crime and Delinquency, 30,* 5–29.

Higgins, G. E. (2005). Can low self-control help with the understanding of the software piracy problem? *Deviant Behavior, 26,* 1–24.

Higgins, G. E., Fell, B. D., & Wilson, A. L. (2006). Digital piracy: Assessing the contributions of an integrated self-control theory and social learning theory using structural equation modeling. *Criminal Justice Studies, 19,* 3–22.

Higgins, G. E., & Wilson, A. L. (2006). Low self-control, moral beliefs, and social learning theory in university students' intentions to pirate software. *Security Journal, 19,* 75–92.

Hinduja, S., & Ingram, J. R. (2008). Self-control and ethical beliefs on the social learning of intellectual property theft. *Western Criminology Review, 9,* 52–72.

Hirschi, T. (1989). Explaining alternatives to integrated theory. In S. F. Messner & A. E. Liska (eds.), *Theoretical Integration in the Study of Deviance and Crime* (pp. 37–49). Albany: State University of New York Press.

Holt, T.J. (2007). Subcultural evolution? Examining the influence of on- and off-line experiences on deviant subcultures. *Deviant Behavior, 28,* 171–198.

Holt, T. J., Burruss, G. W., & Bossler, A. M. (2010). Social learning and cyber deviance: Examining the importance of a full social learning model in the virtual world. *Journal of Crime and Justice, 33,* 31–62.

Holt, T. J., & Kilger, M. (2008). Techcrafters and makecrafters: A comparison of two populations of hackers. *WOMBAT,* 67–78.

Ingram, J. R., & Hinduja, S. (2008). Neutralizing music piracy: An empirical examination. *Deviant Behavior, 29,* 334–366.

Lee, G., Akers, R. L., & Borg, M. J. (2004). Social learning and structural factors in adolescent substance use. *Western Criminology Review, 5,* 17–34.

Morris, R. H., & Higgins, G. E. (2010). Criminological theory in the digital age: The case of social learning theory and digital piracy. *Journal of Criminal Justice, 38,* 470–480.

Piquero, A. R., & Tibbetts, S. (1996). Specifying the direct and indirect effects of low self-control and situational factors in offenders' decision making: Toward a more complete model of rational offending. *Justice Quarterly, 13,* 481–510.

Pratt, T. C., & Cullen, F. T. (2000). The empirical status of Gottfredson and Hirschi's general theory of crime: A meta-analysis. *Criminology, 38,* 931–964.

Pratt, T. C., Cullen, F. T., Sellers, C. S., Winfree, L. T. Jr., Madensen, T. D., Daigle, L. E., Fearn, N. E., & Gau, J. M. (2009). The empirical status of social learning theory: A meta-analysis. *Justice Quarterly, 27,* 765–802.

Schreck, C. J., Wright, R. A., & Miller, J. M. (2002). A study of individual and situational antecedents of violent victimization. *Justice Quarterly, 19,* 159–180.

Skinner, B.F. (1953). *Science and Human Behavior.* New York: Macmillan.

Skinner, W. F., & Fream, A. M. (1997). A social learning theory analysis of computer crime among college students. *Journal of Research in Crime and Delinquency, 34,* 495–518.

Spear, S., & Akers, R. L. (1988). Social learning variables and the risk of habitual smoking among adolescents: The Muscatine study. *American Journal of Preventative Medicine, 4,* 336–348.

Sutherland, E. H. (1947). *Principles of criminology, 4th ed.* Philadelphia: J. B. Lippincott.

Wolfe, S. E., & Higgins, G. E. (2009). Explaining deviant peer associations: An examination of low self-control, ethical predispositions, definitions, and digital piracy. *Western Criminology Review, 10,* 43–55.

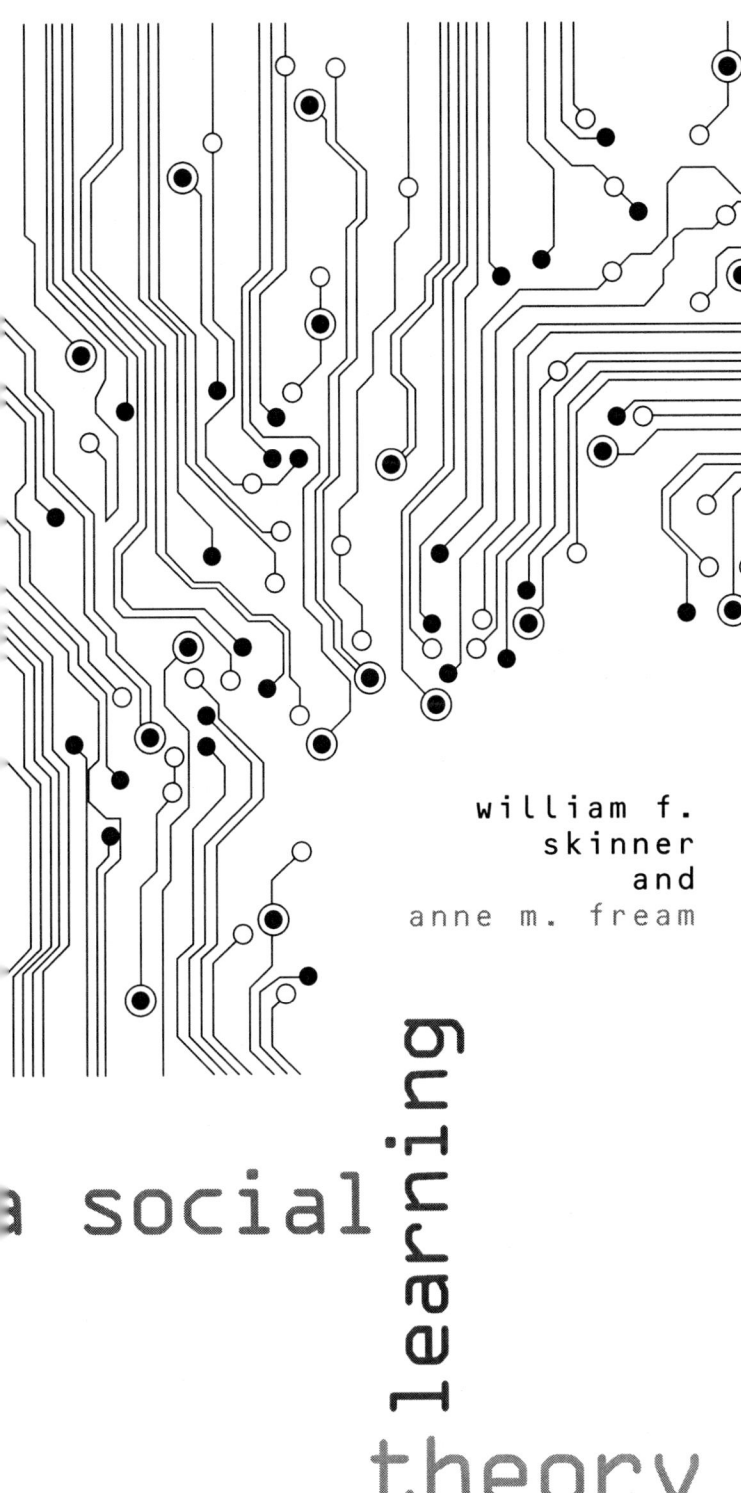

william f.
skinner
and
anne m. fream

## analysis of computer crime among college students

*Computer crime is a fairly new area of research in criminology and deviance. With the exception of Hollinger, few studies have examined the occurrence of illegal computer acts and virtually none have tried to offer a theoretical explanation for the behavior. In this article, the authors provide data on the lifetime, past year, and past month prevalence of five illegal computer activities from a multistage sample (N = 581) of students at a southern university. The authors also examine the etiology of computer crime by testing the ability of social learning theory to explain these behaviors. Using multiple regression procedures, they demonstrate that measures of differential association, differential reinforcement and punishment, definitions, and sources of imitation are significantly related to computer crime. Findings from this study are compared with Hollinger's data and discussed in terms of why social learning theory is an appropriate and useful theoretical perspective for understanding why college students commit illegal computer acts.*

Computer crime is a fairly new area of research in the field of criminology and deviance. Awareness of computer crime emerged in the early 1960s (Parker 1976), and since then, estimates of damage done by computer hackers or thieves have ranged between $145 million to $5 billion annually in the United States alone (American Bar Association 1984; McEwen, Fester, and Nugent 1989; Parker 1987). And there are estimates that "the average computer crime costs about $630,000" (Gottleber 1988:47). Of the few studies conducted on computer crime, most have been directed toward identifying individual and corporate victims of computer crime, consequences of the crime, profiles of the perpetrators, and the criminalization of computer crime (American Bar Association 1984; Gottleber 1988; Parker 1976; Schwartz, Rothfeder, and Lewyn 1990; Wong and Farquhar 1986).

These studies tend to represent the most extreme (costly) instances of computer crime that were detected. To date, little is known about the majority who have managed to escape detection. Hollinger (1988, 1991, 1992) was one of the first criminologists to examine computer crime among college students. He found that during a 15-week semester, 10 percent of his college-based sample reported being involved in software piracy and 3.3 percent had gained unauthorized access to another computer account. Although his study is highly informative and provides the groundwork for the current analysis, Hollinger examined only two types of illegal computer activity and did not provide an organized theoretical analysis of why college students commit computer crime.

There are two main objectives to this study. First, using a multistage sample of students at a southern university, we examine the lifetime, past year, and past month occurrence of five illegal computer activities—software piracy, guessing passwords to gain unauthorized access, gaining unauthorized access solely for the purpose of browsing, gaining unauthorized access for the purpose of changing information, and writing or using a program like a virus that destroys computerized data.[1] Second,

---

1   The Penal Code of the Kentucky Revised Statutes Sections 434.845, 434.850, and 434.855 relating to unlawful access to a computer and misuse of computer information became effective on July 13,1984. Section 434.845 entitled "Unlawful Access to a Computer in the First Degree" states the following:

(1) A person is guilty of unlawful access to a computer in the first degree when he knowingly and willfully, directly or indirectly accesses, causes to be accessed, or attempts to access any computer software, computer program, data, computer, computer system, computer network, or any part thereof, for the purpose of: (a) Devising or executing any scheme or artifice to defraud; or (b) Obtaining money, property, or services for themselves or another by means of false or fraudulent pretenses, representations, or promises; or (c) Altering, damaging, destroying or attempting to alter, damage, destroy any computer, computer system, or computer network, or any computer software, program, or data; (2) Accessing, attempting to access, or causing to be accessed any computer software, computer program, data, computer, computer system, computer network, or any part thereof, even though fraud, false or fraudulent pretenses, representations, or promises may have been involved in the access or attempt to access shall not constitute a violation of this section, if the sole purpose of the access was to obtain information and not to commit any other act proscribed by this section; and (3) Unlawful access to a computer in the first degree is a Class C felony.

Section 434.850 entitled "Unlawful Access to a Computer in the Second Degree" states the following:

(1) A person is guilty of unlawful access in the second degree when he without authorization knowingly and willfully, directly or indirectly accesses, causes to be accessed, or attempts to access any computer software, computer program, data, computer, computer system, computer network, or any part thereof and (2) Unlawful access to a computer in the second degree is a Class A misdemeanor.

Section 434.855 entitled "Misuse of Computer Information" states the following:

because virtually no research has examined the etiology of computer crime, we examine the ability of social learning theory to explain these behaviors (Akers 1985). On the basis of multiple regression procedures, we demonstrate that measures of differential association, differential reinforcement and punishment, definitions, and sources of imitation are significantly related to computer crime.

## previous literature

Most studies on computer crime have been done on the victims of computer crime rather than the perpetrator. This literature has centered on documenting which businesses were being targeted as victims of computer crime and how much it cost them (O'Donoghue 1986; Schwartz et al. 1990; Wong and Farquhar 1986). For instance, the American Bar Association (1984) found in its survey of 283 businesses and organizations (banks, accounting or financial services, computer and electronic firms, and major federal government departments and agencies) that 25 percent had been victims of computer crime and that individually, average losses were between $2 to $10 million. And although 39 percent of the companies could not identify the perpetrators of specific crimes, in 77 percent of the cases where the companies actually caught a computer criminal, the offender was a company employee.

One of the first statistical studies on unknown perpetrators of computer crime was done by Hollinger (1992) at the University of Florida. The computer-related crimes that 1,766 students responded to dealt with (1) giving or receiving "pirated" computer software and (2) accessing another person's computer account or files without the owner's knowledge or permission. The findings showed that during a 15-week semester, 10 percent of the respondents had broken copyright laws on computer software and 3.3 percent had unauthorized access to someone else's computer account or files. Although these figures may not seem to pose a real threat to computer security, Hollinger extrapolated this information to the rest of the student body to show that there would be more than 3,500 instances of felony piracy on campus and over 1,000 instances of illegal intrusions per semester.

Hollinger's examination of correlates of computer crime indicated that those students most likely to be involved in piracy were male, 22 years of age and older, seniors and graduate students, Asian or Hispanic, cohabitating with someone of the opposite sex, and enrolled in majors dealing with forestry, engineering, business, liberal arts, and science. For involvement in unauthorized computer accounts access, the only significant difference occurred for gender, with male students significantly more likely than female students to engage in this type of computer crime. All other variables, although showing some trends, were not significantly correlated with unauthorized access.

Hollinger did find two variables that were strongly correlated with computer crime—friends' involvement and perceived certainty of being caught. When students in Hollinger's study reported that none of their best friends had been occasionally involved in piracy, less than 2 percent had committed the act. On the other hand, when more than half of the students' best friends had occasionally committed

---

(1) A person is guilty of misuse of information when he: (a) Receives, conceals, or uses, or aids another in doing so, any proceeds of a violation of KRS 434.845; or (b) Receives, conceals, or uses or aids another in doing so, any books, records, documents, property, financial instrument, computer software, computer program, or other material, property, or objects, knowing the same to have been used in or obtained from a violation of KRS 434.845 and (2) Misuse of computer information is a Class C felony.

According to Section 532.020 of the Penal Code of the Kentucky Revised Statues, a class C felony has a prison term of at least 5 years but not more than 10 years. A person convicted of a class A misdemeanor can be sentenced to prison at least 90 days but not more than 12 months and could be fined up to a maximum of $500.

piracy, almost 40 percent had committed the act themselves. Similarly, about one-third of the students who had more than half their best friends involved in illegal computer account access had engaged in the same activity. Hollinger also found that when the source of social control was university officials, there was a moderately strong negative relationship between perceived certainty of being caught and frequency of piracy. A similar negative relationship was found between perceived certainty of being caught by fellow students and self-reported piracy. These two deterrence variables did not, however, significantly relate to unauthorized access to computer accounts.

We are in the very beginning stages of understanding and explaining computer crime. Most information to date has been anecdotal, based on face-to-face interviews with a few known computer criminals, or gleaned from victim surveys that were more interested in whether the perpetrators were employees. Although Hollinger's (1992) study was highly informative and lays the groundwork for future research, it was limited: (1) Only two acts of computer crime were included in the questionnaire, (2) the prevalence and incidence of computer crime were restricted to the previous four months, (3) the analysis did not examine a theoretical model explaining computer crime, and (4) no multivariate analysis was done.

This study attempts to overcome these limitations by first providing additional epidemiological information about computer crime. This includes the lifetime, past month, and past year prevalence of five types of illegal computer activity (see note 1). Second, we test hypotheses that relate social learning theory variables (Akers 1985) to the past year frequency of three types of computer crime and a computer crime index using multivariate procedures.

\* \* \*

Definitions are attitudes about certain behavior learned through the process of differential association, imitation, and general interaction or exposure to various sources of learning located in one's social environment. In essence, they are "orientations, rationalizations, definitions of situations, and other evaluative and moral attitudes that define the commission of an act as right or wrong, good or bad, desirable or undesirable, justified or unjustified" (Akers 1994:97). Definitions can be of a general nature (e.g., moral or religious norms that guide general behavior) or specific to particular conforming and nonconforming behavior. Moreover, social learning distinguishes between positive, negative, and neutralizing definitions. Positive definitions define illegal behavior as desirable, acceptable, and permissible. Negative definitions define illegal behavior as undesirable, unacceptable, and wrong. And neutralizing definitions define illegal behavior as excusable, justifiable, and tolerable.

Differential reinforcement/punishment is a concept that captures the diversity of anticipated and actual consequences of engaging in certain behavior. It refers to the balance of social and nonsocial (i.e., physical) rewards and punishments associated with behavior. As Akers (1997) contends, positive reinforcers (e.g., approval from friends, family, teachers) and negative rein forcers (e.g., the avoidance of unpleasant experiences) tend to increase the likelihood that a certain act will occur. On the other hand, positive punishers such as reprimands or more punitive reactions to behavior and negative punishers such as the removal or retraction of rewards, praise, or affection tend to decrease the likelihood that a certain act will occur. Both reinforcers and punishers can, and most of the time do, exist for any behavior. Therefore, it is the balance between these two exigencies that predicts behavior: "Whether individuals will refrain from or commit a crime at any given time (and whether they will continue or desist from doing it in the future) depends on the past, present, and anticipated future rewards and punishment for their actions" (Akers 1994:98).

Finally, imitation refers to the modeling of certain behavior through the observation of others. Sources of imitation or modeling come primarily from salient social groups (parents, peers, teachers) and other sources such as the media. Imitation tends to be more important in the initial stages of learning deviant behavior and less important, although still having some effect, in the maintenance and cessation of behavior.

Because of its complexity, any full test of social learning theory requires operationalizing and measuring numerous variables (Akers et al. 1979; Akers and La Greca 1991; Krohn et al. 1985). We do not claim in this study to completely test social learning theory and, in some instances, do not operationalize the concepts as directly as more extensive studies. However, learning theory does provide a theoretical basis for hypothesizing relationships among selected learning variables and computer crime. Therefore, findings of hypothesized relationships provide support for the theory, and findings counter to the hypothesized relationships detract from the theory.

\* \* \*

The first stage involved a selection of colleges from among the 17 within the university that had the highest levels of computer usage by students. The three colleges chosen were Arts and Sciences, Business and Economics, and Engineering. These particular colleges were specifically selected on the basis of the findings from Hollinger's (1992) study, which indicated that the highest rates of computer crime would come from the departments that belonged to those three colleges. Also, the university's computer security and contingency planning officer suggested that illegal computer activity, if it has occurred, would most likely be committed by students within those three colleges more so than any of the other 14 colleges.

In the second stage, departments were selected from the three colleges. The 13 departments chosen within the College of Arts and Sciences were limited to the social sciences and natural sciences.[2] These departments have typically required some degree of computer expertise other than basic word processing skills to be applied to course work and assignments. All five departments within the College of Business and Economics and all eight departments from the College of Engineering were incorporated into the sampling frame.[3]

In the third stage, undergraduate classes were randomly selected from those departments. The list of undergraduate classes offered in the spring of 1993 was reduced to include only those classes that were required or considered as departmental electives by the university for degree status. This excludes internships, independent studies, fieldwork, or self-directed reading courses. A random selection of 45 classes was taken from the edited sampling frame until about 950 students had been chosen, based on

---

2 The social science departments chosen from the College of Arts and Science were composed of Anthropology, History, Economics, Geography, Political Science, Psychology, and Sociology. The natural sciences contained the following departments from the College of Arts and Sciences: Biology, Chemistry, Computer Science, Mathematics, Physics and Astronomy, and Statistics. This excludes a total of 12 departments in the College of Arts and Sciences: Classical Languages, English, French, German, Latin American Studies, Linguistics, Military Science, Philosophy, Russian and Eastern Studies, and Spanish and Italian. The following Interdisciplinary Minors were also excluded: African American Studies, Appalachian Studies, Religious Studies, and Women's Studies.

3 For the College of Business and Economics, these included Accounting, Decision Sciences, Economics, Finance, Management, and Marketing. For the College of Engineering, these included Agricultural Engineering, Chemical Engineering, Civil Engineering, Electrical Engineering, Engineering Mechanics, Geological Sciences, Material Science Engineering, Mechanical Engineering, and Mining Engineering.

the maximum enrollment figures given for each class.[4] Of those 45 classes, 30 were scheduled to be surveyed. A total of 581 students participated in the study, which represented a 60.2 percent response rate of the 965 students enrolled in the classes.

\* \* \*

In general, there is a 3:1 to 2:1 ratio of male students to female students among those who admitted committing the activities. And as the far right columns in Table 2 indicate, writing or using a virus is strictly the province of male college students. [editor's note: The tables have been removed for the sake of brevity. Please see original manuscript for all statistical figures.] With the exception of lifetime and past year prevalence of guessing passwords, White and Asian students are more likely to engage in illegal computer acts than other racial groups (Swinyard, Heikki, and Ah 1990). There does not seem to be a consistent relationship between the prevalence of illegal computer activity and the student's college. For instance, engineering students report the highest involvement in pirating software, whereas agricultural students tend to have the highest prevalence for guessing passwords, gaining access to accounts to change files, and writing or using a virus. Finally, except for the unusually high percentage of graduate students who pirate software, there does not appear to be any substantial relationship of computer crime to age and year in school. Indeed, subsequent correlational analysis indicated that age had a small, negative relationship with only frequency of guessing a password ($r = .07$).

Table 3 shows both how often those involved in computer crime committed the act and an estimated minimum and maximum incidence figure. Most of the students who had admitted to committing a computer crime had done so fairly infrequently. For instance, most password guessers (73.4 percent), browsers (63.1 percent), and virus writers/users (85.7 percent) had done this act one to two times in the past year. However, it is interesting to note that whereas about 44 percent of students who pirate software did so only 1 to 2 times in the past year, about one-third (31.8 percent) had committed this crime 10 times or more. By taking the minimum number for each of the following categories (1–2 times, 3–5 times, 6–9 times, and 10 times or more), we calculated the minimum and maximum number of occurrences for each of the five crimes in the past year. These figures indicate that 198 students pirated software at least 906 times and possibly more than 1,167 times. Assuming that the pirated software was priced between $100 and $500, these students cost software companies and distributors between about $90,600 and $453,000 in lost revenues. Also, in the past year, there were between 223 and 335 occurrences of students who tried to guess passwords to gain unauthorized access to computer accounts or files. Illegally gained access, whether the purpose was to just browse the files or to change information, occurred between 312 and 451 times in the past year. And although an extremely small number of students were involved in writing or using viruses, they did so at the very least 9 times and possibly more than 17 times in the past year.

---

4 Additional classes whose combined enrollments were in excess of the needed 500 to 600 students were chosen for several reasons. It was reasonable to assume that some faculty members would prefer that their classes not be surveyed or that the time period of data collection may conflict with class curriculums that would not be able to be adjusted to include the administration of the survey. Also, the number given on the database was the maximum number of available openings for each class. However, fewer students may actually have enrolled in any of the classes that were chosen or they may have dropped the class during the drop/add process at the beginning of the semester. The reverse was also a possibility if the faculty member allowed more than the stated number of students in his or her classroom. In addition, those students who attended more than one class where the survey was conducted were asked not to complete the survey for a second time. Also, students who were enrolled in one of the randomly selected classes and were minors (under the age of 18) were asked not to complete a questionnaire because of the necessity and difficulty associated with acquiring written parental consent and any breaches to confidentiality that could occur.

These findings add to a small store of knowledge on the extent and seriousness of computer-related violations. They do not help, however, in explaining individual differences in committing computer crimes. We have argued that the explanation lies at least, in part, in differences in exposure to models of association with other offenders, taking on definitions favorable to engaging in unlawful computer uses, and failing to be deterred by fear of being caught and punished for such acts. We turn now to examining these social learning hypotheses.

* * *

We have not conducted a full test of social learning, and one could argue that if we had conducted such an analysis, we would have explained even more variance in computer crime. However, this study has demonstrated the utility of social learning in understanding a variety of illegal computer activities among college students. Future research should expand on these measures and test more complete social learning models. Moreover, because gender was found to influence some types of computer crime, additional research could focus on possible interaction effects between gender and the learning variables. Other types of samples should also be used to further investigate computer crime. Systematic studies of business employees, Internet companies, and Internet users could offer some valuable insights for understanding the breadth and depth of computer crime, its threat to the security of private information, and its monetary cost to society. Clearly, widespread illegal computer acts are being committed every day. Because educational institutions are teaching students how to use computers and provide access to computer technology, the best place to start teaching them computer ethics and laws should be in the classrooms.

## references

Akers, Ronald L. 1973. *Deviant Behavior: A Social Learning Approach.* Belmont, CA: Wadsworth.

———. 1977. Deviant Behavior: A Social Learning Approach. 2d ed. Belmont, CA: Wadsworth.

———. 1985. Deviant Behavior: A Social Learning Approach. 3d ed. Belmont, CA: Wadsworth.

———. 1994. Criminological Theories: Introduction and Evaluation. Los Angeles: Roxbury.

———. 1997. Criminological Theories: Introduction and Evaluation. 2d ed. Los Angeles: Roxbury.

Akers, Ronald L., Marvin D. Krohn, Lonn Lanza-Kaduce, and Marcia Radosevich. 1979. "Social Learning and Deviant Behavior: A Specific Test of a General Theory." *American Sociological Review* 44 (4): 636–55.

Akers, Ronald L. and Anthony LaGreca. 1991. "Alcohol Use among the Elderly: Social Learning, Community Context, and Life Events." Pp. 242–62 in *Society, Culture, and Drinking Patterns Re-Examined*, edited by David Pittman and Helene Reskin White. New Brunswick, NJ: Rutgers Center of Alcohol Studies.

American Bar Association. 1984. *Report on Computer Crime: June 1984*. Chicago: Task Force on Computer Crime, Section on Criminal Justice.

Bandura, Albert. 1986. Social Foundations of Thought and Action: A Social Cognitive Theory. Englewood Cliffs, NJ: Prentice Hall.

Burkett, Stephen and Eric Jensen. 1975. "Conventional Ties, Peer Influence, and Fear of Apprehension: A Study of Adolescent Marijuana Use." *Sociological Quarterly* 16:522–33.

Fream, Anne. 1993. The Prevalence and Social Learning Predictors of Computer Crime among College Students. Unpublished master's thesis, University of Kentucky, Lexington.

Gottleber, T. T. 1988. "Teaching Ethics in the Community College Data Processing Curriculum." *Community/Junior College Quarterly* 12:47–54.

Hacker is said to agree to a plea bargain. 1995. *New York Times,* July 2, pp. VI44, 22.

Hafner, Katie and John Markoff. 1991. *Cyberpunk.* New York: Simon & Schuster.

Hanson, Gayle. 1991. "Computer Users Pack a Keypunch in a High-Tech World of Crime." *Insight,* April 15, pp. 8–17.

Hollinger, Richard C. 1988. "Computer Hackers Follow a Guttman-Like Progression." *Sociology and Social Research* 72 (3): 199–200.

———. 1991. "Hackers: Computer Heros or Electronic Highwaymen?" *Computers & Society* 21 (1): 6–17.

———. 1992. "Crime by Computer: Correlates of Software Piracy and Unauthorized Account Access." *Security Journal* 2 (1): 2–12.

Hollinger, Richard C. and Lonn Lanza-Kaduce. 1988. "The Process of Criminalization: The Case of Computer Crime Laws." *Criminology* 26:101–26.

Kandel, Denise, Donald Treiman, Richard Faust, and Eric Single. 1976. "Adolescent Involvement in Legal and Illegal Drug Use: A Multiple Classification Analysis." *Social Forces* 55:438–58.

Kentucky Council on Higher Education. 1992. University of Kentucky fall 1992 enrollment figures.

*Kentucky Revised Statutes.* 1984. Sections 434.845, 434.850 and 434.855.

Krohn, Marvin L., William F. Skinner, James L. Massey, and Ronald Akers. 1985. "Social Learning Theory and Adolescent Cigarette Smoking: A Longitudinal Study." *Social Problems* 32 (5): 455–73.

Lewyn, Mark and Evan Schwartz. 1991. "Why the Legion of Doom Has Little Fear of the Feds." *Business Week,* August 6, p. 31.

McEwen, J. Thomas, Dennis Fester, and Hugh Nugent. 1989. *Dedicated Computer Crime Units.* Contract no. OJP-85-C-006. Washington, DC: National Institute of Justice.

O'Donoghue, Joseph. 1986. Mercy College Report on Computer Crime in Forbes 500 Companies: The Strategies of Containment. Dobbs Ferry, NY: Mercy College.

Parker, Donn B. 1976. *Crime by Computer.* New York: Scribner.

———. 1987. "Information Crime and Security." *Computer Fraud & Security Bulletin* 9 (5): 1–4.

Pfuhl, Edwin H., Jr. 1987. "Computer Abuse: Problems of Instrumental Control." *Deviant Behavior* (2): 113–30.

Schwartz, Evan I., Jeffrey Rothfeder, and Mark Lewyn. 1990. "Viruses? Who You Gonna Call 'Hackbusters.'" *Business Week,* August 6, pp. 71–72.

Skinner, B. F. 1953. *Science and Human Behavior.* New York: Macmillan.

Soma, John T., P. Smith, and R. Sprague. 1985. "Legal Analysis of Electronic Bulletin Board Activities." *Western New England Law Review* 7:571–626.

Sutherland, Edwin H. and Donald R. Cressey. 1974. *Criminology.* New York: J. B. Lippincott.

Swinyard, William R., Rinne Heikki, and Keng Kau Ah. 1990. "Morality of Software Piracy." *Journal of Business Ethics* 9:655–64.

Wong, Ken and Bill Farquhar. 1986. "Computer Fraud in the UK—The 1986 Picture." *Computer Fraud & Security Bulletin* 9 (1): 3–11.

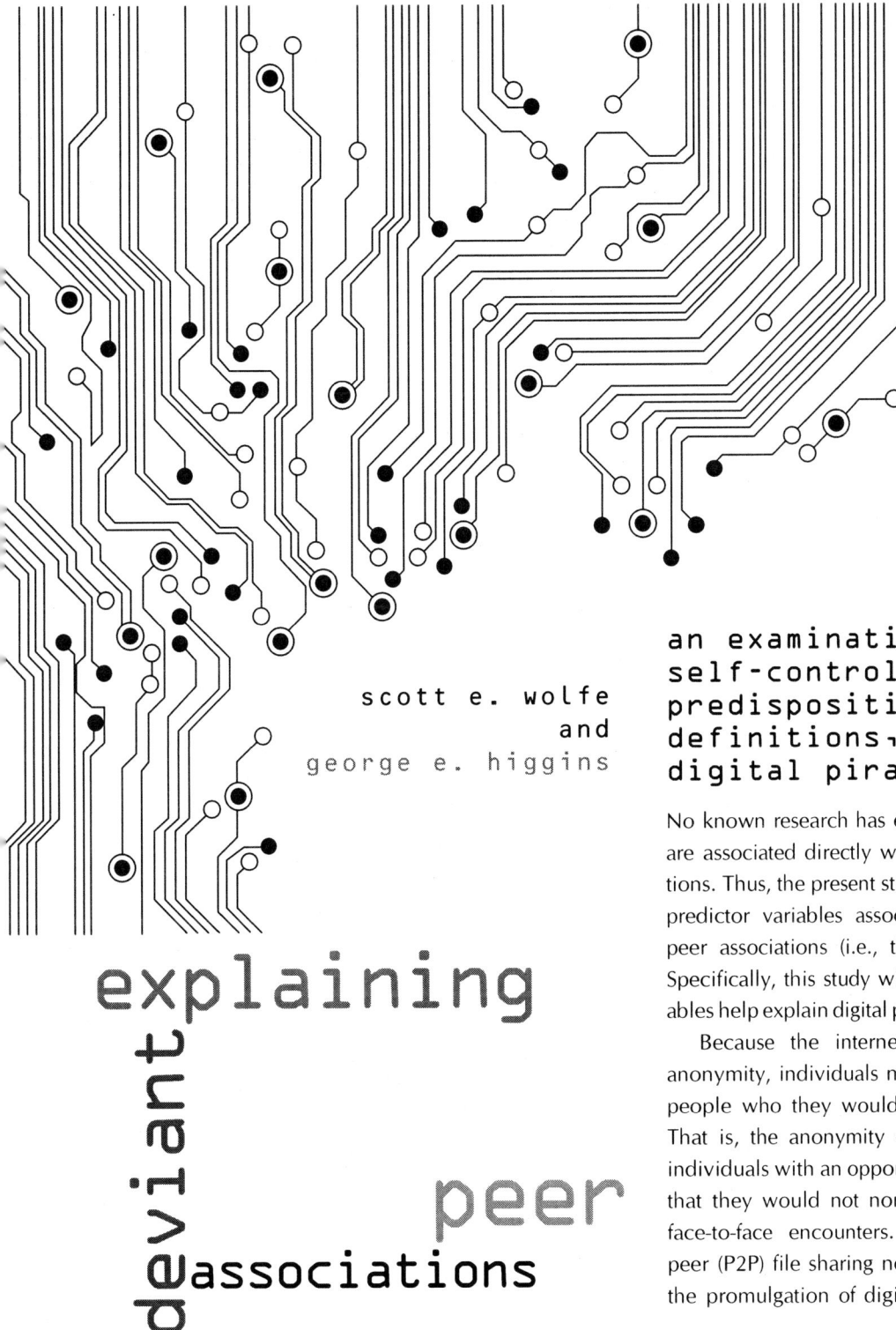

scott e. wolfe
and
george e. higgins

# explaining

deviant

peer

associations

## an examination of low self-control, ethical predispositions, definitions, and digital piracy

No known research has examined what variables are associated directly with deviant peer associations. Thus, the present study will explore possible predictor variables associated with the deviant peer associations (i.e., the dependent variable). Specifically, this study will determine which variables help explain digital pirating peer associations.

Because the internet provides a cloak of anonymity, individuals may be likely to befriend people who they would not normally befriend. That is, the anonymity of the internet provides individuals with an opportunity to behave in ways that they would not normally engage in during face-to-face encounters. For instance, peer-to-peer (P2P) file sharing networks are important in the promulgation of digital piracy. The Business

Software Alliance (BSA) (2003) reported that the increased availability of pirated software over the internet via P2P networks is contributing to rising piracy rates. The BSA indicated that almost 60 percent of all internet traffic is driven by P2P networks. Thus, the roles of peers and their networking systems are important in the development and continuation of digital piracy. However, little is known about the development of digital pirating peer associations. This knowledge may provide information to others about P2P networks and their relation to the tendency to perform the behavior. Therefore, a gap exists in the literature for understanding digital piracy peer associations.

The present study will explore the possible predictor variables associated with deviant peer associations (i.e., the dependent variable). Specifically, this study will determine what variables help explain digital pirating peer associations. This study contributes to the literature in two ways. First, this study will advance our understanding of social learning theory. Specifically, it will address areas that explain deviant peer associations. This theoretical development will be valuable in future explorations of other deviant and criminal behaviors and will assist in the formation of policies directed at the reduction of such behaviors. Second, it will help to further explain the act of digital piracy. The present study will shed light on what contributes to the formation of digital pirating peer associations, which will allow for policy interventions that can help reduce instances of digital piracy.

* * *

## the present study

The purpose of the present study is to examine the factors that contribute to the development of associations with digital pirating peers. Much of the extant literature has shown that differential association (Hinduja 2006; Higgins et al. 2007; Higgins et al. 2006; Higgins and Makin 2004a; Higgins and Wilson 2006; Hollinger 1993; Skinner and Fream 1997; Wolfe et al. in-press), definitions (Higgins et al. 2007; Higgins and Wilson 2006), ethical and moral beliefs (Al-Rafee and Cronan 2006; Gopal et al. 2004; Higgins and Makin 2004; Higgins and Wilson 2006; Im and Van Epps 1991; Solomon and O'Brien 1990; Thong and Yap 1998), and self-control all have links with digital piracy behavior. Additionally, many of these studies have shown correlations and interactive effects between each of the variables. However, little research has examined whether such variables explain associating with deviant, software-pirating peers. Regression will be used in the present study to determine whether low self-control, ethical predispositions (Gopal et al. 2004), definitions, gender, or age have a link with differential association.

This study is important to the development and understanding of differential association from social learning theory (Akers 1985), self-control theory (Gottfredson and Hirschi 1990), and ethical predispositions (Gopal et al. 2004) in the context of digital piracy. Additionally, this study will provide information on the factors that are associated with deviant peer associations, which can then be used to implement policies aimed at reducing instances of digital piracy. Finally, results from the present study will guide future research on digital piracy and other forms of criminal behavior.

## methods

The methods section of the paper will discuss the sampling procedure, sample, measures, and analytic process used in the analysis.

## procedure and sample

A self-report questionnaire was administered to college students at an eastern university in the United States in the fall 2004 semester after Institutional Review Board and Human Subject Protection review. Prior to administration of the survey, the researchers stressed the voluntary nature of study and explained that answers would be anonymous and confidential. The researchers ensured anonymity by requiring no identifying marks or personal information on the survey instrument. Further, confidentiality was ensured by the researchers storing all completed surveys in a locked filing cabinet housed in a locked room within the researchers' academic building. This set of procedures produced 392 questionnaires. However, due to listwise deletion for missing data, 337 completed questionnaires remained for the analysis. The sample consisted of a non-random sample of students in seven classes from the College of Arts and Sciences. These classes consisted of general education courses open to all students.

Table 1 presents the demographic characteristics of the sample. Males represented 39.2 percent of the sample, which is somewhat unrepresentative of the overall student population, which consisted of 47.4 percent males. About 81.5 percent of the sample was white, which is slightly higher than the university population, which is 76.7 percent white. The mean age category of the student sample was 4.37, which is between the ages of 21 and 22. Age information was not available from the university to compare to this sample. The sample consisted of 9.5 percent freshmen, 33.1 percent sophomores, 21.8 percent juniors, and 35.6 percent seniors. This is compared to the university population from which the sample was drawn, which consisted of 27.4 percent freshmen, 18.9 percent sophomores, 19.7 percent juniors, and 25.1 percent seniors. Thus, the sample is somewhat less representative of the overall university population in terms of class rank. Lastly, the present study oversampled criminal justice majors at 52.0 percent of the sample. While the sample is not perfectly representative of the university population from which it was drawn, it contains few drastic departures in terms of demographic characteristics.

Table 1.  Sample Descriptive Statistics

| Variable | Valid N | Mean | Median | Std. Deviation | Variance | Skewness | Kurtosis | Minimum | Maximum |
|---|---|---|---|---|---|---|---|---|---|
| Sex | 390 | .392 | 0 | .489 | .239 | .443 | −1.813 | 0 | 1 |
| Race | 379 | .815 | 1 | .389 | .151 | −1.632 | −.665 | 0 | 1 |
| Age | 391 | 4.371 | 4 | 2.274 | 5.172 | .742 | −.320 | 1 | 9 |
| Class Rank | 390 | 2.836 | 3 | 1.021 | 1.042 | −.206 | −1.249 | 1 | 4 |
| Major | 392 | .520 | 1 | .250 | .250 | −.082 | −2.004 | 0 | 1 |

## measures

The measures for this study included differential association (pirating peers), low self-control, ethical predispositions, and the control variables of age (1 = 18 to 9 = Over 25), sex (1 = male, 0 = female), race (1 = white, 0 = non-white), and previous software piracy ("How many times in the past month have you pirated software?").

*Differential association.* The dependent measure for this study was differential association. A composite of six items from Krohn et al. (1985) was used to form the measure of association with software-pirating peers. The items asked respondents to answer the following questions: "How many of your best *male* friends copied software in the last 12 months without paying for it?," "How many of your *male* friends that you have known the longest have copied software without paying for it in the last 12 months?," "How many of your *male* friends whom you are around the most copied software in the last 12 months without paying for it?," "How many of your best *female* friends copied software in the last 12 months without paying for it?," "How many of your *female* friends that you have known the longest have copied software without paying for it in the last 12 months?," and "How many of your *female* friends whom you are around the most copied software in the last 12 months without paying for it?" The answers were gathered using a five-point Likert-type scale (1 = none, 2 = just a few, 3 = about half, 4 = more than half, and 5 = all or almost all). Higher composite scores indicated more association with deviant peers or differential association. Internal consistency was shown to be acceptable for this measure (a = .96). Further, factor analysis and scree test showed that the scale was unidimensional.

*Definitions.* Respondents' definitions were measured using a set of 11 questions regarding their attitudes toward illegally copying or downloading digital software. A list of the items used in the definitions scale is presented in the Appendix. Such questions are consistent with Akers (1998) but have been formulated to be offense specific. A four-point Likert-type scale, ranging from 1 = strongly disagree to 4 = strongly agree, was used to measure each of the questions. A definitions scale was created by summing the ten questions together. Internal consistency for the scale was acceptable (a = .92) and was demonstrated to be unidimensional through factor analysis and scree test. Higher scores on the scale indicated positive definitions in favor of piracy.

*Low self-control.* Respondents' level of self-control was measured utilizing the 24-item Grasmick, Tittle, Bursik, and Arneklev (1993) scale. Response answer choices were measured on a four-point Likert-type scale, ranging from 1 = strongly disagree to 4 = strongly agree. The scale had an acceptable internal consistency (a = .86) and was shown to be unidimensional through factor analysis and scree test. Higher scores on the scale indicated *lower* levels of self-control.

*Ethical predisposition.* Overall ethical predispositions were measured using a composite of four items from Gopal et al. (2004), who demonstrated the utility of such a scale in research on digital piracy. The items asked the respondents to respond to the following statements: all individuals deserve equal treatment before the law; man's capacity for justice makes democracy possible, but man's inclination to injustice makes democracy necessary; to no man will we sell, or deny, or delay right or justice; and all human beings are born free and equal in dignity and rights. Answer choices were captured using a four-point Likert- type scale, ranging from 1 = strongly disagree to 4 = strongly agree. There was acceptable internal consistency (a = .72), and factor analysis and scree test show unidimensionality.

Table 2.  Regression Results with Differential Association as the Dependent Variable (n = 337)

| Variables | Unstandardized Coefficients | Standardized Coefficients | | t | Sig. | Collinearity Statistics | |
|---|---|---|---|---|---|---|---|
| | b | Std. Error | Beta | | | Tolerance | VIF |
| Age | −.331 | .113 | −.161 | −2.927 | .004 | .902 | 1.109 |
| Sex | .877 | .544 | .091 | 1.610 | .108 | .853 | 1.172 |
| Race | −.613 | .633 | −.051 | −.968 | .334 | .969 | 1.032 |
| Previous Piracy | .217 | .046 | .243 | 4.670 | .000 | .964 | 1.037 |
| Low Self-Control | .074 | .032 | .130 | 2.302 | .022 | .850 | 1.176 |
| Ethical Predis. | .291 | .217 | .111 | 2.074 | .039 | .953 | 1.049 |

F = 8.935**
$R^2$ = .146
**Correlation is significant at 0.01 level (2-tailed).
*Correlation is significant at 0.05 level (2-tailed).

Ordinary least squares (OLS) regression was used in the present study because the data were appropriate for such a technique. Specifically, the data are approximately normally distributed, which allows for the use of OLS regression. Table 3 summarizes the first regression analysis (i.e., without definitions in the model) to determine what factors are associated with deviant peer associations [Editor's note: Table 3 has been removed for the sake of brevity. Please see the original manuscript for all statistical figures]. Low self-control has an impact on differential association (b = .074, B = .130, t = 2.302). The lower an individual's self-control level, the greater deviant peer associations tend to be. This finding is consistent with literature concerning self-control theory and digital piracy. Further, the regression demonstrates that age is significantly related to deviant peer associations (b = -.331, B = -.161, t = -2.927). Specifically, as age increases, individuals are less likely to associate with digital pirating peers.

A unique finding from the first regression model is that ethical predispositions are associated with differential association in the opposite direction from what previous literature (Gopal et al. 2004) would suggest (b = .291, B = .111, t = 2.074). According to the regression, individuals with stronger ethical predispositions have more association with deviant peers. This is an important and interesting finding, given previous literature that implicates strong ethical predispositions (Gopal et al. 2004) with having a deterrent effect on digital piracy. The results of the present study suggest that strong ethical predispositions do not hinder the formation of deviant peer associations and may, in fact, lead to more encounters with software pirating friends. An examination of the tolerance and VIF values in the first model indicates that multicollinearity is not a problem with the data.

The next step in the present study was to examine the impact of definitions on the first model. Table 4 summarizes the findings for the second regression with definitions in the model. The results of the second regression are different from those in the first. With definitions in the model, the effect of low self-control and ethical predispositions on differential association was taken away. Age (b = -.283, B = -.138, t = -2.538) was still shown to impact differential association, with older respondents experiencing less association with deviant peers. Additionally, previous software piracy (b = .171, B

Table 4.  Regression Results with Definitions included in Model and Differential Association as the Dependent Variable (n = 337)

| Variables | Unstandardized Coefficients b | Standardized Coefficients Std. Error | Beta | t | Sig. | Collinearity Statistics Tolerance | VIF |
|---|---|---|---|---|---|---|---|
| Age | −.283 | .112 | −.138 | −2.538 | .012 | .887 | 1.127 |
| Sex | .669 | .541 | .069 | 1.236 | .217 | .839 | 1.192 |
| Race | −.259 | .630 | .024 | −.468 | .640 | .963 | 1.038 |
| Previous Piracy | .171 | .046 | .197 | 3.709 | .000 | .936 | 1.068 |
| Low Self-Control | .045 | .032 | .078 | 1.376 | .170 | .809 | 1.236 |
| Ethical Predis. | .204 | .139 | .078 | 1.471 | .142 | .930 | 1.075 |
| Definitions | .205 | .043 | .258 | 4.753 | .000 | .893 | 1.120 |

F = 8.935**
$R^2$ = .146
**Correlation is significant at 0.01 level (2-tailed).
*Correlation is significant at 0.05 level (2-tailed).

= .197, $t$ = 3.709) was still a significant predictor of differential association. Further, results from this regression demonstrate that individuals with favorable definitions for software piracy had significantly more associations with pirating peers ($b$ = .205, B = .258, $t$ = 4.753).

## discussion

The purpose of the present study was to determine what variables explain associating with software pirating peers by using differential association from social learning theory (Akers, 1985) as the dependent variable. Software piracy has been shown to be a serious crime problem in the United States (Business Software Alliance 2003; Peace et al. 2003; Seale et al. 1998). A number of criminological studies have examined digital piracy using social learning theory (Hinduja 2006; Higgins et al. 2007; Higgins et al. 2006; Higgins and Makin 2004a; Higgins and Wilson 2006; Hollinger 1993; Skinner and Fream 1997; Wolfe et al. in-press), self-control theory (Higgins 2005; Higgins et al. 2006; Higgins et al. 2005; Higgins and Wilson 2006; Wolfe et al. in-press), and ethical predispositions (Al- Rafee and Cronan 2006; Gopal et al. 2004; Higgins and Makin 2004b; Higgins and Wilson 2006; Im and Van Epps 1991; Solomon and O'Brien 1990; Thong and Yap 1998). However, no study to date has attempted to explicitly explain digital pirating peer associations. Doing so is important for two reasons. First, explaining digital pirating peer associations will assist in the formulation of policies aimed at reducing digital piracy. Secondly, understanding digital pirating peer associations will advance our understanding of social learning theory and will improve its utility in explaining various types of criminal behavior.

Results from the present study come with the use of two regression models. The first model examines the ability of age, sex, race, previous piracy behavior, low self-control, and ethical predispositions in explaining deviant peer association. This model does not include any social learning measures except the dependent variable of differential association. The results indicate that as an individual's age increases, he or she tends to associate with fewer deviant peers. Previous research on digital piracy has not found any significant associations with age and digital piracy (Higgins et al. 2007; Higgins and Wilson 2006). However, these studies did not use differential association as the dependent variable. While age may not help explain intentions to digitally pirate, the present study contributes to the literature by showing that age is an important predictor of association with pirating peers. Additionally, previous piracy behavior was shown to influence differential association. Specifically, those individuals who engage in more software piracy have more friends who engage in the same behavior. This is a fairly consistent finding in the social learning and digital piracy literature. These findings suggest that the robustness of social learning theory may be mediating the effect of demographics. Further, the first regression model demonstrates that low self-control is associated with deviant peer association, which tends to be a similar finding to previous literature showing low self-control to be a predictor of intentions to pirate (Higgins 2005; Higgins et al. 2006; Higgins et al. 2005; Higgins and Wilson 2006; Wolfe et al. in-press). The finding from the present study shows that an individual's level of self-control can not only be used to predict his or her intention to pirate but also to predict his or her association with deviant pirating peers. However, the relative impact of low self-control on deviant peer associations may not be as strong as Gottfredson and Hirschi (1990) contend in their general theory of crime when other variables are taken into consideration.

A unique finding from the first regression was that ethical predispositions were positively related to deviant peer association. This finding is counter to what would be hypothesized after examining previous literature on the subject. Studies have shown that individuals with lower ethical predispositions are

142

more likely to commit digital piracy (Gopal et al. 2004; Higgins and Makin 2004b; Higgins and Wilson 2006). As such, one would believe that lower ethical predispositions would be associated with more deviant peer relationships. However, the present study contributes to the literature by demonstrating that this is not the case. Rather, the more ethical an individual is the more likely she or he is to have deviant peer relationships. This suggests that ethical predispositions may not be important in reducing peoples' association with software pirating peers. Further, this finding suggests that software piracy may be a behavior that is often socially accepted and thus accepted within many peer groups. Essentially, associating with peers who commit software piracy may not be viewed as an unethical behavior.

Important to the present study was the second regression that included definitions from social learning theory in the model. This measure was included to see what effect it had on the other variables in the model. Interestingly, definitions took away the effect of low self-control and ethical predispositions. With definitions taken into consideration, an individual's level of self-control or ethical predispositions did not have an impact on his or her deviant peer associations. While the second regression still demonstrates that older individuals associate with fewer deviant pirating peers and those who have pirated themselves associate with more deviant peers, definitions was the only other measure with a significant relationship to the dependent variable. Specifically, individuals who have definitions that favor digital piracy are more likely to associate with peers who engage in the behavior. This finding is important to both the digital piracy and social learning theory literature. Importantly, the present study shows that when definitions are included into the model, the effect of low self-control and ethical predispositions on differential association is reduced to insignificancy. It appears that definitions have such a strong effect in explaining association with deviant peers that the impact of all other variables (with the exception of age) is negligible.

## references

Akers, Ronald L. 1985. *Deviant Behavior: A Social Learning Approach* (Third Edition). Belmont, CA: Wadsworth. Reprinted 1992. Fairfax, VA: Techbooks.

Akers, Ronald L. 1998. Social Learning and Social Structure: A General Theory of Crime and Deviance. Boston, MA: Northeastern University Press.

Akers, Ronald L. and Christine S. Sellers. 2004. Criminological Theories: Introduction, Evaluation, and Application (Fourth Edition). Los Angeles, CA: Roxbury.

Al-Rafee, Sulaiman and Timothy P. Cronan. 2006. "Digital Piracy: Factors that Influence Attitude toward Behavior." *Journal of Business Ethics* 63:237–259.

Bichler-Robertson, Gisela, Marissa C. Potchak, and Stephen G. Tibbetts. 2003. "Low Self-Control, Opportunity, and Strain in Students' Reported Cheating Behavior." *Journal of Crime and Justice* 26:23–53.

Brownfield, David. 2003. "Differential Association and Gang Membership." *Journal of Gang Research* 11:112.

Burgess, Robert L. and Ronald L. Akers. 1966. "A Differential Association Reinforcement Theory of Criminal Behavior." *Social Problems* 14:128–147.

Business Software Alliance. 2003. "Software Piracy Fact Sheet." Retrieved October 22, 2007 (http://www.bsa.org).

Chiou, Jyh-Shen, Chien-yi Huang, and Hsin-hui Lee. 2005. "The Antecedents of Music Piracy: Attitudes and Intentions." *Journal of Business Ethics* 57:161–174.

Cochran, John K., Peter B. Wood, Christine S. Sellers, W. Wilkerson, and Mitchell B. Chamlin. 1998. "Academic Dishonesty and Low Self-Control: An Empirical Test of a General Theory of Crime." *Deviant Behavior* 19:227–255.

d'Astous, Alain, Francois Colbert, and Daniel Montpetit. 2005. "Music Piracy on the Web—How Effective are Anti-Piracy Arguments? Evidence from the Theory of Planned Behaviour." *Journal of Consumer Policy* 28:289–310.

Durkin, Keith F., Timothy W. Wolfe, and Gregory A. Clark. 2005. "College Students and Binge Drinking: An Evaluation of Social Learning Theory." *Sociological Spectrum* 25:255–272.

Durkin, Keith F., Timothy W. Wolfe, and Daniel W. Phillips. 1996. "College Students' Use of Fraudulent Identification to Obtain Alcohol: An Exploratory Analysis." *Journal of Alcohol and Drug Education* 41:92–104.

Evans, T. David, Francis T. Cullen, Velmer S. Burton, R. Gregory Dunaway, and Michael L. Benson. 1997. "The Social Consequences of Self-Control: Testing the General Theory of Crime." *Criminology* 35:475–504.

Gibbs, John J. and Dennis Giever. 1995. "Self-Control and Its Manifestations among University Students: An Empirical Test of Gottfredson and Hirschi's General Theory." *Justice Quarterly* 12: 231–256.

Gibbs, John J., Dennis Giever, and Jamie Martin. 1998. "Parental Management and Self-Control: An Empirical Test of Gottfredson and Hirschi's General Theory." *Journal of Research in Crime and Delinquency* 35:40–70.

Glaser, Daniel. 1956. "Criminality Theories and Behavioral Images." *American Journal of Sociology* 61:433–444.

Gopal, Ram D., G. Lawrence Sanders, Sudip Bhattachaijee, Manish K. Agrawal, and Suzanne C. Wagner. 2004. "A Behavioral Model of Digital Music Piracy." *Journal of Organizational Computing and Electronic Commerce* 14 :89–105.

Gottfredson, Michael R. and Travis Hirschi. 1990. *A General Theory of Crime*. Stanford, CA: Stanford University Press.

Gottfredson, Michael and Travis Hirschi. 1987. *Positive Criminology*. Newbury Park, CA: Sage.

Grasmick, Harold G., Charles R. Tittle, Robert J. Bursik, and Bruce J. Arneklev. 1993. "Testing the Core Empirical Implications of Gottfredson and Hirschi's General Theory of Crime." Journal of Research in Crime and Delinquency 30:5–29.

Gupta, Pola B., Stephen J. Gould, and Bharath Pola. 2004. "To Pirate or Not to Pirate: A Comparative Study of the Ethical Versus Other Influences on the Consumer's Software Acquisition-Mode Decision." *Journal of Business Ethics* 55:255–274.

Higgins, George E. 2005. "Can Self-Control Theory Help Understand the Software Piracy Problem?" *Deviant Behavior* 26:1–24.

Higgins, George E., Brian D. Fell, and Abby L. Wilson. 2007. "Low Self-Control and Social Learning in Understanding Students' Intentions to Pirate Movies in the United States." *Social Science Computer Review* 25:339–357.

Higgins, George E., Brian D. Fell, and Abby L. Wilson. 2006. "Digital Piracy: Assessing the Contributions of an Integrated Self-Control Theory and Social Learning Theory Using Structural Equation Modeling." *Criminal Justice Studies* 19:3–22.

Higgins, George E. and David A. Makin. 2004a. "Does Social Learning Theory Condition the Effects of Low Self-Control on College Students' Software Piracy?" *Journal of Economic Crime Management* 2:1–22.

Higgins, George E. and David A. Makin. 2004b. "Self-Control, Deviant Peers, and Software Piracy." Psychological Reports 95:921–931.

Higgins, G.E. and A.L. Wilson. 2006. "Low Self-Control, Moral Beliefs, and Social Learning Theory in University Students' Intentions to Pirate Software." *Security Journal* 19:75–92.

Higgins, George E., Abby L. Wilson, , and Brian D. Fell. 2005. "An Application of Deterrence Theory to Software Piracy." *Journal of Criminal Justice and Popular Culture* 12:166–194.

Hinduja, Sameer. 2006. *Music Piracy and Crime Theory.* New York: LFB Scholarly, Inc.

Hirschi, Travis. 2004. "Self-Control and Crime." Pp. 537–552 in *Handbook of Self-Regulation: Research, Theory, and Applications,* edited by Roy F. Baumeister and Karen D. Vohs. New York: Guilford Press.

Hollinger, Richard C. 1993. "Crime by Computer: Correlates of Software Piracy and Unauthorized Account Access." *Security Journal* 4:2–12.

Hunt, Shelby D. and Scott. Vitell. 1986. "A General Theory of Marketing Ethics." *Journal of Macromarketing* 6:5–16.

Im, Jin H. and Pamela D. Van Epps. 1991. "Software Piracy and Software Security in Business Schools: An Ethical Perspective." The Database for Advances in Information Systems 15–21.

International Federation of Phonographic Industries (IFPI). 2006. "*The Recording Industry 2006 Piracy Report: Protecting Creativity in Music.*" Retrieved October 16, 2007 (http://www.ifpi.org).

Kini, Ranjan B., H.V. Ramakrishna, and B.S. Vijayaraman. 2004. "Shaping of Moral Intensity Regarding Software Piracy: A Comparison Between Thailand and U.S. Students." *Journal of Business Ethics* 49:91–104.

Koen, Clifford M. and Jin H. Im. 1997. "Software Piracy and Its Legal Implications." *Security Journal* 31:265–272.

Krohn, Marvin D., William F. Skinner, James L. Massey, and Ronald L. Akers. 1985. "Social Learning Theory and Adolescent Cigarette Smoking: A Longitudinal Study." *Social Problems* 32:455–471.

Liang, Zhili and Zheng Yan. 2005. "Software Piracy Among College Students: A Comprehensive Review of Contributing Factors, Underlying Processes, and Tackling Strategies." *Journal of Educational Computing Research* 33:115–140.

Moores, T.T. and J.C. Chang. 2006. "Ethical Decision Making in Software Piracy: Initial Development and Test of a Four-component Model." *MIS Quarterly* 30:167–180.

Peace, A. Graham, Dennis F. Galletta, and James Y.L. Thong. 2003. "Software Piracy in the Workplace: A Model and Empirical Test." *Journal of Management Information Systems* 20:153–177.

Piquero, Alex R. and Stephen G. Tibbetts. 1996. "Specifying the Direct and Indirect Effects of Low Self-Control and Situational Factors in Offenders' Decision Making: Toward a More Complete Model of Rational Offending." *Justice Quarterly* 13: 481–510.

Pratt, Travis C. and Francis T. Cullen. 2000. "The Empirical Status of Gottfredson and Hirschi's General Theory of Crime: A Meta-Analysis." *Criminology* 38:931–964.

Seale, Darryl A., Michael Polakowski, and Sherry Schneider. 1998. "It's Not Really Theft! Personal and Workplace Ethics that Enable Software Piracy." *Behavior and Information Technology* 17:27–40.

Siegfried, Robert M. 2004. "Student Attitudes on Software Piracy and Related Issues of Computer Ethics." *Ethics and Information Technology* 6:215–222.

Skinner, William F. and Anne M. Fream. 1997. "A Social Learning Theory Analysis of Computer Crime among College Students." *Journal of Research in Crime and Delinquency* 34:563–581.

Solomon, S. and J. O'Brien. 1990. "The Effects of Demographic Factors on Attitudes toward Software Piracy." *Journal of Computer Information Systems* 30:40–46.

Sutherland, Edwin D. 1947. *Principles of Criminology* (Fourth Edition). Philadelphia, PA: J.B. Lippincott.

Tan, Benjamin. 2002. "Understanding Consumer Ethical Decision Making with Respect to Purchase of Pirated Software." *Journal of Consumer Marketing* 19:96–112.

Taylor, Susan L. 2004. "Music Piracy: Differences in the Ethical Perceptions of Business Majors and Music Business Majors." *Journal of Education for Business* 79:306–310.

Thong, James L. and Chee-Sing Yap. 1998. "Testing an Ethical Decision-Making Theory: The Case of Softlifting." *Journal of Management Information Systems* 15:213–237.

Tibbetts, Stephen G. 1997. "Gender Differences in Students' Rational Decisions to Cheat." *Deviant Behavior* 18: 393–414.

Tibbetts, Stephen G. and Denise C. Herz. 1996. "Gender Differences in Factors of Social Control and Rational Choices." *Deviant Behavior* 17: 183–208.

Tibbetts, Stephen G. and David L. Myers. 1999. "Low Self-Control, Rational Choice, and Student Test Cheating." American Journal of Criminal Justice 23:179–200.

Turner, Michael G. and Alex R. Piquero. 2002. "The Stability of Self-Control." *Journal of Criminal Justice* 30:457–471.

Tyler, Tom R. 1996. "Compliance with Intellectual Property Laws: A Psychological Perspective." *Journal of International Law and Politics* 29:219–235.

Wagner, Suzanne C. and G. Lawrence Sanders. 2001. "Considerations in Ethical Decision-making and Software Piracy." *Journal of Business Ethics* 29:161–167.

Wall, David S. 2006. "Surveillant Internet Technologies and the Growth in Information Capitalism: Spams and Public Trust in the Information Society." Pp. 340–362 in *The New Politics of Surveillance and Visibility,* edited by K. Haggerty and R. Ericson. Toronto, Canada: University of Toronto Press.

Winfree, L. Thomas and Francis P. Bernat. 1998. "Social Learning, Self-Control and Substance Abuse by Eighth Grade Students: A Tale of Two Cities." *Journal of Drug Issues* 28: 539–558.

Wolfe, Scott E., George E. Higgins, and Catherine D. Marcum. 2008. "Deterrence and Digital Piracy: A Preliminary Examination of the Role of Viruses." *Social Science Computer Review* 26:317–333.

adam m. bossler
and
thomas j. holt

the effect of

self-control

victimization    in the    on    cyberworld

Despite the increasing threat of cybercrime, little is known about the theoretical causes and correlates of cybercrime victimization (see Holtfreter, Reisig, & Pratt, 2008 for a similar discussion of fraud). Although lifestyle/routine activities theory may be useful in understanding cybercrime victimization (Grabosky & Smith, 2001; Holt & Bossler, 2009; Newman & Clarke, 2003; Pease, 2001; see Yar, 2005 for opposing viewpoint), support is limited. Risky lifestyles, including the participation in cyber-deviance or associating with peers who commit cyber-deviance, had been found to increase the odds of on-line harassment (Holt & Bossler, 2009) and malware infection leading to data loss (Bossler & Holt, 2009). Most measures of general computer usage, however, such as time spent on-line, as well as physical guardianship measures including anti-virus software and other protective programs, had little influence on the likelihood of cybercrime victimization (Bossler & Holt, 2009; Holt & Bossler, 2009). Thus, these studies provided partial support for Yar's (2005)

Adam M. Bossler and Thomas J. Holt, "The Effect of Self-control on Victimization in the Cyberworld," *Journal of Criminal Justice*, vol. 38, no. 3, pp. 227-236. Copyright © 2010 by Elsevier Ltd. Reprinted with permission.

argument that cybercrime is substantively different from traditional victimization in that virtual environments are spatially and temporally disconnected and relatively unstable, unlike physical space. Given the limited success of these studies, there is a need to examine theories that explore the relationship between individual characteristics and victimization.

To that end, recent research found merit for the expansion of Gottfredson and Hirschi's general theory of crime into the field of traditional victimization (Holtfreter et al., 2008; Piquero, MacDonald, Dobrin, Daigle, & Cullen, 2005; Schreck, 1999; Schreck, Stewart, & Fisher, 2006; Schreck, Wright, & Miller, 2002; Stewart, Elifson, & Sterk, 2004). This expansion suggests that individuals with low self-control make impulsive decisions, which increase their vulnerability as well as their exposure to offender populations, thereby increasing their risk of victimization. In addition, previous research found a significant relationship between self-control and cyber-deviance, suggesting that this theory may have utility for explaining cybercrime victimization as well (e.g., Buzzell, Foss, & Middleton, 2006; Higgins, 2005; Higgins et al., 2006; Higgins & Makin, 2004).

The current study attempted to improve the theoretical and empirical knowledge of cybercrime victimization by exploring the impact of self-control on the probability of being victimized in cyberspace. Specifically, this study explored the impact of self-control, respondent offending, and peer offending on five forms of cybercrime victimization: unauthorized access to one's computer; having information added, deleted, or changed on one's computer without knowledge or permission; data loss due to malware infection; having one's credit card information electronically obtained without knowledge or permission; and on-line harassment. Furthermore, this study considered whether low self-control had a direct or indirect effect on victimization. The effect may be direct as individuals with inadequate levels of self-control make impulsive, shortsighted, and risky decisions that may increase their risk of victimization. The effect of self-control on victimization, however, may be mediated by offending measures, indicating that self-control only influences victimization if it places individuals in closer proximity to offenders (Schreck, 1999). Thus, this study built on the work of past scholars by examining the link between self-control and previously unexplored forms of victimization that differ substantively from traditional forms. These findings raise theoretical and empirical questions for the entire field of victimization regarding the importance of individual characteristics in comparison with offending measures.

## self-control and victimization

In the traditional victimization literature, scholars have explored the link between low levels of self-control (Gottfredson & Hirschi, 1990) and various forms of victimization (e.g., Piquero et al., 2005; Schreck, 1999; Schreck et al., 2006). Michael Gottfredson and Travis Hirschi's (1990) general theory of crime is a classic control theory which argues that motivation is invariant among all individuals, but levels of constraint differentiate criminals from non-criminals. They argue that humans are rational beings who weigh the costs and benefits of potential behavior, including crime, and act accordingly. Crime is an efficient and effective means to satisfy immediate gratification, though the benefits are usually meager with severe long-term consequences, such as incarceration or retaliation from rival gangs. Thus, individuals with low self-control commit crimes because they do not recognize or care that the consequences of offending are greater than the benefits. Since its inception, low self-control has consistently been linked to various forms of crime and deviance, ranging from student cheating to more serious street crime (e.g., Gibson & Wright, 2001; Grasmick, Tittle, Bursik, & Arneklev, 1993; Piquero

& Tibbetts, 1996) and can be considered one of the strongest correlates of crime regardless of how it has been measured (Pratt & Cullen, 2000).

Although Gottfredson and Hirschi (1990) considered self-control theory to be a *general theory of crime*, and not technically a theory of victimization, they argued that the high correlation between offending and victimization is because both are a result of inadequate levels of self-control (pp. 92–94). The same characteristics of low self-control (i.e., shortsighted, insensitive, impatient, risk-taking) that increase the odds of committing crime also increase the likelihood of victimization through various mechanisms. Individuals with lower levels of self-control do not accurately consider and perceive the consequences of their actions, both increasing the probability of crime and victimization. They place themselves in risky situations and possibly act in an unadvised manner. Thus, participating in imprudent behavior not only increases crime opportunities, but also increases victimization as well (Forde & Kennedy, 1997).

Individuals with lower levels of self-control are furthermore more likely to associate with deviant others, which not only increases their opportunity and likelihood of committing crime (Gibson & Wright, 2001; Higgins et al., 2006; Longshore, Chang, Hsieh, & Messina, 2004), but also increases their victimization risks (Jensen & Brownfield, 1986; Lauritsen, Sampson, & Laub, 1991; Sampson & Lauritsen, 1990). Associating with delinquent peers increases contact with motivated offenders because these delinquent peers will not have to alter their normal routines significantly to find suitable targets with a lack of social guardianship (Holt & Bossler, 2009; Schreck & Fisher, 2004; Schreck et al., 2002). In addition, participation in a delinquent group can increase the odds of victimization if group norms favor the use of violence to settle disputes within the group (Baron, Forde, & Kennedy, 2001). Finally, associating with delinquent peers can increase victimization risk because of other peer groups retaliating for previous perceived or actual injuries (Jensen & Brownfield, 1986; Schreck et al., 2002).

These findings lead to the linkage between the individual-level theory of self-control and elements of the situational theory of routine activities theory to create a conceptual framework of victimization (Forde & Kennedy, 1997; Schreck et al., 2002). This framework argues that low self-control has both *indirect* and *direct* effects on victimization. An indirect effect on victimization is observed because individuals with inadequate levels of self-control are more likely to place themselves in risky situations and associate with delinquent others. Self-control maintains a direct effect on victimization because individuals with low self-control make decisions exclusive of the situation that increases their vulnerability.

\* \* \*

## cybercrime victimization and self-control

Although no previous tests examined whether inadequate levels of self-control are related to higher *cybercrime* victimization rates, the connection between the two seemed plausible. Recent cybercrime scholarship found that individuals with low levels of self-control were more likely to commit various forms of cyber-deviance, including the downloading and viewing of pornographic images (Buzzell et al., 2006), digital piracy (Higgins, 2005; Higgins et al., 2006; Higgins, Wolfe, & Marcum, 2008), movie piracy (Higgins, Fell, & Wilson, 2007), and software piracy (Higgins, 2005, 2006; Higgins & Makin, 2004). These studies indicated that self-control might predict crime in the cyberworld as well as it does in the terrestrial world. Additionally, preliminary research suggested the victim/offender overlap found in real world crime (e.g., Jensen & Brownfield, 1986) also exists in virtual environments (Bossler &

Holt, 2009; Holt & Bossler, 2009). Given this relationship, self-control may be related to cybercrime victimization since it is related to cybercrime offending.

Schreck's (1999) framework connecting the elements of low self-control to traditional victimization appeared to apply to cybercrime victimization in a variety of ways. Individuals with low self-control often have a "here and now" mentality and place little weight on long-term consequences, focusing instead on short-term immediate gratification (Gottfredson & Hirschi, 1990). They are often risk-taking and can be considered thrill-seekers. This decreases the safety of oneself and one's property, increasing vulnerability to victimization (Schreck, 1999). These same principals apply to on-line environments, as individuals with low self-control tend to engage in risky behaviors, such as pirating media (Higgins, 2005; Higgins et al., 2006; Higgins & Makin, 2004) and viewing pornography (Buzzell et al., 2006). These acts provide immediate gratification while also increasing the likelihood of malicious software infection and other forms of victimization (Bossler & Holt, 2009; Holt & Bossler, 2009). Individuals may also interact with others they do not know in chatrooms and virtual environments that may lead to on-line harassment or cyber-stalking (Gilboa, 1996; Hinduja & Patchin, 2008a, 2008b; Holt & Bossler, 2009).

Individuals with low self-control have little empathy, making it difficult to relate to others and leading to fewer and weaker social ties. They may also misunderstand other people's intentions (Gottfredson & Hirschi, 1990; Schreck, 1999). As a result, they experience a decrease of social support and an increase in vulnerability to victimization (Schreck, 1999). Individuals who have difficulty evaluating the intentions of others in face-to-face interactions are at a significant disadvantage in on-line environments (see Herring, 1999; Wall, 2001). Electronic communications, such as e-mail and instant messaging, provide a degree of anonymity and detachment that allow individuals to fraudulently present themselves as any age, race, or gender they choose (see Bocij, 2004; Finn, 2004). Thus, the risk of providing sensitive personal or financial information to criminals is extremely high on-line, increasing the risk of harassment or theft.

In addition, low tolerance can increase vulnerability to victimization in two ways. Individuals with low self-control are commonly physically-oriented and can be easily frustrated or angered (Gottfredson & Hirschi, 1990). These characteristics can unnecessarily escalate situations toward violent outcomes that may increase the likelihood of victimization (Gottfredson & Hirschi, 1990; Schreck, 1999). Inconsiderate or aggressive on-line behavior can lead to victimization in the virtual world as well. Individuals who are easily frustrated may not be capable of dealing with others on-line, as conflict and aggressive language are a regular part of on-line communications (Bocij, 2004; Gilboa, 1996; Herring, 1999). Those with low tolerance may be more likely to be harassed, called names, and threatened in social interactions on-line.

People with low tolerance can also become frustrated with complex security devices, such as steering wheel locks or alarm systems (Schreck, 1999). These individuals stop using the devices completely or use them carelessly, making them more vulnerable to victimization. Security programs meant to protect a system are not necessarily intuitive or simple (see Furnell, 2002; Wall, 2001). Obtaining a security device is not enough to minimize victimization risk in cybercrime. To fully secure a computer, users must regularly update the protective software that is in place to guard against new viruses and other forms of malware that are discovered every day (PandaLabs, 2007). If users do not take these steps, their vulnerability to infection, system compromise, data loss, and other forms of cybercrime victimization increases significantly (see Chien, 2003; Szor, 2005; Taylor et al., 2006). Thus, individuals who become easily frustrated or who lack diligence will not consistently take the available precautions to protect themselves and their property from on-line criminals.

In addition, self-control appears to be related to cybercrime victimization indirectly by its influence on peer associations, as is found in the traditional victimization literature. Individuals with inadequate levels of self-control are more likely to associate with peers who support cybercrime (e.g., Higgins et al., 2006). This increases their proximity to motivated offenders while also decreasing social guardianship (Holt & Bossler, 2009). Deviant peers often harass and victimize the most suitable and convenient targets, even in the virtual world (Holt & Bossler, 2009). Often these suitable targets are their own "friends." Deviant peers may even cause unintentional victimization as malware may be downloaded and spread to others by those who commit computer deviance (e.g., viewing on-line pornography) (Bossler & Holt, 2009).

Not all deviant associations, however, are virtual in nature. Many individuals interact with their peers in both the real and virtual world. Although deviant peers might not victimize their acquaintances in the physical world, they might rely on the anonymous nature of the Internet to harass their peers, hack into their computers, steal their identities, or send malware. For example, hackers gain information and expertise from their associations with other hackers both on- and off-line (Holt, 2007; Jordan & Taylor, 1998; Rogers, Smoak, & Liu, 2006). Many of these associations are not strong, but they still reinforce hacker behavior and place individuals in closer proximity to motivated offenders. Hackers often experience harassment and computer attacks by their fellow hackers because of their sex, skill level, or inappropriate on-line etiquette (Holt, 2007; Jordan & Taylor, 1998). Thus, individuals who associate with deviant peers, whether on- or off-line, increase their probability of being victimized in cyberspace.

\* \* \*

## the present study

This study examined whether self-control theory was useful for understanding cybercrime victimization in comparison to the importance of offending measures. Specifically, this study hypothesized that individuals with lower levels of self-control were more likely to be victims of five forms of cybercrime: unauthorized access to one's computer; having information added, deleted, or changed on one's computer without knowledge or permission; data loss due to malware infection; having one's credit card information electronically obtained without knowledge or permission; and on-line harassment. In addition, this study considered the direct and indirect effects of self-control on victimization after controlling for both respondent and peer offending behavior. It was hypothesized that the relationship between self-control and cybercrime victimization would have been partially mediated by respondent and peer offending. Self-control, however, was expected to retain its direct effect on cybercrime victimization.[1]

Data were collected from a self-report survey administered to students at a southeastern university during the fall of 2006. Five of the ten courses in which the surveys were administered allowed students of any major to enroll. Five hundred seventy-three students answered all questions necessary for the analyses. The analyzed data set was 59 percent female and 88 percent non-Black, similar but slightly overrepresenting the larger university population (52.5 percent female; 75 percent White).

---

1   It should be noted that scholars throughout the self-control-victimization literature refer to peer delinquency measures as part of the "delinquency peer context" (Schreck et al., 2006, p. 323) or "peer context" (Schreck & Fisher, 2004, p. 1021). Delinquency measures, however, are normally described as situational antecedents, situational risk factors, or situational predictors of victimization (Jensen & Brownfield, 1986; Lauritsen et al., 1991; Schreck et al., 2002). Thus, these measures were referred to as "offending measures" or "situational factors" in this study.

\* \* \*

## measures

### *dependent variable*

### *cybercrime victimization*

Respondents were asked how many times they experienced cybercrime victimization over the past twelve months.[2] On a five-point ordinal scale (0 = never, 1 = one to two times, 2 = three to five times, 3 = six to nine times, 4 = ten or more times), students were asked how many times they had been victimized by each of the following five cybercrimes: (1) someone obtaining your password to access your computer account or files (Y1); (2) someone adding, deleting, or changing information in your computer files without your knowledge or permission (Y2); (3) someone sending a computer virus, worm, or Trojan that destroyed computerized data (Y3); (4) someone electronically obtaining your credit card number without your knowledge or permission (Y4); and (5) someone harassing you in a chatroom, IRC, or IM (Instant Messaging) (Y5) (Rogers, 2001). Few students experienced repeat victimization, decreasing variation.[3]

Receiving malicious software that destroyed computerized data (Y3) was the most common form of cybercrime victimization, with 36.5 percent reporting this type of victimization within the last twelve months. On-line harassment (Y5) was the second highest reported form of victimization (18.8 percent); followed by 16.8 percent who were victims of password access (Y1); 9.8 percent who had someone add, delete, or change computer information without their permission (Y2); and only 4.4 percent who were victims of credit card theft via electronic means (Y4). The five dependent variables were dichotomized into five dummy measures, which was consistent with the perception of victimization as a probabilistic event in self-control theory (see Schreck, 1999, p. 644) and because of the skewed data and limited variation in the dependent variable.

---

2  It should be noted that recall periods were shorter in other studies examining on-line behavior. For example, the General Social Survey had a question assessing how often respondents viewed sexually explicit Web sites in the last thirty days (see Buzzell, 2005; Stack et al., 2004). The National Crime Victimization Survey (NCVS) asked about identity theft over the last six months (Baum, 2007). While a longer recall period can decrease the respondent's ability to remember information accurately, most forms of cybercrime victimization do not occur frequently enough to have thirty-day recall periods. Within this sample, credit card theft via electronic means affected only 4.4 percent of the sample over the last twelve months, similar to the NCVS's estimate that 5 percent of the population suffers from identity theft yearly (Baum, 2007). Aside from malware victimization, all other forms of victimization occurred to less than 20 percent of the sample. If a shorter recall period were used, it would have been necessary to combine all the victimization measures into one measure.
3  Y1 = 83.2 percent never, 14.7 percent one to two times, 1.0 percent three to five times, .5 percent six to nine times, .5 percent ten or more times; Y2 = 90.2 percent never, 7.5 percent one to two times, 1.6 percent three to five times, .3 percent six to nine times, .3 percent ten or more times; Y3 = 63.5 percent never, 30.2 percent one to two times, 4.9 percent three to five times, 1.0 percent six to nine times, .3 percent ten or more times; Y4 = 95.6 percent never, 4.4 percent one to two times; Y5 = 81.2 percent never, 14.0 percent one to two times, 3.5 percent three to five times, .7 percent six to nine times, .7 percent ten or more times.

## Independent variables

### Low self-control

This study utilized the twenty-four-item Grasmick et al. (1993) scale. The response categories ranged from strongly disagree (1) to strongly agree (4). The twenty-four items were standardized and summed, producing a measure ranging from -31.35 to 53.74 (mean = .00; SD = 12.73). Higher scores indicated less self-control. The Cronbach's alpha was 0.89, indicating very good reliability (no item could have been deleted to increase reliability). Similar to past studies, principal components analysis revealed six factors with eigenvalues over one (e.g., Grasmick et al., 1993). The Kaiser rule, however, can over-estimate the number of significant factors with a large number of items. The scree discontinuity test indicated a one-factor solution with the largest drop between the first and second factors.

The debate on the strengths and weaknesses of attitudinal and behavioral measures of self-control is not rehashed because of space considerations. It should be noted, however, that Pratt and Cullen's (2000) meta-analysis found self-control to be an important predictor of crime regardless of whether it was measured via an attitudinal or behavioral scale. In addition, most scholars have utilized some derivative of the Grasmick et al. (1993) attitudinal scale to examine the effects of self-control on *deviance* (e.g., Arneklev, Grasmick, Tittle, & Bursik, 1993; Hay, 2001; Piquero, Gomez-Smith, & Langton, 2004; Vazsonyi & Belliston, 2007) and *victimization* (Forde & Kennedy, 1997; Schreck, 1999; Schreck et al., 2006; Schreck et al., 2002; Stewart et al., 2004). Behavioral measures of self-control in victimization studies are rare (Holtfreter et al., 2008; Piquero et al., 2005). Thus, this study followed suit with the majority of the self-control-victimization literature in order to better compare findings.

### Cyber-deviance

Respondents were asked how many times in the past twelve months they had either used their own computer or another person's to: (1) knowingly use, make, or give to another person a "pirated" copy of commercially-sold computer software; (2) knowingly use, make, or give to another person "pirated" media (music, television show, or movie); (3) look at pornographic or obscene materials; (4) guess another's password to get into his/her computer account or files; (5) access another's computer account or files without his/her knowledge or permission to look at information or files; (6) add, delete, change, or print any information in another's computer files without the owner's knowledge or permission; and (7) use someone else's wireless Internet connection without their authorization to surf the Web or otherwise access on-line content (Rogers, 2001; Skinner & Fream, 1997). The options were: never, one to two times, three to five times, six to nine times, and ten or more times. Responses to these seven items were standardized and then averaged. The range for this measure was between -.44 and 4.26 (mean = 0; SD = .66) and the Cronbach's alpha was .79.

A measure of cyber-deviance was included in these analyses for three reasons. First, previous research had found a strong connection between victimization and offending both off-line (Osgood et al., 1996; Sampson & Lauritsen, 1990; Zhang et al., 2001) and on-line (Bossler & Holt, 2009; Holt & Bossler, 2009). In fact, scholars found a relationship between on-line and off-line offending, as evidenced by research on bullying (Hinduja & Patchin, 2008b) and pornography (Stack, Wasserman, & Kern, 2004). Thus, respondent offending was included in the analysis to understand its role as an indicator of victimization. Second, it was imperative to control for offending in order to assess the direct effect of self-control on victimization and not the residual effects of the situation, such as proximity to motivated offenders or retaliation (Schreck, 1999). The inclusion of respondent offending measures allowed for the study to assess the effect of illegal behavior that does not occur in their peers' presence on victimization. Considering the anonymity of the Internet, and that most computer deviance occurs in the absence of others (e.g., see Holt, 2007), it seemed plausible that individuals could place themselves at risk for victimization by committing crime that was not related to their peers. Third, including a measure of cyber-deviance limited the bias posed by asking respondents to report their peers' deviance. Respondents often project their beliefs and qualities onto their friendships (Haynie & Osgood, 2005). Controlling respondent deviance thus alleviated this potential bias as much as possible using this measurement approach (Schreck et al., 2006).

## peer offending

To more fully test whether self-control had a direct effect on victimization, net of offending, a measure of peer offending was included with measures that matched the types of victimization being examined. Following the most common approach in measuring peer deviance (Lauritsen et al., 1992), respondents were asked how many of their friends in the past twelve months had: (1) knowingly used, made, or given to another person a "pirated" copy of commercially-sold computer software; (2) knowingly used, made, or given to another person "pirated" media (music, television show, or movie); (3) looked at pornographic or obscene material; (4) guessed another's password to get into his/her computer account or files; (5) accessed another's computer account or files without his/her knowledge or permission to look at information or files; and (6) added, deleted, changed, or printed any information in another's computer files without the owner's knowledge or permission (Rogers, 2001; Skinner & Fream, 1997). The response categories were: none of them; very few of them; about half of them; more than half of them; and all of them. Responses were standardized and averaged, creating a measure ranging from -.77 to 3.69 (mean = 0; SD = .73). The Cronbach's alpha was .82.

## control variables

This study controlled for sex, being Black, employment, and age since these factors have been found to be related to "traditional" victimization (see Lauritsen et al., 1992; Miethe & Meier, 1994; Sampson & Lauritsen, 1990; Stewart et al., 2004). Sex (female = 1) and race (Black = 1) were dummy measures. The sample was 59 percent female and 11.5 percent Black. Employment was a three-point ordinal measure (unemployed, part-time/temporary, full-time): 28.8 percent were unemployed, 60.4 percent were part-time workers, and 10.8 percent worked full-time. Finally, age was a four-point ordinal measure with 42.8 percent reporting they were eighteen to nineteen, 36.6 percent were twenty to twenty-one, 14.3 percent were twenty-two to twenty-five, and 6.3 percent were twenty-six and over. Controls for school and social ties were not included since past research did not find these variables to be direct or indirect predictors of victimization (Schreck et al., 2006; Schreck et al., 2002).

# results

A correlation matrix is presented in Table 1.[4] The results were consistent overall with the hypothesized relationships. Low self-control was positively related, although weakly, with three different types of

---

4   The tests of significance were one-tailed between the dependent and independent variables because the hypotheses were directional (see also Piquero et al., 2005). This study hypothesized that individuals with low self-control were more likely to be victimized. In addition, this provided a more conservative test of Schreck's (1999) argument that self-control needed to be related to victimization, net of offending.

cybercrime victimization—password access, having computer information changed, and being harassed on-line. Self-control was not significantly correlated with data loss from malware infection or having one's credit card stolen electronically. As the literature suggested, cybercrime offending and peer offending were positively related with all five victimization types.

Following past research on the self control-victimization relationship (Schreck, 1999; Stewart et al., 2004), descriptive statistics and t-tests of the means were examined to assess significant differences between victims and non-victims for each victimization type for the main independent variables (self-control, cyber-deviance, and peer offending) (see Table 2). Only victims of password access and having computer information changed reported lower levels of self-control than non-victims. Harassment victims did not differ from non-victims on any of these three variables. Credit card victims only differed because of having more delinquent friends. Cybercrime victims were generally more likely to commit cyber-deviance and to associate with those who commit cybercrime. Although the correlations and t-tests analyses illustrated that self-control did not have a strong relationship with certain types of cybercrime victimization and no relationship with other types, these univariate analyses provided enough evidence to further explore the relationship between self-control and cybercrime victimization via multivariate analyses.

Logistic regression was used to estimate the probability of cybercrime victimization (see Holtfreter et al., 2008; Schreck, 1999 for similar approaches in the victimization literature). Logistic regression was an appropriate technique for these analyses as the dependent variables were dichotomous and skewed. In addition, victimization is seen as a probabilistic event in both Gottfredson and Hirschi's (1990) general theory of crime and its expansion to victimization (e.g., Schreck, 1999). For each cybercrime victimization type, three models were tested (presented in Table 3) (see Stewart et al., 2004 for similar approach). Model 1 was a baseline model that included the measures of female, Black, age, and employment. In Model 2, low self-control was added to the equation. In Model 3, cybercrime offending and peer offending were added to the equation in order to examine whether these risky behaviors mediated the effect of self-control on victimization and if self-control retained a direct effect on victimization when controlling for the offending measures.

Multicollinearity did not appear to bias the parameter estimates for these models. Peer offending and the commission of cyber-deviance were moderately correlated ($r = .57$; see Table 1). Multicollinearity diagnostics found that the highest variance inflation factor (1.63) and lowest tolerance estimate (.61) were for the peer offending measure. The self-control measure, however, had a variance inflation factor of 1.23 and a tolerance estimate of .81, illustrating that multicollinearity was not a problem even with significant relationships between the independent variables (Menard, 1995).

The Model 1s indicated that demographic factors did not predict different types of cybercrime victimization equally and that demographic risk factors are not the same in the virtual world as they are in the physical world. Traditional victimization research typically finds that males are generally more likely than females to be victimized (e.g., Messerschmidt, 1993). This model found different gender relationships. Males were only more likely to be victims of having their information changed on their computer, while females were more likely to be harassed in the virtual world, just as they are in the physical world (Fisher, Cullen, & Turner, 2002; Logan, Leukefeld, & Walker, 2000; Tjaden & Thoennes, 1998). In addition, being Black did not increase the risk of any cybercrime victimization type. Although younger respondents are traditionally more likely to be victimized (Fisher et al., 2002; Lauritsen et al., 1992; Logan et al., 2000), the models illustrated that age was not related to cybercrime victimization, with the exception of harassment. Older respondents spend less time on-line, which decreases their harassment victimization risks (Holt & Bossler, 2009). Finally, employed students were more likely to have

Table 1.  Descriptive statistics and zero-order correlations (n = 573)

| | Y1 | Y2 | Y3 | Y4 | Y5 | X1 | X2 | X3 | X4 | X5 | X6 | X7 |
|---|---|---|---|---|---|---|---|---|---|---|---|---|
| Y1  Password access | -- | | | | | | | | | | | |
| Y2  Changing info | .48** | -- | | | | | | | | | | |
| Y3  Malware | .20** | .14** | -- | | | | | | | | | |
| Y4  Credit card theft | .09* | .10* | .05 | -- | | | | | | | | |
| Y5  Harassment | .36** | .20** | .18** | .16** | -- | | | | | | | |
| X1  Low self-control | .12** | .13** | .03 | -.00 | .08* | -- | | | | | | |
| X2  Cyber-deviance | .19** | .24** | .12** | .07* | .13** | .25** | -- | | | | | |
| X3  Peer offending | .26** | .35** | .15** | .11** | .16** | .32** | .57** | -- | | | | |
| X4  Female (1 = yes) | -.00 | -.11* | .05 | .04 | .15** | -.30** | -.25** | -.25** | -- | | | |
| X5  Black (1 = yes) | -.00 | -.05 | -.07 | .00 | -.00 | -.07 | -.06 | -.11* | .08 | -- | | |
| X6  Age | -.00 | -.03 | .00 | .00 | -.12** | -.15** | .05 | -.07 | -.17** | .09* | -- | |
| X7  Employed | .10* | .07 | .11** | .08 | .03 | -.02 | .06 | .09* | .03 | -.02 | .25** | -- |
| Mean = | .17 | .10 | .36 | .04 | .19 | 12.73 | .00 | .00 | .59 | .12 | 1.84 | 1.82 |
| SD = | .37 | .30 | .48 | .20 | .39 | | .66 | .73 | .49 | .32 | .89 | .60 |

Note: All tests of significance are two-tailed except for x1-x3 with y1-y5. *p < .05. **p < .01.

Table 2.  Descriptives of low self-control, cybercrime offending, and peer offending by victimization type

| Variables | Password access | | Changing info | | Malware | | Credit card theft | | Harassment | |
|---|---|---|---|---|---|---|---|---|---|---|
| | Yes | No | Yes | No | Yes | No | Yes | No | Yes | No |
| Self-control | 3.42 (11.81) t-value = -2.90** | -.69 (12.81) | 5.01 (12.59) t-value = -3.13' | -.54 (12.64) | .44 (11.83) t-value = .62 | -.25 (13.23) | -.07 (11.09) t-value = .03 | .00 (12.81) | 2.10 (12.08) t-value = -1.91 | -.49 (12.84) |
| Offending | .28 (.98) t-value = -3.25** | -.06 (.57) | .48 (1.09) t-value = -3.63* | -.05 (.58) | .11 (.77) t-value = -2.70** | -.06 (.59) | .23 (1.15) t-value = -1.05 | -.01 (.63) | 0.18 (.89) t-value = -2.44 | -.04 (.59) |
| Peer offending | .42 (.92) t-value = -5.10** | -.08 (.65) | .78 (1.05) t-value = -6.00' | -.08 (.63) | .14 (.77) t-value = -3.65** | -.08 (.69) | .39 (.94) t-value = -2.75** | -.02 (.71) | .24 (.84) t-value = 3.39 | -.05 (.69) |
| N | 96 | 477 | 56 | 517 | 209 | 364 | 25 | 548 | 108 | 465 |

Note: Means with SD in parentheses; one-tailed significance tests. *p < .05. **p < .01.

their password obtained to access their accounts, have someone change their computer information, and receive malware that destroyed computerized information. These findings were consistent with the traditional literature, which found that income levels are positively related to property victimization. This has been traditionally interpreted as higher levels of income increasing target attractiveness (see Miethe & Meier, 1994; Osborn & Tseloni, 1998; Schreck, 1999).

The Model 2s, which included the self-control measure, confirmed the results of the correlation matrix. Low levels of self-control increased the risk of three different types of cybercrime victimization (password access, changing information, and harassment), but did not increase the risk of data loss due to malware infection or electronic credit card theft.[5] None of the demographic measures lost significance or had their coefficients decrease substantially with the inclusion of self-control. Thus, self-control did not substantively mediate the relationship between demographic variables and cybercrime victimization.

The Model 3s, which included all measures from the previous models as well as cyber-deviance and peer offending, consistently illustrated the significant relationship between peer offending and cyber-crime victimization. Associating with others who commit cybercrime increased the risk for all five types of cybercrime victimization. This was consistent with the traditional victimization literature, which found that associating with delinquent friends places individuals in risky situations where victimization can occur (see Lauritsen et al., 1992). In addition, delinquent friends may view the respondent as a suitable target for various forms of cybercrime (Holt & Bossler, 2009). Individual participation in cyber-deviance, however, was only positively related with harassment victimization. Although involvement in cyber-deviance was positively correlated with other forms of victimization (see Table 1), these relationships disappeared when controlling for peer offending. Thus, it appeared that the relationship between offending and victimization in cyberspace is primarily explained by with whom one associates.

In addition, low self-control was not a significant predictor of any form of cybercrime victimization when controlling for relevant offending measures, contrary to previous traditional victimization research that found low self-control had a direct effect on victimization (Schreck, 1999; Schreck et al., 2002; Stewart et al., 2004). Self-control lost its significance in the password access (Y1), changing information (Y2), and harassment (Y5) models.[6] Thus, it appeared that associating with delinquent peers mediated the effect of self-control on victimization in the virtual world as it can in the physical world (see Schreck et al., 2002). Individuals with inadequate levels of self-control choose to associate with peers who commit computer deviance, who in turn intentionally (i.e., harassment) or unintentionally (e.g., malware infection) victimize their peers.

This finding was further supported by the relationships found in the correlation matrix table (see Table 1) and further regression models (results not shown). Low self-control was correlated with three forms of cybercrime victimization and both peer offending ($r = .32^{**}$) and respondent offending ($r = .25^{**}$). In addition, when low self-control was regressed on the peer offending measure, self-control significantly predicted whether one associated with cyber-deviants, even when controlling for his/her own computer deviance. Individuals with inadequate levels of self-control, regardless of whether they

5   For Y1 (password access), the difference in $x^2$ values between Models 1 and 2 was 8.41 (df = 1; p < .01). For Y2 (changing information), the difference in $x^2$ values between Models 1 and 2 was 4.45 (df = 1; p < .05). For Y3 (malware infection), the difference in $x^2$ values was only .87 (df = 1) and was not significant. For Y4 (credit card theft), the difference in $x^2$ values between Models 1 and 2 was .04 (df = 1) and was not significant. For Y5 (harassment), the difference in $x^2$ values between Models 1 and 2 was 6.75 (df = 1; p < .01). This suggested that Model 2s for password access, changing information, and harassment were an improvement over the baseline models because of the inclusion of self-control.
6   Comparing the difference in $x^2$ values (df = 2) between Models 2 and 3 for all five dependent variables found that Model 3s were an improvement over Model 2s. For Y1, the difference in $x^2$ values was 28.46 (p < .01). For Y2, the difference in $x^2$ values was 40.62 (p < .01). For Y3, the difference in $x^2$ values was 13.99 (p < .01). For Y4, the difference in $x^2$ values was 7.67 (p < .05). For Y5, the difference in $x^2$ values was 48.88 (p < .01).

Table 3. Logistic regression models

| Variables | Password access (Y1) | | | Changing info (Y2) | | | Malware (Y3) | | | Credit card theft (Y4) | | | Harassment (Y5) | | |
|---|---|---|---|---|---|---|---|---|---|---|---|---|---|---|---|
| | 1 | 2 | 3 | 1 | 2 | 3 | 1 | 2 | 3 | 1 | 2 | 3 | 1 | 2 | 3 |
| Female | -.09 | .15 | .47 | -.83** | -.63* | -.20 | .21 | .27 | .44* | .36 | .39 | .72 | .72** | .93** | 1.25** |
| | (.23) | (.25) | (.27) | (.29) | (.31) | (.34) | (.18) | (.20) | (.20) | (.45) | (.48) | (.51) | (.24) | (.26) | (.28) |
| | [.92] | [1.16] | [1.61] | [.44] | [.54] | [.82] | [1.24] | [1.32] | [1.55] | [1.44] | [1.48] | [2.06] | [2.06] | [2.54] | [3.48] |
| Black | .06 | .08 | .23 | -.39 | -.37 | -.15 | -.49 | -.48 | -.42 | .07 | .07 | .22 | -.03 | -.01 | .08 |
| | (.36) | (.36) | (.37) | (.54) | (.55) | (.57) | (.30) | (.30) | (.30) | (.64) | (.64) | (.65) | (.35) | (.35) | (.36) |
| | [1.06] | [1.09] | [1.26] | [.68] | [.69] | [.86] | [.62] | [.62] | [.66] | [1.07] | [1.07] | [1.24] | [.97] | [1.00] | [1.09] |
| Age | -.11 | -.03 | .04 | -.31 | -.24 | -.16 | -.03 | -.01 | .01 | -.09 | -.08 | -.01 | -.38** | -.31* | -.30* |
| | (.14) | (.14) | (.15) | (.18) | (.19) | (.20) | (.10) | (.11) | (.11) | (.25) | (.26) | (.26) | (.14) | (.15) | (.15) |
| | [.89] | [.98] | [1.04] | [.73] | [.79] | [.86] | [.97] | [.99] | [1.01] | [.91] | [.92] | [.99] | [.68] | [.73] | [.74] |
| Employed | .51** | .49* | .38 | .53* | .51* | .38 | .39** | .39* | .33* | .67 | .67 | .55 | .25 | .24 | .13 |
| | (.20) | (.20) | (.20) | (.25) | (.25) | (.26) | (.15) | (.15) | (.15) | (.36) | (.37) | (.36) | (.19) | (.19) | (.20) |
| | [1.66] | [1.62] | [1.46] | [1.69] | [1.66] | [1.46] | [1.48] | [1.47] | [1.39] | [1.96] | [1.95] | [1.72] | [1.29] | [1.27] | [1.13] |
| Self-control | -- | .03** | .02 | -- | .03* | .01 | -- | .01 | .00 | -- | .00 | -.01 | -- | .02* | .01 |
| | | (.01) | (.01) | | (.01) | (.01) | | (.01) | (.01) | | (.02) | (.02) | | (.01) | (.01) |
| | | [1.03] | [1.02] | | [1.03] | [1.01] | | [1.01] | [1.00] | | [1.00] | [.99] | | [1.02] | [1.01] |
| Cyber-deviance | -- | -- | .19 | -- | -- | .16 | -- | -- | .20 | -- | -- | .14 | -- | -- | .33* |
| | | | (.18) | | | (.20) | | | (.16) | | | (.28) | | | (.18) |
| | | | [1.21] | | | [1.18] | | | [1.22] | | | [1.15] | | | [1.39] |
| Peer offending | -- | -- | .71** | -- | -- | 1.06** | -- | -- | .36** | -- | -- | .67** | -- | -- | .46** |
| | | | (.18) | | | (.21) | | | (.15) | | | (.29) | | | (.18) |
| | | | [2.04] | | | [2.88] | | | [1.44] | | | [1.95] | | | [1.58] |
| Constant | -2.30** | -2.60** | -2.83** | -2.19** | -2.44** | -2.86** | -1.30** | -1.36** | -1.41** | -4.46** | -4.49** | -4.74** | -1.72** | -1.97** | -2.06** |
| | (.43) | (.45) | (.48) | (.53) | (.55) | (.60) | (.33) | (.34) | (.35) | (.84) | (.86) | (.89) | (.43) | (.45) | (.46) |
| Model χ² | 6.78 | 15.19** | 43.65** | 13.48** | 17.94** | 58.55** | 11.48** | 12.35* | 26.34** | 4.45 | 4.50 | 12.16 | 21.41** | 28.16** | 47.04** |
| $R^2$ | .02 | .04 | .12 | .05 | .07 | .21 | .03 | .03 | .06 | .03 | .03 | .07 | .06 | .08 | .13 |

Notes: Entries (b) are unstandardized logistic regression coefficients, standard errors are in parentheses, and odds ratios are in brackets. One-tailed tests of significance were used for self-control, offending, and peer offending. Pseudo $R^2$ are Nagelkerke $R^2$. *p < .05, **p < .01,

commit crime, like associating with adventurous, risky, impulsive individuals who commit computer deviance. When self-control was regressed on the respondent offending measure, self-control was not significant when controlling for peer offending. Thus, it appeared that peer offending mediated the effect of self-control on both cybercrime victimization and cyber-deviance in this sample.

Finally, the significant effects of employment on password access victimization (Y1) and employment and sex on changing information victimization (Y2) disappeared when controlling for peer offending, implying another mediating effect for peer offending. The implications of these major findings for the expansion of self-control theory to both victimization in general and cybercrime is discussed in the next section.

## conclusion

Theories with a situational-focus (e.g., lifestyles/routine activities theory) have dominated the field of victimology. Unfortunately, individual-level theories have primarily been overlooked. Building on the work of past scholars, this study assessed the ability of Gottfredson and Hirschi's (1990) self-control theory to explain several forms of cybercrime victimization in a college sample while controlling for demographics, respondents' computer deviance, and peer computer offending.

Consistent with previous research illustrating a link between self-control and traditional forms of victimization (e.g., Schreck, 1999; Schreck et al., 2002; Stewart et al., 2004), individuals with low levels of self-control were more likely to experience: (1) someone obtaining their password without authorization to access their computer files; (2) someone adding, deleting, or changing their information in their computer files; and (3) on-line harassment. Self-control, however, did not increase the odds of losing computerized data due to malware infection or someone electronically obtaining credit card numbers without permission or knowledge. In addition, self-control did not retain a direct effect on the odds of victimization when controlling for respondent and peer offending.

These findings may indicate that individual characteristics and choice are less important in understanding certain forms of cybercrime victimization than others, particularly since some forms of cybercrime victimization can occur through no fault of the victim. For example, malicious software infections can occur with little or no direct interaction between victims and offenders (see Chien, 2003; PandaLabs, 2007; Taylor et al., 2006). Worms can replicate and send copies of its code to other computers using e-mail addresses stored in the computer. Malware writers also tend to target an entire population of computer users rather than any one individual, decreasing the importance of individual characteristics (see Chien, 2003; Taylor et al., 2006). Credit card theft can also result from hackers obtaining data through compromising data bases that maintain consumer financial and personal data (Newman & Clarke, 2003; Wall, 2001).

In fact, a factor analysis of the five dependent variables indicated that they separated into two factors: (1) person-based offenses where the specific individual was the target (someone obtaining one's password to access computer files; having information in a computer file changed; on-line harassment); and (2) computer-based, where the individual was not the target but computers in general were (data loss because of malware infection; electronic credit card theft) (results not shown). When these two factors (i.e., person-based and computer-based victimization) were treated as dichotomous dependent variables, further regression models provided support for the argument that self-control might influence a specific category of cybercrime victimization (see Table 4). Inadequate levels of self-control predicted person-based cybercrime victimization, but it was not related with computer-based victimization.

Self-control did not, however, significantly predict person-based cybercrime victimization once offending measures were controlled for, as noted in the earlier analyses (see Table 3). Thus, peer offending appeared to mediate the influence of self-control on all forms of person-based cybercrime victimization. This suggested that self-control has a role in explaining cybercrime victimization when victimization is nonrandom and affected by individual choice, but the role is limited to whether it affects with whom the individual associates.

While the factor analysis and regression models (see Table 4) indicated that these five dependent measures can be collapsed into two categories, future research is needed to examine whether individual and situational risk factors predict all types of cybercrime victimization equally. The authors caution that researchers must not automatically collapse cybercrime victimization types into various categories. In this study, the demographic measures did not consistently predict all forms of cybercrime victimization (see Table 3). For example, being female decreased the odds of having one's information changed on one's computer, but it increased the odds of being harassed on-line. Age was only related to harassment while employment was related to two forms of person-based cybercrime victimization (having someone access one's computer without authorization and having information on one's computer changed) and one form of computer-based victimization (malware). Thus, simply collapsing victimization into categories could overlook important differences.

An alternative argument to the conclusion that self-control only influences person-based cybercrime victimization may be that self-control has the same role in explaining victimization in cyberspace as it does in the physical world—minimal. Past studies normally found the effects of self-control on

Table 4.   Logistic regression models for person-based and computer-based cybercrime victimization

Logistic regression models for person-based and computer-based cybercrime victimization

| Variables | Person-based | | | Computer-based | | |
|---|---|---|---|---|---|---|
| | 1 | 2 | 3 | 1 | 2 | 3 |
| Female | .05 | .15 | .37 | .28 | .31 | .48* |
| | (.18) | (.19) | (.19) | (.18) | (.19) | (.20) |
| | [1.05] | [1.16] | [1.45] | [1.32] | [1.37] | [1.61] |
| Black | -.45 | -.43 | -.35 | -.44 | -.44 | -.37 |
| | (.28) | (.28) | (.28) | (.29) | (.29) | (.29) |
| | [.64] | [.65] | [.71] | [.64] | [.65] | [.69] |
| Age | -.09 | -.05 | -.02 | -.03 | -.02 | .01 |
| | (.10) | (.10) | (.11) | (.10) | (.11) | (.11) |
| | [.92] | [.95] | [.99] | [.97] | [.98] | [1.01] |
| Employed | .47** | .46** | .38* | .37* | .36* | .30* |
| | (.15) | (.15) | (.15) | (.15) | (.15) | (.15) |
| | [1.59] | [1.58] | [1.46] | [1.44] | [1.44] | [1.35] |
| Self-control | -- | .01* | .00 | -- | .00 | -.00 |
| | | (.01) | (.01) | | (.01) | (.01) |
| | | [1.01] | [1.00] | | [1.00] | [1.00] |
| Cyber-deviance | -- | -- | .17 | -- | -- | .18 |
| | | | (.17) | | | (.16) |
| | | | [1.18] | | | [1.20] |
| Peer offending | -- | -- | .64** | -- | -- | .39** |
| | | | (.16) | | | (.15) |
| | | | [1.90] | | | [1.49] |
| Constant | -.87** | -.99 | -1.05** | -1.19** | -1.23** | -1.28** |
| | (.32) | (.33) | (.34) | (.33) | (.34) | (.34) |
| Model x² | 13.49** | 16.29** | 46.20** | 11.42* | 11.67* | 26.84** |
| R² | .03 | .04 | .10 | .03 | .03 | .06 |

Notes: Entries (b) are unstandardized logistic regression coefficients, standard errors are in parentheses, and odds ratios are in brackets. One-tailed tests of significance were used for self-control, offending, and peer offending. Pseudo $R^2$ are Nagelkerke $R^2$. *p < .05. **p < .01.

victimization to be small (e.g., Piquero et al., 2005; Schreck et al., 2006), to the extent that Piquero et al. (2005) warned authors to avoid making strong conclusions concerning the influence of self-control. The small correlations and low effect sizes found in this study did not radically depart from the traditional literature. Instead it may mean that self-control is a statistically significant, but small, predictor of victimization on- and off-line.

# references

Arneklev, B. J., Grasmick H. G., Tittle, C. R., & Bursik, R. J. (1993). Low self-control and imprudent behavior. *Journal of Quantitative Criminology, 9,* 225–247.

Baron, S. W., Forde, D. R., & Kennedy, L. W. (2001). Rough justice: Street youth and violence. *Journal of Interpersonal Violence, 16,* 662–678.

Baum, K. (2007). Identity theft, 2005 (NCJ 219411). Retrieved from Bureau of Justice Statistics Web site: http://www.ojp.usdoj.gov/bjs/abstract/it05.htm

Bocij, P. (2004). Cyberstalking: Harassment in the Internet age and how to protect your family. Westport, CT: Praeger.

Bossler, A. M., & Holt, T. J. (2009). On-line activities, guardianship, and malware infection: An examination of routine activities theory. *International Journal of Cyber Criminology, 3,* 400–420.

Buzzell, T. (2005). The effects of sophistication, access and monitoring on use of pornography in three technological contexts. *Deviant Behavior, 26,* 109–132.

Buzzell, T., Foss, D., & Middleton, Z. (2006). Explaining use of online pornography: A test of self-control theory and opportunities for deviance. *Journal of Criminal Justice and Popular Culture, 13,* 96–116.

Chien, E. (2003). *Malicious threats of peer-to-peer networking.* Retrieved July 15, 2007, from Symantec AntiVirus Research Center Web site: http://enterprisesecurity.symantec.com/content/knowledgelibrary.cfm?EID=0

Computer Security Institute. (2007). *Computer crime and security survey.* Retrieved June 3, 2007, from http://www.cybercrime.gov/FBI2006.pdf

Finn, J. (2004). A survey of online harassment at a university campus. *Journal of Interpersonal Violence, 19,* 468–483.

Fisher, B. S., Cullen, F. T., & Turner, M. G. (2002). Being pursued: Stalking victimization in a national study of college women. *Criminology and Public Policy, 1,* 257–308.

Forde, D. R., & Kennedy, L. W. (1997). Risky lifestyles, routine activities, and the general theory of crime. *Justice Quarterly, 14,* 265–294.

Furnell, S. (2002). Cybercrime: Vandalizing the information society. Boston: Addison-Wesley.

Gibson, C., & Wright, J. (2001). Low self-control and coworker delinquency: A research note. *Journal of Criminal Justice, 29,* 483–492.

Gilboa, N. (1996). *Elites, lamers, narcs and whores: Exploring the computer underground.* In L. Cherny & E. R. Weise (Eds.), *Wired women: Gender and new realities in cyberspace* (pp. 98–113). Seattle, WA: Seal Press.

Gottfredson, M. R., & Hirschi, T. (1990). *A general theory of crime.* Stanford, CA: Stanford University Press.

Grabosky, P. N., & Smith, R. (2001). *Telecommunication fraud in the digital age: The convergence of technologies.* In D. Wall (Ed.), *Crime and the Internet* (pp. 29–43). New York: Routledge.

Grasmick, H. G., Tittle, C. R., Bursik, R. J., Jr., & Arneklev, B. J. (1993). Testing the core empirical implications of Gottfredson and Hirschi's general theory of crime. *Journal of Research in Crime and Delinquency, 30,* 5–29.

Hay, C. (2001). Parenting, self-control, and delinquency: A test of self-control theory. *Criminology, 39,* 707–736.

Haynie, D. L., & Osgood, D. W. (2005). Reconsidering peers and delinquency: How do peers matter. *Social Forces, 84,* 1109–1130.

Herring, S. C. (1999). The rhetorical dynamics of gender harassment online. *The Information Society, 15,* 151–167.

Higgins, G. E. (2005). Can low self-control help with the understanding of the software piracy problem? *Deviant Behavior, 26,* 1–24.

Higgins, G. E. (2006). Gender differences in software piracy: The mediating roles of self-control theory and social learning theory. *Journal of Economic Crime Management, 4,* 1–30.

Higgins, G. E., Fell, B. D., & Wilson, A. L. (2006). Digital piracy: Assessing the contributions of an integrated self-control theory and social learning theory using structural equation modeling. *Criminal Justice Studies, 19,* 3–22.

Higgins, G. E., Fell, B. D., & Wilson, A. L. (2007). Low self-control and social learning in understanding, students' intentions to pirate movies in the United States. *Social Science Computer Review, 25,* 339–357.

Higgins, G. E., & Makin, D. A. (2004). Self-control, deviant peers, and software piracy. *Psychological Reports, 95,* 921–931.

Higgins, G. E., Wolfe, S. E., & Marcum, C. (2008). Digital piracy: An examination of three measurements of self-control. *Deviant Behavior, 29,* 440–460.

Hinduja, S. (2001). Correlates of Internet software piracy. *Journal of Contemporary Criminal Justice, 17,* 369–382.

Hinduja, S., & Patchin, J. W. (2008a). Personal information of adolescents on the Internet: A quantitative content analysis of MySpace. *Journal of Adolescence, 31,* 125–146.

Hinduja, S., & Patchin, J. W. (2008b). Cyberbullying: An exploratory analysis of factors related to offending and victimization. *Deviant Behavior, 29,* 129–156.

Holt, T. J. (2007). Subcultural evolution? Examining the influence of on- and off-line experiences on deviant subcultures. *Deviant Behavior, 28,* 171–198.

Holt, T. J., & Bossler, A. M. (2009). Examining the applicability of lifestyle-routine activities theory for cybercrime victimization. *Deviant Behavior, 30,* 1–25.

Holt, T. J., & Graves, D. C. (2007). A qualitative analysis of advanced fee fraud schemes. *International Journal of Cyber-Criminology, 1,* 137–154.

Holtfreter, K., Reisig, M. D., & Pratt, T. C. (2008). Low self-control, routine activities, and fraud victimization. *Criminology, 46,* 189–220.

Jensen, G. F., & Brownfield, D. (1986). Gender, lifestyles, and victimization: Beyond routine activity theory. *Violence and Victims, 1,* 85–99.

Jordan, T., & Taylor, P. (1998). A sociology of hackers. *Sociological Review, 46,* 757–780.

Lauritsen, J. L., Laub, J. H., & Sampson, R. J. (1992). Conventional and delinquent activities: Implications for the prevention of violent victimization among adolescents. *Violence and Victims, 7,* 91–108.

Lauritsen, J. L., Sampson, R. J., & Laub, J. H. (1991). The link between offending and victimization among adolescents. *Criminology, 29,* 265-292.

Logan, T. K., Leukefeld, C., & Walker, R. (2000). Stalking as a variant of intimate violence: Implications from a young adult sample. *Violence and Victims, 15,* 91–111.

Longshore, D., Chang, E., Hsieh, S. C., & Messina, N. (2004). Self-control and social bonds: A combined control perspective on deviance. *Crime and Delinquency, 50,* 542–564.

Menard, S. (1995). *Applied logistic regression analysis.* Thousand Oaks, CA: Sage.

Messerschmidt, J. W. (1993). *Masculinities and crime: Critique and reconceptualization of theory.* Lanham, MD: Rowman and Littlefield.

Miethe, T. D., & Meier, R. F. (1994). *Crime and its social context: Toward an integrated theory of offenders, victims, and situations.* Albany: State University of New York Press.

Newman, G., & Clarke, R. (2003). *Superhighway robbery: Preventing e-commerce crime.* Cullompton, UK: Willan Press.

Osborn, D. R., & Tseloni, A. (1998). The distribution of household property crimes. *Journal of Quantitative Criminology, 14,* 307–330.

Osgood, D. W., Wilson, J. K., O'Malley, P. M., Bachman, J. G., & Johnston, L. D. (1996). Routine activities and individual deviant behavior. *American Sociological Review, 61,* 635–655.

PandaLabs. (2007). Malware infections in protected systems. Retrieved November 1, 2007, from http://research.pandasecurity.com/blogs/images/wp_pb_malware_infections_in_protected_systems.pdf

Payne, B. K., & Chappell, A. (2008). Using student samples in criminological research. *Journal of Criminal Justice Education, 19,* 175–192.

Pease, K. (2001). *Crime futures and foresight: Challenging criminal behavior in the information age.* In D. Wall (Ed.), *Crime and the Internet* (pp. 18–28). New York: Routledge.

Piquero, A. R., Gomez-Smith, Z., & Langton, L. (2004). Discerning unfairness where others may not: Low self-control and unfair sanction perceptions. *Criminology, 42,* 699–733.

Piquero, A. R., MacDonald, J., Dobrin, A., Daigle, L. E., & Cullen, F. T. (2005). Self-control, violent offending, and homicide victimization: Assessing the general theory of crime. *Journal of Quantitative Criminology, 21,* 55–71.

Piquero, A. R., & Tibbetts, S. (1996). Specifying the direct and indirect effects of low self control and situational factors in offenders' decision making: Toward a more complete model of rational offending. *Justice Quarterly, 13,* 481–510.

Pratt, T. C., & Cullen, F. T. (2000). The empirical status of Gottfredson and Hirschi's general theory of crime: A meta-analysis. *Criminology, 38,* 931–964.

Rantala, R. R. (2008). Cybercrime against businesses, 2005 (NCJ 221943). Retrieved from Bureau of Justice Statistics Web site: http://www.ojp.usdoj.gov/bjs/abstract/cb05.htm

Rogers, M. K. (2001). A social learning theory and moral disengagement analysis of criminal computer behavior: An exploratory study. Unpublished doctoral dissertation, University of Manitoba, Winnipeg, Manitoba, Canada.

Rogers, M. K., Smoak, N. D., & Liu, J. (2006). Self-reported deviant computer behavior: A big-5, moral choice, and manipulative exploitive behavior analysis. *Deviant Behavior, 27,* 245–268.

Sampson, R. J., & Lauritsen, J. L. (1990). Deviant lifestyles, proximity to crime, and the offender-victim link in personal violence. *Journal of Research in Crime and Delinquency, 27,* 110–139.

Schreck, C. J. (1999). Criminal victimization and self control: An extension and test of a general theory of crime. *Justice Quarterly, 16,* 633–654.

Schreck, C. J., & Fisher, B. S. (2004). Specifying the influence of family and peers on violent victimization: Extending routine activities and lifestyle theories. *Journal of Interpersonal Violence, 19,* 1021–1041.

Schreck, C. J., Stewart, E. A., & Fisher, B. S. (2006). Self control, victimization, and the influence on risky lifestyles: A longitudinal analysis using panel data. *Journal of Quantitative Criminology, 22,* 319–340.

Schreck, C. J., Wright, R. A., & Miller, J. M. (2002). A study of individual and situational antecedents of violent victimization. *Justice Quarterly, 19,* 159–180.

Skinner, W. F., & Fream, A. M. (1997). A social learning theory analysis of computer crime among college students. *Journal of Research in Crime and Delinquency, 34,* 495–518.

Stack S., Wasserman, I., & Kern, R. (2004). Adult social bonds and use of Internet pornography. *Social Science Quarterly, 85,* 75–88.

Stewart, E. A., Elifson, K. W., & Sterk C. E. (2004). Integrating the general theory of crime into an explanation of violent victimization among female offenders. *Justice Quarterly, 21,* 159–181.

Szor, P. (2005). *The art of computer virus research and defense.* Upper Saddle River, NJ: Addison Wesley.

Taylor, R. W., Caeti, T. J., Loper, D. K., Fritsch, E. J., & Liederbach, J. (2006). *Digital crime and digital terrorism.* Upper Saddle River, NJ: Pearson Prentice Hall.

Tjaden, P., & Thoennes, N. (1998). Stalking in America: Findings from the National Violence Against Women Survey (NCJ 169592). Washington, DC: U.S. Department of Justice, National Institute of Justice.

Vazsonyi, A. T., & Belliston, L. M. (2007). The family, low self-control, and deviance: A cross cultural and cross-national test of self-control theory. *Criminal Justice and Behavior, 34,* 505–530.

Wall, D. S. (2001). *Cybercrimes and the Internet.* In D. S. Wall (Ed.), *Crime and the Internet* (pp. 1–17). New York: Routledge.

Yar, M. (2005). The novelty of "cybercrime": An assessment in light of routine activity theory. *European Journal of Criminology, 2,* 407–427.

Zhang, L., Welte, J. W., & Wiecxorek, W. F. (2001). Deviant lifestyle and crime victimization. *Journal of Criminal Justice, 29,* 133–143.

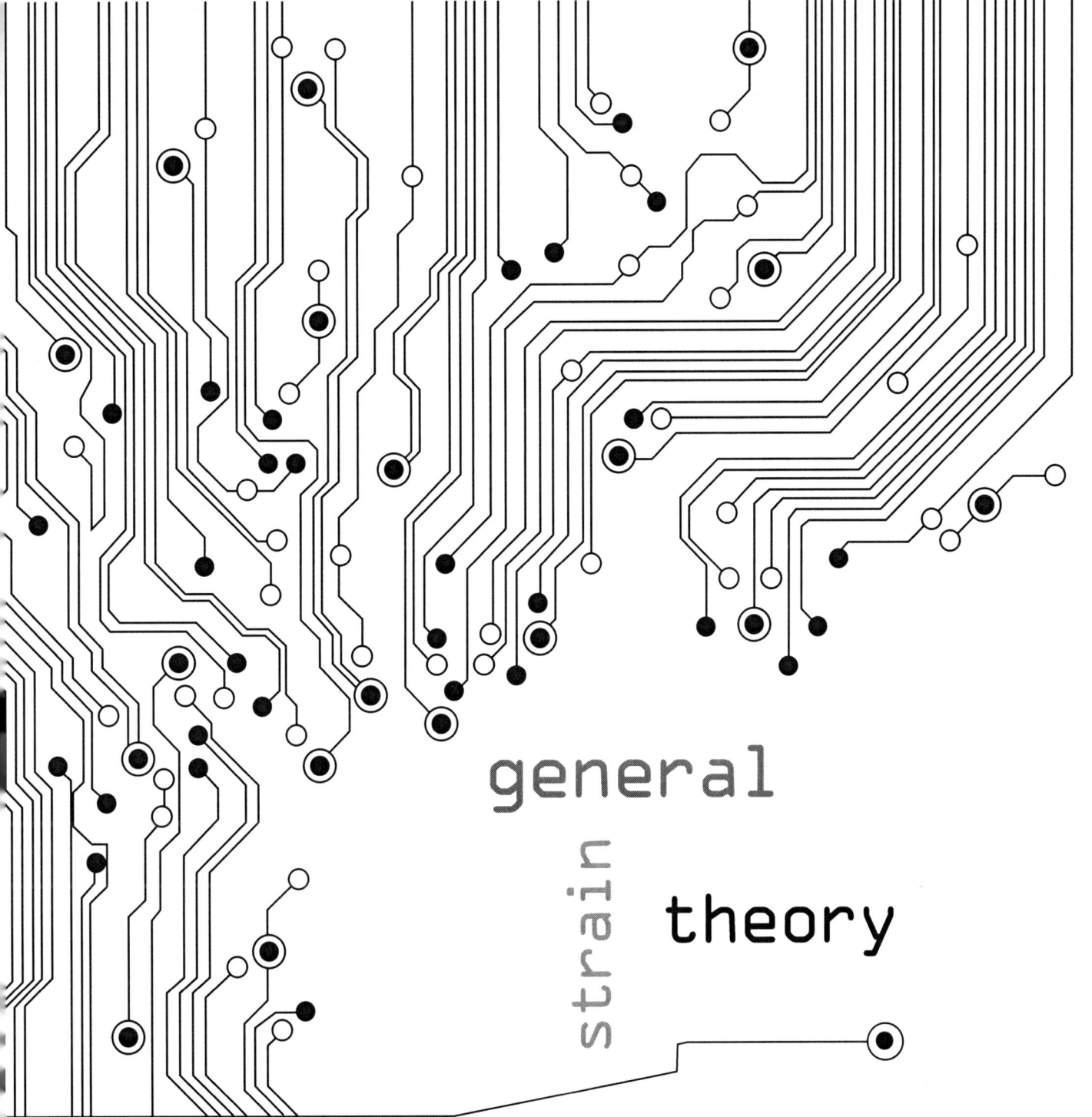

general

strain

theory

thomas  j.  holt

Though Gottfredson and Hirschi's (1990) general theory of crime and Akers's (1998) social learning theory have been extensively explored within cybercrimes, a small literature is emerging on the applicability of other existing theories. In particular, a number of studies have been published examining the utility of Robert Agnew's (1992, 2006) General Strain Theory. This individual-level theory was developed as an expansion of Merton's (1938) classic strain theory, which emphasizes the role of blocked access to a desired goal, particularly economic success. From this perspective, individuals who are unable to achieve the goal of economic achievement will feel a substantive sense of frustration and find other ways to satisfy their needs, including criminal activity.

Agnew's General Strain Theory, however, moved beyond blocked economic success to identify various sources of strain and its role in offending, specifically among juvenile populations. Agnew argued that individuals who report anger, frustration, disappointment, or depression do so as a consequence of various strains in their lives. In fact, there are three strains that have a substantive impact on an individual's emotional state. The first strain a person may experience stems from the failure to achieve positively valued goals. This is similar to the argument presented by Merton (1938) in that a person may aspire to get good grades or excel in sports. Those who are unable to achieve their goals are likely to experience strain as a consequence. In addition, Agnew (1992) argued that strain can be caused by the removal of positively valued stimuli, such as losing a parent or loved one or having driving privileges taken away. This sort of experience can lead to a substantive sense of frustration over their experiences. Finally, strain may result from the presentation of negative stimuli. For instance, family conflict, school failure, or physical and emotional abuse can present a significant sense of anger and sadness, which may be directed internally or unleashed upon others around that person.

Exposure to any of these strains may have a cumulative effect, such that the more frequent and intense a strain is present in an individual's life, the more likely they are to experience negative emotions. From Agnew's (1992, 2006) perspective, strains can produce emotional reactions, including anger, frustration, and a need for revenge. These feelings produce pressure for an individual to respond to their strain in some way. As a consequence, negative emotions produced by strains, especially anger, increase the likelihood that an individual will engage in crime.

The response to strain can also be conditioned by multiple factors, including individual coping strategies. For instance, individuals who are able to vent their anger through healthy outlets such as physical exercise may be less likely to engage in criminal acts. Some may, however, choose to engage in coping techniques like drug or alcohol use, which may actually increase the risk of offending behaviors. Furthermore, positive social relationships may decrease criminal responses to strain by allowing individuals to vent their frustrations to pro-social others. Connections with deviant peer groups will, however, increase the likelihood that an individual may engage in crime because of the acceptance and internalization of deviant or criminal values (Agnew, 2006). Finally, a lack of self-control, as identified by Gottfredson and Hirschi (1990), may make it difficult for individuals to resist the opportunity to respond to strain with criminal activity (Agnew, 2006).

While a number of studies have found some support for general strain theory (Agnew & White, 1992; Hoffman & Miller, 1997; Mazerolle, 1998; Mazerolle, Burton, Cullen, Evans, & Payne, 2000; Mazerolle & Piquero, 1997), there have been few tests of this theory with regard to cybercrime. The emerging studies in this area have commonly used person-based cybercrimes like bullying and harassment. This is sensible, given that the virtual environment allows individuals to immediately and easily vent frustration and anger at others in a detached way that does not require direct interaction with their victim.

The following papers in this section provide initial insights into the value of General Strain Theory (GST) to account for bullying behaviors on- and off-line. In addition, these works provide substantive discussions on the overlap between offending and victimization in the same milieu. The increasing intersection of our virtual and real lives has been given generally short shrift in the research literature, calling to question how our experiences in one environment may affect our lives in the other. As a result, these papers have twofold value for the research community by addressing various aspects of cybercrime and criminological theory.

The first paper, by Patchin and Hinduja (2011), examines the predictive value of GST for involvement in bullying on- and off-line with a population of almost 2,000 middle school students in the United States. The findings suggest that bullying is related to both the experiences of strains and negative emotions across both cyber- and real-world bullying behaviors. The second piece, by Hay, Meldrum, and Mann (2010), considers the impact of bullying victimization as a source of strain, predicting participation in delinquency, self-harm, and suicidal thoughts. This analysis is unique in that it considers the influence of on-line experiences on real-world offending through measures related to minor acts of delinquency. Both studies provide timely explorations of bullying from different viewpoints using similar theoretical orientations.

At the same time, there is a substantive need for greater exploration on the utility of General Strain Theory to account for cybercrime and deviance. While most researchers have focused on social learning and self-control to account for involvement in piracy and hacking for their utilitarian purpose, few have considered how Agnew's structure could explain participation in these offenses from an expressive framework. In addition, Agnew (2006) argued that strain interacts with other correlates of crime, such as delinquent peer associations and self-control (as in Hay et al., 2010). The inclusion of these variables as conditioning factors for strain in models for offending that are also direct predictors of offending call to question the true significance of strain. Thus, future research is needed to better examine these issues in depth in order to assess the empirical value of strain theory generally.

## discussion questions

1.  Are there any forms of cybercrime that may be more difficult to account for through the use of General Strain Theory? For instance, could computer hacking or digital piracy serve as a way to cope with strains?
2.  Are there any strains that may be more likely to result in individual participation in cybercrimes? Which type of strain do you think may have the strongest relationship to cybercrime generally?
3.  How might individual technology use affect the relationship between strain and cybercrime? Since individual coping strategies affect the likelihood of crime as a response to strain, is it possible that those people who spend less time on-line will be less generally inclined to engage in cybercrimes if they experience anger or frustration?

## references

Agnew, R. (1992). Foundation for a general strain theory of crime and delinquency. *Criminology, 30,* 47–87.

Agnew, R. (2006). General strain theory: Current status and directions for further research. In F. T. Cullen, J. P. Wright, & K. R. Blevins (eds.), *Taking Stock: The Status of Criminological Theory* (Advances in Criminological Theory, vol. 16, pp. 137–158). New Brunswick, NJ: Transaction.

Agnew, R., & White, H. R. (1992). An empirical test of general strain theory. *Criminology, 30,* 475–499.

Akers, R. L. (1998). *Social Learning and Social Structure: A General Theory of Crime and Deviance.* Boston: Northeastern University Press.

Gottfredson, M. R., & Hirschi, T. (1990). *A General Theory of Crime.* Stanford, CA: Stanford University Press.

Hay, C., Meldrum, R., & Mann, K. (2010). Traditional bullying, cyber bulling, and deviance: A general strain theory approach. *Journal of Contemporary Criminal Justice, 26,* 130–147.

Hoffman, J., & Miller, A. (1998). A latent variable analysis of general strain theory. *Journal of Quantitative Criminology, 14,* 83–110.

Mazerolle, P. (1998). Gender, general strain, and delinquency: An empirical examination. *Justice Quarterly, 15,* 65–91.

Mazerolle, P., Burton, V. S., Cullen, F. T., Evans, T. D., & Payne, G. L. (2000). Strain, anger, and delinquent adaptations: Specifying general strain theory. *Journal of Criminal Justice, 28,* 89–101.

Mazerolle, P., & Piquero, A. (1997). Violent responses to strain: An examination of conditioning influences. *Violence & Victims, 12,* 323–343.

Merton, R. K. (1938). Social structure and anomie. *America Sociological Review, 3,* 672–682.

Patchin, J. W., & Hinduja, S. (2011). Traditional and nontraditional bullying among youth: A test of general strain theory. *Youth & Society, 43,* 727–751.

justin w. patchin
and
sameer hinduja

traditional

nontraditional and

bullying among youth: a test strain theory of general

## introduction

School bullying has long been a concern among parents, educators, and students alike. Accordingly, many researchers have focused a significant amount of attention on this topic over the past three decades (Besag, 1989; Ericson, 2001; Limber & Nation, 1998; Olweus, 1978; Tattum, 1989). Though there has been much research on the prevalence of bullying among students (Boulton & Underwood, 1992; Finkelhor, Turner, Ormrod, & Hamby, 2005; Haynie et al., 2001; Seals & Young, 2003; Stephenson & Smith, 1989), fewer studies have attempted to identify the causes and correlates of bullying behaviors (Borg, 1998; Hawker & Boulton, 2000; Rigby, 2003; Roland, 2002). In addition, the nature of bullying has changed dramatically over the past several years. Whereas traditional bullying historically took place in or near the school, bullies in

Justin W. Patchin and Sameer Hinduja, "Traditional and Nontraditional Bullying Among Youth: A Test of General Strain Theory," *Youth and Society*, vol. 43, no. 2, pp. 727-751. Copyright © 2011 by SAGE Publications. Reprinted with permission.

the 21st century have enlisted technology to inflict harm on their peers through what has been termed *cyberbullying*.

Cyberbullying has been defined as "willful and repeated harm inflicted through the use of computers, cell phones, and other electronic devices" (Hinduja & Patchin, 2009, p. 5). This definition includes many of the important constructs common in definitions of traditional bullying (e.g., intentionality, repetition, actions that cause harm) but highlights the changing nature of adolescent communication and interaction by acknowledging the technology most commonly used by teens. Without question, both forms of bullying are (and remain) significant social concerns that warrant attention, empirical examination, and response.

To that end, the current study uses a popular contemporary criminological theory—general strain theory (GST)—to contribute to what is known about the factors associated with both traditional and nontraditional (electronic) forms of bullying. GST argues that individuals who experience strain, and as a result of that strain feel angry or frustrated, are more at risk to engage in criminal or deviant behavior (Agnew, 1992). As such, the primary question examined here is "Are youth who experience strain more likely to engage in bullying?" To explore this question, a brief review of the bullying and emergent cyberbullying literature is first provided. This is followed by a succinct summary of GST and a discussion of the theorized relationship between strain and bullying. Next, methods and analyses are described and results presented. Finally, the implications of this study are discussed along with recommendations regarding areas for future research into the causes and consequences of interpersonal adolescent aggression.

* * *

According to GST, strain does not directly cause crime. Rather, Agnew (1992) argued that experiencing strain first produces negative emotions such as anger and frustration and that crime is one adaptation or coping mechanism that strained individuals may use in response to those negative emotions. Therefore, not all youth who experience strain commit crime—only those who become angry or frustrated as a result of the strain (as those feelings create pressure for corrective action, potentially in the form of wrongdoing; Agnew, 2006a). In the relatively short amount of time that GST has been a mainstream theory, a solid body of evidence has accumulated for its support and relevance (see, for example, Agnew, 2006b; Agnew & White, 1992; Aseltine, Gore, & Gordon, 2000; Mazerolle, Burton, Cullen, Evans, & Payne, 2000; Paternoster & Mazerolle, 1994).

## the relationship between strain and bullying

Although a few previous studies have examined bullying as a source of strain (Hinduja & Patchin, 2007; Wallace, Patchin, & May, 2005), no study has yet examined bullying as a potential outcome of strain. Nevertheless, there is good reason to explore this relationship. First, bullying makes sense as a response to strain when considered within the context of GST. According to Agnew (2000) experiencing strain "makes us feel bad; that is, it makes us feel angry, frustrated, depressed, anxious, and the like. These bad feelings create pressure for corrective action; we want to do something so that we will not feel so bad" (p. 109). Clearly, bullying others—whether in person or online—is one such corrective action strained youth might adopt. Teasing, taunting, belittling, and otherwise tormenting others provides a bully with a sense of power and superiority (Olweus, 1978, 1993; Rigby & Slee, 1993), and so it is reasonable to hypothesize that strained youth who wish to ameliorate certain negative feelings might engage in this behavior to improve the way they feel about themselves. Particularly with respect to cyberbullying, technology may equip youth who otherwise would not be willing or able to respond with the perceived anonymity and tools to lash out with little concern for immediate retribution (Hinduja & Patchin, 2009).

Second, GST is purported to be one of a select few "general theories of crime" capable of explaining a wide variety of deviant behaviors (which would include bullying). Moreover, bullying itself has been linked to broader delinquent outcomes of the type more commonly studied by criminologists. For example, teens who bully others are four times more likely to appear in court on delinquency-related charges than their nonbullying counterparts (Rigby, 2003). Moreover, bullying is associated with other forms of antisocial behavior such as vandalism, shoplifting, truancy, dropping out of school, fighting, and drug use (Ericson, 2001; Loeber & Disheon, 1984; Magnusson et al., 1983; Olweus, 1999; Rigby, 2003; Tattum, 1989) as well as negative emotions which are sometimes resolved in deviant ways (Borg, 1998; Ericson, 2001; Rigby, 2003; Roland, 2002; Seals & Young, 2003). Further exploration of bullying appears necessary to gain more clarity about its causes and consequences. Accordingly, it is hypothesized that some youth may engage in bullying behaviors (both traditional and nontraditional) as a response to strainful life events and the negative emotions that they produce.

## current study

### data and sampling strategy

The data for this study came from a survey distributed in the spring of 2007 to approximately 2,000 students in 30 middle schools (6th through 8th grades) in one of the largest school districts in the United States.[1] Students were selected to participate if they were enrolled in a district-wide peer conflict class that all students are required to take at some point in their middle school tenure. Created by a leading educational nonprofit organization, this class seeks to reduce violence among youth and teach problem-solving and conflict-resolution skills. It combines in-class instruction with strategies to manage personal aggressive reactions and often includes supplemental activities such as fact sheets and educational games.

\* \* \*

### measures

### dependent variables

The general outcome of interest, bullying, was examined using two measures designed to represent different manifestations of current-day adolescent aggression. First, traditional bullying was a dichotomous variable (1 = *bully*; 0 = *not a bully*) representing whether a youth had engaged in bullying behaviors in the previous 30 days (see Table 2). The behaviors that encompass the bullying scale were

---

1   The survey was pretested among a group of 266 students at two randomly selected middle schools in the same district. Modifications were made to increase the clarity of each survey item and to ensure that they related to the constructs they were designed to measure.

Table 1.  Sample Demographic Characteristics ($N$ = 1,963)

| | | |
|---|---|---|
| Gender | | |
| Female | 50.1 | 48.0 |
| Male | 49.8 | 52.0 |
| Missing | 0.1 | |
| Grade | | |
| 6th | 34.7 | 33.9 |
| 7th | 35.6 | 32.2 |
| 8th | 29.2 | 33.9 |
| Missing | 0.5 | 0.0 |
| Age (mean = 12.8) | | |
| 10 | 0.4 | 1.2 |
| 11 | 11.0 | 24.4 |
| 12 | 29.5 | 31.9 |
| 13 | 32.7 | 31.4 |
| 14 | 20.0 | 8.8 |
| 15 | 4.8 | 2.0 |
| 16 | 1.5 | .3 |
| Missing | 0.2 | 0.1 |
| Race | | |
| White | 40.6 | 41.0 |
| Black/African American | 23.4 | 28.0 |
| Hispanic or Latin American | 19.6 | 23.0 |
| Multiracial | 7.1 | 4.7 |
| American Indian or Native | 1.3 | 0.6 |
| Other | 3.5 | 2.5 |
| Missing | 0.4 | 0.0 |

adapted from Kaufman et al. (2000), and are typical of those employed in previous studies (Besag, 1989; Olweus, 1978; Tattum, 1989). As noted in Table 2, the bullying measure includes a variety of behaviors representing relatively minor and common forms (e.g., "I called another student mean names") to more serious and less common forms (e.g., "I threatened or forced another student to do things he or she didn't want to"). As bullying represents a pattern of behavior and not just one isolated incident, responses were dichotomized as follows: youth who reported no involvement in bullying or just one incident were coded as "0" whereas those who responded that they had participated in bullying behaviors two or more times were coded as "1." The dichotomous measure had a mean of 0.34 and a standard deviation of 0.474 (Cronbach's α = .88). As reported in Table 2, 34.1% of respondents admitted to participating in bullying behaviors two or more times in the previous 30 days. This number is somewhat higher than those found in other studies, which tend to average between 15% and 25% (Ericson, 2001; Finkelhor et al., 2005; Seals & Young, 2003).

The second outcome measure of interest in this analysis was the dichotomous variable cyberbullying (1 = cyberbully; 0 = not a cyberbully). As with the measure of traditional bullying, a variety of cyberbullying behaviors were examined (see Table 2), and youth who reported no involvement or just one incident were coded as "0" whereas those who responded that they had participated in cyberbullying behaviors more than once were coded as "1." The dichotomous measure had a mean of 0.22 and a standard deviation of 0.413 (Cronbach's α = .76). Here, more than 21% of youth admitted that they had participated in cyberbullying behaviors two or more times in the previous 30 days. This number is in line with those found in other cyberbullying studies which range between 15% and 25% (Hinduja

Table 2. Descriptive Statistics (N = 1,963)

| | M | SD | Range/Percentage |
|---|---|---|---|
| **Dependent variables** | | | |
| Traditional Bullying Scale (α = .88) | 0.34 | 0.474 | 0–1 |
| I called another student mean names, made fun of or teased him or her in a hurtful way | | | 27.7% |
| I have taken part in bullying another student or students at school | | | 20.5% |
| I kept another student out of things on purpose, excluded him or her from my group of friends or completely ignored him or her | | | 19.9% |
| I hit, kicked, pushed, or shoved another student around or locked another student indoors | | | 15.3% |
| I spread false rumors about another student and tried to make others dislike him or her | | | 10.8% |
| I bullied another student with mean names, comments, or gestures with a sexual meaning | | | 9.9% |
| I bullied another student with mean names or comments about his or her race or color | | | 8.6% |
| I took money or other things from another student or damaged another student's belongings | | | 7.9% |
| I threatened or forced another student to do things he or she didn't want to do | | | 6.5% |
| I bullied another student in another way | | | 11.7% |
| One or more of the above, two or more times | | | 34.1% |
| Cyberbullying Scale (α = .76) | 0.22 | 0.413 | 0–1 |
| I posted something online about another person to make others laugh | | | 22.8% |
| I sent someone a computer text message to make them angry or to make fun of them | | | 13.5% |
| I have taken a picture of someone and posted it online without their permission | | | 11.9% |
| I posted something on on MySpace or similar site to make them angry or to make fun of them | | | 11.2% |
| I sent someone an email to make them angry or to make fun of them | | | 9.0% |
| One or more of the above, two or more times | | | 21.5% |
| **Independent variables** | | | |
| Strain (α = .77) | 3.30 | 2.462 | 0–9 |
| I received a bad grade on an exam in school or in a class | | | 35.3% |
| I got into a bad disagreement with a family member | | | 29.0% |
| I got into a bad disagreement with a friend | | | 28.3% |
| I have been treated unfairly by someone | | | 28.2% |
| I broke up with a boyfriend or girlfriend | | | 28.1% |
| A close friend of mine died or spent time in the hospital | | | 20.8% |
| I have had money problems | | | 19.1% |
| I moved to a new school | | | 13.6% |
| I was a victim of a crime | | | 11.5% |
| Anger/frustration (α = .86) | 0.99 | 0.770 | 0–4 |
| I lose my temper | | | 59.9% |
| I let little things irritate me | | | 55.7% |
| I stay mad at someone who hurts me | | | 54.5% |
| I feel like yelling at a parent or teacher | | | 51.9% |
| I feel like getting even with someone who has harmed me | | | 49.9% |
| I feel like other people are always lucky and they get all of the breaks in life | | | 46.4% |
| I feel like life has given me a raw deal (has been unfair) | | | 46.1% |
| I am jealous of other people | | | 40.4% |
| I feel like a powder keg ready to explode | | | 33.9% |
| I feel like physically lashing out against a parent or teacher | | | 25.4% |
| **Control variables** | | | |
| Gender | 0.50 | 0.500 | 0–1 |
| Male | | | 50.2% |
| Female | | | 49.8% |
| Race | 0.41 | 0.491 | 0–1 |
| White | | | 40.6% |
| Non White | | | 59.1% |
| Age | 12.81 | 1.124 | 10–16 |

Note: Percentages may not add to 100 due to rounding and missing data.

& Patchin, 2008; Li, 2006, 2007; Patchin & Hinduja, 2006; Ybarra, Espelage, & Mitchell, 2007; Ybarra & Mitchell, 2004).[2]

## independent and control variables

Agnew's (2006b) GST is innovative because it suggests several different kinds of strain. As such, the current study used a very broad measure that includes a variety of experiences seemingly common among adolescents (e.g., breaking up with a significant other, receiving a bad grade, getting into a disagreement with a family member) but also less common sources of strain (e.g., moving to a new school or being the victim of a crime; see Table 2).[3] The strain measure was a 9-item variety scale (ranging from 0 to 9) with higher values representing increased levels of strain $(M = 3.3; SD = 2.46;$ Cronbach's α = .77). To note, respondents were asked whether they experienced strain in the previous 6 months—a longer time-frame than the outcome measures which looked at participation in bullying and cyberbullying during the previous 30 days.[4]

GST also maintains that negative affect is an important mediator in the relationship between strain and deviance. To be sure, not all strained individuals turn to criminal behavior as a coping strategy or adaptive response. The current study therefore included a 10-item anger/frustration scale, derived from Brezina (1996), as an indicator of negative affect (see Table 2). With this mean scale (ranging from 0 to 4), higher values represented higher levels of anger and/or frustration $(M = 0.99; SD = 0.77;$ Cronbach's α = .86).

In addition to the above variables, the analyses also included other demographic measures to control for any potentially spurious relationships. Male was a dichotomous item where 1 = *male* and 0 = *female*. As reported in Table 1, the sample was evenly divided across gender. White was a dichotomous variable where 1 = *White* and 0 = *non-White*. Approximately 41% of respondents were White. Finally, Age was included as a continuous variable representing the respondents age in years $(M = 12.8)$.

## analysis

Statistical analyses were conducted in two phases. First, ordinary least squares (OLS) regression was used to estimate the effect of strain on anger/frustration. GST argues that anger and frustration mediate the relationship between strain and deviance, and for this relationship to exist, strain must first be significantly related to anger/frustration. Next, logistic regression analysis was used to examine the

---

2  Research has also shown that traditional bullying and cyberbullying are significantly correlated (Hinduja & Patchin, 2008), though the strength of the relationship (r = .303; see correlation matrix in the appendix) suggests that there may be differing mechanisms that correspond to different forms of bullying.

3  A meaningful body of literature has suggested a significant relationship between victimization and offending (Esbensen & Huizinga, 1991; Fagan, Piper, & Cheng, 1987; Jensen & Brownfield, 1986; Lauritsen, Laub, & Sampson, 1992; Loeber, Kalb, & Huizinga, 2001; Sampson & Lauritsen, 1990, 1993). As an astute reviewer pointed out, there is the possibility that including the victimization measure in the strain scale may bias the actual relationship between strain and bullying/cyberbullying. A decision was made to keep the victimization measure in the strain scale for a number of reasons. Reliability and factor analyses suggested that it was a good indicator of strain, and analyses conducted with the victimization measure removed from the strain scale retrieved substantively identical findings. This is also an operationalization of strain commonly found in the extant literature.

4  Although the data were cross-sectional in nature, the fact that the strain measures focus on a period prior to (and including) the outcome variables allowed proper temporal ordering to be approximated. As the data were not collected over time, temporal ordering could not be determined as precisely as would have been desired. Future research should replicate this analysis using longitudinal data to see if the patterns observed remain.

effect of strain and anger/frustration on bullying. Logistic regression is appropriate when dichotomous outcome variables are used (Menard, 1995).[5] Overall, a series of step-wise logistic regression models were computed to estimate the effect of strain on both traditional and nontraditional forms of bullying, the effect of anger and frustration on both outcome variables, and the effect of strain while controlling for anger and frustration. If GST is correct, the effect of strain should diminish or be rendered insignificant when anger/frustration was included in the multivariate models.

## results

Within the sample, gender and grade level was distributed relatively evenly (see Table 1). Concerning age, respondents were between 10 and 16 years old with most aged 12 (29.5%), 13 (32.7%), or 14 (20%). With regard to race, 40.6% were White, 23.4% were Black, and 19.6% were Hispanic. As reported in Table 2, a meaningful number of adolescents reported participating in bullying behaviors—both traditional and nontraditional forms. The most frequently cited type of bullying reported was "I called another student mean names, made fun of or teased him or her in a hurtful way" (27.7%). In all, more than one third (34.1%) of students reported engaging in traditional bullying two or more times during the previous 30 days. Cyberbullying was also relatively common among these middle schoolers. More than 21% of respondents reported cyberbullying others two or more times during the previous 30 days, with "I posted something online about another person to make others laugh" being the most frequently reported form. These findings are consistent with previous research that demonstrates a meaningful proportion of middle school students are involved in various types of bullying (Nansel et al., 2001; Nofzinger, 2001; Schreck, Mitchel, & Gibson, 2003; Whitney & Smith, 1993).

Table 3.  Ordinary Least Squares Regression Coefficients Representing the Effect of Strain on Anger/ Frustration

|  | B (SE) | Beta | t value |
| --- | --- | --- | --- |
| Strain | .064 (.01)*** | .205 | 7.332 |
| Male | −.288 (.04)*** | −.148 | −5.369 |
| White | .083 (.04) | .053 | 1.910 |
| Age | .049 (.02)* | .070 | 2.477 |
| Constant | .205 (.25) |  | 0.418 |

*p < .05. ***p<.001, two-tailed.

Next, the relationship between strain and anger/frustration was examined. Table 3 shows that strain was positively and significantly related to anger. That is, the more strained a respondent was, the more anger and frustration he or she reported. Also noted was the finding that boys experienced significantly less anger/frustration than girls (also see Mirowsky & Ross, 1995) and older youth experienced more anger and frustration than younger youth (also see Wallace et al., 2005).

Finally, the relationship between strain and traditional and nontraditional forms of bullying was analyzed (see Table 4). As presented in Models 1 and 2, both strain and anger/frustration were significantly related to traditional bullying (p < .001), even after controlling for the effects of gender, race, and age. That is, youth who experienced strain or anger and frustration were more likely to bully others than

---

5   We also computed the analyses using continuous dependent OLS regression, retrieving virtually identical results.

Table 4. Logistic Regression Coefficients Representing Effects of Strain and Anger/Frustration on Bullying

| | DV = Traditional bullying | | | | | | DV = Nontraditional (cyber) bullying | | | | | |
| | Model 1 | | Model 2 | | Model 3 | | Model 4 | | Model 5 | | Model 6 | |
| | B (SE) | Exp(B) | B (SE) | Exp(B) | B (SE) | Exp(B) | B (SE) | Exp(B) | B (SE) | Exp(B) | B (SE) | Exp(B) |
|---|---|---|---|---|---|---|---|---|---|---|---|---|
| Strain | .16 (.03)*** | 1.18 | | | .14 (.03)*** | 1.15 | .12 (.03)*** | 1.13 | | | .12 (.03)*** | 1.13 |
| Anger/frustration | | | .85 (.07)*** | 2.34 | .71 (.09)*** | 2.03 | | | .43 (.07)*** | 1.53 | .29 (.09)*** | 1.33 |
| Male | .01 (.12) | 0.93 | .13 (.11) | 1.14 | .18 (.13) | 1.19 | .03 (.14) | 1.03 | .01 (.12) | 1.01 | .06 (.14) | 1.06 |
| White | -.22 (.13) | 0.80 | -.36 (.11)*** | 0.70 | -.29 (.13)* | 0.75 | -.32 (.15)* | 0.73 | -.32 (.12)* | 0.73 | -.37 (.15)* | 0.69 |
| Age | .17 (.06)** | 1.18 | .16 (.05)** | 1.17 | .13 (.06)* | 1.14 | .21 (.06)*** | 1.23 | .24 (.05)*** | 1.28 | .19 (.07)** | 1.20 |
| Constant | -3.29 (.74)*** | | -3.47 (.65)*** | | -3.51 (.78)*** | | -4.29 (.83)*** | | -4.71 (.71)*** | | -4.27 (.85)*** | |
| Nagelkerke $R^2$ | .07 | | .14 | | .15 | | .05 | | .06 | | .07 | |

*$p < .05$. **$p < .01$. ***$p < .001$, two-tailed.

those who had not experienced strain or anger/frustration. To note, though, the nature of this relationship did not change when both were concurrently included (see Model 3). As such, the mediating relationship purported by GST (and partially supported in Aseltine et al., 2000; Brezina, 1996; Broidy, 2001; Hoffmann & Su, 1997; Mazerolle, Piquero, & Capowich, 2003) was not present in these data (also see Hoffman & Miller, 1998; Mazerolle et al., 2000; Mazerolle & Piquero, 1998; Tittle, Broidy, & Gertz, 2008). Similar findings emerged with respect to cyberbullying (see Models 4 through 6). Youth who reported strain or anger/frustration were more likely to participate in cyberbullying, though anger/frustration did not appear to mediate this relationship either.

It is also noteworthy that in all models, age was positively related to bullying and cyberbullying. That is, older students were more likely to report participating in bullying and cyberbullying. It is important to remember, however, that as this sample was based on a middle school population, it is only accurate to say that bullying increases as students age through 6th, 7th, and 8th grade. Subsequent research should examine these relationships among older students to see the point at which these behaviors diminish. In addition, White students were less likely to report involvement in bullying and cyberbullying (ns in Model 1). Further inquiry is also necessary to disentangle any racial effects that exist among these behavioral outcomes.

# discussion

A significant proportion of youth engage in, or are affected by, bullying at school. In addition, the 21st century has enabled bullies to extend their reach beyond the schoolyard through cyberbullying. The current study explored one potential cause of both forms of interpersonal harm by using GST as a theoretical roadmap. This theory argues that individuals who experience strain and its resultant negative emotions are at risk to engage in deviant behavior. Like many previous studies, the current work found partial support for GST's explanatory relevance.

First, there was a clear direct relationship between strain and both types of bullying. Middle schoolers who reported strain were significantly more likely to have engaged in bullying and cyberbullying. Second, bullying seemed to be related to feelings of negative emotions. Respondents who revealed feeling angry and/or frustrated were more likely to have participated in bullying and cyberbullying. Third, contrary to GST, anger and frustration did not appear to mediate the relationship between strain and either form of bullying. Rather, this finding suggests that strain and anger/frustration have an influence on both types of bullying independent of each other. In short, results from the current work are consistent with much of the previous strain literature and highlight the robustness of the basic GST model in its theoretical applicability to both bullying and cyberbullying.

## implications

Results from the current study point to several recommendations for policy and practice in working with youth. To preempt youth from attempting to reconcile strainful circumstances and negative emotions in an unconstructive or deviant manner, findings suggest that schools provide health education programming and emotional self-management skills to reduce the likelihood of significant strain resulting from interpersonal strife and conflict (including those occurring online; De Wolfe & Saunders, 1995; Hampel, Meier, & Kummel, 2008; McCraty, Atkinson, Tomasino, Goelitz, & Mayrovitz, 1999). Through the use of classroom teaching modules or schoolwide assemblies, educators might cover personal safety and defense; the defusement of potentially explosive interactions; stress management; the types of hostile behavior of which law enforcement should be made aware; and a clear reminder that absolutely no one deserves to be mistreated (Matheny, Aycock, & McCarthy, 1993; Miller, Telljohann, & Symons, 1996).

Second, students must feel comfortable to openly approach and speak to faculty and staff on their school campus—which requires the provision and maintenance of an empathic and nonthreatening environment. Students may need to vent, obtain solace and emotional support, and try to understand why their specific instance of victimization may have happened (de Anda et al., 2000; Frydenberg & Lewis, 1993; Kobus & Reyes, 2000). Such a climate should also promote a continued open line of communication between youth and adults within the school setting. Consequently, this should reduce the occurrence of, and negative outcomes stemming from, interpersonal conflicts that arise among adolescents (Anderson, 1998; Riley & McDaniel, 2000). Incipient research in this area has identified a relationship between a positive school climate and cyberbullying. That is, students who perceived their school climate to be more positive experienced less bullying and cyberbullying (Hinduja & Patchin, 2009). Further research is necessary to determine what characteristics of the school climate are effective at reducing the amount of interpersonal aggression that affects this age group.

Third, and as previously mentioned, strain produces "pressure for corrective action" and requires some kind of release (Thaxton & Agnew, 2004, p. 764). This release may be positive or negative. Indeed, research has shown that adolescents between ages 11 and 15 increasingly cope with strain in maladaptive ways, such as resignation, avoidance, and hostility (Compas, Orosan, & Grant, 1993; Hampel & Petermann, 2005). As such, educators and other youth-serving adults must make available positive outlets at school and elsewhere to provide youth with a way to disengage from what weighs them down. This might include physical or mental extracurricular activities that occupy students' time and help them find satisfaction and self-worth in exploring personal interests (Frydenberg & Lewis, 1993; Miller & McCormick, 1991). These activities may provide a much-needed break from self-consuming thoughts related to any stressful life events experienced.

## references

Agnew, R. (1992). Foundation for a general strain theory of crime and delinquency. *Criminology, 30(1),* 47–87.

Agnew, R. (2000). Strain theory and school crime. In S. Simpson (Ed.), *Of Crime and Criminality: The use of theory in everyday life* (pp. 105–120). Thousand Oaks, CA: Pine Forge Press.

Agnew, R. (2006a). General strain theory: Recent developments and directions for further research. In F. T. Cullen, J. Wright, & M. Coleman (Eds.), *Advances in criminological theory, taking stock: The status of criminological theory* (Vol. 15, pp. 101–123). New Brunswick, NJ: Transaction Publishers.

Agnew, R. (2006b). *Pressured into crime: An overview of general strain theory.* New York: Oxford University Press.

Agnew, R., & White, H. R. (1992). An empirical test of general strain theory. *Criminology, 30,* 475.

Anderson, D. C. (1998). Curriculum, culture and community: The challenge of school violence. In M. Tonry & M. Moore (Eds.), *Youth violence* (pp. 317–363). Chicago: University of Chicago Press.

Aseltine, R. H., Gore, S., & Gordon, J. (2000). Life stress, anger and anxiety, and delinquency: An empirical test of general strain theory. *Journal of Health and Social Behavior, 41,* 256–275.

Besag, V. E. (1989). *Bullies and victims in schools.* Milton Keynes, UK: Open University Press.

Bjorkqvist, K., Ekman, K., & Lagerspetz, K. (1982). Bullies and victims: Their ego picture, ideal ego picture, and normative ego picture. *Scandinavian Journal of Psychology, 23,* 307–313.

Borg, M. G. (1998). The emotional reaction of school bullies and their victims. *Educational Psychology, 18,* 433–444.

Boulton, M. J., & Underwood, K. (1992). Bully victim problems among middle school children. *British Journal of Educational Psychology of Addictive Behaviors, 62,* 73–87.

Bowers, L., Smith, P. K., & Binney, V. (1992). Cohesion and power in the families of children involved in bully/victim problems at school. *Journal of Family Therapy, 14,* 371–387.

Brezina, T. (1996). Adapting to strain: An examination of delinquent coping responses. *Criminology, 34*(1), 39–60.

Brezina, T., Piquero, A. R., & Mazerolle, P. (2001). Student anger and aggressive behavior in school: An initial test of Agnew's macro-level strain theory. *Journal of Research in Crime and Delinquency, 38,* 362–386.

Broidy, L. M. (2001). A test of general strain theory. *Criminology, 39*(1), 9.

Brownfield, D., & Sorenson, A. (1993). Self-control and juvenile delinquency: Theoretical issues and an empirical assessment of selected elements of a general theory of crime. *Deviant Behavior, 14,* 243–264.

Compas, B. E., Orosan, P. G., & Grant, K. E. (1993). Adolescent stress and coping: Implications for psychopathology during adolescence. *Journal of Adolescence, 16,* 331–349.

Crick, N. R., & Bigbee, M. A. (1998). Relational and overt forms of peer victimization: A multi-informant approach. *Journal of Consulting and Clinical Psychology, 66,* 337–347.

de Anda, D., Baroni, S., Boskin, L., Buchwald, L., Morgan, J. N., Ow, J., et al. (2000). Stress, stressors and coping among high school students. *Children and Youth Services Review, 22,* 441–463.

De Wolfe, A. S., & Saunders, A. M. (1995). Stress reduction in sixth-grade students. *Journal of Experimental Education, 63,* 315–329.

Dollard, J., Doob, L., Miller, N., Mowrer, O., & Sears, R. (1939). *Frustration and aggression.* New Haven, CT: Yale University Press.

Endresen, I. M., & Olweus, D. (2001). Self-reported empathy in Norwegian adolescents: Sex differences, age trends, and relationship to bullying. In A. C. Bohart, C. Arthur, & D. J. Stipek (Eds.), *Constructive and destructive behavior: Implications for family, school, and society* (pp. 147–165). Washington, DC: American Psychological Association.

Ericson, N. (2001). *Addressing the problem of juvenile bullying.* Washington, DC: U.S. Government Printing Office, U.S. Department of Justice, Office of Justice Programs, Office of Juvenile Justice and Delinquency Prevention.

Esbensen, F., & Huizinga, D. (1991). Juvenile victimization and delinquency. *Youth & Society, 23,* 202–228.

Fagan, J., Piper, E. J., & Cheng, Y. (1987). Contributions of victimization to delinquency in inner cities. *Journal of Criminal Law & Criminology, 31,* 586–613. Finkelhor, D., Turner, H. A., Ormrod, R. K., & Hamby, S. L. (2005). The victimization of children & youth: A comprehensive, national survey. *Child Maltreatment, 10*(1), 5–25.

Frydenberg, E., & Lewis, R. (1993). Boys play sport and girls turn to others: Age, gender and ethnicity as determinants of coping. *Journal of Adolescence, 16,* 253–266.

Hampel, P., Meier, M., & Kummel, U. (2008). School-based stress management training for adolescents: Longitudinal results from an experimental study. *Journal of Youth and Adolescence, 37,* 1009–1024.

Hampel, P., & Petermann, F. (2005). Age and gender effects on coping in children and adolescents. *Journal of Youth and Adolescence, 34,* 73–83.

Hawker, D. S. J., & Boulton, M. J. (2000). Twenty years' research on peer victimization and psychological maladjustment: A meta-analysis review of cross-sectional studies. *Journal of Child Psychology and Psychiatry, 41,* 441–445.

Haynie, D., Nansel, T., Eitel, P., Crump, A., Saylor, K., & Yu, K. (2001). Bullies, victims and bully/victims: Distinct groups of at-risk youth. *Journal of Early Adolescence, 21*(1), 29–49.

Himmelweit, H., Biberian, M., & Stockdale, J. (1978). Memory for past vote: Implications of a study of bias in recall. *British Journal of Political Science, 8,* 365–375.

Hinduja, S., & Patchin, J. W. (2007). Offline consequences of online victimization: School violence and delinquency. *Journal of School Violence, 6*(3), 89–112.

Hinduja, S., & Patchin, J. W. (2008). Cyberbullying: An exploratory analysis of factors related to offending and victimization. *Deviant Behavior, 29*(2), 1–29.

Hinduja, S., & Patchin, J. W. (2009). *Bullying beyond the schoolyard: Preventing and responding to cyberbullying.* Thousand Oaks, CA: Sage (Corwin Press).

Hoffman, J. P., & Miller, A. S. (1998). A latent variable analysis of general strain theory. *Journal of Quantitative Criminology, 14*(1), 83–110.

Hoffmann, J. P., & Su, S. S. (1997). The conditional effects of stress on delinquency and drug use: A strain theory assessment of sex differences. *Journal of Research in Crime and Delinquency, 34*(1), 46–78.

Horvath, F. (1982, March). Forgotten unemployment: Recall bias in retrospective data. *Monthly Labor Review,* 40–43.

Jensen, G. F., & Brownfield, D. (1986). Gender, lifestyles, and victimization: Beyond routine activity. *Violence and Victims, 1,* 85–99.

Kaufman, P., Chen, Z., Choy, S. P., Ruddy, S. A., Miller, A. K., Fleury, J. K., et al. (2000). *Indicators of school crime and safety, 2000* (No. NCES 2001-017/NCJ-184176). Washington, DC: U.S. Departments of Education and Justice.

Kobus, K., & Reyes, O. (2000). A descriptive study of urban Mexican American adolescents' perceived stress and coping. *Hispanic Journal of Behavioral Sciences, 22,* 163–178.

Kowalski, R. M., & Limber, S. P. (2007). Electronic bullying among middle school students. *Journal of Adolescent Health, 41,* S22–S30.

Lagerspetz, K., Bjorkvqvist, K., Bertz, M., & King, E. (1982). Group aggression among school children in three schools. *Scandinavian Journal of Psychology, 23,* 45–52.

Lauritsen, J. L., Laub, J. H., & Sampson, R. J. (1992). Conventional and delinquent activities: Implications for the prevention of violent victimization among adolescents. *Violence and Victims, 7,* 91–108.

Li, Q. (2006). Cyberbullying in schools: A research of gender differences. *School Psychology International, 27,* 157–170.

Li, Q. (2007). New bottle but old wine: A research on cyberbullying in schools. *Computers and Human Behavior, 23,* 1777–1791.

Limber, S. P., & Nation, M. N. (1998). *Bullying among children and youth. Combating fear and restoring safety in schools.* Retrieved January 20, 2006, from http://ojjdp.ncjrs.org/jjbulletin/9804/bullying2.html

Loeber, R., & Disheon, T. J. (1984). Early predictors of male delinquency: A review. *Psychological Bulletin, 94,* 68–99.

Loeber, R., Kalb, L., & Huizinga, D. (2001). *Juvenile delinquency and serious injury victimization.* Washington, DC: Office of Juvenile Justice and Delinquency Prevention, U.S. Department of Justice.

Magnusson, D., Statten, H., & Duner, A. (1983). Aggression and criminality in a longitudinal perspective. In K. T. V. Dusen & S. A. Mednick (Eds.), *Prospective studies of crime and delinquency* (pp. 277–301). Amsterdam: Kluwer Nijoff.

Manning, M., Heron, J., & Marshal, T. (1978). Style of hostility and social interactions at nursery school and at home: An extended study of children. In A. Lionel, M. B. Hersov, & D. Shaffer (Eds.), *Aggression and antisocial behavior in childhood and adolescence* (pp. 29–58). Oxford, UK: Pergamon.

Matheny, K. B., Aycock, D. W., & McCarthy, C. J. (1993). Stress in school-aged children and youth. *Educational Psychology Review, 5*(2), 109–134.

Mazerolle, P., Burton, V., Cullen, F. T., Evans, D., & Payne, G. L. (2000). Strain, anger, and delinquent adaptations: Specifying general strain theory. *Journal of Criminal Justice, 28,* 89–101.

Mazerolle, P., & Piquero, A. (1998). Linking exposure to strain with anger: An investigation of deviant adaptations. *Journal of Criminal Justice, 26,* 195–211.

Mazerolle, P., Piquero, A., & Capowich, G. E. (2003). Examining the links between strain, situational and dispositional anger, and crime. *Youth & Society, 35,* 131–158.

McCraty, R., Atkinson, M., Tomasino, D., Goelitz, J., & Mayrovitz, H. N. (1999). The impact of an emotional self-management skills course on psychosocial functioning and autonomic recovery to stress in middle school children. *Integrative Psychological and Behavioral Science, 34,* 246–268.

Menard, S. (1995). *Applied logistic regression analysis* (Vol. 106). Thousand Oaks, CA: Sage.

Merton, R. K. (1938). Social structure and anomie. *American Sociological Review, 3,* 672–682.

Miller, D. F., Telljohann, S. K., & Symons, C. W. (1996). *Health education in the elementary and middle-level school* (2nd ed.). Madison, WI: Brown & Benchmark.

Miller, N. E. (1941). The frustration-aggression hypothesis. *Psychological Review, 48,* 337–342.

Miller, S., & McCormick, J. (1991). Stress: Teaching children to cope. *Journal of Physical Education, Recreation, and Dance, 62*(2), 53–70.

Mirowsky, J., & Ross, C. E. (1995). Sex differences in distress: Real or artifact? *American Sociological Review, 60,* 449–468.

Morgenstern, R., & Barrett, N. (1974). The retrospective bias in unemployment reporting by sex, race and age. *Journal of the American Statistical Association, 69,* 355–357.

Nansel, T. R., Overpeck, M., Pilla, R. S., Ruan, W. J., Simons-Morton, B., & Scheidt, P. (2001). Bullying behaviors among U.S. youth: Prevalence and association with psychosocial adjustment. *Journal of the American Medical Association, 285,* 2094–2100.

Nofzinger, S. (2001). *Bullies, fights, and guns: Testing self-control theory with juveniles.* New York: LFB Scholarly.

Olweus, D. (1978). *Aggression in the schools: Bullies and whipping boys.* Washington, DC: Hemisphere Press (Wiley).

Olweus, D. (1993). *Bullying at school.* Oxford, UK: Blackwell.

Olweus, D. (1999). Norway. In P. K. Smith, Y. Morita, J. Junger-Tas, D. Olweus, R. Catalano, & P. Slee (Eds.), *Nature of school bullying: A cross-nationalperspective.* London: Routledge.

Patchin, J. W., & Hinduja, S. (2006). Bullies move beyond the schoolyard: A preliminary look at cyberbullying. *Youth Violence and Juvenile Justice, 4,* 148–169.

Paternoster, R., & Mazerolle, P. (1994). General strain theory and delinquency—A replication and extension. *Journal of Research in Crime and Delinquency, 31,* 235–263.

Patterson, G. R. (2002). Recent developments in our understanding of parenting: Bidirectional effects, causal models, and the search for parsimony. In M. H. Bornstein (Ed.), *Handbook of parenting: Vol. 5. Practical issues in parenting* (2nd ed., pp. 59–88). Mahwah, NJ: Erlbaum.

Rigby, K. (2003). Consequences of bullying in schools. *Canadian Journal of Psychiatry, 48,* 583–590.

Rigby, K., & Slee, P. T. (1993). Dimensions of interpersonal relating among Australian school children and their implications for psychological well-being. *Journal of Social Psychology,* 133(1), 33–42.

Rigby, K., & Slee, P. T. (1999). Australia. In P. Smith, Y. Morita, J. Junger-Tas, D. Olweus, R. Catalano, & P. Slee (Eds.), *The nature of school bullying: A cross-national perspective* (pp. 324–339). London and New York: Routledge.

Riley, P., & McDaniel, J. (2000). School violence prevention, intervention, and crisis response. *Professional School Counseling, 4,* 120–125.

Roland, E. (1980). *Terror i skolen.* Stavanger, Norway: Rogaland Research Institute.

Roland, E. (2002). Bullying, depressive symptoms and suicidal thoughts. *Educational Research, 44,* 55–67.

Salmivalli, C., Kaukiainen, A., Kaistaniemi, L., & Lagerspetz, K. M. (1999). Self- evaluated self-esteem, peer-evaluated self-esteem, and defensive egotism as predictors of adolescents' participation in bullying situations. *Personality and Social Psychology Bulletin, 25,* 1268–1278.

Sampson, R. J., & Lauritsen, J. L. (1990). Deviant lifestyles, proximity to crime, and the offender-victim link in personal violence. *Journal of Research in Crime and Delinquency,* 27(1), 110–139.

Sampson, R. J., & Lauritsen, J. L. (Eds.). (1993). *Violent victimization and offending: Individual-, situational-, and community-level risk factors* (Vol. 3). Washington, DC: National Research Council.

Schreck, C. J., Mitchel, J. M., & Gibson, C. (2003). Trouble in the school yard: A study of the risk factors of victimization at school. *Crime & Delinquency, 49,* 460–484.

Seals, D., & Young, J. (2003). Bullying and victimization: Prevalence and relationship to gender, grade level, ethnicity, self-esteem and depression. *Adolescence, 38,* 735–747.

Slee, P. T., & Rigby, K. (1993). The relationship of Eysenck's personality factors and self esteem to bully/victim behaviour in Australian school boys. *Personality and Individual Differences, 14,* 371–373.

Steinberg, L., & Silk, J. S. (2002). Parenting adolescents. In M. H. Bornstein (Ed.), *Handbook of parenting: Volume 1. Children and parenting* (2nd ed.). Mahwah, NJ: Erlbaum.

Stephenson, P., & Smith, D. (1989). Bullying in junior school. In D. P. T. D. A. Lane (Ed.), *Bullying in schools* (pp. 45–58). Stroke-on-Trent, UK: Trentham.

Tattum, D. P. (1989). Violence and aggression in schools. In D. P. Tattum & D. A. Lane (Eds.), *Bullying in schools* (pp. 7–19). Stroke-on-Trent, UK: Trentham.

Thaxton, S., & Agnew, R. (2004). The nonlinear effects of parental and teacher attachment on delinquency: Disentangling strain from social control explanations. *Justice Quarterly, 21,* 763–792.

Tittle, C. R., Broidy, L. M., & Gertz, M. G. (2008). Strain, crime, and contingencies. *Justice Quarterly, 25,* 283–312.

Wallace, L. H., Patchin, J. W., & May, J. D. (2005). Reactions of victimized youth: Strain as an explanation of school delinquency. *Western Criminology Review,* 6(1), 104–116.

Whitney, I., & Smith, P. K. (1993). A survey of the nature and extent of bullying in junior/middle and secondary schools. *Educational Research,* 31(1), 3–25.

Ybarra, M. L., Espelage, D. L., & Mitchell, K. J. (2007). The co-occurrence of Internet harassment and unwanted sexual solicitation victimization and perpetration: Associations with psychosocial indicators. *Journal of Adolescent Health, 41,* S31–S41.

Ybarra, M. L., & Mitchell, J. K. (2004). Online aggressor/targets, aggressors and targets: A comparison of associated youth characteristics. *Journal of Child Psychology and Psychiatry, 45,* 1308–1316.

carter hay
ryan meldrum
and
karen mann

# traditional bullying, and deviance: a general strain theory approach

## cyber bullying,

The purpose of this study is to address three issues that we see as neglected, substantively important, and logically linked to one another. The first of these involves the need to learn more about the criminogenic effects of bullying. In a significant elaboration of GST, Agnew (2001) identified bullying—or "peer abuse"—as a strain that should be especially consequential for delinquency. Yet even as bullying has received continued attention as an adolescent social problem (e.g., White & Loeber, 2008) GST research has neglected its effects on crime and delinquency. This study addresses this void, and we do so with data that allow us to examine not only traditional notions of bullying (e.g., physical and verbal harassment) but also cyber bullying, which has garnered significant recent attention (Hinduja & Patchin, 2009; Wang, Iannoti, & Nansel, 2009).

A second goal of our study is to examine the effects of bullying not just on crime but also on noncriminal, internalizing forms of deviance. GST tests often assess the effects of strain on

Carter Hay, Ryan Meldrum and Karen Mann, "Traditional Bullying, Cyber Bullying, and Deviance: A General Strain Theory Approach," *Journal of Contemporary Criminal Justice*, vol. 26, no. 2, pp. 130-147. Copyright © 2010 by SAGE Publications. Reprinted with permission.

"externalizing" crimes—acts committed against others or their property. Some individuals, however, may respond with "internalizing" acts that harm themselves. Although neglected, this possibility is consistent with GST's position that individuals cope in different ways and deviant adaptations can come in many forms (Agnew, 1992). We consider this issue by examining the effects of bullying not just on crimes committed against others but also on internalizing deviance, including suicidal ideation and acts of self-harm such as "cutting" or burning oneself. These outcomes are especially important to consider when examining the effects of bullying—those who are bullied may be socially isolated and ostracized, and this may lead to self-directed responses to strain (Moon, Morash, McCluskey, & Hwang, 2009).

Our final focus is on the possibility that these relationships vary across males and females. Broidy and Agnew (1997) identified important ways in which strain-crime relationships may be moderated by sex, and a number of empirical studies support their arguments (e.g., Piquero & Sealock, 2004). This issue has not, however, been examined with respect to the above two issues—issues that may especially call for a consideration of sex-specific patterns. There still is uncertainty about whether males and females experience bullying to the same degree and whether they react to it in similar ways (see Espelage, Mebane, & Swearer, 2004). Sex differences also are important to consider when studying the effects of strain on internalizing deviance. As Broidy and Agnew noted, when confronted with strain, males may resort to externalizing responses, whereas females may be more susceptible to internalizing responses. This hypothesis rarely, however, has been tested in GST research, and it has not been examined with respect to bullying. Also, recent evidence contradicts the conventional wisdom that internalizing deviance is largely a problem among females—rates of deliberate self-harm and suicidal ideation are far from trivial among males in industrialized nations (Kerr, Owen, Pears, & Capaldi, 2008; Patton et al., 2007).

## the present study

The purpose of this study is to examine the effects of bullying on externalizing and internalizing forms of deviance and to assess whether these relationships vary across males and females. Our central hypothesis is that, consistent with GST, bullying is significantly related to both types of deviance. Testing this hypothesis reveals insight on the accuracy of Agnew's (2001) claims regarding the importance of exposure to bullying, and it clarifies whether GST can be extended to explain aggression directed against the self. With respect to sex differences, two hypotheses are tested, both of which draw from Broidy and Agnew (1997) and the related research. We predict that the effects of bullying should be greater for males than females when the dependent variable is externalizing behavior. Conversely, the effects of bullying should be greater for females for dependent variables that involve internalizing deviance. We should emphasize, however, that these hypotheses are offered tentatively. The stress and coping literature upon which Broidy and Agnew based their arguments has not focused on adolescent stressors like bullying. Moreover, its concern with internalizing deviance often has emphasized emotional (e.g., depression) rather than behavioral outcomes. Thus, our test of how these relationships vary according to sex is exploratory to some degree.

## data

These issues are considered with data collected from a sample of roughly 400 adolescents in a Southeastern state of the United States in the spring of 2008. Respondents were sampled from two participating schools—one high school and one middle school—located in a rural and relatively poor county.[1] Using the standards set by the school district, a passive consent procedure was followed. Permission forms were distributed to all students 1 week prior to the survey administration, and students were excluded from the study if parents returned the form asking that their child be excluded. Each participating student then completed an anonymous, self-administered questionnaire during normal school hours and was given a small reward (a candy bar) for completion. This procedure allowed for a near complete census of the two schools' populations, with 93% of attending students participating in the study.[2] This produced a fairly diverse sample. The average age of participants was 15 but ranged from 10 to 21. The sample was split evenly between males and females, and non-Whites represent 34% of the sample. Additionally, family disruption was common, with only 50% of respondents living in a household with both biological parents.

Admittedly, the use of a school sample from a nonmetropolitan county raises concerns about the sample's generalizability. Again, however, our sample is diverse, and there is nothing about it that would appear to bias the results in one direction or another. Moreover, the dearth of studies on this set of issues justifies smaller-scale efforts that are more feasible and less costly. We hope that an initial test of this kind may stimulate and inform more elaborate data collection efforts in the future.

## measures

The survey allowed for multiple-item scales for most variables, and there are two features common to the measures that we used. First, all items in multiple-item scales included ordinal response categories, with almost all using a 4-point scale. For measures that assess frequencies, responses ranged from 1 = *never* to 4 = *often*. For items asking respondents to rate themselves on some characteristic, responses ranged from 1 = *strongly disagree* to 4 = *strongly agree*. Second, with respect to scale construction, each scale was computed by averaging its constituent items.

*Independent variables.* To assess the effects of bullying, two measures were used. The first is a 6-item measure ($\alpha$ = .85) that captures the traditional emphasis on physical and verbal harassment. Respondents indicated how often during the prior 12 months they were (a) the target of lies or rumors; (b) the target of attempts to get others to dislike them; (c) called names, made fun of, or teased in a hurtful way; (d) hit, kicked, or pushed by another student; (e) physically threatened by other students; and (f) picked on by others. Our second bullying measure is a 3-item scale ($\alpha$ = .80) that captures the more recent interest in cyber bullying. Respondents were asked to indicate how frequently during the previous 12 months they were (a) the target of "mean" text messages; (b) sent threatening or hurtful statements or pictures in an e-mail or text message; and (c) made fun of on the Internet.

*Dependent variables.* Externalizing delinquency was measured with a 5-item scale ($\alpha$ = .86) of self-reported offending during the prior 12 months. Respondents indicated how often they had (a) stolen something worth less than $50; (b) stolen something worth more than $50; (c) damaged, destroyed, or tagged property that did not belong to them; (d) entered a building or house without permission from the owner; and (e) hit, kicked, or struck someone with the idea of seriously hurting them. Two measures of internalizing behavior were used, with both measured with a single item. The first is a measure of suicidal ideation in which respondents were asked how often "you think about killing yourself." Self-harm was measured by asking respondents how often "you purposely hurt yourself without wanting to die," with "cutting or burning" offered as examples.

---

1   The data were collected as part of a larger project concerned with improving the quality of data collected and reported by public schools in the state.

2   Exceptional and special education students were not eligible for the study and were excluded from the sampling design.

*Control variables.* A number of demographic control variables were included in the analyses to protect against concerns about spuriousness. These included five demographic variables: age (measured in years), sex *(male = 1, female = 0)*, race *(non-White = 1, White = 0)*, nonintact family structure *(non-intact = 1, living with both biological parents = 0)*, and place of birth *(foreign-born = 1, native born = 0)*. Also, to better isolate the independent relationship between exposure to bullying and the outcomes of interest, controls were included to capture key aspects of respondents' school, family, peer, and personal characteristics. This included measures of school grades (as indicated by self-reported grades on the most recent report card); parental control, as indicated by a 10-item scale ($\alpha = .92$) of parental monitoring and discipline; and unstructured time spent with peers, as indicated by a 2-item scale ($r = .56$) measuring time spent with friends with no adults present and time spent with friends at a mall, restaurant, or street corner. And last, all analyses include an 8-item measure ($\alpha = .85$) of self-control, which included the 8 items used in the Grasmick et al. scale (Grasmick, Tittle, Bursik, & Arneklev, 1993) to measure impulsivity and risk seeking.[3]

## results

The first step in the analysis was to consider the effects of bullying on our externalizing and internalizing outcomes. Given the high correlation ($r = .67$) between traditional and cyber bullying, the effects of the two were estimated in separate equations. Thus, with two measures of bullying and three outcomes of interest (delinquency, self-harm, and suicidal ideation), we estimated six ordinary least squares (OLS) equations, each of which included all of the controls.

The results for these equations are shown in Table 2, which reveals a consistent effect of bullying—the effects of bullying are statistically significant and relatively large in all six equations (with betas ranging from .22 to .41).[4] Cyber bullying has modestly higher effects than traditional bullying—standardized effects of .33 for delinquency, .39 for self-harm, and .41 for suicidal ideation, which compares to effects of .22, .33, and .39 for traditional bullying. Also, both types of bullying have greater effects on self-harm and suicidal ideation than on delinquency. For traditional bullying, for example, the effect on suicidal ideation ($B = .39$) is nearly 80% higher than the effect on delinquency ($B = .22$). The pattern is less extreme but still true for cyber bullying, which has an effect on suicidal ideation ($B = .41$) that is 24% higher than its effect on delinquency ($B = .33$). Thus, bullying has a consistent, relatively strong association with delinquency, self-harm, and suicidal ideation, but this is especially true for cyber bullying in particular and for outcomes that involve internalizing rather than externalizing deviance.[5]

---

3   Table 1 provides descriptive statistics for the full sample and for the males and females subsamples (for key variables of interest).

4   The effects of bullying are relatively high when compared to the effects of other variables in the model. To be clear, several of the controls (especially non-White, parental control, and self-control) had relatively consistent effects. In the case of self-control, these significant effects were limited to the models for self-harm and suicidal ideation—self-control had no effect on delinquency. Because self-control has a significant bivariate correlation (-.23) with delinquency, our best explanation for its lower-than-expected multivariate effect is its correlation with other variables in the model (-.27 with poor grades, .27 with parental control, -.28 with traditional bullying, and -.16 with cyber bullying). Some recent studies find that the effects of self-control (or related concepts) are diminished in equations that include controls for other key theoretical variables (Agnew et al., 2002; Antonaccio & Tittle, 2008).

5   We estimated additional equations to consider how sensitive our results were to various modifications in measurement or modeling. First, we considered whether verbal and physical bullying—which were combined in our traditional bullying measure—had effects that differed from one another. We found that the effects of physical bullying were consistently stronger. However, both measures were significantly related to the dependent variable in all equations. Second, we considered whether the effects of bullying were greater on violent or property crime. We found significant effects on both types

Table 1.   Descriptive Statistics

| Total sample | N | M | SD | Minimum | Maximum |
|---|---|---|---|---|---|
| Age | 424 | 14.99 | 2.18 | 10.00 | 21.00 |
| Male | 420 | 0.50 | 0.50 | 0.00 | 1.00 |
| Non-White | 422 | 0.34 | 0.48 | 0.00 | 1.00 |
| Foreign-born | 423 | 0.07 | 0.26 | 0.00 | 1.00 |
| Nonintact family | 407 | 0.50 | 0.50 | 0.00 | 1.00 |
| Poor school grades | 391 | 2.02 | 1.04 | 1.00 | 5.00 |
| Parental control | 416 | 3.08 | 0.76 | 1.00 | 4.00 |
| Time spent with peers | 407 | 2.65 | 1.78 | 0.00 | 5.00 |
| Self-control | 422 | 2.79 | 0.64 | 1.00 | 4.00 |
| Cyber bullying victimization | 417 | 1.33 | 0.64 | 1.00 | 4.00 |
| Traditional bullying victimization | 419 | 1.74 | 0.72 | 1.00 | 4.00 |
| Delinquency | 415 | 1.23 | 0.51 | 1.00 | 4.00 |
| Self-harm | 418 | 1.31 | 0.75 | 1.00 | 4.00 |
| Suicidal ideation | 417 | 1.33 | 0.76 | 1.00 | 4.00 |
| Male sample | | | | | |
| Cyber bullying victimization | 204 | 1.30 | 0.62 | 1.00 | 4.00 |
| Traditional bullying victimization | 205 | 1.76 | 0.72 | 1.00 | 4.00 |
| Delinquency | 205 | 1.28 | 0.54 | 1.00 | 4.00 |
| Self-harm | 205 | 1.25 | 0.70 | 1.00 | 4.00 |
| Suicidal ideation | 204 | 1.31 | 0.74 | 1.00 | 4.00 |
| Female sample | | | | | |
| Cyber bullying victimization | 209 | 1.37 | 0.65 | 1.00 | 4.00 |
| Traditional bullying victimization | 209 | 1.72 | 0.72 | 1.00 | 4.00 |
| Delinquency | 205 | 1.16 | 0.43 | 1.00 | 4.00 |
| Self-harm | 210 | 1.37 | 0.80 | 1.00 | 4.00 |
| Suicidal ideation | 210 | 1.35 | 0.79 | 1.00 | 4.00 |

Our next step in the analysis was to examine whether these relationships vary across males and females; in short, do males and females differ in their response to traditional and cyber bullying? It is first useful to consider whether there were sex differences in exposure to these forms of bullying. The descriptives provided in Table 1 reveal that there were not. On scales that ranged from 1 to 4 (indicating exposure as 1 = *never*, 2 = *rarely*, 3 = *sometimes*, or 4 = *often*), both males and females had average values of approximately 1.75 for traditional bullying and 1.35 for cyber bullying. (The differences between males and females were not significant.) Thus, if bullying victimization is to produce divergent outcomes for males and females, it will result not from their differing extent of exposure, but instead, from their differing reactions.

---

of offending, but the effects were greater for property offending. However, this pattern could be the result of our limited measure of violent offending. It was measured with a single item pertaining to assaults against others, whereas property offending was measured with a 4-item scale. And third, we considered whether the effects of traditional and cyber bullying could be estimated in the same equation. The two have a correlation of .67, and including them in the same model produced variance inflation factors that often approached 2.00; this level is seen as problematic by some standards (Fox, 1991). That being said, these equations generally found cyber bullying to be the more consequential form of victimization. Its effects were significant and substantively larger than the effects of traditional bullying in all equations. Indeed, although traditional bullying continued to have significant effects on self-harm and suicidal ideation, its effect on delinquency was reduced to zero in the model that also included cyber bullying.

cybercrime and criminological theory

Table 2. OLS Regressions of Dependent Variables on Traditional and Cyber Bullying Victimization

| Predictor | Delinquency (N = 363) | | | Self-harm (N = 365) | | | Suicidal ideation (N = 364) | | |
|---|---|---|---|---|---|---|---|---|---|
| | b | SE | B | b | SE | B | b | SE | B |
| Age | 0.02 | 0.012 | 0.07 | 0.00 | 0.017 | 0.01 | 0.02 | 0.017 | 0.05 |
| Male | 0.09 | 0.049 | 0.09 | -0.18 | 0.070 | -0.12** | -0.08 | 0.071 | -0.05 |
| Non-white | 0.14 | 0.055 | 0.13* | 0.21 | 0.079 | 0.13** | 0.19 | 0.080 | 0.12* |
| Foreign-born | 0.01 | 0.098 | 0.00 | 0.06 | 0.141 | 0.02 | 0.27 | 0.142 | 0.10 |
| Nonintact family | 0.10 | 0.051 | 0.10* | 0.09 | 0.073 | 0.06 | 0.10 | 0.073 | 0.07 |
| Poor school grades | 0.00 | 0.025 | 0.01 | -0.01 | 0.036 | -0.02 | -0.06 | 0.037 | -0.09 |
| Parental control | -0.16 | 0.035 | -0.24** | -0.14 | 0.050 | -0.14** | -0.17 | 0.051 | -0.17** |
| Time with peers | 0.04 | 0.014 | 0.13** | 0.03 | 0.020 | 0.06 | 0.00 | 0.020 | 0.00 |
| Self-control | -0.04 | 0.042 | -0.05 | -0.21 | 0.061 | -0.18** | -0.13 | 0.062 | -0.11* |
| Traditional bullying | 0.15 | 0.035 | 0.22** | 0.34 | 0.050 | 0.33** | 0.41 | 0.051 | 0.39** |
| Constant | 1.10 | 0.264 | — | 1.62 | 0.379 | — | 1.29 | 0.382 | — |
| Adjusted R2 | — | 0.21 | — | — | 0.24 | — | — | 0.26 | — |
| Age | 0.01 | 0.011 | 0.02 | -0.02 | 0.016 | -0.06 | -0.01 | 0.017 | -0.03 |
| Male | 0.12 | 0.047 | 0.12* | -0.14 | 0.069 | -0.10* | -0.04 | 0.070 | -0.03 |
| Non-White | 0.13 | 0.053 | 0.12* | 0.18 | 0.077 | 0.11* | 0.15 | 0.078 | 0.10 |
| Foreign-born | 0.02 | 0.094 | 0.01 | 0.09 | 0.137 | 0.03 | 0.31 | 0.140 | 0.11* |
| Nonintact family | 0.12 | 0.048 | 0.12* | 0.14 | 0.070 | 0.09 | 0.16 | 0.072 | 0.11* |
| Poor school grades | 0.01 | 0.024 | 0.01 | -0.01 | 0.035 | -0.01 | -0.05 | 0.036 | -0.07 |
| Parental control | -0.17 | 0.034 | -0.24** | -0.15 | 0.049 | -0.15** | -0.18 | 0.050 | -0.18** |
| Time with peers | 0.02 | 0.014 | 0.08 | 0.00 | 0.020 | 0.01 | -0.02 | 0.020 | -0.05 |
| Self-control | -0.05 | 0.040 | -0.06 | -0.24 | 0.058 | -0.21** | -0.018 | 0.059 | -0.16** |
| Cyber bullying | 0.26 | 0.038 | 0.33** | 0.45 | 0.054 | 0.39** | 0.49 | 0.055 | 0.41** |
| Constant | 1.21 | 0.231 | — | 2.08 | 0.336 | — | 1.94 | 0.344 | — |
| Adjusted R² | — | 0.27 | — | — | 0.29 | — | — | 0.28 | — |

*$p < .05.$ **$p < .01.$

Table 3. Z-Score Test for Differences in Effects of Bullying for Males and Females

| Type b | Delinquency | | | Self-harm | | | Suicidal ideation | | |
|---|---|---|---|---|---|---|---|---|---|
| | SE | Z | b | SE | Z | b | SE | Z |
| Traditional bullying | | | | | | | | | |
| Males 0.135 | 0.057 | -0.54 | 0.366 | .067 | 0.46 | 0.454 | 0.074 | 0.63 |
| Females 0.174 | 0.044 | — | 0.319 | .077 | — | 0.389 | 0.071 | — |
| Cyber bullying | | | | | | | | | |
| Males 0.274 | 0.062 | 0.12 | 0.578 | .069 | 2.20* | 0.648 | 0.078 | 2.41* |
| Females 0.265 | 0.045 | — | 0.342 | .082 | — | 0.382 | 0.078 | — |

Note: All equations included controls for age, non-White, foreign born, nonintact family, poor school grades, parental control, time spent with peers, and self-control. *p<.05.

To consider this possibility, we estimated OLS regression equations identical to those presented in Table 2, except that they were estimated separately for males and females. Table 3 provides a summary of the key results from these equations. For each male-female comparison, we provide the unstandardized coefficient and standard error for the bullying measure in question. Also, we provide the z-score statistic used to determine whether the coefficients for males and females significantly differed. We used the formula recommended by Paternoster and his colleagues (Paternoster, Brame, Mazerolle, & Piquero, 1998) that takes $b1-b2$ (the difference between the two coefficients) as the numerator and the square root of $SE\ b_1^2 + SE\ b_2^2$ (the estimated standard error of the difference) as the denominator. If this formula yields a value for z that exceeds 1.96, the null hypothesis that $b1 = b2$ is rejected for a two-tailed test with an alpha level of .05.

The figures in Table 3 reveal that in four of the six bullying-deviance combinations, there are no significant differences in effects between males and females. Traditional bullying has effects (shown in the top panel of Table 3) that are similar for males and females across all three dependent variables—each effect is significant, and the differences between the coefficients for males and females are negligible and insignificant. This pattern also is true for cyber bullying (shown in the bottom panel of Table 3) when delinquency is the dependent variable—the effect of cyber bullying on delinquency is almost identical for males and females.

A different pattern emerges, however, for the effects of cyber bullying on self-harm and suicidal ideation—these effects are significantly greater for males. To be clear, exposure to cyber bullying is associated with heightened internalizing deviance for both males and females. For males, however, the effects on these two outcomes are about 70% higher than what is observed for females, and these effects for males are quite large in absolute terms, with standardized effects (not shown) of .52 on self-harm and .54 on suicidal ideation. Indeed, these effects of cyber bullying on male self-harm and suicidal ideation are nearly double the standardized effect of cyber bullying on male delinquency $(B = .29)$.

Taken as a whole, these results are consistent with the possibility that males and females sometimes differ in their responses to strain. However, support for this idea emerged only when considering the effects of cyber bullying on internalizing deviance. Moreover, the exact pattern of differences was unexpected—internalizing responses to strain were higher among males rather than females.

# references

Agnew, R. (1992). Foundation for a general strain theory of crime and delinquency. *Criminology, 30,* 47–87.

Agnew, R. (2001). Building on the foundation of general strain theory: Specifying the types of strain most likely to lead to crime and delinquency. *Journal of Research in Crime and Delinquency, 38,* 319–361.

Agnew, R. (2002). Experienced, vicarious, and anticipated strain: An exploratory study on physical victimization and delinquency. *Justice Quarterly, 19,* 603–632.

Agnew, R., & Brezina, T. (1997). Relational problems with peers, gender, and delinquency. *Youth & Society, 29,* 84–111.

Agnew, R., Brezina, T., Wright, J. P., & Cullen, F. T. (2002). Strain, personality traits, and delinquency: Extending general strain theory. *Criminology, 40,* 43–72.

Antonaccio, O., & Tittle, C. R. (2008). Morality, self-control, and crime. *Criminology, 46,* 479–510.

Baron, S. W. (2004). General strain, street youth and crime: A test of Agnew's revised theory. *Criminology, 42,* 457–483.

Brezina, T. (1998). Adolescent maltreatment and delinquency: The question of intervening processes. *Journal of Research in Crime and Delinquency, 35,* 71–99.

Broidy, L. (2001). A test of general strain theory. *Criminology, 39,* 9–36.

Broidy, L., & Agnew, R. (1997). Gender and crime: A general strain theory perspective. *Journal of Research in Crime and Delinquency, 34,* 275–306.

Capowich, G. E., Mazerolle, P., & Piquero, A. (2001). General strain theory, situational anger, and social networks: An assessment of conditioning influences. *Journal of Criminal Justice, 29,* 445–461.

Centers for Disease Control and Prevention. (2008). Youth risk behavior surveillance—United States, 2007. *Surveillance summaries, June 6, 2008. Morbidity and Mortality Weekly Report 2008, 57* (No. SS–4).

Crick, N. R., & Grotpeter, J. F. (1995). Relational aggression, gender, and social-psychological adjustment. *Child Development, 66,* 710–722.

Espelage, D. L., Mebane, S. E., & Swearer, S. M. (2004). Gender differences in bullying: Moving beyond mean level differences. In D. L. Espelage & S. M. Swearer (Eds.), *Bullying in American schools: A social-ecological perspective on prevention and intervention* (pp. 15–35). Mahwah, NJ: Lawrence Erlbaum.

Fox, J. (1991). *Regression diagnostics.* Newbury Park, CA: Sage.

Gottfredson, M., & Hirschi, T. (1990). *A general theory of crime.* Palo Alto, CA: Stanford University Press.

Grasmick, H. G., Tittle, C. R., Bursik, R. J., & Arneklev, B. (1993). Testing the core empirical implications of Gottfredson and Hirschi's general theory of crime. *Journal of Research in Crime and Delinquency, 30,* 5–29.

Hawker, D. S. J., & Boulton, M. J. (2000). Twenty years' research on peer victimization and psychosocial maladjustment: A meta-analytic review of cross-sectional studies. *The Journal of Child Psychology and Psychiatry, 41,* 441–445.

Hawton, K., Rodham, K., & Evans, E. (2006). *By their own hand.* Philadelphia: Jessica Kingsley Publishers.

Hay, C. (2003). Family strain, gender, and delinquency. *Sociological Perspectives, 46,* 107–135.

Hay, C., & Evans, M. (2006). Violent victimization and involvement in delinquency: Examining predictions from general strain theory. *Journal of Criminal Justice, 34,* 261–274.

Hinduja, S., & Patchin, J. W. (2007). Off-line consequences of online victimization: School violence and delinquency. *Journal of School Violence, 6*, 89–112.

Hinduja, S., & Patchin, J. W. (2009). *Bullying beyond the schoolyard: Preventing and responding to cyberbullying.* Thousand Oaks, CA: Corwin Press.

Hoffmann, J. P., & Cerbone, F. G. (1999). Stressful life events and delinquency escalation in early adolescence. *Criminology, 37*, 343–373.

Hoffmann, J. P., & Miller, A. S. (1998). A latent variable analysis of general strain theory. *Journal of Quantitative Criminology, 14*, 83–110.

Kerr, D. C. R., Owen, L. D., Pears, K. C., & Capaldi, D. M. (2008). Prevalence of suicidal ideation among boys and males assessed annually from ages 9 to 29 years. *Suicide and Life-Threatening Behavior, 38*, 390–402.

Lauritsen, J. L., Sampson, R. J., & Laub, J. H. (1991). The link between offending and victimization among adolescents. *Criminology, 29*, 265–292.

Lenhart, A., Madden, M., & Hitlin, P. (2005). *Teens and technology: Youth are leading the transition to a fully wired and mobile nation.* Washington, DC: Pew Internet and American Life Project. Retrieved July 6, 2009, from http://www.pewinternet.org/~/media//Files/ Reports/2005/PIP_Teens_Tech_July2005web.pdf.

Mason, K. L. (2008). Cyberbullying: A preliminary assessment for school personnel. *Psychology in the Schools, 45*, 323–348.

Mazerolle, P. (1998). Gender, general strain, and delinquency: An empirical examination. *Justice Quarterly, 15*, 65–91.

Mazerolle, P., & Piquero, A. (1997). Violent responses to strain: An examination of conditioning influences. *Violence and Victims, 12*, 323–343.

Moon, B., Morash, M., McCluskey, C. P., & Hwang, H. (2009). A comprehensive test of general strain theory: Key strains, situational and trait-based negative emotions, conditioning factors, and delinquency. *Journal of Research in Crime and Delinquency, 46*, 182–212.

Paternoster, R., Brame, R., Mazerolle, P., & Piquero, A. (1998). Using the correct statistical test for the equality of regression coefficients. *Criminology, 36*, 859–866.

Paternoster, R., & Mazerolle, P. (1994). General strain theory and delinquency: A replication and extension. *Journal of Research in Crime and Delinquency, 31*, 235–263.

Patton, G. C., Hemphill, S. A., Beyers, J. M., Bond, L., Toumbourou, J. W., McMorris, B. J., et al. (2007). Pubertal stage and deliberate self-harm in adolescents. *Journal of the American Academy of Child and Adolescent Psychiatry, 46*, 508–514.

Piquero, N. L., & Sealock, M. D. (2000). Generalizing general strain theory: An examination of an offending population. *Justice Quarterly, 17*, 449–484.

Piquero, N. L., & Sealock, M.D. (2004). Gender and general strain theory: A preliminary test of Broidy and Agnew's gender/GST hypotheses. *Justice Quarterly, 21*, 125–158.

Sharp, S. F., Terling-Watt, T. L., Atkins, L. A., Gilliam, J. T., & Sanders, A. (2001). Purging behavior in a sample of college females: A research note on general strain theory and female deviance. *Deviant Behavior, 22*, 171–188.

Vajani, M., Annest, J. L., Crosby, A. E., Alexander, J., & Millet, L. M. (2007). Nonfatal and fatal self-harm injuries among children aged 10–14 years—United States and Oregon, 2001–2003. *Suicide and Life-Threatening Behavior, 37*, 493–506.

Wang, J., Iannotti, R. J., & Nansel, T. R. (2009). School bullying among adolescents in the United States: Physical, verbal, relational, and cyber. *Journal of Adolescent Health, 45*, 368–375.

Warr, M. (1996). Organization and instigation in delinquent groups. *Criminology, 34,* 11–37.

White, N. A., & Loeber, R. (2008). Bullying and special education as predictors of serious delinquency. *Journal of Research in Crime and Delinquency, 45,* 380–397.

Ybarra, M., & Mitchell, K. (2004). Online aggressor/targets, aggressors, and targets: A comparison of associated youth characteristics. *Journal of Child Psychology and Psychiatry, 45,* 1308–1316.

cybercrime and criminological theory

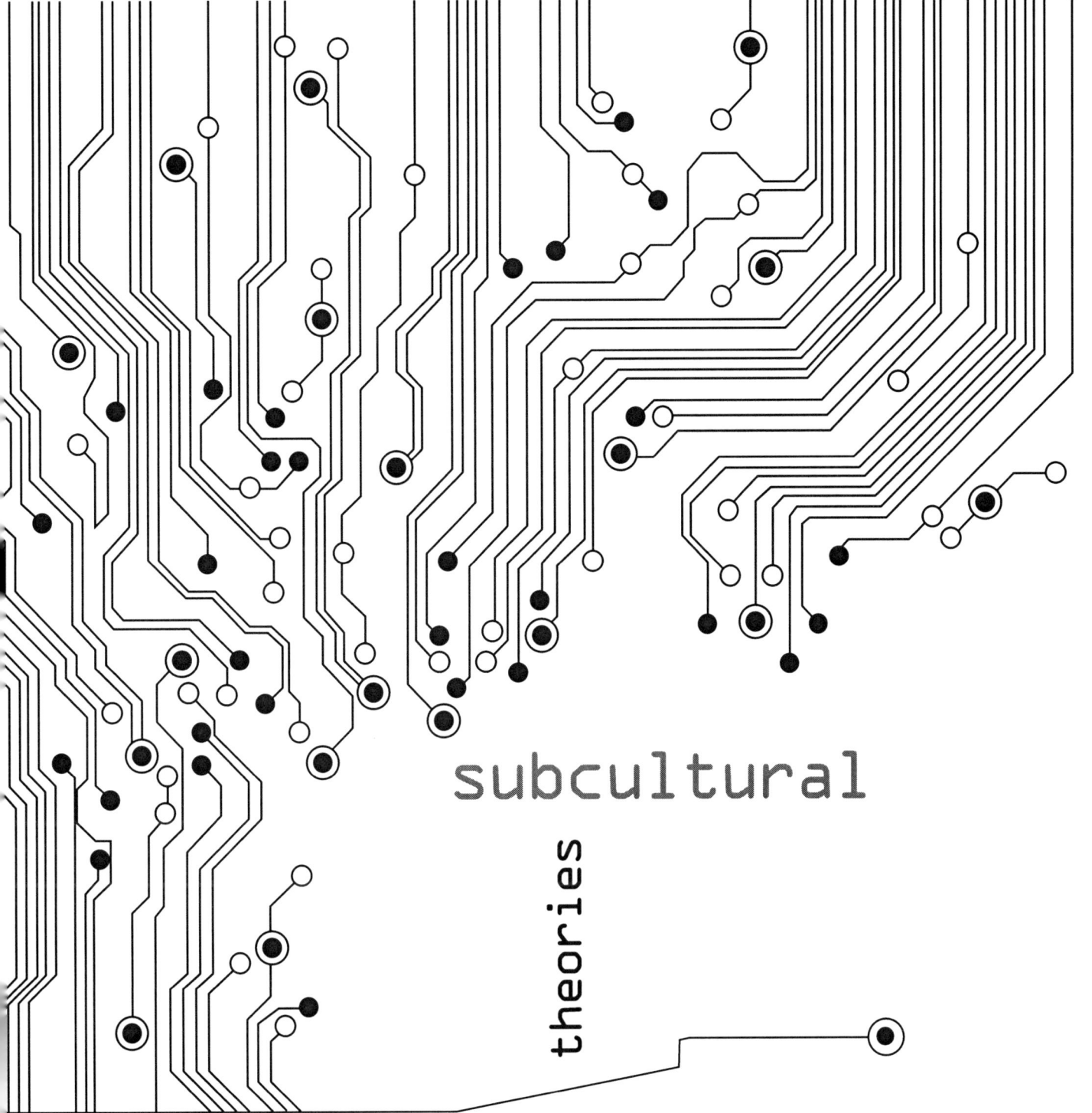

subcultural

theories

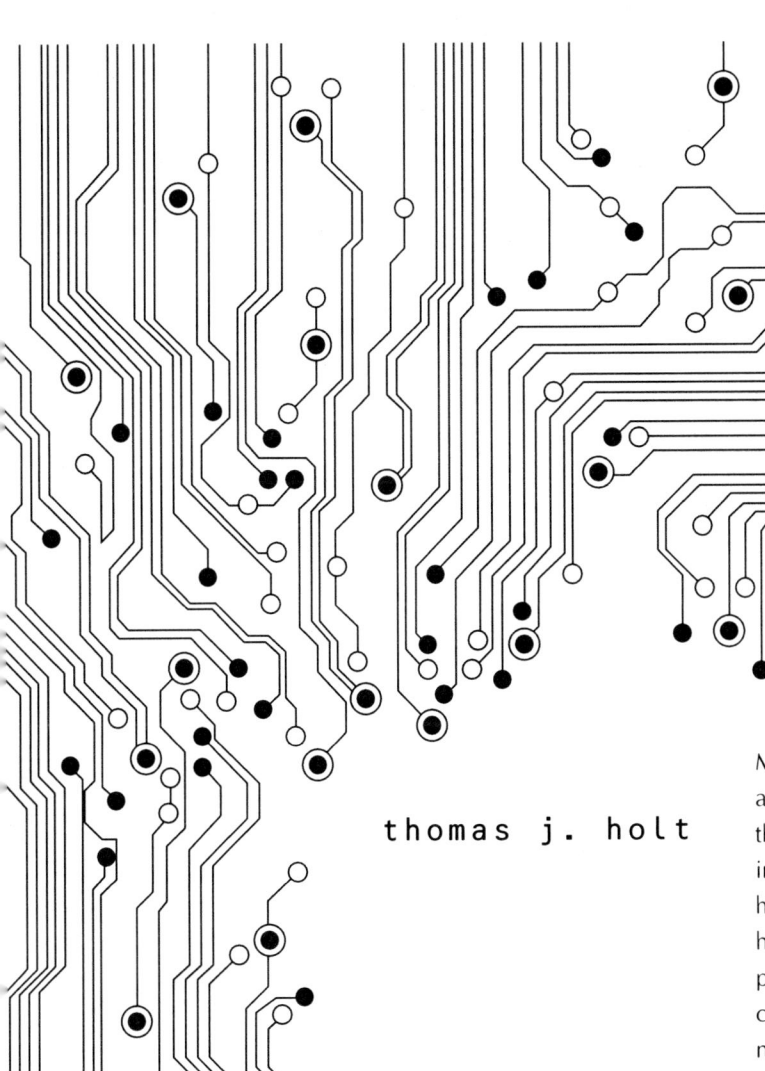

thomas  j.  holt

Most criminological theories focus on offending as a consequence of individual-level factors that may be affected through properly targeted intervention strategies. These theories do not, however, explore the meaning that offending has for some individuals and the depth of their participation in peer networks that may facilitate criminal activity. Researchers who explore criminality through a subcultural lens can, however, provide substantive depth on the how and why of criminal behavior (Miller, 1958; Short, 1968). Defined from a broad perspective, a subculture is any group having certain values, norms, traditions, and rituals that set them apart from the dominant culture (Kornblum, 1997; Brake, 1980). In fact, subcultures form as a response to either a rejection of the dominant culture (see Miller, 1958), or around a distinct phenomenon that may not be valued by the larger society (Quinn & Forsythe, 2005; Wolfgang & Ferracuti, 1967). This includes an emphasis on performing certain behaviors or developing skill sets (Maurer, 1981) and learning the rules or codes of conduct that structure how individuals view and interact with different groups

(Foster, 1990). Subcultures also utilize special terms and slang, called an argot, and may also have some outward symbols of membership like tattoos or informal uniforms (Maurer, 1981). Thus, demonstrating such knowledge illustrates an individual's reputation, status, and adherence to a particular subculture.

In some ways, subcultures share common elements of differential association (Sutherland, 1947) and social learning (Akers, 1998), as involvement in a subculture influences behavior by providing individuals with beliefs, goals, and values that approve of and justify particular types of activities, including crime (Herbert, 1998). In fact, the transmission of subcultural knowledge increases the likelihood of involvement in criminal behavior despite potential legal consequences for these actions (Miller, 1958; Short, 1968). As such, subcultural frameworks provide an important perspective to explain how the values and ideas espoused by members of a group affect the behavior of its members.

The development of the Internet and computer technology have had a dramatic impact on the formation of and participation in deviant or criminal subcultures (DiMarco & DiMarco, 2002; Quinn & Forsyth, 2005). The anonymity and distributed nature of the Internet enables individuals to connect to groups that share similar likes, dislikes, behaviors, opinions, and values, regardless of the participants' location in the real world (DiMarco & DiMarco, 2002). Some individuals may not be able to discuss their interests or activities with others in the real world due to fear of legal reprisal or concerns that others around them may reject them because they do not share their interests. Technology allows individuals to connect to others without these fears, and even enable individuals who are curious about a behavior or activity to learn more in an on-line environment without fear of detection (Blevins & Holt, 2009; Holt, 2007; Quinn & Forsyth, 2005). In fact, individuals can readily communicate subcultural knowledge through e-mail and other forms of computer-mediated communication, such as techniques of offending that may reduce their risk of detection from victims and law enforcement (Holt, Soles, & Leslie, 2008; Holt & Copes, 2010). Such information can increase the likelihood of success for illicit behavior despite potential legal consequences for these actions. Thus, the value of the Internet and computer-mediated communications with individuals across the globe are pivotal in the pursuit of crime and deviance on- and off-line.

The following selections demonstrate the value of subcultural frameworks to our understanding of offender behavior in on-line environments and cybercrimes generally. The first piece, by Cooper and Harrison (2001), provides unique insights into the subculture of piracy in Internet Relay Chat, or IRC. These channels were immensely important for individuals engaged in music piracy during the late 1990s and early 2000s, until the creation of torrents in recent years (Holt & Copes, 2010; Nhan, 2010). While IRC channels have declined in popularity, this qualitative study explores what individual participants valued and how their communications and activities were structured by the online medium they engaged in.

The second piece is by Holt (2010) and gives an exploration of the specialized language, or argot, of computer hackers. This analysis considers the way that subcultural values are communicated through the various terms for hackers, and the meanings they have for those inside and outside of the subculture. In addition, this study gives some insight into the ways that real-world experiences shape participation in a subculture that is focused almost entirely on technology. While most assume that hackers operate in an on-line environment only due to their manipulation of technology, many hackers interact with peers at meetings and conferences in the real world. As a result, on-line communications and off-line interactions affect the values, beliefs, and experiences of hackers.

Both of these studies give substantive insights into the ways that cybercriminals interact and how their perspectives on offending are structured by on- and off-line experiences. However, we need a great deal of research to better understand subcultures in a modern context. For example, some forms of offending occur off-line only, such as prostitution, though there are on-line subcultures that have emerged in forums that support and justify their activities (Blevins & Holt, 2009; Holt & Blevins, 2007). In these instances, it is not clear how offender behaviors off-line are impacted by their on-line experiences. Furthermore, the constant evolution in technologies and communications methods requires continuous investigation to understand how offender subcultures adapt to these changes. Finally, the global nature of the Internet allows a single subculture to vary based on regional preferences and attitudes, as noted in hacker communities within China, Russia, Turkey, and the United States (Chu, Holt, & Ahn, 2010; Holt, Soles, & Leslie, 2008; Holt, 2009). Research is needed to document the contours of a subculture, and the similarities and differences that may exist across the world.

## discussion questions

1. Are there any on-line subcultures in which you participate? For instance, do you belong to a forum, newsgroup, or fan site for a band, TV show, or book series? What is it about this subculture that you enjoy or identify with? How does involvement in this subculture affect your outlook on the world?

2. Given the proliferation of technology and Internet access, do you think it may be more difficult for individuals to leave an on-line subculture? For instance, smart phones can give individuals immediate access to e-mail, websites, and social networking sites. As a consequence, how do individuals disconnect from a subculture that they can access at any time?

3. Is it sensible that traditional subcultures in the real world will develop a substantive on-line presence? For instance, why would members of a street gang utilize Facebook or YouTube to further their goals or support individual activity?

## references

Akers, R. L. (1998). *Social Learning and Social Structure: A General Theory of Crime and Deviance.* Boston: Northeastern University Press.

Blevins, K. R., & Holt, T. J. (2009). Examining the virtual subculture of johns. *Journal of contemporary Ethnography, 38,* 619–648.

Brake, M. (1980). *The Sociology of Youth Cultures and Youth Subcultures.* London: Routledge and Kegan Paul.

Chu, B., Holt, T. J., & Ahn, G. J. (2010). *Examining the Creation, Distribution, and Function of Malware On-Line.* Washington, DC: National Institute of Justice. [Online] Available online at: www.ncjrs.gov/pdffiles1/nij/grants/230112.pdf

Cooper, J., & Harrison, D. M. (2001). The social organization of audio piracy on the Internet. *Media, Culture, and Society, 23,* 71–89.

DiMarco, A. D., & DiMarco, H. (2003). Investigating Cybersociety: A Consideration of the Ethical and Practical Issues Surrounding Online Research in Chat Rooms. In Y. Jewkes (ed.), *Dot.cons: Crime, Deviance and Identity on the Internet.* Portland, OR: Willan Publishing.

Foster, J. (1990). *Villains: Crime and Community in the Inner City.* London: Routledge.

Herbert, S. (1998). Police subculture reconsidered. *Criminology, 36,* 343–369.

Holt, T. J. (2007). Subcultural evolution? Examining the influence of on- and off-line experiences on deviant subcultures. *Deviant Behavior, 28,* 171–198.

Holt, T. J. (2009). The Attack Dynamics of Political and Religiously Motivated Hackers. In T. Saadawi & L. Jordan (eds.), *Cyber Infrastructure Protection* (pp. 161–182). New York: Strategic Studies Institute.

Holt, T. J. (2010). Examining the Role of Technology in the Formation of Deviant Subcultures. *Social Science Computer Review, 28,* 466–481.

Holt, T. J., & Blevins, K. R. (2007). Examining sex work from the client's perspective: Assessing johns using online data. *Deviant Behavior, 28,* 333–354.

Holt, T. J., & Copes, H. (2010). Transferring Subcultural Knowledge Online: Practices and Beliefs of Persistent Digital Pirates. *Deviant Behavior, 31,* 625–654.

Holt, T. J., Soles, J., & Leslie, L. (2008). *Characterizing Malware Writers and Computer Attackers in Their Own Words.* Paper presented at the 3rd International Conference on Information Warfare and Security, April 24–25, in Omaha, Nebraska.

Kornblum, W. (1997). *Sociology in a Changing World, 4th ed.* Fort Worth, TX: Harcourt Brace and Company.

Maurer, D. W. (1981). *Language of the Underworld.* Louisville: University of Kentucky Press.

Miller, W. B. (1958). Lower-class culture as a generating milieu of gang delinquency. *Journal of Social Issues,* 14, 5–19.

Nhan, J. (2010). *Policing Cyberspace: Structural and Cultural Issues.* El Paso, TX: LFB Publishing.

Quinn, J. F., & Forsyth, C. J. (2005). Describing sexual behavior in the era of the Internet: A typology for empirical research. *Deviant Behavior, 26,* 191–207.

Short, J. F. (1968). Introduction. In J. F. Short (ed.), *Gang Delinquency and Delinquent Subcultures* (pp. 7–16). New York: Harper and Row.

Sutherland, E. H. (1947). *Principles of Criminology, 4th ed.* Philadelphia: J. B. Lippincott.

Wolfgang, M. E., & Ferracuti, F. (1967). *The Subculture of Violence: Towards an Integrated Theory in Criminology.* London: Tavistock Publications.

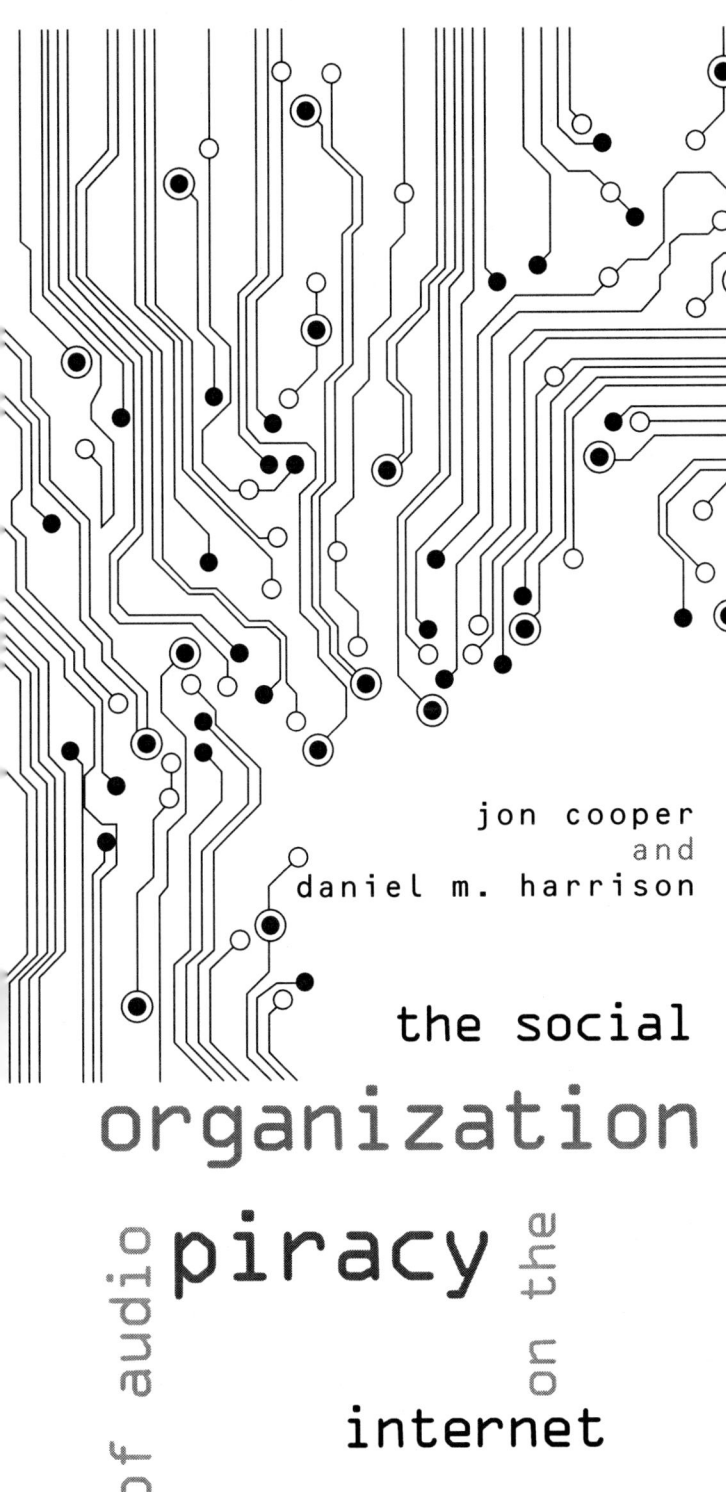

jon cooper
and
daniel m. harrison

# the social

# organization

of audio **piracy** on the

# internet

We attempt to advance sociological study of 'virtual communities' by embarking on an extremely focused study of one particular Internet subculture that is literally revolutionizing the production and consumption of popular music—audio pirates. Audio piracy, in a very basic sense, refers to the process of methodically encoding copyrighted music and distributing it without paying royalties. In our day, these encodings take place in a rich and highly textured social system mediated by electronic communication networks.

Audio pirates operate in a complex and highly structured social and economic environment that has its own particular matrix of roles, norms and mores. We present the first sociological analysis of this system, one that seeks to explain not only the internal social structure of the MP3 community, but which also strives to understand how the entire network of musical distribution and production around the globe may be affected by these developments. In analyzing the social organization of the audio piracy subculture, we aim to communicate three main concerns: (a) the activities of audio pirates; (b) how they maneuver in cyberspace; and (c) the underlying motivations for the audio piracy movement.

\* \* \*

## the technological facilitators and emergence of the mp3 subculture

The audio piracy subculture is inscribed and embedded almost entirely within the Internet. While exchanges of MP3 files are sometimes mediated by way of face-to-face interaction,[2] most of the time exchange participants will never meet in 'physical' space. In fact, in many cases participants don't even meet virtually, as parties often prefer conditions of anonymity. Before explicating the culture of online audio pirates, we first address the various communications technologies that make this subculture possible.

Finnish programmer Jarkko Oikarinen wrote IRC (Internet Relay Chat) in 1988 so that he could communicate simultaneously with multiple partners—a feature that the then-current synchronous text conversation technology could not provide. As the IRC program grew in popularity, it spread like wildfire around the network, and within months IRC was an Internet institution, pre-dating the World Wide Web (WWW) by two years and vastly surpassing it in popularity for at least another four. IRC is thus one of the oldest social institutions on the Internet, rivaled only by Usenet newsgroups. From its modest beginning as a method to bring a few people together in one forum, it has expanded into a massive international communication network.[1] There are currently five major IRC networks, with hundreds of servers and thousands of users at any one time on each network, and dozens of smaller networks. The largest network, *EFnet* has, at the time of writing, 50 servers, all interconnected by high-speed links, and it serves 43,179 simultaneous users chatting in 17,410 channels. It is estimated that at any one time there are over 100,000 people on IRC, most of them extremely computer literate and network savvy.

IRC serves as the focal point for the audio piracy subculture. It is the electronic common ground to which all audio pirates return, and in which primary contacts are made and relationships formed. Each user selects a nickname (or 'nick') such as '_sub-bass', 'niceGuy' or 'BiGFiSH' to signify themselves. By selecting and joining a 'channel' from a larger set of alternative channels with varying access rituals, audio pirates come to be categorized by musical genre, type of computer connection, sort of pirate group and other social attributes. Presently, of the 17,410 available EFnet channels, there appear to be 135 channels devoted to MP3 file exchanges, with an average of 20 users in each channel.

The reader can gain a rudimentary understanding of the sort of communication to be found in these channels through the following example of a simple IRC session. We entered a channel called #mp3leech:

```
/join #mp3leech
Now talking in #mp3leech
> Has anyone got the new Method Man album, Tikal 2000?
< _sub-bass > Has anyone got the new Method Man album, Tikal 2000?
< z0rtie > beta is big h0zer
< fleg > yuh
```

---

1   IRC gained notoriety as a social facilitator during the Persian Gulf war when thousands of people from around the world gathered to talk with people in the war zone in real time during the fighting, the first author of this paper among them.

Our discourse (as '_sub-bass'), is distinguished by the symbol '>' which precedes our text as we type into the IRC client software. This discourse is then echoed back as the other users see it when it goes out through the network and comes back into our client. In this extract, we can also see the random conversation of two other users named 'z0rtie' and 'fleg', respectively.

Channels are often operated on a long-term basis by a group of individuals who take responsibility for the channel and who wield what is known as 'operator' status. Operators control who can access the channel and who gets permission to speak. Aiding the operator staff of a channel are 'bots', which can number as many as 10 per channel. Bots are computer programs (agents) that connect to the IRC network just like any ordinary (human) user but they also perform special functions, some public and some private. A typical example of public bot usage is the following:

```
>! seen edz-
< _sub-bass > !seen edz-
<MAJOR > I saw edz- last, 2 days 23 hours 36 minutes ago. – last signoff: suicide.......< rB! >
```

In this example we asked the bot ('MAJOR') when another user ('edz-') was last seen in the channel. Bots create an additional level of social infrastructure in the IRC beyond simple chatting. They can be used to protect a channel from hostile takeover, to enforce class distinctions, to spy on other channels, to send asynchronous messages to other users, and to also catalog and transfer files.

A special kind of bot is the *FServ bot*. These bots provide a library of audio files which may be downloaded either free of charge or in exchange for a certain ratio of files which the user 'uploads' into the channel (more on which later). Another example should be illustrative:

```
/join #mp3jazz
 > !swingman
 < _sub_bass > !swingman
*DCC chat request from swingman [rewt@128.49.26.32]
 > /dcc chat swingman
*DCC chat session established with swingman [rewt@128.49.26.32] = < swingman >
SwingMAN fileserv running Polaris v1.0
 = < swingman > Ratio: OFF
 = < swingman > Commands: cd, ls, dir, read, get, quit, bye, exit
 = < swingman > stats, credit, ratio, who, sends, gets, top10, queues
 = < swingman > To get more information about these commands, type help
 = < swingman > [\]
 > /msg = swingman ls
 = < swingman > [\*. * ]
 = < swingman > COLTRANE MIXED JAMS VOLUME 1 – RNS
 = < swingman > End of list.
```

In this example, we connected to a bot named 'swingman' that inhabits '#mp3jazz', a channel for the exchange of jazz music. Since we were connected by *DCC* (Direct Client to Client) chat instead of through the regular IRC network, our messages went directly between host computers without bouncing through the IRC servers (thus reducing latency and adding security). DCC allows files to be transferred directly between two IRC users (or a user and a bot). This method of exchange is most frequently employed when two users are exchanging files in a trade, or when one is providing a single file as a gift to another user.

*XDCC* (extended DCC) is a set of client extensions that allow users to automatically offer a set of files for download via DCC to all participants in a channel. Running an XDCC requires fewer resources than running a fully-fledged web-site and they are also more fleeting. As such, XDCC is popular with users who would like to give something back to the subculture but who lack the resources or inclination to run a larger system. Most of the time, XDCC offers are known as 'leech', which means that nothing is expected in return for the files that are provided. Here is an example of an interaction with an XDCC offer script:

> *Red{Out} plays □ drunken_rasta.mp3 □ 5899kb □ Type @Bonghit drunken_ rasta.mp3 to leech
> > @Bonghit drunken_rasta.mp3
> < _sub_bass > @Bonghit drunken_rasta.mp3
> *DCC SEND request 'drunken_rasta.mp3' from Red{Out} [red-out@24.17.82.33] /dcc get Red{Out} drunken_rasta.mp3
> *DCC GET 'drunken_rasta.mp3' initiated with Red{Out} [red-out@24.17.82.33]

In this example we triggered the offer script running in Red{Out}'s client to send us a song by typing a command into the channel, and the program responded by transmitting the file.

Moving files directly between IRC clients is convenient for small and infrequent file exchanges, but it does not meet the needs (measured in terms of reliability, performance, and stability) for large scale users who exchange hundreds of megabytes of files per day in dozens of transactions. A much more robust system of file exchange exists for these participants—*FTP* (File Transfer Protocol). FTP was one of the first network applications deployed in the infancy of the *Arpanet* (the military computer network which became the Internet we know today). A user who wishes to become more seriously involved in the trading of MP3 files will often put up a 'site' (shorthand for 'FTP site'), and run a server on his or her computer that provides other users with access to audio files by way of an FTP client. Sites may be public (open to access by anyone knowing the coordinates of the computer in cyberspace), or private (open to access only by those with their own login accounts). Frequently a site will run with a 'ratio', which means that a user must upload (give) files in order to receive permission to download (take) files from the site. A typical ratio is 1:5, meaning that for each 1 byte the user uploads in a session he or she may download 5. This prevents 'leeches' from simply downloading an entire collection without contributing anything back to the site.[2]

These technologies collectively provide the substrate upon which the audio piracy subculture grows. We now strive to explicate this subculture in action.

---

2   The five to one ratio is interesting in that it corroborates insights concerning the social importance of the number five. As Harrison White (1992: 10) observes:

> One thousand, and five, more or less, should be the two principal numbers for the human species. A thousand, on the one hand, because that is where it all begins, the size in number of individual creatures of a primitive tribe which is a more or less isolated aggregation able to subsist and to reproduce itself ... Five is the median number of comparable selves that work together effectively enough to keep reproducing the arrangement. The size of five cuts across all contexts and levels: nuclear family, men in a fishing party, producing firms making up a market, and so on.

# inside the audio piracy subculture: roles of exchange

In the remainder of this article, we provide a brief ethnography of the culture of audio pirates. As will soon become evident, their culture is extremely dynamic—a state of more or less continuous flux—as participants must cope with technological advances and other changes in their virtual environment. Our primary purpose in this section is to sketch out the fundamental social distinctions and differential relationships in the audio piracy subculture.[3]

The audio pirate often uses several computerized tools simultaneously, sometimes with multiple and distinct windows open at any one time to different destinations in each.[4] A typical 'upper-class' audio pirate might have open two FTP clients, an IRC client talking in four channels, a web browser and an FTP server. By rapidly multiplexing which of these interactions to focus upon, the pirate will never run out of things to do, and can spin about for an unbounded amount of time, moving files from place to place, building social status and all the while continuously conversing with others.

Audio pirates spend varying amounts of their daily lives involved in these activities—the lower and upper limits in this study being about 30 minutes, and eight hours a day, respectively. The users we encountered typically felt that their interactions are of real social significance, as friendships are made and destroyed, and conflicts created and resolved day in and day out. Above all, however, their raison d'être is to move data at a dizzying pace. Let's wade in.

The audio piracy community's nominal purpose is to exchange high-quality audio files between people, making it easy to locate, share and store them for later playback and re-transmission. There are three dominant modes or roles into which a pirate's online activities may fall, that of leech, trader and citizen, which we now address in turn. The links to existing sociological discourse on social action will be made by applying these constructs to the three main routes of 'getting action' found in network theorist Harrison White's (1992) recent work, *Identity and Control*.[5]

Files obtained via the leech approach are provided to the receiver completely free of charge and without social obligation, as noted above. An agent locates a file that is available gratis either by waiting on an IRC channel for an FServ bot to offer it for download or by using a search engine on the Web or as part of a bot. Having found the file, the user then downloads it via FTP or DCC, and moves on to obtaining the next one he or she desires. When a file is received under the sign 'leech', the person offering it is not expecting a favor or even necessarily a word of thanks; he or she is simply doing it for the good of the community as a whole. In White's terminology, the leech would fit in the scheme of getting action by 'reaching through' the MP3 network. No objective change in social position or status is obtained by acting as a leech. According to White,

> Reaching through is a phenomenological term about strategic efforts to get action and control through and despite ... complex deposits of social organization ... Reaching through is a matter of occasion and process as much as structuration ... Reaching through is as much selectivity as it is persevering through multiple connections. (White, 1992: 260)

---

3 The reader should be aware that these models will undoubtedly change over time. Part of what makes this culture so interesting for sociological inquiry is the very swift mutations that it undergoes, changes which are facilitated by the fact that there are no real physical objects to move when the infrastructure undergoes fundamental changes in nature.

4 Internet cultures are, in general, a boon for the ADD/ADHD ridden post-television generation and its kin, since an infinite number of stimuli are simultaneously and efficiently available at any moment, and the typical audio pirate embodies the fragmented attention-span typical of serious Internet users.

5 For more on the theoretical ideas of Harrison White, see Harrison (forthcoming).

Leeches that 'reach through' to get action are mainly treading water. New information is sought out and short-term connections established, but none of this involves a longer range plan for further control and action within the subculture.

A trader's approach is based on a system of pure exchange value. Someone who is trading files will typically enter a chat channel and request a specific song or album he or she desires, hoping to find someone who has it in their collection. Upon finding a person who possesses the file, a deal is struck to exchange the desired file for another file or set of files that the requesting user either has in his or her collection, or knows where to go to find it. Here is a simple example of a trading session:

> < _sub-bass > anyone got DJ Qbert's 'Demolition Pumpkin Squeeze Music'
> japanese promo?
> *m1x* yuh
> *m1x* u got other turntablism shit?
> < _sub-bass > yep, got cut chemist, prince paul, and umm I think some dj shadow
> *m1x* sweet the whole cd iz 80 megs what link r u on?
> < _sub-bass > cable
> *m1x* word herez a dcc
> *DCC SEND request 'dj_qbert_demolition_pumpkin_squeeze_music_jp_ promo_full_album.zip'
> from mix [richard@think.com]
> /dcc get mix 'dj_qbert_demolition_pumpkin_squeeze_music_jp_promo_full_ album.zip'
> *DCC GET 'dj_qbert_demolition_pumpkin_squeeze_music_jp_promo_full_album.zip'
> initiated
> with m1x [richard@think.com]
> < _sub-bass > so what did you want?
> *m1x* which dj shadow
> < _sub-bass > endtroducing. . .
> *m1x* sure
> *m1x* send it
> /dcc send m1x /home/_sub-bass/mp3/dj_shadow_endtroducing_full_album.zip
> *DCC SEND 'dj_shadow_endtroducing_full_album.zip' initiated with mix [richard@think.com]

A typical trader repeats this simple interaction many times a day. Traders sometimes impose more stringent conditions for a swap if a file is particularly difficult to find, for example, if it is a pre-release copy or a 'bootleg' of a live show. Occasionally a trader will demand a file the requesting trader does not have in his or her collection, and the requesting trader will be forced to seek out the file in order to make the trade. An ability to fulfill difficult requests is a sign of status within the audio pirate community (more on which later).

> < _sub-bass > has anyone heard of 'swollen member' out of new york? I think they have
> everlast from house of pain
> < spinner > nope
> < daz > pretty ill, right?
> < daz > my boy in ny got a copy, it's only on vinyl, mad underground shit
> *daz* what u got to trade?

<_sub-bass > got some dj rectangle, squarepusher, the new xzibit

*daz* nah fuck that spacy shit

*daz* what u got datz underground?

<_sub-bass > what are you looking for?

*daz* hmm.. dj honda?

<_sub-bass > huh hang a few I think I saw it on a site

The trader role appears to fit nicely in to Harrison White's second mode of getting action, that of 'reaching up' (White, 1992: 256). Reaching up is a matter of shifting one's social location, from present position to someplace 'upstream'. Traders reach up into a channel to obtain a coveted file and in the process often, in fact, 'upload' files into that domain. They are the entrepreneurs who get action by reaching up to become further embedded in the subculture. The more upward their orientation, the larger their net of audio files, and thus their social action potential.

The most respected role structure in the audio piracy community, however, is that of the citizen. Someone who exchanges files in citizen mode is willing to give files away in order to benefit the community as a whole, sometimes trading, sometimes leeching, sometimes providing things for the leechers to consume. The citizen role is the most common for committed members of the audio piracy subculture. The citizen role seems to have an elective affinity with White's (1992: 262–5) remarks about 'reaching down'. As White (1992: 263) suggests, 'reaching down is seen as a positive opportunity for action in that it allows for the continued outreach to wider and changing scopes which is indispensable to continuing to get action'. Reaching down is primarily a matter of elite actions; using one's power to generate action for oneself and others, which thereby enlarges identity.

It is important to compare and contrast the social roles of leech, trader, citizen, and to examine the attendant social ramifications that falling into any one of these subgroups provides. Membership in these subgroups changes over time, of course, as a user's relation (e.g. time, devotion and social position) to the subculture changes. For example, someone who is primarily a citizen may engage in leeching when he or she is simply looking for new audio wares, and a citizen might occasionally engage in trading in order to get a really hard-to-find file.

Leeches are the bottom of the social heap, and are at the mercy of philanthropist citizens to provide them with the files they need. In a given channel containing 60 users, only five or ten might be actively conversing at any one time, while a large number of leeches (also called 'lurkers') hang around the channel waiting for someone to offer a file for download, at which point they snap into action and acquire it. Here is an example of leeches doing what they do best in a channel:

<RapMstr > | RAPMASTER FSERV // RMS 1998, BIATCH!

<RapMstr > | type !get #X to get pack #X

<RapMstr > | -------------------------------------------------------------------

<RapMstr > | #1: De La Soul, (classic) 3 Feet High and Rising [album]: 65m: 16 gets

<RapMstr > | #2: Method Man, Tikal 2000: Judgement Day [album]: 70m: 177 gets

<RapMstr > | #3: Blackstar, Blackstar [album]: 68m: 115 gets

<RapMstr > | -------------------------------------------------------------------

<RapMstr > 10 of 10 slots open, 10 of 10 queue slots open, record speed 88k/sec

<vBeeF > !get #2

<RiZZUH > !get #2

<RiZZUH > !get #3

```
<vBeeF > !get #3
<tekNO > !get #1
<s1k0 > !get #3
<smash > !get #2
```

In this example, an FServ bot called 'RAPMASTER' operated by a pirate group called RMS (Rock Mighty Syndicate) offers some popular albums for download to everyone in a channel, and within seconds five leeches begin to download the files, two of them requesting two separate files each. The chief advantage of being a leech is that it is very low maintenance, requires no regular social interaction and no real investment in the community beyond time. Competition between pirate groups to supply the largest number of leech requests results in a surplus of recent popular songs being widely available for leeching, but since leeching requires almost no social effort the leech remains a member of the lowest social class within the subculture.

Traders, by contrast, are more complicated characters. It is often difficult to determine whether a given trader actually wants a given file for personal use, for trading capital or simply because they like to transmit data around cyberspace. Sites typically provide private login accounts to traders who maintain an adequate upload ratio and they build a reputation on the site on this basis. The login identifier is authenticated by a password and an 'ipmask' (a numeric network identification that uniquely identifies the trader's computer so that he cannot share his account on the site with other traders).

There is much competition between traders who frequent a given site or channel to see who can upload the most data to an important site or who can wield the largest array of files to trade. Here's an example of the way in which a trader gets an account on a site:

```
< _sub-bass > trading recent hiphop on a fast connection. /msg me for info
*meKKa* yo I run a phat site.
*meKKa* t3/15 gig/hiphop only
< _sub-bass > gimme a ratio acct, I will ul
*meKKa* l/p and ipmask please
< _sub-bass > _sub-bass/bas1k 24.3.78.188
*meKKa* okey: BaSS meKKA 182.15.22.16 port 357 1:5 ratio
*meKKa* upload lame shit and be banned
```

Essentially, the trader brags about the speed of his or her connection and the amount and type of files he or she possesses, and then site operators offer temporary trial accounts to see if the trader can really deliver the goods. It is social protocol to upload a large amount of files before downloading from a site in order to thank the site operator for the account. However, if the trader perceives the site operator or the site to be 'lame'—in the sense that it doesn't contain files of interest—he or she may not upload at all or upload only enough files to get the files he or she wants.

Citizens represent the highest social strata of the audio piracy subculture. There exists some overlap between the role of trader and the role of citizen, but the main difference is that traders are primarily focused on their own data acquisition, while citizens are more attuned to social interaction and status. This is not to say that citizens are uninterested in transferring files (as data exchange is the central activity of this subculture), but citizens are distinguished by taking an active interest in one another as human beings rather than mere bargaining chips. Those who act in citizen role are the philanthropists of the subculture, and they run the FServ bots that serve the leeches. They gain social status through these activities. Citizen users make up the majority of the members of pirate groups and channel operators because they enjoy the status and power of their social position as much and sometimes more than the actual exchange of files.

We interviewed a citizen-class user about why he participates in the MP3 subculture. Part of this exchange is reproduced here:

< _sub-bass > thanks for letting me interview you.

<Magias > np

< _sub-bass > so, a) why do you run an FServ?

<Magias > It's kind of nice to give people things that make them happy, and it only takes me like ten minutes a day to give a lot of leeches a lot of recent music. What goes around comes around, you know?

< _sub-bass > you don't get anything in return but social status?

<Magias> I'm not really sure I get social status. I mean people give me shell accounts and accounts on their sites, but that's not really why I do it. Well I guess I do get social status but I'm not in it to compete, just to have fun.

< _sub-bass > yeah. b) where do you get the mp3s you put onto your FServ?

Magias > From my sites. From other people I know. The usual. I just have some good sites.

< _sub-bass > c) would you call the people you know online 'friends'?

<Magias > What?!

<Magias > Ummmm. . .huh. Well some of them are, of course. It's just like anything else, some people are dicks and some people are just like aquaintances and some people I talk to almost every day. It all depends.

Most of the pirates we interviewed, however, had for the most part failed to think reflexively about their involvement with the audio piracy subculture. Some even expressed contempt at our attempt to document and analyze the power relations within their community, viz.: '*tim* FUCK YOU, COLLEGE BOY'.

For the most part it seems that audio pirates view this social system as just another network in which they participate. They talk to the people they like, ostracize those they don't and, on the whole, seem to have a pretty good time in the process. As in all social organizations, there are power relations among the social actors, and in the audio piracy subculture, these relationships shape the flow of data between participants.

## status symbols and power signifiers

The most common status symbols we discovered in the audio piracy subculture are fast bandwidth and large disk storage capacity. Since the dissemination and accumulation of data are the primary activities for the members of this subculture, the ability to store massive amounts of data and to move it rapidly from place to place are necessary for inflating a pirate's status within the scene. Certain channels exist for users with particular sorts of links who are unwilling to transmit data at speeds slower than their link will permit.[6] Another important status symbol for traders is the speed with which they can get released files. 'Zero-day' traders, for example, receive new sound files on the day they are released to the network by a pirate group, while 'zero-hour' traders take it one step further and get the files within

---

6   At the time of writing, these included: #mp3t1, #mp3-t3 and #mp3cable.

an hour. A final marker of status is affiliation with pirate groups, which are ranked according to an internal ordering scheme, relative to each other.

Respect is the metric of status within this social system, and an increase in respect tends to increase the amount of power wielded in the subculture. Some forms of cultural capital can increase a pirate's status simply because he possesses them, but others must be earned by hard work and apt social maneuvering, just as in real life. Traders earn respect by having the largest number of recently released files, and by uploading them very quickly to the sites and people with whom they trade. They compete with one another on sites to see who can upload the most files to a respected site, which may earn them the coveted 'uploader-top' title, a distinction bestowed when they outperform all other users during a given period of time.

The way citizens gain respect is more complex and depends upon the services they provide to the community or group, but it is also often based on social intangibles such as the extent of one's social connections and ability to handle adverse situations. Power is wielded mainly in terms of controlling or restricting the ability of others to transmit and receive data.

Once granted admission to a channel, the pirate may be granted '+v' status—which means that he or she is a member in good standing of the channel or group—or '+o (operator)' status—which means that he or she helps to control the channel or group. On channels belonging to audio pirate groups, +v and +o status tend to signify whether or not a user is a member or a senior member, while on more public channels these signs indicate status on the channel. Those with +o permissions may excommunicate people from a channel, remove their ability to speak, change the channel topic, make the channel invitation-only, and apply a host of other restrictive criteria to a pirate's account.

Access to sites also obviously involves relations of power and control. The bargain is that, once granted access to a site, pirates will provide quality files (in terms of release date and type) that fill the needs of the site—the better the site, the higher the quality of the files the pirate is expected to provide. 'Leech' access on excellent sites is granted only to individuals of the highest rank or those who know the site administrator personally. Pirate membership in diverse social networks and the capacity of high-speed links can exert power on the site operator, and force him or her to provide the user with an account in order to improve his site. By way of illustrating this phenomenon, compare the interaction we quoted earlier when we were granted access to a fairly low-grade site (this in spite of its operator labeling it 'phat'), with the interaction in which we bargain for an account on a high-end site (one with a T3 connection, 45 gigabytes of storage and which is US headquarters for a major MP3 piracy group):

```
< _sub-bass > hey, mark0z told me to ask you about an account on your site.
*tek9* did he
*tek9* what are your affiliations
< _sub-bass > I run bots and do some couriering for steppaz
*tek9* my site only allows > 50k/s transfers
< _sub-bass > yeah I can do that
*tek9* hmm
*tek9* u can have a trial acct
*tek9* make uptop10 this week and u get a perm acct
*tek9* read the site rules
*tek9* l/p and ipmask?
< _sub-bass > subbass/sp4ng ipmask 24.3.78.188
< _sub-bass > thanks
```

```
*tek9* wait
*tek9* ArmoryFTP / 128.180.118.102: 187
```

This site operator granted us access based upon the fact that we were recommended to him by a user the operator knew had an account on his system, as well as the fact that we were a member in a mid-tier MP3 piracy group called 'steppaz'. It is quite likely that *tek9* had a private conversation with the user (mark0z) who recommended us, to ensure that we were telling the truth. Even with this recommendation, the operator required us to be one of the top ten uploaders in terms of bytes uploaded for the next week in order to keep our account. The power dynamic weighed heavily in his favor because *tek9* controlled the resource we wished to access, and as such he was able to name the terms under which we could participate on the site.

## references

Harrison, Daniel M. (forthcoming) 'The Madness of Harrison White: Theory, Networks, and Social Domination', PhD Dissertation, Department of Sociology, Florida State University.

Lyotard, Jean-Francois (1991) *The Postmodern Condition: A Report on Knowledge,* trans. Geoff Bennington and Brian Massumi. Minneapolis: University of Minnesota Press. (Orig. pub. 1979.)

Kellner, Douglas (1995) 'Marxism, the Information Superhighway and the Struggle for the Future', *Humanity and Society* 19(4): 41–56.

Stone, Rosanne Allucquere (1996) *The War of Desire and Technology at the Close of the Mechanical Age.* Cambridge, MA: MIT Press.

thomas j. holt

examining

the role of

technology

in the deviant

formation of

subcultures

Few researchers have considered the development and structure of technologically focused criminal subcultures and what insights they provide on the nature of technology and crime. This study will attempt to address this gap in the literature by examining one of the most well recognized forms of technology-focused crimes: computer hacking. Hackers have a profound interest in computers and technology and use their knowledge to access computer systems with or without authorization (Schell, Dodge, & Moutsatsos, 2002). The origin of hacking can be traced directly to the development of computer technology in the 1950s, though hackers have become known for malicious and criminal activities over the last two decades (see Furnell, 2002; Holt, 2007; Schell et al., 2002).

To understand the role of technology in hacking, this study will explore the argot of computer hacker subculture.[1] An argot is a specialized and

---

1    All argot terms identified in this study are highlighted in italic in the text and detailed separately in the Appendix.

secret language within a subculture that serves multiple functions within the group, such as communicating the structure, norms, and values of a given subculture to its members (Einat & Einat, 2000; Hamm, 1993; Hensley, Wright, Tewksbury, & Castle, 2003; Johnson, Bardhi, Sifaneck, & Dunlap, 2006; Kaplan, Flores Farfan, & Kampe, 1990; Lerman, 1967; Maurer, 1981). Those who correctly use the argot when speaking to others may indicate their membership and status within the subculture (see Hensley et al., 2003; Maurer, 1981). This specialized language also functions to conceal deviant or criminal activities and communications from outsiders (Johnson et al., 2006; Maurer, 1981). Thus, argots reflect the values, norms, and beliefs of a group and their attitudes toward conforming and deviant behavior.

Several researchers have examined hacker subculture, demonstrating the norms, values, and beliefs that structure hacker behavior online and off-line (Holt, 2007; Jordan & Taylor, 1998; Taylor, 1999; Thomas, 2002). The findings suggest that a number of terms are used to differentiate between actors in hacker subculture. A limited number of studies have also catalogued the terms used by hackers (Furnell, 2002; Schell & Martin, 2006) or developed typologies of hackers using some terms from within hacker subculture (see Taylor et al., 2006). As a whole, these examinations have provided little insight into the ways hacker argot is dynamically applied and how it reflects the influence of technology within this subculture. This study explores these issues using three qualitative data sets, including posts from six hacker web forums, interviews with active hackers, and observations at a hacker convention. The findings provide an exploration of the dynamic use of hacker argot and the enculturation process of hacker subculture. In turn, this can inform our understanding of the ways that technology shapes deviant and criminal subcultures.

\* \* \*

## the current study

This study uses three qualitative data sets to examine hacker argot and its function in hacker subculture, including a series of 367 strings from six hacker web forums, interviews with active hackers, and observations from Defcon 12, a hacker convention held annually in Las Vegas, Nevada. These multiple data sources are triangulated and used to understand how hackers define and differentiate between those inside and out of hacker subculture. This is followed by an exploration of the argot used in exchanges between hackers and how these terms express the importance of technology in the socialization process and normative structure of hacker subculture.

\* \* \*

Terms and their meanings were inductively derived from the repeated appearance of a specific phrase or idea in the data. The value of each term is derived from positive or negative comments of the respondents. In turn, theoretical links between these concepts are derived from the data to highlight its role within hacker subculture. These data sets were triangulated, allowing the distinct social settings of the data to be connected, while situating each order in its specific social setting and context (Silverman, 2001, p. 235). These methods are used to critically explore the structure and meaning of the argot of hacker subculture.

# findings

This analysis will consider the terms used to describe the behaviors of hackers as well as the descriptive labels that define the boundaries of hacker subculture and their use in each social context. The data will also consider the ways argot structures identity and status within hacker subculture, using passages from the data sets as appropriate.

## terms for the act of hacking

Hackers use unique terms both online and off-line to refer to the variety of behaviors they engage in on a day-to-day basis. The most critical of these terms are *hacks* and *cracks,* referring to the ways an individual uses technology to suit his or her needs. A person may engage in a hack or a crack depending on its "hack value," measured by the application and its positive or negative value (see Taylor, 1999; Turkle, 1984). Specifically, a hack refers to any legitimate and useful alteration or adjustment to computer hardware or software, which enables technology to be used in an innovative or unusual way. For example, Mutha Canucker described one of the first hacks he performed to circumvent an Internet filtering program in a public library's web browser. He altered the code of the bookmarking program in the browser to link to a search engine, allowing them to surf to different sites. While this sounds complex to the uninitiated, he suggested that "it was a piece of cake really, it just required some creativity." This sort of description and behavior was evident across all the data sets, though defining an act as a hack varied based on the individual's ethical beliefs (Holt, 2007; Jordan & Taylor, 1998; Taylor, 1999).

In fact, the term crack is typically applied when a hacker alters technology for a negative or potentially criminal application. For instance, Mack Diesel suggested he performed a crack when he:

> downloaded what's called a password dictionary file which contains hundreds of words and used it to hack [a University's] password system and … get a number of passwords for accounts. I just let this program run and I got the information for access to a number of different accounts.

Mack occasionally used these accounts to steal Internet access and considered this to be a crack because he used this service without authorization. Mack used hacking skills to gain access to these accounts, but he did not view it a hack because of his intentions and beliefs about the illegal use of services. Thus, the attribution of "hack value" has significant weight within hacker subculture as hackers differentiate between individuals on the basis of their use of hacks and cracks (Schell et al., 2002; Turkle, 1984). There is, however, no consensus on these terms, as the same act may be perceived as a hack or crack depending on individuals' ethics and beliefs (see also Holt, 2007).

The term crack is also used to describe the process of removing the copyright protections on a piece of software or media. When someone "cracks" media, they can then distribute the material free of charge to others. Cracks are also called *warez* and are hosted on web sites that allow hackers to obtain software and media at no charge (see also Furnell, 2002, p. 44). A variety of materials can be found on warez sites, such as operating systems and tools that may help hackers. For example, Kamron stated that he became a better hacker in part by "participating in hacker warez." Similarly, Dark Oz described participating in "The Elusive Dream BBS" in the 1980s, which "was a great 0-day warez BBS, so they had every piece of software you could imagine, usually uploaded there on the same day it was released (thus, 0-day)." In addition, individuals traded warez at Defcon in various open areas around the conference hotel.

Hackers also use a variety of other technologies beyond computer software and hardware. Some individuals had an interest in *phreaking*, where they attempt to hack telephone networks and systems. For example, Indiana Tones suggested that several of his friends "were more into the phreaking. You know, hacking the phone company kind of deals. Uh, getting free phone calls, calling long distance then getting it billed to somebody else." Interviewees and forum users suggested that phreaking helped further their general knowledge of technology and development as a hacker. Phreaking was also discussed at Defcon in the panel titled "Phreaking in the Age of Voice Over IP." The presentation was described as "a basic new age phreaking presentation that will show the latest techniques that phreaks are using today—it's not just about free calls either, hell you get that with VoIP anyways!"

Hackers also discussed attempts to surreptitiously obtain information from people that may enable them to complete a hack. This process is known as *social engineering* and involves physical or verbal misrepresentation of self to a person or company to gain information (see also Furnell, 2002; Mitnick & Simon, 2002). One of the forum users succinctly described the process of social engineering, stating that:

> Social Engineering works on the premise of understanding "tells" and hidden signals and how to manipulate people into getting them to give up information or perform a task that they would normally not do ... imposing your will on others in such a way that they don't know they are being manipulated.

Similarly, some Defcon attendees wore T-shirts that read "social engineering expert: because there is no patch for human stupidity." The common use of the term social engineering across the data sets suggests that social engineering is an important activity in hacker subculture.

Hackers have also begun to engage in *wardriving* as a result of the increasing popularity of wireless technology. This term refers to the process of driving or travelling through an area using a laptop and various pieces of equipment to look for wireless Internet (or Wi-Fi) access points (see also Hurley, Puchol, Rogers, & Thornton, 2004). For example, a multistage wardriving game was held at Defcon. In one game, competitors had to drive around Las Vegas seeking out and logging all open wireless Internet access points. The individual who found the largest number of points won, though the game required driving through Las Vegas for 48 hr strait to log the largest number of Wi-Fi points. However, the practice of wardriving was discussed in only two of the forums and by two interviewees, suggesting this may be a small activity of interest in hacker subculture.

## terms within hacker subculture

The hacker argot also uses a range of terms for individuals within the subculture. These labels communicate subcultural values by indicating an individual's progress as a hacker along a continuum of knowledge, technical skill, and moral or ethical ideals. At one end of the continuum lie *noobs, newbies,* or *neophytes* who have just begun to learn to hack. These terms were commonly applied in web forums to those individuals who were new to the subculture and its value system. In fact, new forum users commonly used this term to identify themselves at the outset of any post they made. The use of this term helped them avoid potential negative comments from other forum users, particularly when seeking answers to questions. For instance, the user s0ck0 started a post stating, "I'm a noob so dont [sic] bash me please." This strategy had some success, though noobs were often disrespected by more experienced members of the subculture because of their lack of knowledge.

As an individual is brought further into hacker subculture, the individual's knowledge and skill with technology increase. Budding hackers begin to access information and resources online and off-line.

Their understanding and appreciation for technology expands through peer relationships in cyberspace and the real world as well as by reading technical manuals and tutorials (Holt, 2007). Hackers across the data sets suggested that the resources needed to learn to hack are available online. The wealth of materials posted in cyberspace is a huge asset, but it can negatively affect the developing hacker. Specifically, premade programs or *scripts* that automate the process of hacking are freely available in a variety of outlets online. In fact, four of the six forums provided access to a variety of scripts to automate attacks. Individuals need only to download a script and they may be able to complete a hack without necessarily understanding the methods or mechanics behind their attack.

As a result, scripts allow hackers to engage in relatively successful hacks but not as a consequence of their level of knowledge or skill. This has led to the development and application of the term *script kiddie*, referencing those individuals who use scripts to hack. Rose Kennedy explained this term succinctly, stating a script kiddie is "someone who hacks by downloading an application that can hack something without requiring any background knowledge of how computers or networks function." This term is often used in a derogatory or pejorative context, as it suggests the person has a limited knowledge of computers and hacking and is unwilling to learn. For instance, an individual in one of the forums asked about identifying an exploit but did not want to have to do any of the programming work needed to actually run the attack. Users replied to his questions with comments such as "you probably have no clue how the exploit works, or even what it'll produce in the end. Get your head out of your ass, fuck off, and read a book." Another wrote "Get off your dead ass and code your own exploits, you fucking script kiddie."

These comments plainly demonstrate the significance of understanding how hacks actually work, which can only be gleaned through hard work and dedication. If an individual does not seem willing or able to perform the technical tasks needed to complete a hack, he or she will be disrespected and derogatorily referred to as a script kiddie. They may also be referred to as a *lamer* because of their actions (see also Furnell, 2002). For example, a poster who asked about using a malicious script called Sub7 was told to "Be shot and therefore removed from the internet, lamer!" Such instances of labeling occurred in conjunction with *flames* or "subtle varieties of insult and verbal jab" (Taylor et al., 2006). The blatant negative applications of the term script kiddie led many forum posters to advise new hackers against becoming script kiddies. For example, Slappywag explained, "don't become an Sk [script kiddie] it is illogical. It doesn't hold half of the internal enjoyment as knowing the stuff." As a consequence, being a script kiddie may be one step in the process of being a hacker. Several forum users commented on this issue, suggesting noobs can develop into script kiddies over time. OvR18 wrote:

> I think most of the people who started getting interested in computers and/or hacking in an early state of age (such as 12 or so) were script-kiddies/lamers how ever you wanna call it. Then or stayed lame theire [sic] hole life or developed to what they are now, newbies, neophytes (↓ spelled correct?) hackers. People have to start somewhere.

Several interviewees agreed with this notion, making reference to their own experiences. For instance, Mack Diesel noted that "being a script kiddie can be a transitory stage. It could be someone who does want knowledge, who does want to learn, but does not have the skill set right then to do these things for himself. I think yes … they can eventually become a hacker." Thus, script kiddies are individuals with limited hacking skill, though they may be able to progress beyond this point if they are interested in technology and how hacks are actually completed.

Over time, if a noob or script kiddie explores the ways the tools they use actually work, then they may eventually have enough skill to be labeled a *hacker*. However, there is significant variation based on when and how a person may define themselves as a hacker. Some hackers indicated that there are behavioral benchmarks that could be used to identify their skill development, such as completing a certain task or understanding a complicated process. For example, nad15 suggested that he thought he might be a hacker because

> I have completed most of the things which fit the social role of hacker, for example I have found various types of security flaws ... and used them to gain remote access to a bunch of my targets, most of which have been my test machines, but a few have been machines out in the wild.

There were also attitudinal components that must be present to be a hacker. Phreakphan suggested that a hacker is an individual who "enjoys exploring the details of computers and how to enhance their capabilities." Many people across the data sets argued that a certain sense of curiosity or desire to learn was a vital component of hacker identity. Lazaraus considered a hacker to be "any person with a sincere desire for knowledge about all things and is constantly trying to find it." The forum user baXter echoed this sentiment suggesting, "I am a hacker, because I am willing to learn, fix my mistakes, and help others learn."

Individual variation in the definition of hacker led forum users to discuss whether they could call themselves hackers at all. A few posters felt others must identify them as a hacker to truly be a hacker. Gribblefan explained this perspective, suggesting, "I don't think you know when you're a hacker and you can't call yourself a hacker, its [sic] one of those titles that you can only receive from others." Recognition of skill was key to this perspective, as wAyNeBrAdY wrote:

> I started calling myself a Hacker once some other people had called me one a few times. I few computer specialists I worked with for a summer term at a government office a few years ago called me a Hacker, many of my teachers have called me a Hacker and I've had friends call me a Hacker before. All of these people meant it in a positive way and respected me for it, therefore I figured I really had become a Hacker.

However, most forum users did not agree with this perspective. Those who considered themselves to be hackers made no mention of being labeled by others outside of the subculture. Rather, they were hackers because of personal achievement or a motivation to learn and understand computers. Hence, personal opinion significantly influenced the identity and construction of the term hacker online and off-line.

Similar arguments were found in web forums concerning the labels used to differentiate between skilled hackers. Specifically, the terms *white, black,* and *gray hats* were used to describe individuals who use their knowledge as a hacker based on their ethical perspective. For example, white hats were thought to use their abilities for relatively benevolent purposes. jRose suggested a *white hat* is "someone who looks for security problems to tell the potential victim to solve them before they are exploited." *Black hats* were thought to engage in malicious hacks against a range of targets. Lazarus provided a simple definition for a black hat, as "A 'hacker' who is willing to break laws to get the information he desires." The division was succinctly described by the forum user j@ck0 who suggested that "the black hats use their knowledge to destroy things. The whitehats use it to build things." It must be noted that there was some disagreement over the nature of white and black hat activities in online environments. This was exemplified in a post by the forum user snakey who wrote:

> They [blackhats] hack for their own good, to learn, and explore … in fact the skilled blackhats don't destroy, they keep root and even secure the box [computer] they got access to for free so you got a hidden "security expert" which patches your box from the latest (even private) bugs so noone [sic] else will get access.

As a consequence, arguments over the meaning of black and white hat hackers appeared to be based on personal opinion.

Similarly, some hackers argued that they were *gray hats,* in that they completed ethical or unethical hacks depending on their mood. Vile Syn suggested this is an individual who is a "mix between black and white hats" and were common in hacker subculture. In fact, gray hats did not align themselves with any specific moral philosophy but rather acted to achieve some specific goal. They were willing to act within and outside of existing ethical parameters based on each unique situation. Some hackers indicated that such a stance was key to better understand and use technology for their own purposes. For example, phreakphan suggested that she was a gray hat hacker because she used "both standard security methods taught in many colleges and unorthodox methods that are right out of the core of hacker culture." She felt that this knowledge and capacity to attack and defend would better prepare her for a role in computer security, stating:

> What good is having a security officer at a company that can only defend against well known and publicly known attacks if hackers are going to attack the company with unorthodox methods. They will be extremely unprepared.

Beyond the use of hats, the phrase *elite* or *1337* was used to describe a hacker with great skill. Interestingly, this term was rarely used and appeared to be held as an ideal to strive for rather than a regular part of hacker argot. The forum user jQuizon explained this notion, stating:

> id [sic] say nearly everyone who calls themselves 1337 is a liar I mean to call your self that surely youd [sic] have to know nearly every thing about programming hacking network system files hardware and much more.

Cerberus agreed with this sentiment, suggesting, "I really don't think I am '1337' or particularly a hacker. I just think of myself as being more experienced on computer. If you would as[k] me you won't every truly become 1337 as this, in my opinion, is impossible."

A final subcategory of hacker present in the data was the *cracker,* though this type was described more often by interviewees than in any other data set. Forum users differentiated between hacks and cracks but spent little time elaborating the term cracker. However, the interviewed hackers were asked how they defined this term and there was a relatively even split in their responses. Six hackers indicated a cracker was someone who tried, as Indiana Tones suggested, "to crack passwords … writin' programs that do the serial numbers for the pirated software." For these individuals, a cracker was involved in breaking protections to copy or otherwise misuse software in much the same way as a software pirate (Furnell, 2002, p. 44). A *pirate* or "warez d00d" is a type of cracker who breaks copyright protections on software, then distributes illegal copies (Furnell, 2002, pp. 44–45).

The other seven hackers suggested a cracker was a more malicious form of hacker, not unlike a black hat or script kiddie. Spuds elaborated this concept, stating:

> A cracker would be the SUREST word for someone who breaks into systems for whatever reason. A hacker can be a cracker if his goal is to break into a system. A hacker has a means and a goal and they have curiosity. Crackers are ONLY there to break into a system.

His definition recognizes the similarities between the hacker and cracker and also emphasizes the cracker's desire to damage systems. In fact, the term "cracker" was developed by hackers as a defense against media misuse of the term hacker (Furnell, 2002, p. 42). This may explain why Vile Syn wrote "A cracker (media's hacker) is someone who solely dedicates their time to maliciously crack systems." Similarly, Mack Diesel suggested that "a cracker is probably a black hat, so a hacker on the inside … a hacker is somebody who wants to learn. The 'cracker' hacks into systems to destroy or harm them." Furthermore, many hackers could be labeled as crackers and their actions are quite similar to those of black hats. True hackers, however, consider these individuals to be "a lower form of life" because of their destructive behavior, though they have more skill and ability than the "script kiddie" (Furnell, 2002, p. 44).

The variation present in the meaning of cracker as well as black and white hat hackers illustrated the variation of terms within hacker argot. Labels may have specific connotations, as with black or white hat hackers, but individuals can accept or reject that meaning. In turn, hackers formed boundaries between themselves and others in the subculture based on their definition of hacker. The conflicted meanings of some terms in hacker argot suggest that there may be a lack of uniformity in hacker subculture, thus, individuals create their own meanings for some terms (see also Holt, 2007). This may also explain the general disagreement over definitions for hacker within the larger research literature (see Furnell, 2002; Schell et al., 2002).

## discussion and conclusions

This study sought to explore the argot of hacker subculture to better understand the ways that technology structures deviant subcultures. The findings suggest that hacker argot reflects the importance of technology for hackers and fulfils several roles within this subculture. Although hacker argot appears to do little to facilitate secrecy, the terms communicate norms and values of hacker subculture as well as its boundaries (see also Einat & Einat, 2000).

\* \* \*

Hacker argot also indicates status within the loose hierarchy of this subculture based on an individual's understanding of and skill with computer technology. For example, noobs are shown less respect than others due to their relatively recent involvement in the subculture. Derogatory labels such as script kiddie are applied to those who hack but do not fully understand the technology they use. Individuals who have an affinity for technology may be considered hackers, while others may perceive this as an unattainable ideal in much the same way as being 1337. The hacker argot serves to structure social relationships based on subcultural values, much like the argot of prisoners (Einat & Einat, 2000; Hensley et al., 2003) and the marijuana subculture (Johnson et al., 2006).

Hacker argot can also communicate the ethical beliefs and values of a hacker. Individuals who identify themselves as white or black hat hackers provide an outward indication of their beliefs on the act of hacking (see also Holt, 2007; Jordan & Taylor, 1998; Taylor, 1999). Some may suggest that black hat hacking is not always malicious, but the term contextualizes their actions and gives some insight into their potential motivations. Individuals who describe themselves as gray hats may have a less rigid ethical orientation, thus, they may engage in malicious or beneficial hacks depending on their mood or other factors.

This study also identified an important overlap in the use of argot in both online and off-line discussions. The appearance and practical use of argot across these environments illustrates an important overlap in the experiences of individuals in cyberspace and the real world (see also Holt, 2007). Yet, these findings may not be applicable to other criminal subcultures, regardless of their use of technology. Further research is needed examining the virtual and real subcultural experiences of other deviant and criminal groups to identify variations in their normative structure as a consequence of online and off-line communications. This will improve our understanding of the ways the Internet acts as a conduit for deviant communication and crime as well as its role in the development of deviant subcultures.

There is also a need for research examining online behavior to consider the impact that off-line experiences have on individual action through the collection and triangulation of multiple data sets. Most research considering online deviance uses data collected from either virtual or real environments, providing only a partial exploration of a phenomenon (see Holt, 2007). As a result, there is a need for researchers to develop data that address activities in cyberspace from multiple perspectives online and off-line. Through increased data collection, triangulation, and careful analyses, social science research can significantly improve our understanding of both cybercrime and virtual interactions as well as inform how experiences in both environments affect human behavior.

In addition, this research points to the importance of technology in our understanding of crime and deviance and the need to carefully consider how new technologies may produce deviant subcultures. Computer hacking is an excellent example of such an adaptation, however, it is one of several crimes that stem directly from technological innovations (see also Taylor et al., 2006). Research is needed exploring other technology-centered criminal subcultures to understand the ways they differ from traditional street-crime subcultures, such as gangs and drug cultures. This will improve our understanding of the influence of technology on the nature of crime and deviance in the 21st century.

# appendix
## argot of hacker subculture

**1337 speak:** the replacement of characters and numbers in lieu of letters in certain words and phrases used in computer-mediated communications.

**Black hat hacker:** a skilled hacker who breaks into systems without authorization or permission to engage in malicious behaviors.

**Con:** real-world hacker conference or convention.

**Crack:** (a) a malicious or damaging hack and (b) breaking the security protections on software enabling users to copy the materials at any time for free.

**Cracker:** (a) a hacker who engages in malicious or damaging hacks and (b) someone who breaks the security protections on software allowing the materials to be copied freely at any time.

**Elite:** a very skilled, proficient hacker (also 'leet, leet, and 1337).

**End user:** an individual with very little knowledge of computer systems who uses technology for simple means only.

**Exploit:** a script or code that takes advantage of vulnerabilities in computer software and hardware to attack or manipulate the system in unintended ways.

**Fed:** a law enforcement officer or federal agent.

**Flame:** a text-based insult or jab.

**Gray hat hacker:** a skilled hacker who engages in malicious or ethical hacking depending on his or her mood or a given situation.

**Hack:** a legitimate, useful alteration or adjustment of computer hardware or software, which enables technology to be used in an unusual or innovate way.

**Hacker:** a skilled computer user with a profound interest in technology who alters technological devices to work in innovative or new ways.

**Lamer:** hackers who engage in either criminal or negative hacks as well as weak or simple hacks.

**Newbie:** someone who is either new to hacking or web forums (also noob, n00b, newb, neophite).

**Phreaker:** individual who hacks telephone networks and related technologies.

**Pirate:** an individual who creates and trades illegal copies of copyrighted material.

**Scene whore:** individual who is not involved in hacking or hacker subculture but attends hacker conventions and fraternizes with hackers.

**Script:** a prewritten series of codes that operate or execute automatically.

**Script kiddie:** hacker with limited skill who relies on scripts or programs created by others to perform actual attacks.

**Social engineering:** the verbal or physical misrepresentation of self to gain information.

**Wardriving:** driving around a city or area using technological devices to look for wireless internet access points.

**Warez:** cracked or pirated software often traded between hackers.

**White hat hacker:** a skilled hacker who uses his or her knowledge and skill to protect and secure systems.

**Vulnerability:** a hole, flaw, or error in a computer program that can be used to attack and enter a system.

## references

Andersson, L., & Trudgill, P. (1990). *Bad language.* Oxford, UK: Blackwell.

Bryant, C. D. (1984). Odum's concept of the technicways: Some reflections on an underdeveloped sociological notion. *Sociological Spectrum, 4,* 115–142.

Cherbonneau, M., & Copes, H. (2006). Drive it like you stole it: Auto theft and the illusion of normalcy. *British Journal of Criminology, 46,* 193–211.

Corbin, J., & Strauss, A. (1990). Grounded theory research: Procedures, canons, and evaluative criteria. *Qualitative Sociology, 13,* 3–21.

DiMarco, A. D., & DiMarco, H. (2003). Investigating cybersociety: A consideration of the ethical and practical issues surrounding online research in chat rooms. In Y. Jewkes (Ed.), *Dot.cons: Crime, deviance and identity on the Internet.* Portland, OR: Willan Publishing.

Durkin, K. F., & Bryant, C. D. (1995). Log on to sex: Some notes on the carnal computer and erotic cyberspace as an emerging research frontier. *Deviant Behavior, 16,* 179–200.

Einat, T., & Einat, H. (2000). Inmate argot as an expression of prison subculture: The Israeli case. *The Prison Journal, 80,* 309–325.

Forsyth, C. (1986). Sea daddy: An excursus into an endangered social species. *Maritime Policy and Management: The International Journal of Shipping and Port Research, 13,* 53–60.

Furnell, S. (2002). *Cybercrime: Vandalizing the information society.* Boston, MA: Addison-Wesley.

Hamm, M. S. (1993). American skinheads: The criminology and control of hate crime. Westport, CT: Praeger.

Hensley, C., Wright, J., Tewksbury, R., & Castle, T. (2003). The evolving nature of prison argot and sexual hierarchies. *The Prison Journal, 83,* 289–300.

Holt, T. J. (2007). Subcultural evolution? Examining the influence of on- and off-line experiences on deviant subcultures. *Deviant Behavior, 28,* 171–198.

Holt, T. J., & Blevins, K. R. (2007). Examining sex work from the client's perspective: Assessing johns using online data. *Deviant Behavior, 28,* 333–354.

Hurley, C., Puchol, M., Rogers, R., & Thornton, F. (2004). *WarDriving: Drive, detect, defend: A guide to wireless security.* San Diego, CA: Syngress Press.

Jacobs, B. (1999). *Dealing crack: The social world of streetcorner selling.* Boston, MA: Northeastern University Press.

Johnson, B. D., Bardhi, F., Sifaneck, S. J., & Dunlap, E. (2006). Marijuana argot as subculture threads: Social constructions by users in New York City. *British Journal of Criminology, 46,* 46–77.

Jordan, T., & Taylor, P. (1998). A sociology of hackers. *The Sociological Review, 46,* 757–780.

Kaplan, C. D., Flores Farfan, J. A., & Kampe, H. (1990). Argots as a code-switching process: A case study of sociolinguistic aspects of drug subcultures. In R. Jacobson (Ed.), *Codeswitching as a worldwide phenomenon.* New York: Peter Lang.

Landreth, B. (1985). *Out of the inner circle.* Washington: Microsoft Press.

Lerman, P. (1967). Argot, symbolic deviance, and subcultural delinquency. *American Sociological Review, 32,* 209–224.

Lucas, A. M. (2005). The work of sex work: Elite prostitutes' vocational orientations and experiences. *Deviant Behavior, 26,* 513–546.

Malesky, L. A. Jr., & Ennis, L. (2004). Supportive distortions: An analysis of posts on a pedophile internet message board. *Journal ofAddictions and Offender Counseling, 24,* 92–100.

Mann, D., & Sutton, M. (1998). Netcrime: More change in the organization of thieving. *The British Journal of Criminology, 38,* 201–229.

Mativat, F., & Tremblay, P. (1997). Counterfeiting credit cards: Displacement effects, suitable offenders and crime wave patterns. *The British Journal of Criminology, 37,* 165–183.

Maurer, D. W. (1981). *Language of the underworld.* Louisville: University of Kentucky Press.

Melbin, M. (1978). Night as frontier. *American Sociological Review, 43,* 3–22.

Mills, R. (1998). Cyber: Sexual chat on the Internet. *Journal of Popular Culture, 32,* 31–46.

Mitnick, K. D., & Simon, W. L. (2002). *The art of deception: Controlling the human element of security.* Indianapolis, IN: Wiley.

Quayle, E., & Taylor, M. (2002). Child pornography and the Internet: Perpetuating a cycle of abuse. *Deviant Behavior, 23,* 331–361.

Quinn, J. F., & Forsyth, C. J. (2005). Describing sexual behavior in the era of the Internet: A typology for empirical research. *Deviant Behavior, 26,* 191–207.

Schell, B. H., Dodge, J. L., & Moutsatsos, S. S. (2002). *The hacking of America: Who's doing it, why, and how.* Westport, CT: Quorum Books.

Schell, B. H., & Martin, C. (2006). *Webster's new world hacker dictionary*. Indianapolis, IN: Wiley.

Sharp, K., & Earle, S. (2003). Cyberpunters and cyberwhores: Prostitution on the Internet. In Y. Jewkes (Ed.), *Dot cons. Crime, deviance and identity on the Internet*. Portland, OR: Willan Publishing.

Silverman, D. (2001). *Interpreting qualitative data: Methods for analyzing talk, text, and interaction* (2nd ed.). Thousand Oaks, CA: Sage.

Soothhill, K., & Sanders, T. (2005). The geographical mobility, preferences and pleasures of prolific punters: A demonstration study of the activities of prostitutes' clients. *Sociological Research On-Line, 10*. Retrieved October 10, 2006, from http://www.socresonline.org.uk/10/17soothill.html

Taylor, P. A. (1999). *Hackers: Crime in the digital sublime*. New York: Routledge.

Taylor, R. W., Tory, J., Caeti, T. J., Loper, D. K., Fritsch, E. J., & Liederbach, J. (2006). *Digital crime and digital terrorism*. Upper Saddle River, NJ: Pearson Prentice Hall.

Thomas, D. (2002). *Hacker culture*. Minneapolis: University of Minnesota Press.

Turkle, S. (1984). *The second self: Computers and the human spirit*. New York: Simon and Schuster.

Wall, D. S. (2001). Cybercrimes and the Internet. In D. S. Wall (Ed.), *Crime and the Internet* (pp. 1–17). New York: Routledge.

CPSIA information can be obtained at www.ICGtesting.com
Printed in the USA
BVOW050716070313

314931BV00003B/136/P

9 781609 274962